AF432007

RAISED BY WOLVES, POSSIBLY MONSTERS

Raised by Wolves, Possibly Monsters

Michael Swerdloff

Mystical Michael Publishing

Copyright © 2024 Michael Swerdloff / Mystical Michael Publishing

All rights reserved. No part of this book may be reproduced in any form or by an electronic or mechanical means, including information storage and retrieval systems, without permission in writing from the publisher, except by a reviewer who may quote brief passages in a review.

Editing: Jane Gerhard
Proofreading: Lisa Nigro & Susanna Baker
Layout: Kate Winter
Cover Design: Kiran Sarvana
Illustrations: Joanna Read

Paperback ISBN: 979-8-218-48779-9
Hardcover ISBN: 979-8-218-48627-3
Ebook ISBN: 979-8-3303-4205-1

Printed in the United States of America

Contents

"The Guest House"

This being human is a guest house.
Every morning a new arrival.

A joy, a depression, a meanness,
some momentary awareness comes
as an unexpected visitor.

Welcome and entertain them all!
Even if they're a crowd of sorrows,
who violently sweep your house empty of its furniture,
still, treat each guest honorably.
He may be clearing you out
for some new delight.

The dark thought, the shame, the malice,
meet them at the door laughing,
and invite them in.

Be grateful for whoever comes,
because each has been sent
as a guide from beyond.

Jalāl ad-Dīn Muhammad Rūmī
translated by Coleman Barks

"Caring for myself is not self-indulgence, it is self-preservation, and that is an act of political warfare."

Audre Lorde

"Our deepest fear is not that we are inadequate. Our deepest fear is that we are powerful beyond measure. It is our light, not our darkness that most frightens us. We ask ourselves, 'Who am I to be brilliant, gorgeous, talented, fabulous?' Actually, who are you not to be? You are a child of God. Your playing small does not serve the world. There is nothing enlightened about shrinking so that other people won't feel insecure around you. We are all meant to shine, as children do. We were born to make manifest the glory of God that is within us. It's not just in some of us; it's in everyone. And as we let our own light shine, we unconsciously give other people permission to do the same. As we are liberated from our own fear, our presence automatically liberates others."

Marianne Williamson

Introduction

This story is intense, but it is also beautiful, joyful, inspiring, and hopeful. I invite you to take care of yourself as we walk together and explore my life.

The Vision of a Book

I was in Costa Rica at a seven-day Himalayan Tantric Retreat. I was exhausted by Friday morning; individually and collectively, our intense work pushed me to the edge. I believe about 10 minutes into a guided meditation, I fell asleep. I don't know if I fell asleep or lost consciousness for five or forty minutes. When I was not conscious, I had a vision instructing me to write a book about my experiences of being raised by a misogynistic father, bullied by a sociopathic brother, and the impact both men had on me and my view of women in adolescence and early adulthood. You are reading the outcome of that vision. It was clear, specific, and forceful. It was not until I started writing that the content expanded to include other aspects of my life.

I've made every effort to maintain the truth in this story, achieving about 90% accuracy. I've had a photographic memory most of my life. I do not know if that is a trauma response, a gift from birth, or a combination of both. My memory is what made the details of the book possible. There are instances where I've altered the narrative for clarity and impact. Additionally, I changed many characters' names to protect their anonymity and ensure their safety. I am adamant about not re-traumatizing or exposing anyone to potentially negative consequences from my book.

There are a few instances where I have jumped around, leaving gaps in my life. The book is long enough already.

I have written this book for many reasons:

First, I didn't feel like I had a choice; it wrote itself.

Second, I want to share the message that men can change! We do not have to be stuck in an endless cycle of avoiding unwanted feelings through hate, anger, numbness, and addiction. Men can do better than this, and men deserve better than this. Certainly, the people in our lives deserve better. Many of us were raised in environments that didn't support us being kind, loving, tender, and humble or acknowledged unwanted thoughts, feelings, and emotions as OK and just part of being human. I get it; changing the core of what has kept men up and running our whole lives is hard. I want to share with you that change is absolutely worth it! We can experience tenderness, connection, intimacy, and love beyond our imagination. And it's incredible. You, the reader, are part of the motivation for writing this book.

Lastly, I want to offer a window for women to see what change in men may look like and let them see how long and challenging the process of transformation can be. While most men do not stoop to the levels of pain, hate, and addiction that I did, the majority of men on the planet take their power for granted and, to a greater or lesser extent, use it against those they perceive to be less powerful. They may harm people they love without understanding what they did or why. I wrote this book in hopes that my experience may help readers understand that the true source of all strength and determination lies within, not by replicating the strategies of wolves and monsters.

In the two and a half years I've been working on this project, one of the driving motivations that has kept me focused is the understanding that, at some point, a man needs to come forward and share his story. I'm willing to be that man. I am taking this stand because it aligns with my values and commitments and is what I need to do. Nobody has caught me doing anything I don't willingly speak about here. I'm not in trouble professionally because of my past. I'm not running for political office or doing damage control. There are no videos from my past that are about to go public. I am doing this, knowing that my current life might get ripped apart, which I love and am utterly grateful for. I'm doing it not because I want my life ripped apart but because I want to say, "I'm a man, and I've done some horrible things in my life to girls, women, and myself. I've changed, and so can other men."

My experience of writing this book has been strengthening, humbling, and inspiring. The original draft was somewhat effortless since everything was "written" from voice to text. Telling it has not been challenging. However, reading it was. I was shaken by reading and rereading the awful experiences I've had and those done to others. I confronted yet again the fact that in many of these stories, I had been the violent person who caused harm.

I've removed some of the situations in which I've hurt women emotionally, mentally, physically, sexually, and spiritually because, at a certain point, it became counterproductive and ran the risk of potentially turning readers off. My story is of redemption and change, and I made editorial choices to make that clear. I also took out significant chunks of the National Institutes of Health process in testing and the initial stages of recovery from Tumor-Induced Osteomalacia. I shrunk the six years of being unable to walk well, even with a cane, down to a handful of pages. I included some of my experiences in Mongolia and Central Asia; it felt important to share with you that part of the journey of rediscovering my masculinity.

I want to be clear that my mother was not a wolf or a monster, although she, too, was raised by wolves and monsters.

Thank you in advance for choosing to read this story. My hope for you is that it will create even more compassion, empathy, and understanding for the boys and men in your life who treat their dogs better than the people they love. It would be easy to read this book and think that it is a book about hating men and everything that's wrong with being a man. That is not my feeling or intention. If anything, it's the opposite. This is a story about a boy who knew he was kind, thoughtful, loving, and attentive. One by one, he witnessed all four characteristics disappear gradually until he didn't know who he was anymore. He became what he thought other men wanted him to be. It was a lie. He was never that guy, but he played the part exceptionally well. This is a story about hope. We do not have to be what they did to us, but it's our responsibility to do something about it. I wish for you to experience feeling loved, accepted, respected, and connected, as well as experience a life of being the person you always knew you could be. Thank you again for letting me share my story with you.

Raised by Wolves, Possibly Monsters

PART I
What It Was Like

"We are here to awaken from our illusion of separateness."

Thich Nhat Hanh

Being Raised by Wolves, Possibly Monsters

IT ALL STARTED in Mr. Sobieski's science class in seventh grade. Sure, I had a few wet dreams and even masturbated a time or two beforehand, but those were alone in my bed in the dark. This experience was in the bright lights of a public school classroom in a predominantly white, suburban neighborhood with a real live girl with a real live adolescent girl's body.

Mr. Sobieski summoned the class to the front of the room to his black Formica desk to demonstrate the experiment. I remember nothing about whether it was physics, chemistry, or biology. I do remember that I was leaning on his desk, noticing directly across from me that one of my classmates, Deborah, was already leaning over. Everything stopped. As an adolescent boy, I was lost in the experience of staring at two young breasts exposed from her white cotton shirt. There was nothing unique or different about her breasts besides that they existed, and she was directly across from me. I noticed her soft skin and the curve of her breasts. I even saw part of her bra, also white and cotton: it was enthralling.

What happened inside of me was unique. Before that moment, I had had a few girlfriends and briefly kissed one or two of them. I had a friend who used to invite me over to her house, and we would turn out the lights in her bedroom, much to her mother's chagrin, and "wrestle" on the carpet floor. Those were the days of wall-to-wall shag carpeting. What Lori called "wrestling" was the two of us rolling and grabbing each other on the floor and grabbing my ass over my clothes and me grabbing her ass and breasts over her clothes. Even though I could feel the shape and form of Lori's breasts while wrestling, it was in the dark, and she was wearing a heavy blue sweatshirt.

That moment in science class was the first time my body responded to seeing two beautiful young breasts, not just in my mind. A warmth filled my chest and belly. About a minute later, I was experiencing my first public erection in my dozen years of life in this body! My genitals and entire groin area were alive, warm, and vibrating. While my penis continued to grow, my desire and excitement grew even faster.

I had this deep feeling in my heart for ten or fifteen seconds. I remember for just a flash thinking, "I am in love. I will never love anything or anybody as much as I do her right now."

That joy and wonderment were interrupted by the awareness that if I didn't do something quickly, I was going to ejaculate right then and there with my penis pushing against Mr. Sobieski's desk! I panicked. The handful of times I ejaculated in bed, I was caught off guard by the experience and was alone in my bed in the dark. I didn't have to hide anything. I didn't have to feel ashamed of having an erection. I didn't have to be embarrassed by the potential of having a wet spot on the inside of my right leg.

I faced a dilemma in that I knew nothing. Nobody ever told me I was going to have an erection. Nobody ever told me I was going to have a wet dream. Nobody ever told me I would ejaculate this warm, clear, almost white substance where only urine had come out. Nobody told me that one could feel shame, embarrassment, and excitement for a chemical reaction in my body during science class. Most importantly, nobody told me what to do with this erection in public!

Nobody told me any of these things were going to happen. However, I was given clear instructions and guidance on why I should hate girls. I remember my chest tightening, barely being able to breathe, and my hands clenched together as if I were holding a baseball bat. All I could think about was how I could hurt her for doing this to me; this is what I was taught about girls. They do this to mess with us and manipulate us. They play games with us. Our job is to hurt them and take what we want from them. That's how you win the game. You don't win the game by sharing love, joy, and connection. You win the game by making girls feel beaten, broken, and less than you. The goal was to win, not to be happy.

Our class was seated according to the alphabetical order of the last name; Deborah sat directly before me. The next day, she wore a thin white button-down shirt that showed the outline of her bra on her back. I became turned on by the knowledge of her bra and the memory of her partially bare breasts. I became angry with her again. I hated her for making me feel this way. I was furious. Deborah raised her right hand just as Mr. Sobieski turned around to write something on the green blackboard. There was no precognition or plan. I just reached my right hand around the right side of her body, put my hand over

    Raised by Wolves, Possibly Monsters

her right breast, and cupped it. I squeezed harder than what felt natural or enjoyable. She clamped her right arm down, not realizing that this would keep my hand firmly on her breast because I couldn't move it. A few seconds later, Deborah started crying, grabbed my right hand, and yanked it away. For a moment, I felt sad and ashamed of my actions. A few boys in the back row started laughing and cheering me on. I felt powerful. I felt invincible. I felt unstoppable. This strategy worked as it was supposed to for someone raised by wolves.

This violation was the first of many times I would grab one or both of Deborah's breasts when she was unprepared in Mr. Sobieski's science class. Two weeks later, Deborah was out "sick" for two days. When Deborah returned, I did the same thing, and then she got "the flu" and was out of school for a whole week. After her battle with "the flu," I continued my assault on her body and spirit.

Deborah didn't return to school for the rest of the year. I don't know if she ever told anybody what happened or why Deborah wouldn't go to school. None of the girls ever said anything to me. There were no consequences for my actions. For the first time, I understood why my brother and father acted the way they did. Monsters create fear and terror in others and experience power and supremacy in themselves. This was my first lesson on the male drug named Power.

My Neighborhood

BUT THAT WASN'T all of me, at least, not then. As a kid, I still retained my intrinsic compassion. Sports were a big part of my childhood. I loved running around, I loved playing with balls, and I loved being a team member. One of the neighborhoods that I lived in as a child had a cul-de-sac. It was predominantly a residential neighborhood with a pile of children of all different ages, shapes, and sizes. One of the things we did together was kickball in the cul-de-sac in front of Doreen's house. Doreen was older than me, athletic, and strong, and everybody knew not to mess with her.

Doreen was often one of the team captains. Although she wasn't warm and fuzzy, she was incredibly competitive and fair. She always let the other captain pick first to make the teams equal. Doreen also taught me, without ever saying a word to me, that everybody gets to play, no matter how big or small, whether they are girls, talented, or awful, everybody gets to play. She was not a wolf or a monster. I didn't know she was teaching me this then, but it sunk in. When Doreen got to middle school and didn't play with the kids in the neighborhood as much, I became the person to make sure that everybody got to play and that the teams were fair. It looked so easy when Doreen was doing it. It felt challenging when I was doing it.

There was a boy named Ira who lived across from me and was a year younger than me. Ira and I were not close friends until his body started to change. I was young, so I didn't understand what was happening at first, actually, ever. Ira began wearing a brace around his hips and legs when playing sports and stopped playing football because it was dangerous. I understood what he told me, and his mom and dad tried to explain that something happened with his hips, and the bone was deteriorating or something like that. A year later, Ira was in a wheelchair most of the time with a brace from his hips down to his ankles. The following year, he was in a wheelchair 95% of the time. It was painful to watch, knowing I could do nothing to help Ira. He loved sports and loved to run around.

In sixth grade, I was hanging out at a new friend's house who had a younger brother. Since so many kids were named Michael, his younger brother asked me my last name. I told them my name was Swerdloff, and he kept pronouncing Squirreloff. By the end of the day, my last name became Squirrel. When I was saying goodbye and getting on my bike, he just called me Squirrel, not Michael Squirrel, just Squirrel. My friends liked it, and my name became Squirrel. By about midway through the school year in sixth grade, not only did everybody in my grade and anybody who knew me call me Squirrel, but even my teachers started calling me Squirrel.

On Saturday mornings, Ira used to get up earlier than everybody else in the neighborhood and me. He would roll his wheelchair down the little hill to the house next door to him and put on the parking brake when he got to the corner across from my home. And he would keep saying my name: Squirrel, Squirrel, Squirrel, Squirrel. I could hear his voice as I started to wake up. I would put my hands over my ears so I couldn't listen to him, but it didn't work. My mother would come in and tell me he was outside. My brother would yell at me to get "the kid in the wheelchair to shut up." I felt so ashamed that I was terrible because I didn't want to get out of bed and play with him. He wasn't fun to play with because we couldn't do many things. And he was sad. Now and then, I will remember how bad I felt about "There was nothing I could do to help him."

I became aware there was something I could do.

I couldn't do anything so that he could play football again. Or kickball. Or basketball. Or soccer. But I could be his friend. I could do something with him so he wouldn't be utterly alone on a Saturday morning when everybody else could go out and play somewhere. I could do that. Sometimes, a tear or two would come out of my eyes as I dressed and brushed my teeth. I would ensure I wiped them all away before I went outside the house, crossed the street, unlocked the parking brake on his wheelchair, and pushed him to the picnic table in his backyard or across the street to hang out at my house. Those were things I could do.

Now and then, I remember what it was like to be that kid, Squirrel. I was the kid who made sure girls who didn't know how to play sports, the younger children who didn't understand the rules, and the neighborhood kid who became disabled also participated in whatever we were doing. In contrast to what shifted inside me in the coming years, these memories offer me balance and perspective. Between the beginning of sixth grade and the middle of seventh grade, I became a different kid; an internal monster was forming, raised by wolves who lived by one rule: the winner takes all. I had to choose—be a loser or a monster.

Before I made that choice, sharing what I was like before feels essential. Before, I was defined by hate, loss, pain, and shame. Before, I felt like I didn't have a home, a family, or anybody to protect and care for me. Before the school year ended, I tested in the top one percentile nationwide. I went from one version of being "That Kid" to a different version of "That Kid."

Blood on Snow in Underwear

 ONE WOLF LIFE lesson came when I was ten years old. School was canceled that day due to the volume of snow, so I was playing in the snow in our front yard. I was rolling around in the snow, making

snowballs that weren't wet enough to stick together, and just having a blast being a kid in the snow.

I was out there for a while when an older kid named Kevin, who lived a few blocks away, was walking past. He made a smart-ass remark about my having no friends and playing by myself. I wasn't bothered because it wasn't true. I had things to do with my friends. I wanted to play in the snow and hang out with them later, so I ignored it.

My response didn't meet Kevin's needs. He made a few more stupid comments that had nothing to do with me, so I continued playing in the snow, ignoring him. His irrelevance to me pissed him off; since he was three years my senior, he expected kids my age to show intimidation or respect in his presence . . . but I didn't feel either of those things. I didn't either that day or in general. I thought he was pretty stupid. Kevin was bigger than me, with blond hair, blue eyes, and a red face from the cold wind and snow.

Kevin came towards me since his words weren't affecting me, and he wasn't getting the response he sought. When he got close enough, Kevin started pushing me backward with his hands on my chest. I remember yelling at him, "Kevin, you're a stupid asshole, and I don't like you, so just leave me alone!"

He pushed me harder, and this time, I fell back and landed in the snow. He laughed and stood beside me to intimidate me and kick snow in my face.

About ten seconds later, my brother came running out of the house in his underwear and what we used to call a "Guinea Tee" (which I guess today we would call a "wife beater") with no shoes, jumping over small plants between our porch and the front yard. He attacked and beat Kevin right there in the snow. At first, I was excited about his arrival, especially when he knocked down Kevin and kicked him in the belly. By about the seventh punch in the face, with blood squirting everywhere, I started to panic. David kept swinging and beating Kevin. Blood was all over the snow, David's chest, and his white underwear. "I'm going to keep beating the shit out of you till you apologize to Mike and let him kick you in the face."

Kevin shook his head, and the pounding continued. "I'm giving you one more chance to apologize to him, or I will break your face apart, and your mother won't recognize you."

     Raised by Wolves, Possibly Monsters

Kevin was crying, "Okay, okay, stop." Kevin turned his head towards me; this big kid was already unrecognizable between the blood and beaten face. "I'm sorry, Mike. I won't do it again."

I don't think either of them realized my experience at that moment. Kevin was probably forty pounds heavier than me, and David, with bare feet, no pants in his underwear, and a T-shirt, just beat the shit out of him with no effort whatso-ever; it was a reminder of how powerless I was in David's presence. "It's okay, Kevin. Dave, let him go."

"Now kick him in the fucking face so he understands not to ever fuck with you again."

"I'm sure he understands. I don't want to kick him in the face. Please let him go."

"What kind of pussy are you? No! Kick him in the face before I beat the shit out of you too."

I gathered what little courage and strength were inside me, closed my eyes, and kicked him with my green rubber boots. My foot landed on the area that was the most significant open gash with blood. The blood was now all over my green boots, and when I stepped back, I made a footprint of red blood in the snow. David looked excited and full of glee.

"Now, doesn't that feel better?" He stood up, stepped on Kevin's chest along the way, kicked him in the belly, slapped me as a sign of approval, and casually walked back into the house as if he didn't just pulverize a human being. His lack of effect felt scary, as if he wasn't in bare feet and underwear in the snow in the middle of winter. David paused before opening the front door to the house and entering the little gym my parents made for him with a universal weight system. With his bare feet, he kicked over the red metal ornamental milk can about three feet high. He continued into the house to finish his workout. I have no idea how my parents thought a violent sociopathic teenage boy needed to have a whole system for creating muscle, rage, and intensity made sense, but they did.

How to "Get" a Girl

"JUST KEEP ASKING, no matter what she says." My brother David was four years older than me and fancied himself quite the lady's man. He went on. "Girls don't know what they want. If you keep asking them, they will eventually say yes."

"David's right." My dad decided to join the conversation, which he was watching intently. "They don't know what the hell they want. They can't even figure out what clothes to put on when they get dressed in the morning. It takes them thirty minutes to decide what fucking clothes to wear. Who gives a shit? Listen, they all say yes eventually. It works every time. It worked on both your mother and stepmother." My father leaned back with his hands folded in front of his chest and a triumphant smile.

After my father died in 1995, my mother shared with me how they met, their first date, and how they got married. The reality was much more horrifying than whatever my mind as an adolescent boy was trying to piece together. Here is the story that I remember her telling me.

You could call it "how wolves get girls":

"My best friend and I had run away from home at age sixteen. I can't believe we actually did that! Two high school dropouts, Italian girls from Newark, New Jersey, ran away from home. It's unbelievable to think about. We were both working at a luncheonette counter. We lived in this tiny little place with a Murphy bed from the wall we slept on together. We had saved money and bought bus tickets to California. It's so long ago I don't remember where we were going! I think it was Los Angeles, but I don't remember. All I knew was that we both wanted to get out and away from Newark, New Jersey. We tried to escape our drunk fathers, who cheated, lied, and beat our mothers. My father sometimes dragged me to the bar to watch him get drunk, kiss, and grab all the young girls right before me, Aunt Dee Dee, and Uncle John. He made us watch. Our bus ticket was for Friday, and we were both so excited! No more drunk fathers, no more beat-up mothers, no more gangsters. Friday was our get-out-of-jail-free day!

     Raised by Wolves, Possibly Monsters

"On Tuesday, before we left for California, I cleaned up the counter at the end of the shift before we closed. A good-looking guy comes in and pesters me even though I turned off everything already to make him a coffee and a sandwich. The cook was gone, so I had to make the sandwich myself. It was easier than continuing to fight with him at the counter; besides, I could get out of there quicker by giving him food than arguing. There was about enough for one cup of coffee left in the big coffee maker we used back then. I was saving it for myself but gave it to him. I served the sandwich and the coffee, and then he asked for a milkshake. A coffee milkshake, to be specific. I told him we didn't have coffee syrup, only vanilla, and chocolate, and we had already cleaned the machines. He said we could use coffee ice cream with vanilla or chocolate syrup, and he would be okay with it as if he was doing me a fucking favor! So, I made him his God damn coffee milkshake. He muttered something under his breath about how much better it would taste with coffee syrup and what kind of a luncheonette this was. I held my tongue again.

"So, while he's eating his damn sandwich, talking with his mouth full, he starts flirting with me. He tells me how pretty I am. It is great that a girl like me can have a job my age. And that I did my job well. And he keeps going on and on and on about how pretty I am, how great I am, blah blah blah. The owner had left by now, and I was the only person there alone with him. I was getting a little bit nervous, but not too much. If you grow up in a home as I did, you know how to care for yourself with guys like him. So, I told him it was time to close up, and I needed to finish cleaning the shop. He started asking me out on a date; I said no. He asked again, and I said no. I told him he needed to leave so I could close up. He told me he would only go if I said yes to a date. He said he would borrow his friend's car and come and pick me up and take me to dinner. He knew this would impress me, and it did. None of my friends had cars. None of my friends' parents had cars. He kept badgering me, and eventually, I said yes. He said he would wait outside the shop till I was done closing, and then he would walk me home to make sure I was safe. I saw right through his bullshit and knew he wanted to know where I lived. I tried to feed him an excuse, and it didn't work. He waited there outside the door of the coffee shop, staring at me impatiently.

"He walks me home and tells me he will be waiting outside at seven in his friend's car. I couldn't figure out how to get out of it and didn't want any more problems or trouble between now and Friday to mess up going to California and getting out of New Jersey.

He picked me up in his friend's car, and we ate dinner. He talked the whole time. He was charismatic, fun, and enjoyable. I eventually started laughing and having some fun. He made a big deal by paying for the check as if he were buying me a diamond ring or something. While driving me home, he turned in a different direction and went to an empty parking lot in an area I didn't know. I was worried, but there were streetlights, and I had my fist ready in case I needed to do something. And just like that, he told me he wanted to spend the rest of his life with me and asked me to marry him.

"I said no. He asked again. I said no. He asked again. I told him I was leaving for California on Friday. He became even more insistent. We kept going back and forth, and then, while I was talking, he just leaned over, kissed me, and held his face against me so I couldn't do anything. Eventually, I kissed him back so he would stop holding my head. It was a good kiss, but not outstanding. It was not good enough to talk me out of going to California. He then really pressured me about marrying him. He then threatened to come to our place. And then he threatened not to let me get on the bus. Then he threatened to tell my father where I was living and that I was leaving for California. That's when I said yes. Being with him was still better than being home with my father. He said he would pick me up after I was done with my shift tomorrow, and we will get married tomorrow afternoon.

"Sure enough, he was out there thirty minutes before I was done with my shift. I looked and felt awful from not sleeping the night before. I'm trying to think of ways to escape or hide between now and Friday so we can leave Newark. My girlfriend and I had a big argument before bed about me ruining her dream of moving to California. I pleaded with her to understand that I said no and tried to get out of it, but she didn't believe me. I didn't believe me either.

"We got married. I never moved to California. My best friend stopped talking to me. Two days after we married, he told me he was drafted and leaving for the war the following week! He left for the Goddamn war. I was left in Goddamn Newark, New Jersey, without a family. Without a job. Without my best friend. And without my new husband. That's how our marriage started."

Back at the dinner table with my father and brother, I was trying to make sense of their strategy with girls; I still couldn't picture my father convincing my

     Raised by Wolves, Possibly Monsters

mother by repeatedly asking her. Years later, I learned how well this strategy worked with my mother.

David grabbed me by the right arm just above the elbow. "We wouldn't have this conversation if your strategy wasn't worthless. If you could get a girl, we wouldn't have this conversation. I'm fucking three different girls right now. How many girls do you get to fuck with your stupid strategy?" He paused to let me answer, knowing I didn't have one. "That's what I thought." He folded his hands and arms in front of his chest and leaned back into the chair with the same stupid smile as my father. I remember being terrified that someday I would be telling my son the same stupid shit, with the same folded hands and arms, with the same foolish smile. I forgot to breathe in or out.

My father leaned forward across the table. He was almost sticking his elbow into the bowl full of spaghetti with marinara sauce from a jar. "Michael, girls are all wackos. They don't know what the hell they want. So, you tell them whatever they want to hear, and they shut up. They do whatever you want if you keep asking. And tell them what they want to hear. They all give in eventually. The sooner you figure this out, the sooner you'll have a good life." My father and brother exchanged that same shady grin with each other, nodded, then stuck their forks back into the spaghetti, and that was the end of the conversation.

An Aside About David

 THE ADULTS IN my family told me when I was a child that David demanded significant attention from birth. They said the day I was coming home from the hospital as a baby, David set up a tepee for me to sleep in so that he would sit outside to protect me from anyone or anything. He loved playing the role of an older brother, wanting to teach me sports, games, and King of the Bed. My brother was a good-looking kid and a better-looking teen and young adult. He demanded and received attention everywhere he went.

David was aggressive and violent and did not care who you were or how big or old you were if you stood between him and what he wanted. The list of people he was aggressive and violent with included teachers, school principals, guidance counselors, kids, parents of friends, aunts, uncles, grandmothers, coaches, and especially me.

I remember when I was in sixth grade, and David was in high school, he shoved a security guard at a fast food restaurant through a glass wall because he had dared tell David to quiet down. I started to speak more softly.

When he was a senior in high school, his friends had a rivalry with a nearby town's football team. David and two of his best friends, Billy and Brian, set up a brawl with many kids from that town on a Friday night. The location was in a city, about twenty minutes by car. David had a date with the first of many Lisas, so Brian and Billy were going to meet him at that brawl. Brain and Billy got a flat tire on their way, so David fought six kids by himself. He beat up and hospitalized all six of the boys. Their parents brought it to court. I was too young to understand how it ended up in court. After they explained how David had beaten them violently, the judge responded, "Do you really expect me to believe that this boy, who is smaller than all six of these kids, beat them up by himself and sent them all to the hospital with multiple broken noses?" He paused for a minute. "I am dismissing these charges and want all of you to get out of my courtroom!" No consequences for David, but more intense fear of David for me. If he could do this to them, what would he be capable of doing to me?

David always had plenty of girlfriends. As a kid and young adult, I assumed it was because he was good-looking, tough, and cool, but as I have reflected, it is possibly his strategy of wearing them down by asking until they said yes, which may have been part of that dynamic, too. My brother obsessed over the girls or women who said no to him and kept at them to change their minds. When that tactic did not work, he threatened them or worse. I was aware of this and never did anything about it.

My brother was imprisoned for two long stints. The first sentence was for committing a dozen acts of robbery of old ladies at gunpoint after they left a jewelry store. David was on the front page of the *Star-Ledger*. I had just arrived in a new town as a high school senior. This is how I was known at my new school. He served less than four years on a ten to thirteen-year sentence. Part of his time was spent as a prisoner at Rahway State Prison, a maximum-security facility. I must have visited him with one of my parents during that first year and a half at

     Raised by Wolves, Possibly Monsters

least fifty times. I hated every single one of those visits. Several years after he was released, he was arrested and convicted of counterfeiting and fraud. He served less than two years for that sentence.

When his oldest son was a little boy, they told him that his father was in the army when he left to serve his sentence. He thought his dad was a war hero, not an ex-convict found guilty of multiple felonies.

Growing up, David loved me more than he loved anyone else, and I knew it. He was my protector, teacher, enforcer, role model, and the person I needed the most protection from. When my parents went through their vicious divorce, David also became my parent and caretaker. I loved him dearly and felt terrified of him and his capabilities. I was crushed at my core every time I heard that he had torn another girl or woman's spirit and body from them, like the way monsters do. I still see several of their faces afterward, void of life, soul, or hope. Over the years, I have had the instinct to search for and make amends to all of them for not preventing him from stealing all that was beautiful and sweet from them. I know I could have done little to stop David. He was a wolf or possibly a monster, and I was a squirrel.

After all these years, I am still curious about what could have helped David to become someone different from what he became. Did he need more discipline, less discipline, therapy, institutionalization, medication, God, a different family, etc.? If we had both been born twenty years later and armed with the knowledge and support that are now available, would my brother have turned out to be the man we occasionally caught glimpses of?

The memory I hold dear about David occurred one night on the phone while living on the farm with my friends Charles and Karla. That night, his voice cracked. "Mike, I mean Michael, Carlo is different from us. He loves poetry, animals, happy songs, and playing board games. My son likes poetry and animals!" I could tell he was working hard not to break out in tears. He lowered his voice almost to whisper, as if he didn't want to hear himself speaking, "I hope I don't mess him up. He is such a beautiful boy."

His sons, Carlo and Anthony, are searching to understand who their father was and how he has impacted them as men. I love them both and see my favorite parts of him when I connect with them. At times, I feel my chest tighten and can barely breathe. My brother was born and died on the Jewish holiday Yom Kippur at age forty, and somehow, this feels Biblical, as if he was given forty years to figure out how to be a human and failed. My wish was that even though I kept him out of my life by necessity, David would figure this out and have a measure of joy, peace, and, more than anything else, a sense of safety. I remember he was on guard every moment; you could see it in his eyes.

I have intentionally omitted significant aspects and behaviors of David's life. The blood, pain, hate, guns, knives, recklessness, and carnage he left in his wake was devastating and unimaginable. The impact on the mind, body, spirit, and lives of women, men, children, and families seems vicious and cruel to share with you as readers and for his family to read about in a book. I believe it is that brutal, and it is what separates him from my father, who was just a scared mess. It distinguishes the wolf from the monster, which both left their marks on me and taught me not to trust men or myself. David didn't appear to have a "No matter what happens, I will never do ___." He stocked his car with legal weapons like baseball bats, billy clubs, fourteen-inch screwdrivers, chains, ropes, awls, hand saws, full gas cans, large heavy-duty trash bags, and a Taser, in case he needed them. If this creates an image in your mind that stiffens your spine, you are in the right neighborhood. I am experiencing fear by simply referencing the things I have witnessed without sharing any details.

If We All Hated Her So Much...

IT WAS EMERSON'S twelfth birthday party, and many boys had a sleepover party in his living room. It seemed like twenty of us, but there were probably eight or nine. One of them was a beautiful boy named Sean. I did not know Sean well; he and Emerson were good friends. Sean was often calm, soft, sweet, sensitive, fun to play with, and excellent at sports. I always wanted to get to know Sean and be his friend, but it never happened. I was a little jealous of him because he was good-looking in an authentically beautiful way, intelligent, liked by everybody, and excellent at everything while still humble and confident.

What I remember most about that night was talking and hanging out in the

Raised by Wolves, Possibly Monsters

living room. One by one, we spoke about how much we hated Nina, a girl who transferred to our school and moved from a town about thirty minutes away. And we all kept arguing over who hated her more as if it was a competition.

One of the gifts that Emerson received for his birthday from his parents was this brand-new thing that had just come out called the "Magic 8 Ball." If you have never seen one before, you shake it up, and while you're shaking it, you ask it a question, and then, in dark blue letters, it gives you an answer. I don't remember all of the responses, but I remember it is having things like, "Absolutely," "Never," "Forget about it," or "You must be patient." The Magic 8 Ball was one part fortune cookie and a fun game/toy to play at a party.

As the night wore on and our sugar intake increased, the game of Magic 8 Ball shifted from questions like, "Will I be in the Major League Baseball Hall of Fame?" or "Will I be president of the United States?" to "Will Nina go out with me" and "Will Nina and I get married and have twelve children?"

It's like, individually and collectively, we were straddling being dreamy-eyed little boys with fantasies beyond comprehension to trying to reconcile these new and confusing feelings and experiences around being attracted to girls. None of us knew what to do with these feelings, how to talk about them, or if they were good or bad. Without knowing it, we were aching for a coming-of-age ritual somewhere between prepubescent and adolescence. Asking the Magic 8 Ball if we had a shot with Nina or not was the closest, we had come to that essential ritual.

Nina and I became friends. Sometimes we flirted, but not a lot. I thought she was too pretty and popular for somebody like me. At one point during that school year, I had "Asked Nina out," and she said yes. Nothing changed between us except we talked on the phone sometimes, and when we spoke on the phone, there was more giggling, and the conversations were more extended. There was nervous and exciting energy. Even though people talked about how "stuck up" and "what a bitch" she was, I never saw that. I witnessed boys being rude and mean to Nina because they were confused about their feelings toward her. I saw girls jealous of her popularity and attractiveness as distant and cold to her.

It was fascinating how much attention and drama her presence created by just showing up at our school in the middle of sixth grade and being blonde, tall, thin with soft cheeks and brown eyes. I remember resenting her so deeply on multiple occasions because I wanted to kiss her, hold and touch her body. It got worse when she started showing up in some of my dreams. This was new to me, the experience of fantasizing with girls I knew in real life versus TV or movies.

Near the end of school, several years later, in ninth grade, it was time to vote for who would get yearbook titles. It was a common consensus that everybody in the school thought Nina should win the best-looking girl; it was a given. During the voting week, everybody was gossiping. We were excited and created drama around all the different categories. A girl named Donna, who was dating a boy named Mike (not me), was hurt and angry that he had broken up with her because he had a crush on Nina. A bunch of us were whispering and passing notes about voting for Nina, and Donna said in the heavy black ink of her Bic pen that she was going to vote for Riley. Riley was just extraordinarily beautiful but did nothing to attract attention. She was somehow able to hide in plain sight despite her beauty. And I remember a handful of us simultaneously looking at Riley sitting in the back left-hand corner of the classroom. Riley's face turned bright red, and she appeared to be panicking.

About an hour later, in what felt like a political or social protest, our whole grade decided that we would vote for Riley as the best-looking girl to spite Nina. When the rumor mill reached Nina's best friend, who in turn told Nina, Nina broke down in tears and ran through the cafeteria during lunch to the bathroom. We all laughed at her. We all got revenge on Nina for being too pretty. What a terrible crime she committed.

Collecting Lisas

SOME PEOPLE, ME included, collect music, some collect pottery and crystal, others get excited about their eighteenth pair of shoes, and my brother, in those years, collected Lisas. There was always at least one Lisa in his life. I have no idea if this happened because we lived in an area populated with Italian and Jewish people, but Lisa was a trendy name in the 70s and 80s in the New York City metro area. You could call the name Lisa to a

    Raised by Wolves, Possibly Monsters

woman or girl you found attractive, and it seemed like you had a decent shot of being right without even knowing her. One could also do this with the name Michael.

The first Lisa I remember that my brother was with when he was seventeen, she was sixteen, and I was thirteen. Lisa was cute, flirty, and fun. One day, we decided to play hooky from our respective schools and went down the shore for the day. The ride down in David's Mustang was fun, with the music blaring. Besides Lisa being her playful, flirty self, my brother was in a good, nonviolent mood. We were relaxing on a blanket on the beach in Pt. Pleasant. Like most days on the beach, I napped. I cannot remember any point in my life when sleeping on the beach did not bring me great pleasure, and this day was no different.

What was different about this nap was that I woke to feel breasts, hips, and legs wrapped around my body. I was not sure if I was dreaming or if it was real life. Lisa could tell that I couldn't quite figure out what was happening, so she playfully whispered in my ears, "Hi Mike, rise and shine." She wiggled and rubbed her body all over my back and ran her fingers through my hair. I instantaneously felt a response in my genitals and heart and a tingling throughout my body. I had never had a high school girl with a high school body, high school experience, and high school confidence wrapped up against my junior high school body and laying on top of me that way.

Lisa giggled and played. I felt embarrassed and confused. I didn't know what I was supposed to do or feel. She continued saying flirtatious things, and my urge was to roll her over, lying on top of her, grabbing her breasts and butt. But I was too embarrassed and disoriented to do that or anything but be uncomfortable. My body knew what to do with an almost mature female body against me. My brain is what backfired.

David was interested in exploiting attractive, popular, sexy adolescent girls who liked trouble, but underneath their exteriors were sweet, innocent girls wanting attention and to be desired. I remember him saying, "I like fucking the innocence right out of them and coming inside their virginal pussies."

Every time he said this, I would feel bad, disgusted, ashamed, and still, an erection built inside my pants. I was experiencing lust and desire for being a predator as much as for scoring with physically and personally attractive young girls.

"Mike, what you got to do is get 'em and fuck 'em before they get a driver's license. Once they get a driver's license, they can leave when they want and get independent. You gotta get 'em before they get a driver's license. Remember, the best way is to keep asking and pushin'; eventually, they give in, and bang, you nail 'em! The younger they are, the less it takes before they give in and fuck 'em in the driveway of their house where their father is inside watching football."

Sometimes, when he would say that I would be on the brink of tears for those girls, for all girls, and myself for being complicit in this. I knew what he was doing and did nothing to stop him. All I knew, and all I could truly focus on, was his acceptance and avoiding being on the wrong side of his rampages. My safety overrode their safety. I had to be a wolf to live among them or hide the ways I was not like them.

Making Friends with Cute Girls

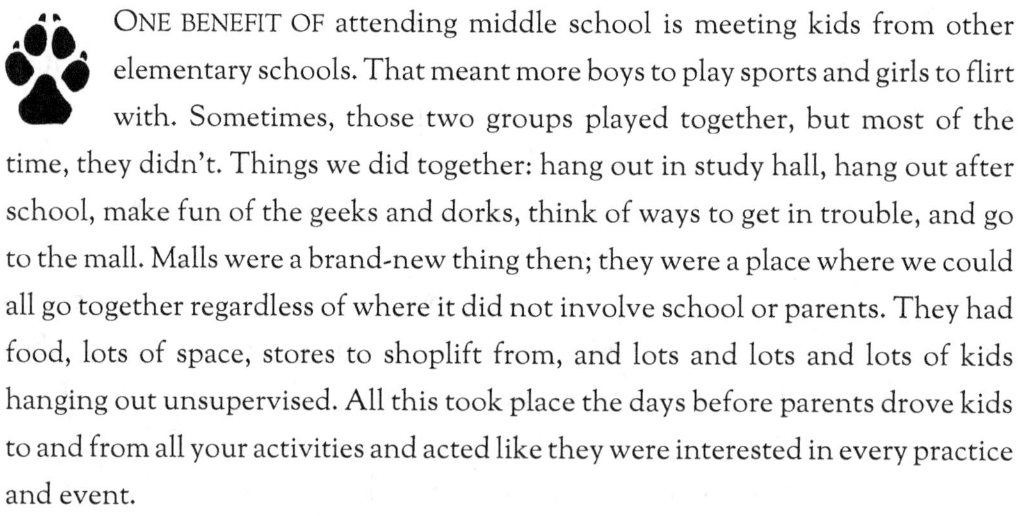

ONE BENEFIT OF attending middle school is meeting kids from other elementary schools. That meant more boys to play sports and girls to flirt with. Sometimes, those two groups played together, but most of the time, they didn't. Things we did together: hang out in study hall, hang out after school, make fun of the geeks and dorks, think of ways to get in trouble, and go to the mall. Malls were a brand-new thing then; they were a place where we could all go together regardless of where it did not involve school or parents. They had food, lots of space, stores to shoplift from, and lots and lots and lots of kids hanging out unsupervised. All this took place the days before parents drove kids to and from all your activities and acted like they were interested in every practice and event.

Hanging out at the mall and meeting girls created new problems. If they lived in another town, we would have no way to see or talk to each other. The entire family typically shared one telephone and one telephone number, and it cost money to call other towns in many cases. So, we would meet these girls at the mall, flirt, play, and hang out with them. Sometimes, we even make out with them in some hidden nook or cranny of the mall. My favorite spot was hiding in

          Raised by Wolves, Possibly Monsters

the hanging rugs in Sears. We would exchange phone numbers, and we were excited about the possibilities. And then, for the most part, nothing happened. We didn't have a way to contact each other because our parents wouldn't let us spend an obscene amount of money to "speak to some girl you met at the mall." Meeting kids at the mall was a great practice ground for social introductions in general, as well as explicitly flirting and meeting those you find attractive.

Another exciting aspect of integrating all these kids from different schools was that no matter what you were like in first, third, or fifth grade, you could reinvent yourself to be whatever you wanted in this new school. That meant that before things became awful in my life and I got perfect scores on tests and assignments, I was now an officially certified troublemaker, which made me this ambiguous thing called "cool." The social rewards of being a problem kid were all the affirmation I needed while fluctuating between good and bad kids. TV and movies taught me that being a troublemaker gets hot girls. It certainly got me their attention and friendship, but my face was starting to change without me knowing it. After two years of being miserable and pissed off based on the chaos and crisis in my family, the soft, sweet, and borderline adorable face was exchanged for a stiff, complex, and angry one. Girls liked and hung out with me; they didn't want to make out with me.

I did not adopt my father and brothers' advice of asking girls out relentlessly into submission. If anything, I went to the other extreme. I would hint that I was interested in them and hope they would pick up on it. I never entirely developed the skill of knowing if they were interested in me or that I was interested in them. These patterns continued into my twenties and possibly even my early thirties. I surrounded myself with a group of girls/women who were considered attractive, with prominent personalities and social cache, who were part of the popular groups, if not the leaders. Having attractive women around me all the time gave people the illusion that I was more successful in dating, romance, and sex than I was in reality. When I eventually "lost my virginity," I was known for being a slut and a guy with a long list of one-night stands. I did nothing to challenge this perception; I did anything I could to encourage it.

My inner belief was that I was ugly and unattractive, in contrast to my father and brother, who were successful with girls and women every time they left home. I was a miserable failure. It had never occurred to me that they might've been full of shit and were not nearly as successful at actually being with the girls and women. Anytime a girl came to our place, either my father or brother made a move on every single one of them! I learned at an early age that I could not bring any girl I was interested in to meet my father or brother because they were so much more exciting and skilled in the art of seduction than I was. Looking back, the idea my dad, in his fifties, was hitting on fourteen-year-old girls blows my mind. And he didn't do it discreetly; he was aggressive and straightforward about it. He would talk about their hair, eyes, clothes, and bodies and compliment them on their appearance and maturity. My brother would put his hands on them, kiss them, and get their phone numbers right while I was standing there.

My brother and father's tenacity in seeing my friends as prey came out into the open at my Bar Mitzvah party when I was thirteen.

My parents thought I should have a Bar Mitzvah for reasons I never understood. It did not make sense since nobody in my family was religious, believed in the Bible or God, or knew what the service was about. They convinced me by telling me how much money I would get as gifts and that I could have a big party with all my friends. I went through the training, and during the actual Bar Mitzvah service, I just decided to leave out all the parts in Hebrew. I remember the Rabbi and the Cantor looking at me and quietly whispering and encouraging and demanding me to do it, but since we were in front of the whole synagogue of people, they didn't want to embarrass me. In my head, this was a great way to give a big fuck you to my parents, religion, and this stupid ceremony.

One of the kids I invited to the party was a girl named Evie.

Before Evie and I started "going out," we had an awkward friendship. We laughed at each other and were sometimes warm and friendly. I remember us being allies when others were disrespectful to either of us. I remember Evie pushing and then almost beating up a boy who poked fun at me. Then it happened. One day, we argued on the playground; the next, we made out behind one of the hallways during the third period. The first time we did it, she laughed at me and slapped me for kissing her too briefly. We made out longer the next day, and she seemed to like it. I most definitely did.

Evie had a warm, soft face, gentle eyes, full lips, and soft dark brown hair that

   Raised by Wolves, Possibly Monsters

matched her dark brown eyes. Evie wore what appeared to be fashionable and expensive clothing, but they were always a mess due to getting in fights, playing sports, and wrestling. Evie wore expensive white sweaters covered with grass stains, dirt stains, and sometimes blood from somebody she punched, kicked, or bit. Evie never pretended to be anything that wasn't her; my first girlfriend wasn't a good or bad student and didn't have many or no friends. She wasn't mean or friendly, fun or boring; she was all of those things and none of them. When I reflect, Evie was about half a century ahead of her time.

Our first official date wasn't just hanging around in school and making out behind a staircase between second and third period; it was at the mall. It was a Saturday afternoon, and I was riding my bike to her side of town, about three miles away. Evie lived in an affluent neighborhood near the mall. At the last minute, she told me her friend Liz was joining us. I didn't like Liz very much. Liz was arrogant and egotistical because she was the smartest kid in the school, and I resented her for being more intelligent than me. I thought she was ugly, and she had no friends but Evie. That was another one of Evie's exciting traits. She seemed to like to hang out with people who either didn't fit in, didn't have friends, or belonged to several different social groups. After we hung out in the mall for a while, Evie took my hand and said, "Let's go back to my house. My parents aren't home, and only the housekeeper is there with my little brother."

I didn't have to think about saying yes. I was overly enthusiastic, and Evie laughed at that as well. While we walked towards her house, she stopped and said, "Okay, let's kiss here." I was caught off guard. Apparently, I licked my lips without thinking. Evie and Liz broke out laughing. What stopped the laughter was her kissing me. We stopped for about five seconds and then started kissing again. I remember her white sweater. I remember her reddish rust-colored corduroy pants. I remember her breath. I remember her small adolescent breasts pressing against me. I remember the way she smelled. When we stopped, she looked happy, content, and softened.

When we arrived at her house, we went straight to her room. She showed me things around her room; I remember everything was white. While I was looking at stuff out of the blue, Evie blurted out, "Okay, Liz, you can leave now so that we can make out." Liz stomped her foot on the floor and then made a dramatic exit. Evie closed and locked the door behind her.

We were now alone, and "something" was about to happen. Evie had more experience than me. She didn't precisely tackle me, but she grabbed me, sat me down on her bed, and sat beside me. She leaned over as if she was about to kiss me and said, "Okay, Squirrel, I want to make out with you and hang out with you, and I'm having fun. And all we're going to do is make out for right now. Unless I change my mind. So don't get any funny ideas." And she was wagging her finger at me while her eyes were soft and sparkling, and her lips, shiny with lip gloss, were about three inches away from my mouth. Before I could say anything, Evie kissed me again. This time, it was different. The other times at school and while walking through her neighbor's backyard were just lips on lips with hands grabbing arms and backs and butts. This kiss was intimate. Everything tingled inside of me. I remember my penis jumping up and surprising me. That had never happened before. I flinched for a second, and she pushed me back and asked me what was wrong. I responded by leaning toward her and kissing her. It was my first time initiating an intimate kiss with a girl. She seemed to like it. Evie became more passionate, and I remember hearing some cooing sounds escaping from inside her. Evie giggled when she realized she was doing so.

Evie and I were in another world. I can say we connected on several levels. I was clueless about anything around me but Evie's lips, hands, body, perfume, and my heart beating. Oh yeah, and my penis alternated between mildly erect to fully erect. At some point, her leg came in contact with my penis, and at first, she flinched, then leaned into it. I could feel her face smiling while we were kissing.

A knock on the door snapped me out of the delightful dream. The person knocked again, this time with more urgency. A young boy's voice cracked and nervous, "Evie? I know you're in there. Can you open the door?" He was crying. I remember being furious that he was ruining our moment. Evie whispered in my ear softly. "That's my brother; I have to see what happened."

Evie squatted low while unlocking and opening the door so she would be at his eye level. He was crying and scared. I had never seen him before, but his face was colorless.

"What happened?" Evie gently wiped the tears off his cheeks. He kept crying. "What's wrong?" He looked up at me for a brief second and then looked at her.

She understood that he didn't know me and was too scared to speak in front of me. She turned around and made eye contact with me, raised her right hand, and put her index finger up, letting me know she would return in one minute. Evie stepped outside the door, leaving it open a crack.

"What's the matter?"

"Liz touched me."

"What do you mean she touched you?" Her voice was curious, with a tinge of anger.

"She touched my peepee." He pointed towards his genitals. Evie was on her feet and in her little brother's room, yelling at, pushing, and shoving Liz around. I could hear all of it. Evie and Liz argued, and I heard Evie command her to leave and never come back, and she would never talk to her again.

Evie turned back to her little brother for a few minutes before entering her room, holding him in her arms. I could see her trying to hold back her tears, but she couldn't. I was doing the same thing and didn't even know him. That was the last time Evie and I made out or had an intimate experience. We have yet to talk about it. Not about what happened to her brother, Liz, or us. It was as if all of it had disappeared. The imprint it left on me was that love, intimacy, and connection with a girl result in awful catastrophes that end. I didn't hang out with her again until my Bar Mitzvah party. I invited her at the last minute and was happy she came.

I don't remember much about the brown pants she was wearing the night of the party, but I remember she wore a green silk button-down shirt tucked in tightly that rested over her breasts enough to show they existed but not sufficient to make her breasts noticed more than her or her shirt. She was also wearing a little bit of mascara and lipstick. It was the first time I saw her wearing makeup. As the day wore on, my brother started paying attention to her. I had a pit in my stomach. No matter what we were doing, I focused on Evie and my brother. We were playing ball in the backyard. I saw them both walking to the front of the house in the corner of my eye. I heard his car racing up the street and screeching tires. Evie was in David's car. They weren't back for a few minutes as I'd hoped. I thought he would drive around the block, show off his Mustang, screech some tires, and be back. Fifteen minutes had passed, and they had not returned.

I went and told my mother. A few minutes later, most of the adults living in the neighborhood went to their houses to check, walked around, and a couple left in cars to see if they could find them. About thirty minutes later, they came back. Evie's shirt was a mess and untucked. One of the buttons was missing. Her face was red, and I could see she had cried. She expressed terror and rage through her face and body language. I had lived with David, so I understood what it meant. When I saw her coming to the backyard, I greeted Evie, "Leave me alone and don't bother me!" her voice shaking and eyes red with tears. She pointed at me, and it was an explicit command. Other kids and adults tried to talk to Evie, and she either physically or verbally pushed them away. She entered the bathroom, locked the door, and didn't come out for a while. Evie was never the same. Neither was I. The problem was that David stayed the same.

Jane and Blair

BRAYDEN AND I met Jane and Blair on a sweltering hot day in July at the town pool. We were about to enter eighth grade, and they were about to enter seventh grade at our school. Jane and Blair were cute, fun, and intelligent in many ways. Jane had brown hair and blue eyes and was tall and thin. She was attractive but relatively simple-looking; you would not notice her in a crowd, but you would see a beautiful teenage girl when you did. Blair was slightly shorter than Jane, had mixed blonde and brown hair and deep blue eyes, and was more physically developed than Jane. Blair was the type you would notice because her eyes, hair, skin, and clothes were an assortment of colors. Jane started connecting with Brayden, who was my other best friend, along with Emerson, and I was connecting with Blair.

We started hanging out together over the next couple of weeks. Brayden was beginning to make out with Jane, and there was nervous energy between Blair and me. We flirted, played, and liked each other but didn't proceed for similar or different reasons. Since I didn't know her previously, she had just recently developed her adolescent body and was beginning to get male attention; therefore, she was inexperienced. For me, it was the usual story. We liked each other,

Raised by Wolves, Possibly Monsters

we connected, the excitement and energy developed, and then I got scared, and the whole thing paused.

We hadn't reached the pause stage yet; it was the 4th of July. We all made up stories of where we would be and with whom so our parents wouldn't know. We met at the fireworks one block away from the pool. We were hanging out in the back, where the older "cool kids" were. Brayden and Jane were making out during the fireworks while we were all lying on our backs, looking up at the stars, the bright lights, and the loud booms. Blair and I exchanged glances, followed by chickening out from making eye contact or kissing. Eventually, we looked at each other simultaneously, leaned too far into each other, and slightly tapped our foreheads, and our lips met. We both started laughing, and a minute later, we were kissing. It was enjoyable and exciting. I felt alive and stimulated by the fireworks, the big bangs, and the little kisses. Neither of us was experienced, so we kissed, rubbed our cheeks against each other, and hugged. Occasionally, we rubbed our noses against each other and giggled. Hands found butts, hands found waists, and hands found breasts. While I was rubbing her breasts over her white T-shirt and bra, I could feel her nipples getting hard. Blair being excited got me even more turned on and excited.

Blair whispered in my ear, "You can touch them." She took my right hand and put it under her T-shirt on her bra. Her skin was soft, warm, and a little bit sweaty. Her nipples became even more erect from my touch over her smooth bra, which felt satiny. I felt brave enough to slide my hand under her bra for a brief moment. She wiggled her body a little bit. I thought she was trying to pull away. I started pulling my hand back, and she grabbed it over her shirt and put it back. "I just wanted to make it easier for you." Now that I had permission and confirmation, I became confident and slid my hand under her bra until I found her nipple. When I first touched them, the world stopped briefly. A tiny sound escaped her mouth, bringing me back to the world. Just a slight little exhale and breathlessness. As I continued to explore her breasts and nipples, Blair became more breathless, and her hips and legs would move around and connect with mine. Our bodies moved closer together; we were tangled in the best way possible.

The fireworks were exploding above us, signaling the finale, and everybody was screaming, shouting, and oohing and aahing. They ended, and everybody clapped. And just like that, everybody got up from the grass and started walking in the direction where the four of us were lying on the grass playing the way adolescent kids do.

One of those people was a sixth-grade teacher from the school Blair had just completed. "Blair? Is that you?" All four of us looked up at this middle-aged woman wearing glasses when I realized my hand was still inside her shirt, and I tried to slowly sneak it out as if she wouldn't notice a hand inside her former student's white T-shirt. "Blair! I am shocked by this. I did not think you were this kind of girl!" She grunted, huffed, and stomped away. The moment was lost. Blair and I never kissed or flirted again.

About three weeks later, Brayden and his family went to Florida to visit his paternal grandparents, who had a boat that they would visit every summer. While Brayden was away, Emerson and I wandered around Jane's neighborhood. We did not know where she lived but assumed it was somewhere in that neighborhood. We weren't specifically looking for Jane; we were floating around looking for friends to hang out with. When we walked past her house, she sat outside drawing on a sketch pad. When we recognized each other, all three of us said hello excitedly. A few minutes later, her mother came outside and told Jane to invite her friends inside since it was getting dark. She awkwardly asked us performatively since her mother was standing there waiting. The three of us entered a room with a couch and a TV. Her mother returned with three lemonades in tall glasses with ice.

Inside her house with bright lights, we were seated on the green leather couch of their den; we didn't know what to say. The three of us had never spent time together. There was the weird thing between Blair and me on the 4th of July, and the obvious was that Jane was Brayden's girlfriend, and my best friend, Brayden, was away on a family vacation. We started by talking about Brayden and making jokes about him, his family, and his grandparents in Florida.

We started asking playful questions of Jane, like if she and Brayden had ever made out, which we already knew the answers to. I had witnessed it several times in person. Had he ever felt her up, she initially got embarrassed and giggled without responding. With some prodding, she said yes. Jane was playing along;

       Raised by Wolves, Possibly Monsters

Emerson asked her if he had ever put his hands "down there"? She jumped up, startling both of us, thinking we had upset her. Instead, Jane quietly closed the door to the den so her parents couldn't hear us talking. She came back to sit between us, and we moved our bodies a little closer. Jane had each of her hips connected to one of us.

"We should stop doing this. If Brayden finds out, he'll be so mad at me."

Emerson was primarily interacting directly with Jane at this point. "Well, why did you shut the door if you didn't want to talk about it or play? Am I right?"

Jane's face turned red with embarrassment. She nodded her head and giggled. Her face turned a deeper shade of red. Jane's eyes sparkled with excitement, as did her whole face. Emerson leaned towards her and kissed her on the cheek. She giggled quietly and put her hand over her mouth sheepishly. He kissed her again on the cheek, holding it a bit longer. When Emerson pulled away, he nodded at me, so I kissed her on the cheek this time. Since it worked for him, I kissed her a second time on the cheek a little longer. Then he kissed her on the cheek, and I kissed her on the cheek. Her excitement was growing by the moment. Emerson became bolder, kissing her on the lips, and she kissed him back. He took his head away and then again made eye contact with me. I kissed her on the lips, and she kissed me back.

We took turns kissing her on the lips and cheeks; sometimes, we simultaneously kissed her on the cheek. The energy in the room was rising. Emerson put his hand on her breast over her white T-shirt, back in the hippie days when almost everybody wore white T-shirts in the summer. At first, she cringed; there was panic in her eyes. Emerson kissed her again and asked her if we should stop. She shook her head. A minute later, my hand was on her breast instead of Emerson's. Jane's father knocked on the door and came in, and there were no hands or lips on her body.

"What's going on here? This door needs to be open!" It was not a question, more an accusation.

"Your TV is so loud that we can't hear the one in here, and we wanted some privacy. Shut the door and leave us alone."

"Don't talk to me like that! We need you to leave the door open." He gave her a stare-down and walked away. She waited till she heard him sit on the couch in the other room, whispering to her mother. The only words that we could hear were "Jane," "door," and "boys." And while they were talking, Jane quietly got up and closed the door. The affirmation we were looking for without knowing we were looking for one. When she sat down between us, kisses, tongues, hands over shirts, under shirts, over bras, under bras, sometimes all of those things were happening at the same time.

I was feeling encouraged for the first time and started rubbing her denim shorts between her legs. She had a powerful reaction and quietly said no without much energy and force behind her demand. A minute later, I tried again; she didn't say anything but wiggled her body in a way that prevented me from doing it. I did it a third time, and she stopped resisting. I was rubbing her between her legs over her blue denim shorts. I could tell she wasn't enjoying this experience at all. She felt small for the first time. While this was happening, her father entered the door again, and everybody's hands returned to where they belonged before he could see us. "I told you to leave this door open! If you don't leave it open, your friends can't stay! Do you understand?"

Jane responded with the standard American white teenage girl tone and energy, "Yess-uh! Now leave us alone!"

I've always wondered if there is a school that American white teenage girls go to teach them how to put an "uh" on the end of any word in the English language when they are frustrated or angry. Jane was no exception. She looked relieved when her father came in to interrupt what was happening. This time, the door stayed open, and we were talking and playing over her shirt on her breasts and fingers touching lips, no kissing, and no hands under T-shirts or bras. We heard her mother get up from the couch in the other room; she stopped before the door and asked if we wanted popcorn. We nodded, and she was back with popcorn a few minutes later. And more lemonade.

The TV was on in the background, starting to joke and play, eating popcorn and drinking lemonade. Everything had become relaxed and easy again. Jane was feeling comfortable. When we finished the bowl of popcorn, she got up and went to the kitchen to get more popcorn, re-entered the room with the bowl full, and clicked the door closed again. There was more kissing, there were breasts, and there was her lifting her hips to touch and rub her butt over her jeans and then

  Raised by Wolves, Possibly Monsters

under her jean shorts. One of those times, I felt excited and cocky, and I slid my hand down the front of her shorts. "No!" she quickly pulled my hand out. Her father appeared three seconds later.

"No," that two-letter word catches every father's attention with a daughter worldwide.

"Is everything okay?"

"Yes. Squirrel and Emerson both started throwing popcorn at me, Dad. I told them to stop because I didn't want it stuck in the couch." She looked at us to stop "the popcorn throwing." She put on her best disapproving face for her dad.

"That's my girl." He walked away, satisfied and proud of his daughter.

When we heard him return to the other room excitedly telling her mother what a good daughter they had, she turned to each of us individually, "No touching down there." She said it quietly, so it didn't activate her father's radar again. There was a firmness in her face and energy. "Do you promise?" We both independently nodded. With that, she got up and closed the door again. I'm not sure what happened, but about three minutes later, we were kissing, hands-on breasts, hands-on butts. We took turns gently taking her hand and putting it on our pants over our penises, which both woke up. Initially, she resisted but then seemed curious.

I think Jane liked having the experience and power of touching a boy's penis through his pants and creating such a response physically. She seemed very turned on and excited. I then slowly slipped my hand down her pants, and my new friend looked at me. Jane was about to say no when my fingers were running through her pubic hair. Again, she looked like she was about to say no, but she didn't. About three seconds later, for the first time, my fingers directly touched a girl's labia. Jane appeared confused and experienced many emotions, thoughts, and feelings. Her nipples showed through her T-shirt, without a bra, which she had removed, and she stuck it in the couch. The same couch she was supposed to be afraid of us getting popcorn stuck. Her face was full of life and energy, but her eyes looked nervous and scared. When I started to insert my finger inside her vagina, she reached down and yanked my hand out of her denim shorts. She grabbed me by the wrist when it was out and glared into my eyes. "You promised!" Her voice was too loud because both her parents came into the room.

"I'm sorry, but your friends have to leave now. You keep shutting the door, and we asked you to keep it open. I'm sorry, Emerson and Squirrel. If you want to come into the living room and watch TV with us, you're welcome to do that. If not, you're going to have to go."

"I'm sorry. We were having a private conversation. Squirrel and I will leave. Thank you for letting us watch TV and hang out with your daughter. Jane is awesome and fun to hang out with. The popcorn and lemonade were delightful, like my mother's." Emerson stood up, and I followed, as did Jane. We exchanged goodbyes with her parents, and Jane walked us out the front door.

We were standing in front of her front stoop under the moonlight. We could see tears rolling down her cheeks. She looked at me with deep sadness, "You promised, Squirrel. I let you do everything else, and the one thing I asked you not to do, which you promised me you wouldn't do, you did! Why did you do that? Do you not like me?"

I felt like I had just been punched in the stomach by my brother after he ate one of his protein shakes with a raw egg. I felt a little wobbly on my feet, and my breathing was tight and constricted. I tried to ensure no tears would leak from my eyes, but I'm not sure I succeeded. "I'm so sorry, Jane. I just got excited. I think you're cool and smart, and I like you. I'm really sorry."

Jane nodded her head. She threw her arms around me and hugged me. I could feel her tears on my cheek now. She held me tight. Part of me was excited about feeling her braless breasts pressed against me and my penis pressed against her body. The other part was feeling the sweetness of the moment and the impact of apologizing for something I did to somebody I liked and did something harmful to.

Her voice was barely audible, "Thank you, Squirrel." She kissed me on the cheek and let go. Some of my shame subsided, but not all of it. Jane turned and hugged Emerson as well. It did not have the same degree of force and warmth as Jane and I shared.

I was never able to be friends with Jane again. I felt such shame and embarrassment over my actions. Jane still wanted to be friends with me, but I didn't dare look her in the eye whenever I saw her. A few weeks later, she was at our school, and I would say hello while passing in the halls without stopping.

 Raised by Wolves, Possibly Monsters

A Flight to Florida

 I WAS A last-minute addition to a vacation my father and brother were going on to visit my aunt and uncle in Florida. The week before the trip, my mother and brother argued at dinner; this was not particularly unusual. What was different was the volume and intensity of my mother. She looked like she was going to kill him. She looked like she would kill every "him" in the world. I remember the spoon shaking in my right hand while trying to eat escarole and bean soup.

What's interesting about this particular argument is that I can't remember what David said or did. I was fourteen then, and by then, I had learned to tune out most of what he did and said, especially when he was angry. In that particular fight, my mother matched his rage.

"I've had enough of you and your father's bullshit! I will not listen to this crap anymore. You're all fucking liars, and I've had enough of it. I had it with my father as a kid, I had it with my brother before he went to prison at age eight in Jamestown, I had it with your goddamn father, and I will not take it from you! Either eat your damn dinner and shut up or just get the fuck out of here!" She banged her right fist on the table, and the silverware and dishes clicked in response.

I have no idea what David said, but I can feel it in my bones right now. It had that dark hate and venom that his eyes, words, and whole being would embrace. In general, when he stepped into this energy, everybody was terrified. My mother was not on that night. He kept yelling, threatening, and taunting her. My mother took her empty can of Coke and threw it at my brother. It bounced off the side of his cheek, and he laughed. His laugh was another taunt and an invitation to battle. She looked like she was about to lose it. She grabbed her butter knife, which flew across the table toward his head. He smacked it out of the way, stood up, and laughed.

"I'm right here in front of you. Now you have a bigger target. Why not get the wooden spaghetti spoon and see if that helps? How many of them do you have to break while smacking me before you realize you can't hurt me? You can't touch me. Nobody can hurt me. I'm untouchable and unstoppable."

My mother's face turned white, and her eyes were wide open. She realized for the first time that she could do nothing to scare or hurt David. When my brother realized he had won, he flipped over his bowl of soup; it spilled across the table. He laughed out loud and walked away like a matador after a bullfight. That night, David moved out. He went to stay at my dad's shitty little studio apartment in Elizabeth. Three days later, I was on a flight to Florida with them, not knowing where I would live or stay when we returned from vacation.

Besides all the chaos and turmoil leading up to the flight, for some reason, there were only ten passengers on that Boeing 727 with four flight attendants, which we called stewardesses back then. Back then, stewardesses were typically aspiring models and actresses trying to earn a living. They successfully utilized their physical attractiveness to make a good living. They were all pretty, flirty, playful, and young. All four of these particular flight attendants were living magazine covers, ready and willing to give us whatever attention and needs we had for a three-hour flight. David and my father flirted with two of them in particular relentlessly. At different times during the flight, my brother disappeared into a bathroom with one flight attendant, and later on, my father disappeared into a separate bathroom with another flight attendant.

The one I was "flirting with" eventually started looking at me with that look of, "What a cute little boy. I'll bet he'll be cute and sweet when he's older." It felt demoralizing how successful and easy it was for the two of them and how dismissed I was. They got whatever they got in private bathrooms, and I got two extra bags of peanuts and pretzels.

I wanted to cry. The week I had was brutal and painful for me. Not one person asked me how I was doing or what I needed, except the flight attendant kept asking me if I needed more peanuts. Nobody knew how crushed I was. Nobody knew this was the night I went from lost and confused to hateful and bitter. Nobody knew that this was the night that I became one of them.

When we arrived at the Fort Lauderdale Airport, my Aunt Doris and Uncle Ben were ecstatic and surprised to see me, my father, and my brother. Somebody was happy to see me. I mattered to somebody.

Parts of that vacation were fun and exciting. Most of the vacation did not feel like a vacation because we were inching toward the inevitable. I would not live

     Raised by Wolves, Possibly Monsters

with my mother, and I would now live with my father and brother in his studio
apartment, which had an open-up loveseat that became a bed and another
loveseat across from it. I knew that that loveseat would be where I slept across
from the monsters swallowing me up.

The Garden Apartments for Single Parents and Their Kids

 WE MOVED INTO a two-bedroom apartment in the West Mill Garden
Apartments with 664 units three weeks later. They were a brand-new
style of architecture with two stories of garden apartments. David had
the big bedroom, I had the small one, and my father brought his open-up
loveseat, where he slept in the living room. The complex was across the street
from the hospital where I had had my tonsils taken out a few years earlier. Most
adults living in this complex were doctors or nurses at the hospital. The other
thing they shared was being the first generation of divorced parents, raising their
kids without a partner. This was the beginning of divorced parents in America.
We were shifting the family unit from the illusion of the perfect nuclear home to
messy and hateful homes without one of their parents and the other one pissed
off and miserable taking care of them.

I remember the day the movers came to the house and took David's and my
bedroom furniture, clothes, and everything else. Even though strangers were in
the house moving furniture, my mother couldn't bring herself to get dressed. All
this happened while she was standing in her slippers, wearing her nightgown in
the living room, and holding tissues in her hand the whole time. She did not say
one word. Her sense of defeat at my father's hands was devastating. My father
had cheated on her the entire time they were married, had gotten away with it,
was not a responsible parent, and somehow ended up taking her children away.
It was worse than her worst nightmare. The sad part was that my father wanted
to "win" so badly that it did not occur to him that "winning" meant he was now
a parent and the adult who takes care of the home.

When I got in my brother's Mustang so we could leave for our new home in
the neighboring town, I knew I was no longer a child. I didn't know what I was

becoming, but I knew I wasn't a kid any longer.

I went from a new kid to a cool kid quickly. Most of the teenagers in the neighborhood were one or two years younger than me. They were more impressed with me than those who were my age. A group of boys hung out every day after school and often at night. We did the things that troubled boys from complicated homes do when they hang out together. We drank alcohol, smoked weed, stole things, broke things, lit stuff on fire, exploded things, and terrorized girls. Most of the girls did what girls do from complicated homes; they hung out with troubled boys and became the target of troubled boys.

Pretty in Pink

JASMINE WORE A lot of pink. Jasmine's mother wore a lot of pink. Jasmine's living room, dining room, and bedroom were temples honoring the gods of pink. Some girls embrace being feminine, or what many people call being "girly." Jasmine was one of them at a young age. Both Jasmine and her mother looked fabulous in pink. I don't think I remember ever seeing either one of them robed in anything but pink or white, except a pair of brand-new designer blue jeans.

Jasmine's mom was warm, friendly, and gorgeous. Vanessa enjoyed being attractive and being a woman. She was intelligent, successful, and strong. I don't know what happened before Jasmine's mother divorced, but the woman I met was a force of nature draped in pink and white with long black hair. She was a superb role model for Jasmine, but adolescent boys aren't as prepared for goddesses as grown men are. For the record, grown men don't impress me with how well they interact and honor goddesses. Vanessa was a goddess, and Jasmine was a goddess in training.

My buddy Asher and I used to visit Jasmine a lot. As we saw it, there were two great reasons to go to Jasmine's house after school. The first and most important reason was that her mother was rarely home after school since she had a business. The second was that Jasmine was still a goddess in training and wasn't strong enough yet to set firm boundaries so that we would leave her alone. We knew this. She knew we knew this. Vanessa knew that we knew this.

I want to be precise. Jasmine did nothing wrong. I repeat, Jasmine did nothing wrong. Her biggest "crime" was having a warm, loving heart, a pretty face, and a desire to be found attractive.

Like all good manipulators and exploiters, we started small and built upon each boundary we broke successfully. That's the way wolves become monsters.

I learned this strategy from my father, brother, and uncles. Jasmine was scared. She was scared of being hurt and abused, of not being accepted, and of not mattering or being noticed. She understood that girls like Amelia and Winnie commanded more attention from boys. They were the most popular girls in our apartment complex. She understood women like her mother demanded attention and to be seen and aspired to walk in her mother's shoes. She understood that receiving attention from older boys was the most effective way to feel noticed and attractive. I also believe that deep down inside, Jasmine liked Asher and me, especially me. She wanted to be my friend. It's possible she also wanted to be my girlfriend, but I never gave that a chance. I removed from Jasmine and myself the opportunity to have a real friendship and forget about being boyfriend and girlfriend.

As I mentioned earlier, we started small. Simple things like flirting, telling Jasmine how pretty she was, and telling her she was more mature than other girls her age. Her eyes would widen and sparkle when I told her how pretty she was. I, too, liked Jasmine and would have liked her to have been my girlfriend. I'm reminding you that I was raised by wolves if not monsters; I understood that taking what I wanted would always override what would make me happy and feel loved and accepted. The taking was the key. Women and their bodies were conquests.

I remember playing with Jasmine's light brown, wavy, almost curly hair that went down below her shoulders. Jasmine often looked like somebody from a black-and-white photo from 1937. I appreciated how consistently well put together and presented she was. Jasmine had soft cheeks, softer lips, and even softer skin. She liked being touched. At the root of it, that was the actual obstacle for Jasmine. She liked it when we touched her arms, her hand, and especially her face and hair. She liked when I would rub my hand over her upper and lower back and possibly her butt. Those moments when Jasmine felt loved and nurtured while experiencing fear and betrayal must have been brutal. Sometimes, I remember seeing her eyes get red and wet; occasionally, a tear dripped down her cheek. I vaguely remember kissing one of her tears once and running my tongue on her cheek with its salty taste.

Jasmine enjoyed having me kiss her. Soft kisses felt nice to her; passionate, forceful, and sexual kisses did not. She was only thirteen. Sometimes, when touching or kissing her, one or both of us "casually" would rub our hand over her breast, and her body would stiffen. She usually asked us to stop with a feeble "Please" at the end of her request. How could she know that her voice shaking with the word "Please" communicated that she was at our mercy? Jasmine sounded powerless, which informed us that we were powerful.

Sometimes, Jasmine wouldn't resist. I'm not going to guess why. Sometimes, I would rub between her legs over her jeans. She would wiggle away with minimal success. I was more successful if I was stroking, rubbing, and caressing her butt because she enjoyed that experience and appeared turned on. However, Jasmine seemed distressed if I had just touched the front. When she wasn't wearing jeans and was wearing one of her soft, flowing dresses or skirts, I could feel the folds of her labia through the clothing, which apparently turned us both on despite her need for this not to happen.

Now and then, I would show up with a friend or two, knocking on her window to her bedroom late enough that she was in her sheer pink nightgown getting ready for bed. She would come to the window and put her finger over her lips, communicating for us to be quiet. We would plead with her, but maybe she thought she'd get rid of us quicker by opening the window before her mother could hear us outside. Those were the first times I could see a young adolescent girl's nipple clearly and protruding. Jasmine was a real-life doll out of the old movies. She always looked pretty, no matter what she was wearing or doing.

A few times, I climbed into her bedroom window and touched Jasmine's breasts over her nightgown. She pleaded for me to stop in a hushed whisper so her mother wouldn't hear. Her nipples became even more erect to my touch. I think one time, I even heard a slight moan escape her mouth. I did adore Jasmine. I did want her to like and be attracted to me. I did want her to break down and

Raised by Wolves, Possibly Monsters

ask me, beg me to have sex with her. I fantasized about convincing Jasmine to let me penetrate her. That never happened. There were a few times that a finger or two briefly penetrated her vagina. Jasmine's body was aroused and confused. Her beautiful, sweet body and heart wanted something that her mind knew she was neither ready for nor wanted.

I am aware even today that there were several times that if I had pushed further, Jasmine and I would've had intercourse for the first time. While she had that inner struggle, she would have given in, as my father and brother said, and parts of her would've enjoyed it. I never felt good when I left Jasmine's home. I cared for and possibly loved Jasmine as a friend and a boy attracted to her. I felt shame and pity about myself, compassion and empathy, and, in some weird way, a deep connection with Jasmine. I wanted to stop what I was doing to her, but I didn't have the power to do something better. It was cruel what I did. I find it informative that my fantasies about Jasmine typically involved tenderness and connection, touching, soft voices, and intimate sex. At my core, I wanted to love and be loved by her. My hate for myself and fear of rejection created resentment, bringing up a force that said, "I need to eradicate her, her beauty, and her purity. I need to annihilate all of her."

Jungle Love

DURING THE SECOND summer of living in the garden apartments, a girl from a few towns away started hanging out at the pool for apartment complex residents. She did not live there, nor did anybody in her family, but her father was supposedly a mob guy, and somehow, that translated to her being able to hang out and swim at the pool. Layla had dreamy blue eyes, black hair, a simple but warm smile, and fun to play and flirt with.

I remember Asher and I being the two primary flirters. At some point, it became clear that she was choosing Asher over me. It was typical for a girl or woman to be excited and interested in me and one of my friends. As I would lose my confidence, as mentioned above, she would choose my friend, regardless of which one.

On a rainy Sunday afternoon, Layla asked Asher and me if we wanted to go to the movies with her and her best friend, Sylvia. Neither of us knew Sylvia, but we had nothing else to do, so I said yes. The four of us giggled, flirted, played, and threw popcorn the whole movie. It was enjoyable.

We were already in our seats when they arrived. I saw reddish-blond hair, full cheeks with freckles, and big, juicy lips in the dim lighting. This new girl's body had curves, and Sylvia was fun to talk and play with. My excitement increased when Asher and Layla made out a few times. There was groping, and she squealed now and then. Layla's squealing turned me on even more. When the lights came on, I was not as attracted to Sylvia, but since we had fun, I figured, why not see where this goes? They had to leave because Layla's mother was waiting outside. Asher and I were petrified of her father. Her parents were strict, so they left promptly.

The following Saturday, Layla and Sylvia would be at the pool. Asher and I ensured we were there but would have been there anyway. As was usual, Asher and I smoked a joint before they showed up since neither of them smoked pot. We played in the pool, and Sylvia often flirted with me. She started getting closer, and we grabbed and touched each other's bodies. I remember at one point rubbing her butt over her bathing suit and even under her bathing suit in the pool while everybody was around. Since she didn't seem to object to that, I rubbed and squeezed her breasts over her bathing suit several times. We decided to leave the pool and walked together to the playground about a hundred yards away. We were swinging on the swings, and for some reason, I started singing "Jungle Love" by Steve Miller Band, which was becoming popular. They joined in, and we had fun being silly and making up ridiculous words, mostly about sex.

I ran into a new dilemma with Sylvia. I liked her, and she was fun. I enjoyed flirting and playing with her. She wanted me and liked flirting and playing with me, too. I thought her body was beautiful, but something about her face turned me off. We made out briefly before Layla's mom came to pick up the two of them. She already had her phone number and name written on paper and stuck it in my pocket before they left.

We hadn't seen them in a couple of weeks. One day, I was listening to WDHA, a local rock station in New Jersey. I was caught off guard when the DJ

     Raised by Wolves, Possibly Monsters

said, "This next song is sent out to somebody named Squirrel from Sylvia. I have no idea who these people are, but the names are funny, and I like the song. Here we go with Steve Miller Band's 'Jungle Love.'" The song came on the radio through my Pioneer audio system. I was excited, mortified, confused, and happy. Halfway through the song, Asher and Richie called me separately, as did Amelia and Winnie. The other three did not know who Sylvia was, but Asher did. We spent a half hour on the phone figuring out if it was Sylvia, Layla's friend, and why she would pick that song. I asked him to call Layla and find out what was going on.

Unbeknownst to me, Sylvia had a massive crush on me. She thought we had something special and was waiting for me to call every day. For her, I was singing this song on the swings because I thought she and I had "Jungle Love." For me, the song was in my head, and I would have sung it even if I was in math class. Nothing further ever happened between Sylvia and me, but it was the first time I had a song dedicated to me on the radio! Whenever I hear that song, I think of the four of us on the swings being ridiculous and having fun. I think about that opportunity and how narrow-minded I was about dating and being attracted to women, and I think about Layla.

The Summer of Sam

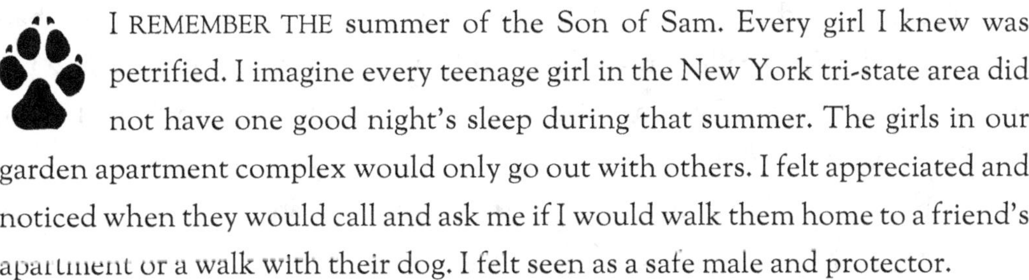I REMEMBER THE summer of the Son of Sam. Every girl I knew was petrified. I imagine every teenage girl in the New York tri-state area did not have one good night's sleep during that summer. The girls in our garden apartment complex would only go out with others. I felt appreciated and noticed when they would call and ask me if I would walk them home to a friend's apartment or a walk with their dog. I felt seen as a safe male and protector.

There are three benefits to living across the street from a large hospital.

1) Many young, attractive nurses in their twenties and thirties regularly walk to and from the hospital.

2) If you get munchies from weed or hash, the cafeteria is open twenty-four hours a day, seven days a week, for microwave popcorn, a brand-new invention

at the time, and you could only find it at hospitals.

3) The one most critical to me was that I often had sharp abdominal pains and cramps. We could quickly and easily get to the hospital. They never had any solutions, but there was a medicine that seemed to help the pain.

After months of visits to the hospital across the street, a doctor referred a gastroenterologist over the hill on Old Short Hills Road. I remember going to the Atkins Building for the first time. The building was modern, with mirror glass windows. The doctor was a nerdy-looking guy who looked like he hadn't smiled or had fun since the 50s. We returned the following week for some new advanced testing to help figure out what was going on in my abdominal region. He told me I'd need to drink special fluids for twenty-four hours before the tests and no other food or drink. He did not tell me that they would be sticking a metal thing with a camera up my asshole to look around.

The doctor explained many words and things I didn't understand to my father. Sometimes, he would look at me, talk slowly, and use elementary words, as if I was six years old, born in another country, and new to the English language. After speaking for about ten minutes to the both of us, with all of his long words, deep voice, and pointing to us with a blue pen, he said, "We don't know what's wrong with you." Then, he asked my father if he could speak privately with me. My father said of course and left the room.

"Mike, I'd like to ask you a few questions. Have you had much stress in your life lately?"

"Yeah. I moved from my mother's, and the courts were involved, and I had to sign a sucky thing called an affidavit, and my mom was a great cook, and my dad's a shitty cook, and I get to do whatever I want, I hate the school that I go to, and I miss my friends."

"What are you doing to help you with the stress? Testing suggests the pains and cramps in your abdomen are from stress or tension."

"Are you trying to say that there's nothing wrong with me when I wake up in the middle of the night screaming in fucking pain!"

"No. What I'm saying is that it does not originate in your body. It appears to be from your stress and tension."

"That's bullshit!"

     Raised by Wolves, Possibly Monsters

"Just give me a minute here. What do you do to relieve the stress from everything that's going on in your life?"

"I play basketball and smoke pot!"

"Well, clearly, you need to play more basketball and smoke more pot because you have a bleeding ulcer, and if you don't do something about it soon, there's gonna be a hole in your gut by the time you're twenty-five for the rest of your life."

I was stunned that this annoying geeky doctor told me to smoke more pot! "One more thing, Mike, I'm prescribing medicine for you when you have stomach cramps. It won't help much, but it may make your father feel better if you take it. When you have stomach cramps, smoke pot and play basketball."

A year later, I was addicted to marijuana and, soon after that, cocaine. It took another two years to complete the triumvirate, including alcohol. The final straws were when my mother's sister, my aunt Dee Dee, died of cancer, followed by John Lennon the next year. John was the one human being who gave me hope that love could exist, peace could exist, and that love matters. He was shot and killed in front of his garden. My Aunt DeeDee was my safe person. Now, there was no Aunt DeeDee, no John Lennon, and, more importantly, no hope or reason to fight any longer. Life sucked. I sucked, and everything sucked.

Mountain Highs and Mountain Lows

FROM THE SECOND I attended Mountain High School (my initials, MHS), I didn't want to be there. They were our rival town. My cousin Carmen was the only person I knew, and we were no longer very close. When we were young, we spent a lot of time together.

As a kid, there are two things I remember about Carmen. He was sensitive and not interested in pop culture or being cool. He only enjoyed eating pasta with butter, cheeseburgers, French fries, and Coke. An odd diet for a boy in an Italian family! Carmen had a younger sister, Carla, who was three years younger than us, and an older brother, who was twelve years our senior. Charlie was drafted and went to Vietnam. He left as a hippie and came back as a hippie, struggling to make sense of his time in Vietnam like many other young men. He married his high school sweetheart Maria when he returned. They have been together ever since and have created a nice life for themselves.

So, when I went to Mountain High School, even though Carmen and I were the same age, he was one grade behind me. Sometimes, our social circles crossed, and because we weren't close any longer, it was awkward for me and appeared as if it was for him as well. We never talked about it. I hated having to make new friends. I hated having to prove myself all over again. I hated the change in environment; I lived in a neighborhood where local kids showed up to share the delicious meals my mother cooked, but I moved into an environment where my father thought making salad was a culinary accomplishment. My brother even avoided dinner often.

I hated getting off the bus and walking up towards our apartment, seeing my father, who was in his fifties, and anywhere from three to five women in their twenties hanging out together. He was always the center of attention because he was a dynamic and exceptional bullshit artist. I don't know if it infuriated me more just how easy it was for him to manipulate and exploit females for attention and sex or that he lost his job and was collecting unemployment and hanging out all day with the local twenty-something-year-old nurses. Did I mention that I also hated having to take a bus ride about forty minutes each way to get to and from school after moving from a town where I was about to go to the high school that was two and a half blocks away? Did I mention that I hated being a total mess and lost in high school and felt like nobody was there to care for and love me?

I got suspended once and expelled for running a blackjack game in the boys' bathroom. We were not playing for change or single-dollar bills. It was a high-stakes game for high school kids, where somebody would lose anywhere from $25 to $75 in fifteen minutes. I also got suspended for selling drugs in the parking lot.

Fortunately for me, while my dad was threatening to sue the school for suspending me and they were negotiating about my being expelled, he decided to marry the twenty-two-year-old model who was working for him part-time in some pyramid scheme he was running. So, instead of being in the town that I initially hated and had no friends, I was leaving that town and leaving behind two towns of friends to live somewhere that I'd only been to once or twice before.

    Raised by Wolves, Possibly Monsters

In this new town where I was the new kid at the beginning of the senior year, I don't think I spoke an entire three paragraphs in class or to any student until the last day of school! I was smoking so much marijuana at this point I was just numb and without interest or excitement about anything but music.

My One Semester in the Dorms

I SPENT ONE semester staying on campus at Glassboro State University (currently Rowan University).

I had 3.5 roommates in a two-bedroom suite. I shared a room with a tall, slim white guy with reddish-blond hair, blue eyes, and freckles, who wore slacks and a button-down shirt. Everybody called him "Opie" like the kid on *The Andy Griffith Show*; it was not a compliment. In the other bedroom, there was this laid-back Italian boy who primarily wore baggy pants that you would see his underwear and the crack of his ass. He shared a room with Samuel, a handsome African American man who was fun, funny, and the life of the party. Samuel was a hardworking student, and everybody liked him; that was why I did not like him. He ruined my plan to be our unit's coolest, most interesting, and fun guy. Samuel got attention wherever he went. And lastly, there was a young man named James, who was also African American. Before I moved in the previous semester, the roommates let James sleep on a cot in the living room. That meant two things: he was living there for free, and somebody was sleeping in the living room in the morning and when you went to bed at night.

I was a DJ at the radio station, that is, until I played the Dead Kennedys' "Too Drunk to Fuck" twenty-seven times and got kicked out.

Unlike most students, I did not take out student loans or receive grants because I had transferred at the last minute. Neither of my parents had money. They were both in debt, and I did not get a scholarship. I was paying for tuition, books, food, and anything else I needed. I considered getting a job at the local Radio Shack but knew I would have to work full-time, and that still wouldn't cover my expenses. I wasn't willing to work that much,

My strategy became clear. I would pick up money DJing in one of the local bars, which I did. I would sell weed, magic mushrooms, and cocaine, which I did. For anything else I needed, including food, I would shoplift, which I did. Before I got to Glassboro, I had been doing these things, but I didn't need to shoplift all my food before being a student on campus. I was good at it. I would walk into stores, make eye contact and small talk with whoever was behind the counter, make sure I made eye contact with the person who looked like the manager or owner, and casually cruise around the store getting what I needed. I was a successful shoplifter and had not been caught stealing for about a decade.

When Samuel and James came with me, shoplifting was not so easy; everyone was watching us because Samuel and James were Black. I didn't try to steal when we were together because I knew it was a waste of time. Every single employee would stop what they were doing to follow us when I was with both of them! For anybody who thinks racism is not real, try shopping with a Brown or Black man present and see what happens.

Things were becoming desperate for me. Not being able to illegally obtain food, alcohol, music, and audio parts for DJing was frustrating, and more importantly, I didn't have enough money to buy drugs to sell. I could not skim drugs off the top for myself to use. It all made me, as an active drug addict, even more of a mess than usual.

One day, I asked Samuel if we could talk. He looked curious because I didn't think Samuel and I had a private conversation besides, "Hey, are you about to use the bathroom?" or "Do you know what happened to the bottle of Molson I put in the fridge?"

"Samuel, we have a problem with us being friends."

Initially, he responded with amusement, "You mean besides you being an asshole?"

"No. You're costing me too much money."

"I ain't costing you nothin'." Then Samuel repeated something about me being an asshole. This was the closest I heard Samuel come to cursing. He came from a religious, wholesome family. My roommate was raised with love, community, and respect.

"As you know, I'm paying myself for school and everything else. And since I've been hanging out with you, every time we go in a store together, I get caught

Raised by Wolves, Possibly Monsters

shoplifting, and it's costing me too much money. So, we can't hang out together in public because I can't afford to live here otherwise."

Samuel's face got tight, looking like he was ready to pop. I had not once witnessed Samuel angry, forget about rageful. He was forgiving and compassionate, even when anger may be justified or warranted. "Let me see if I got this straight; you want to stop hanging around me because of all the racist assholes out there that when I walk in stores, they follow me everywhere you're going, and this is costing you money? Therefore, your solution is not to be friends with the guy who has to go through this every single day of his life; and would never steal anything, or sell drugs, and works a full-time job cleaning the cafeteria while being a full-time student and your racist ass wants to not be in public with me. Do I have this right?"

"Samuel, I'm so sorry. There's no other solution. I'm glad you understand."

Samuel got up, kicked over one of the chairs, and started pacing the room, breathing heavily. "I'll tell you what I understand. I knew you were a self-centered asshole the first minute I met you, but I continued to be nice to you despite being proven time and again that I was right. I've introduced you to my friends, who you've been disrespectful and condescending to. I've hung out with you and brought you to parties and events that we all go to together, and it even turned my head when I knew you were stealing because you seemed desperate. I never said anything to you once about you being a thief and a drug dealer. Not once."

Samuel leaned over the chair in my direction with his eyes open wide and his fist closed tightly. "I'll agree to your racist bullshit idea on one condition. Tomorrow night, when we have that meeting at the radio station, you will sit with us all. You know why we're there, what happened, and you know those two guys that were kicked off the radio station for some stupid reason were just that they were Black and Jamaican. And you know we're having that protest and conversation with the station manager and a program director, and you're going to sit right in the middle of us all because you're a student DJ there, and you're a white guy, and you're a racist pig! If you agree to do that, I agree not to be in public with you because I've never wanted to be in public with you. And I'll be polite and respectful to you here in our dorm because that is how my Mama raised me. But don't expect me to be nice to you, don't expect me to let you always go first when you want to take a shower and act like you're more important than me, and certainly don't think I'm going to keep promoting you as a DJ to all my Black and Hispanic friends ever again!" Samuel banged his right fist on the table.

Samuel had spoken loudly enough that people had gathered in the hallway and poked their heads inside the door. I didn't know they were there for most of the conversation. His friend Alonzo was standing behind the crowd. "Looks like we're going to have DJ Mike sit with us Black and Hispanic kids at the radio station tomorrow night! How about that? We're going to have a White racist punk sitting amongst more than twenty-five Black and Spanish kids in front of his friends and everybody else at the radio station. Good job, Samuel. Glad you convinced this piece of shit, thief, drug dealer, and drug addict for our benefit and our cause."

A lot of the guys gave each other high-fives. There was a lot of chiming in from folks in the background as things were getting heated. I could feel my face getting warmer by the moment. One of the girls who stayed in the room next to ours waited till everybody was almost quiet and watching us intensely, "Besides being a racist pig, we can add pervert to that list. All of us girls know that we must be fully dressed when he's around." That got another round of people making high-fives. "We all know when he's not pissing off all the Black and Hispanic kids, he's pissing off all the white girls." I was running out of allies quickly.

"Yeah, I can do that. I'll sit with all of you tomorrow night. I'll even say something if you want me to."

"No! We don't want you to say a thing! If you open your mouth, somehow, you'll make us look worse for being around you. Just sit there with all of us and shut up. Deal?"

Samuel reached out his hand in what felt like one part aggression and rage and one part forgiveness and reconciliation, his integrity and respect intact. His kindness made me uncomfortable. I was not used to people responding like that. I stood up to shake his hand and banged my knee on the bottom of the table. Mostly, everybody was sticking their heads in the door, and many in the room, at this point, all broke out laughing. We shook hands, and then Samuel took his left hand and put it on top of both of our right hands.

     Raised by Wolves, Possibly Monsters

I felt shame on such a deep level that I just wanted to break into tears, but I didn't have the courage or strength to do it. I wanted to take my left hand and put it on top of Samuel's left hand as a gesture of respect and brotherhood, but I couldn't. I didn't have self-respect, and I was nobody's brother. Most of Samuel's friends were now in the room giving Samuel warm, intimate, and loving hugs, high-fives, and thanking him for getting the racist pig who's a DJ at the radio station to sit with them. They were supporting him for being intelligent and for not stooping to my level.

Opie, whom I was never nice to or paid attention to, came over and put his arm around me. I wanted to hug him right there and cry in his arms, but I couldn't do that either.

Belinda, one of the girls in the suite next door and the girl's roommate, walked over and hugged me. She didn't allow me to say no or do anything else. This young woman held me for a whole moment. Internally, I was vacillating between wanting to take in that somebody was being so kind and loving to me even though we didn't know each other very well. Part of me was getting turned on by her braless breasts being pressed against me. "DJ Mike, you're not an awful person. You've always been nice and respectful to me. I don't condone what you did or said to Samuel, but you stood up and agreed to sit with them tomorrow night. If you'd like, I'll sit next to you so you're not alone."

A few tears escaped my eyes. I'm not sure. I felt like an evil presence, having holy water poured on me and my skin and body being eaten alive by God, love, or possibly both, like in *The Exorcist*. For a brief second, I had the impulse to ask her to marry me. I was sure no kind, loving, beautiful, intelligent girl would ever be this nice to me again.

I broke the hug and stepped back into my role as "the cool guy," or at least that's what I told myself I was. I was seeing evidence that was not how other people thought about me. "Thank you, Belinda. That's nice of you, but I'm cool. I think I need to do this by myself." Brittany had a warm smile on her face. She reached her head forward, kissed me on the cheek, and gave me another hug. The horror of the last ten minutes disappeared for that brief ten seconds.

Belinda slowly pulled away and placed her hands on my elbows, "If you ever need anything, I'm right next door. I want you to know that you have a friend."

It took everything I had not to kiss her on the mouth and grab her ass. And I'm so glad that I didn't! I still had not learned to discern the difference between affection from friends and affection from sexual/romantic partners.

The next night, Samuel and Alonzo came to get me thirty minutes before we had to get to the radio station. A minute later, right behind them were at least fifteen or twenty of their friends piling into our living room. They wanted to do last-minute planning and ensure that I followed through on my promise. We walked across campus as a group, and they made sure I was in the middle at all points. When we arrived at the radio station, they sat me in the middle of the chairs, and everybody sat around me. It was a contentious meeting with the student station manager, program director, and DJ coordinator in the front, sitting on folding chairs facing about forty people. Three white kids in the front were all good-looking, good students, and well-dressed, and a room full of Black and Hispanic kids who looked nothing like them in any shape or form sitting as a group.

As the tension rose, the program director, a cute white girl, responded to a question. She started her sentence with, "Well, if you people . . ." and the room exploded. I made a mental note never to say "you people" again to a group of Black or Hispanic people.

Nothing was resolved at the station. The two Jamaican guys did not get their radio show returned to them, but they promised to speak to the staff advisor about it the next day. The meeting ended, and we all filed out of the room.

As soon as we left, Alonzo turned to me, "Look, we put up with your racist crap with Samuel yesterday because we needed you for tonight. We don't need you anymore. We don't want you around us. You can't walk with us and don't say hello to us. We have a hard enough time on campus full of racism; we don't need some thief, drug addict, and drug dealer making it worse for us. You can walk home by yourself."

They shuffled away and left me standing there. I wanted to run back in and tell the three people from the college radio station that I wasn't supporting them; I was sitting with them because they made me. Fortunately, some part of me quietly and firmly told me to shut up, walk home, and not say a word to anybody. I did. There were about six weeks left in the semester. I had to find a way to

          Raised by Wolves, Possibly Monsters

navigate through the mess I had created with one of the most liked and popular men on campus, who also happened to be my roommate. Any thoughts of ever living in the dorm again evaporated on that walk home.

When I returned, Belinda was standing in the hallway between our rooms. I felt relief when I saw her as I opened the stairway doors to the third floor. "Hi, Mike. How did it go? I saw Samuel and Alonzo, along with some of the rest of the group, stop by your room quickly and then leave. They didn't look happy."

I took a deep breath before speaking, noticing I had not taken a full breath in at least an hour, the night before, or since fifth grade. "It was scary for a minute there. Nothing was resolved, but they are going to talk to the staff advisor tomorrow."

"That sucks. How was it for you to have to do this?"

"It felt weird sitting with people I don't know who hate me, and I treated like an asshole."

"But you did it. You did what you said you would."

"Why are you being so nice to me? I don't deserve it."

"Mike, like I said last night, I am not OK with what you did and how you treat people, like my roommates and Samuel, but everyone deserves nice people, and you have been nice to me whenever I see you. And I get the feeling you can use a friend right now." Belinda shared a warm smile with me. My throat felt dry, and I was not able to answer her. I nodded my head because that was all I could do. She smiled again.

"Hang in there, Mike. I'll see you around." Belinda reached out and touched my left elbow lightly with a gentle squeeze. I felt a jolt of life/electricity entering my body. She smiled one more time and walked back to her room. I stood there catching my breath momentarily before heading into my room to drink tequila and smoke a joint.

I wish I could say I had a spiritual or racial awakening that night, that month, or that semester or decade. And in a way, I did. I learned I only got away with stealing, selling, and using drugs because I wasn't Black or Latino. I also learned how much harder it was for them to do the same things I was doing because of the resistance they received at every turn. None of my behaviors or attitudes improved. But for a brief period, I understood what today we call White Privilege.

Emelie

 AFTER THE DEBACLE at Triad dorms on campus, I was grateful to be "starting fresh again" somewhere else. If there was anything that I had mastered in life by age twenty-one, it was "starting fresh" again. It felt like a lifestyle direction or skill.

I moved across the street from campus to a small apartment complex called Campus Terrace Apartments. Little did I know there was a bizarre secret about this apartment complex. My buddy Asher from West Orange, who had been going to Ithaca College in Upstate New York, was struggling academically and socially. He decided to transfer to Glassboro. The idea of having Asher as my roommate was thrilling. I had already proved myself to him and was not starting at zero or less.

I moved into Campus Terrace in June for multiple reasons. The biggest is that I did not want to go back to North Jersey to stay with either of my parents. My brother was still serving his ten to thirteen-year sentence at Rahway State Prison, and if I went back up north, I would have to visit him in prison. I also wanted to stay in the Glassboro area to get settled. I never had a chance to do that in the Triad dorms.

The first person I met was Jacob, who became my DJ partner. Jacob and I got along spectacularly from the get-go. He was a DJ, and I was a DJ. Jacob dealt drugs on the side, and I sold drugs as a lifestyle choice. He was into taking significant risks and had a lot of "punk" in him. I was a punk when punk got me what I needed. Jacob liked to stay up all night partying and being the center of attention. I can say nothing more here for you to recognize the common ground.

Jacob was an unusually handsome guy. Everybody loved Jacob, especially the most attractive, dynamic, fun, and exciting girls in any situation.

I made a new friend named Emelie, who looked like a Scandinavian model and whose family was originally from Sweden. She had what we used to call back then "dirty blond hair," basically blond hair with streaks of light brown mixed in. Her hair was parted in the middle and went down below her shoulders. I can honestly say I would have fallen for Emelie if all I did was see her hair. Emelie never did anything to make her hair look better or different. Throughout that summer, I would see her walk outside in jean shorts, hair still wet from showering, and that was it, voila! If there was a type of body that was my favorite "type" of the female body, we could call that type of body Emelie.

Despite all that physical beauty, my favorite part of Emelie was being in her presence. Emelie didn't act like anybody else because I'm not sure it ever crossed her mind to be anything but herself. Her best friend Karly became Asher's girlfriend a few months after he moved in with me. Emelie was so much fun. She was rarely, if ever, totally serious or full of stress and worry. I appreciated that Emelie was warm and caring without being friendly or offering fake smiles or polite phrases. She was always present when we were together.

Over the next few months, we became closer and closer. Our friend Emelie would show up wherever Jacob or I were DJing. And she would be there early if we were DJing together.

That December, when everybody was planning to go home for the holidays, neither Emelie nor I were interested in being home with our families. For the next two weeks, we spent every single day and night together, from when we woke up to when we went to sleep. Some of those nights, Emelie slept on one of the two ugly but semi-comfortable couches in our living room. I felt so comfortable with Emelie that some mornings when she knocked on my door, I would answer the door in my underwear—those days meant white Fruit of the Loom briefs. I trusted her more than I did Asher or Jacob.

One night, we were at a small club I'd never been to before, not far from where Emelie grew up. We were doing tequila shots and were pretty plastered when we found our way to the dance floor. I had been waiting since the day I met her for an opportunity like this. Emelie was drunk enough that she started to dance sloppily. She would end up in my arms, with me holding her up several times. Eventually, I held her close while she danced with my arms around her. I could smell her hair; I felt her curves pressing against me. Her closeness in proximity and comfort had me internally dancing, full of desire and affection.

Since we never talked about it, I don't know if she moved closer or held onto me because she was too drunk to hold herself up or if our shared experience also turned her on. I brought her in a little bit closer to me and moved closer to her. Our hips and cheeks were connected, and I could feel Emelie's beautiful hair on my face. I could also feel my erection growing in my Levi's. She could, too, because as soon as it grew, she moved her pelvic area closer and pressed against me. At times Emelie was grinding herself on my mostly erect penis.

I don't remember making the decision, but I just started kissing her on her neck, then her left ear, her soft cheek, and then her lips. When I was kissing her, sounds were escaping her mouth, and she was breathing heavily in my ears. I kissed Emelie on the lips, and she kissed me back. That moment was the most magical experience I had in my twenty-one years. That moment, the fantasy in my dreams at age twelve, came to life in the name and body of Emelie.

My hands were caressing and holding her ass as she wriggled and ground against me. Time was lost.

I have no idea how long Emelie and I kissed and danced like this. It was more than five minutes and less than an hour.

And just like that, it ended.

"Emelie?" A tall guy, semi-preppy with blue eyes, dark hair parted on the side, and white skin tapped her on the shoulder. "Emelie, is that you?"

It took Emelie a minute to pull away from me as she turned around to stare at this guy. He was handsome. Fear and jealousy erased the joy, love, and connection I had experienced sixty seconds before. It looked like her eyes were coming into focus, "Matt? What the fuck are you doing here? I thought you went to Los Angeles!" Reality hit me when she said Matt's name and mentioned Los Angeles. She had a boyfriend when I met her during the summer. They broke up at the end of the summer when he decided to go to grad school in Los Angeles. I froze.

"I came back for Christmas to see my parents. It's so good to see you!" He looked into her eyes, intending to draw her in. It didn't quite work out that way.

"Well, it's not good to see you. And you can go fuck yourself!" Emelie made a fist and gave him a right-handed uppercut into his belly. He bowled over, out of breath. Emelie surprisingly followed by stomping on his foot. With that accomplished, she took my arm and led us out of the club and to my car. The ride home was about twenty-five minutes, in which Emelie had her head on my shoulder, crying about what an asshole he was, how she was unprepared to see him there, and she had just finally gotten over him last month.

     Raised by Wolves, Possibly Monsters

I stopped in front of her apartment, "Mike, can I stay at your place tonight? I don't want to be by myself."

"Of course." Two minutes later, I walked Emelie upstairs. We went into the bedroom I shared with Asher and our separate beds.

She plopped down on Asher's bed. "Can I stay in here tonight?"

"Yes."

I went to the bathroom to brush my teeth and pee. By the time I returned, Emelie was asleep in Asher's bed in her new denim jeans with a hole in the right knee on top of the covers, sleeping. The range of emotions and thoughts I experienced at that moment went from love and appreciation to rape and holding her down to crushing disappointment and rejection. It took me quite a while to fall asleep. My body was turned on in a way I had not experienced. The melding of lust, desire, and pleasure with a penis utterly convinced it should be inside of Emelie somewhere, mixed with the ache in my heart, made it hard to fall asleep. I promised myself that I was not going to masturbate while one of my best friends, who I was possibly in love with and just made out with an hour before, was sleeping six feet away from me. I kept my promise, but at some point during the night, I had an orgasm without even touching myself. All other feelings and experiences were washed away by shame, embarrassment, and humiliation. I felt like an awful friend and a disgusting human being.

In the morning, we didn't talk about anything specific. There were the "last night was crazy," "what a night," and "that's what happens when you drink too much tequila." We never talked about our kiss and that dance. I don't even know if she remembered the kiss or not. We talked about Matt and not about my heartbreak or the regret I assumed she felt. Something was lost that morning between Emelie and me. I lost my safety, comfort, and trust in our relationship between that kiss and shitty coffee with stale bagels for breakfast.

Everybody returned a couple of weeks later. Emelie and I still spent time together, mostly with other people.

A hidden benefit of DJing at a dive bar in the middle of nowhere happens when the bar closes. While carrying out equipment, nobody has a clue you're taking bottles of Tanqueray, Bacardi Gold, and cases of beer. When I returned home, Asher and his girlfriend Alma were hanging out in the living room, finishing the last bottle of Heineken. They were ecstatic when I walked in with gallons of alcohol. We turned up the music and started drinking and smoking pot. Emelie and her best friend Karly were walking home from a party. They heard the music and came upstairs. Asher and Karly had gotten together several times the previous semester but stopped when he started dating Alma until they started again and stopped again.

We moved my DJ equipment, except speakers, onto shelves in our huge bedroom closet. This allowed us to have two couches, two lounge chairs, a coffee table, an end table, plus an antique bar in our living room. Our living room had become a campus party place. The five of us were drinking, smoking pot, and snorting lines, except for Alma, who did not do cocaine. I'd go into the closet to change music frequently, walking through our bedroom.

One of those times, I walked out of the closet, and Karly was topless with her perfect, firm collegiate breasts. She was drunk and high; I think it took her a minute to realize I was standing before her while she was changing her shirt. Her black bra and sweater were lying on my bed. My body instantly woke up. As if nothing had happened, Karly got dressed and casually returned to the living room. Alma had fallen asleep on a couch. We lowered the music volume and our voices. Emelie leaned against me, resting her head on my shoulders for the first time in about two months. I didn't take any full breaths for fear of ruining the experience. A few minutes later, Emelie asked Karly to go to the bathroom with her.

When they came back, Emelie looked uncomfortable. She didn't sit down anywhere; she just stood in the middle of the room. Karly sat beside Asher, even though his girlfriend slept a few feet away. It was my turn to go to the bathroom, and when I came back, Emelie was sleeping on the other couch. I felt frustrated, confused, sensual, lustful, and frustrated. I went to sleep in my bed, turning off the lights.

At some point, Asher and Karly entered the room. A minute later, Asher was inside Karly, and their bodies and mouths were making many noises. I heard Karly whispering to Asher, "He can hear us." He kept making love to her; Karly forgot I was in the room. I became uncomfortable and was too turned on to lie

          Raised by Wolves, Possibly Monsters

there listening to them. I got up and left in my white Fruit of the Loom underwear.

I walked into the living room. Alma was sleeping on one couch, and Emelie was sleeping on the other. I tried to fall asleep in the Lazy Boy chair, but it didn't work. I kept fantasizing about Karly's breasts, Asher and Karly fully immersed in their sexual experience, and Emelie lying on her back with her legs spread, in shorts and a T-shirt and arm's length away.

Finally, I gave up and gently and quietly crawled on Emelie between her legs.

"What are you doing, Mike?"

"Asher and Karly are fucking, and there's nowhere for me to sleep."

Emelie grunted and repositioned herself with me on top.

I moved so my erect penis was directly on her light blue gym shorts. I lasted about a minute like this. I delicately put my hand over her left breast with my right hand. I just held it there. Her nipple got hard, and I gently pressed my thumb on her nipple over her shirt. Emelie moaned and moved her head to the left and right just a little bit. I continued to do that for a moment as her breathing became labored. I put my hand under her shirt over her bra, then inside. I was on fire.

I repositioned my body to create better access. The moans were more pronounced. I removed my hand from Emelie's shirt and slid it under her shorts and underwear. I felt her soft pubic hair. I ran my fingers through it slowly. I moved my body again, and she moved to accommodate my touch. I ran my fingers around her labia briefly before inserting my fingers inside her lubricated vagina. Emelie let out an exhale and a moan upon entry. I rubbed her with more force and pressure as she became moister. Her pelvis was pressing against me as her head was tossing about. Emelie was fully engaged.

It was a whisper, but I heard it. "Fuck me now." She was pressing harder, pulling me in and out. I took a ten-second break to push my underwear down, and my penis slapped up against her belly. Emelie woke, "What the fuck are you doing!?!"

I pretended I was sleeping and didn't know what was happening. My dear friend angrily pulled her shorts up, pushed my penis off her belly, and went back to sleep. However, I had no chance of falling asleep at this point. I waited a few minutes and moved slightly to see if Emelie was awake. She appeared to be out cold again. I again touched her breast and touched her still erect nipples over her T-shirt. Emelie started moaning again. I then slid my hand back under her shorts and underwear. She was pushing her pelvis up against me and moaning loudly. One of her moans was loud enough to wake herself up. "Get the fuck off me!" In one shove, Emelie threw me off the couch, and I landed with a thud on the floor, barely missing my head on the coffee table. Alma slept through all of this.

I tried to fall asleep, but for the second time that winter, I had been brutally beaten again by my shame, embarrassment, and humiliation of being turned on by Emelie. I waited until she fell asleep and tiptoed back into the bedroom since I didn't hear Asher and Karly. I crawled into my bed and fell asleep. Sometime in the middle of the night, I woke up with my hand around my penis. It took thirty seconds for me to ejaculate before I fell asleep.

Alma left before the rest of us woke in the morning. Next up was Emelie, who came into the bedroom and stood between our beds. She looked at me with fire and hate in her beautiful eyes. My trusted friend kicked Karly gently to wake her up. She and Asher both woke groggy. Emelie looked directly at Asher, "Your best friend tried to rape me last night!" She turned to me and gave me a real kick in my thigh. And then she stepped on me two or three times and left. Emelie and I were never friends again after that morning. But there was still one more confession between us.

My brother was released from prison and moved to Elizabeth, yes that Elizabeth. The Elizabeth, where I slept on my father's loveseat till we moved to West Orange. David and I got an apartment together for a little while, and then he moved across the street. One day, a couple of years after I moved out of Glassboro as a full-time criminal with my ex-con brother, Emelie called and put the phone on speakerphone, which was a brand-new feature at the time. Jacob and Toby were in the background. Emelie was angry. "Everybody keeps telling me that I used to give you blowjobs. I've never given you a blowjob. I'm never going to give you a blowjob. You even told them in specific detail how and where I gave you blowjobs, even though it never happened. Tell them right now it never happened."

I didn't say anything.

"Tell them right now it never happened."

     Raised by Wolves, Possibly Monsters

No response.

"I'm giving you one more chance to tell them that I never gave you a blowjob, or I will let everybody know down here what you did to me and how I was your best friend and you treated me like shit. Tell. Them. Now!"

I was shaking. I felt like the lowest form of life on planet Earth. I told awful lies about a close friend, sexually assaulted her, and now faced her anger and hatred towards me that I created. "Emelie never gave me a blowjob. I lied."

"Why did you say those things to our friends? What the hell, Mike? Why would you do this to me?" Emelie was now crying, not shouting.

"I don't know. I guess because I wanted everybody to think I was cool and that you liked me."

Toby spoke for the first time. "There is nothing cool about lying about having sex with one of your best friends, especially when she was so good to you, and you told all of her friends this lie. Nothing cool about this, Dude."

Emelie spoke." I don't want you ever to call or talk to me again, or I will tell them what else you did. Asher already knows, but the rest of them don't. Never speak to me again!"

Jacob said, "Emelie is never angry like this; I don't know what you did to her. You better agree and do what she tells you. She is our friend! And you just don't do this with girls, especially your friends!"

"OK. I won't talk to you again, Emelie." I was now crying profusely. "I am so sorry. I didn't mean to hurt you. I'm just fucked up and do stupid shit. I'm so sorry, Emelie. I want you to know that I feel like shit."

"Good. Now, goodbye forever!" And I could hear the phone slamming on the receiver and then a dial tone.

I got off the phone with Emelie that afternoon and was acutely aware I had now reached the level of my brother and that I, too, was dark, evil, and disgusting. But unlike my brother, I ached in my whole being. There was not any part of me I did not hate and loathe. So, the answer to the question of how my life got even worse was simple: do enough drugs and alcohol to numb the pain and the shame and the self-hate and earn several thousand dollars a week to support your drug use. I didn't have to worry at this point if I was going to become like them. I had now reached their level. I had achieved scum. That's how I became a mob guy. I sexually assaulted one of my best friends and then lied in great detail to all of the guys in our lives about how often and what style she gave me blowjobs, including me telling them how much she liked it when I came all over her face.

If you're trying to figure out how to throw your life away and become a full-time criminal, that's what you do. You do the things you swore you would never do often enough that you recognize you will never be who you were before. That's how you do it. This is how you become the monster you hated your whole life.

Loverboy

 THAT FIRST SUMMER at Campus Terrace, the woman who lived downstairs from me had her teenage niece move in because nobody could take care of her. She was fifteen and going through that phase of wanting to see what she could get away with. The thing about fifteen-year-olds is they don't realize how transparent what they're doing is to people who aren't fifteen anymore.

Tara would play a game with me, and sometimes I would play along. I would hang out on the front steps listening to music, pretending to be reading or doing homework. Each time she heard me, Tara would come out and act surprised to see me. The distinctive feature of Tara beyond being fifteen and having a thirst for trouble was the red lipstick she wore only when coming to hang out with me. Her wardrobe seemed only to include clothes showing most of her breasts and part of her butt.

She was a big fan of the band Loverboy at the time. I knew this, and when their new hit song came, I picked it up at the record store immediately. The next day, when I was hanging outside, I told her about it and asked if she wanted to come up and hear it. Tara looked back to see if anybody was looking. She put her finger before her lips, communicating "quiet," and nodded.

We walked upstairs to my apartment. When I opened the door and Tara came in, she looked ecstatic with joy and fear. I do not know if she was fearful of something I would do to her that she didn't want to happen, or afraid I would do something to her that she did want to happen, or both.

That was the first of several times that summer when Tara came to my apartment to listen to music and hang out. A couple of times, she asked if she could drink some of my vodka or tequila. I said yes. Watching how shocked Tara was by the burn when it went down if you drank it like soda was comical. I had never put my hands on her body at any point. That's why what happened next was bizarre and ironic, given the kind of man I was at that point.

One afternoon, I was leaving for Deptford Mall to get some new music. While driving by the apartment complex's dumpy little pool, I saw Tara in her tiny, black bathing suit. I was turned on and excited at the prospect of her taking a ride with me and ignored my surroundings, which was very unusual for me.

"Hi! I'm riding to Deptford Mall to pick up some music; want to come?"

Tara stiffened and appeared nervous immediately. She shook her head quickly several times as if she didn't want to be noticed or seen talking to me.

I still didn't understand what was happening. "Okay, cool. When I return later, can you come up and listen to the new stuff I will pick up?" She looked even more nervous and scared. She continued to look around, folding her arms in front of her chest nervously. I pulled away, confused.

I was even more confused when, half an hour after I returned, blasting music from the new album by The Clash in my apartment, I heard a loud thumping on the door. I lowered the music, figuring it was one of my friends or somebody wanting to buy drugs. Much to my surprise, it was four cops. They barreled in with their pistols pointing at me.

The second one with his sunglasses blurted out, "Where is she?"

The two in the back brushed right past me and into the bedroom, and the closet door opened. "Who?" I demanded.

"You know who. Tara, the girl from downstairs. Where is she hiding!" The guys from the back room re-entered the living room, "Clear. She's not in the bathroom, bedroom, or bedroom closet."

"Tara, the girl from downstairs? She's not here. Why would she be here? Why are you here?"

"Tara is Louis's granddaughter. Louis and his wife heard you telling her to come here after you returned from Deptford Mall. They asked her about it and how she knew you. She ran away and has been missing since. Nobody knows where she went." His voice went down several octaves. "Where are you hiding her?"

He put his pistol directly in front of my face. It was not the first time somebody put a loaded gun in front of my face, but it was the first time that it wasn't a gangster or drug dealer. "There is going to be an investigation of statutory rape. You can improve things if you tell us where you're keeping her before this worsens." He looked around at all the beer bottles, bongs, wrapping paper, and bags of marijuana. He chuckled and looked back at me, "Based on everything you have here in your apartment already, it looks like this is about to get worse for you real fast if you don't tell us where she is right now!" It looked like he was getting ready to pull the trigger.

"Statutory rape? I've never put my hands on her. She's been here several times, and we've hung out. But I've never put my hands on her, and I have no idea where the fuck she is right now."

"Yeah, that's what they all say." The detective will conduct a full investigation tonight or tomorrow morning." He looked around at the other three officers, giving each other knowing glances and heading out the door and down the steps. He looked back at me, "Watch your step, pal. We're onto you!" They stomped down the stairs in their loud, black shoes, sounding like a herd of elephants.

I symbolically gave them the finger when they closed the outside door.

I kept looking out my window all night to see if Tara would show up. Sometime around nine at night, Tara's Aunt Linda, my downstairs neighbor, Tara's mother, and Tara returned together. Both women had her by her elbows, pulling her along with them. Her aunt looked up in the direction of the living room window I was looking out, and when she saw me, she gave me "That look" that mothers give to men like me when their daughters or nieces are in danger. I turned from the window to act like I hadn't seen her. About twenty minutes later, Tara had her suitcase in her left hand, with her mother pulling her by the right hand.

"I don't want to go home. I hate you. Mike never touched me. We used to hang out, and he was nice to me and gave me attention. He never even kissed me.

     Raised by Wolves, Possibly Monsters

Let go of my arm before I kick you! Why are you doing this to me? I hate you! I hate you! I hate you!"

"I think you're full of shit, and I think what he told the cops is bullshit too. If you don't watch it, you'll end up sixteen, pregnant like I was with you and Grandma was with me."

That was the last time I saw Tara. The detective asked many questions in the morning but didn't press hard. Tara's Aunt Linda would give me That Stare whenever I went up and down the outside steps. Everybody in the neighborhood called me The Cradle Robber for the next month or two. I was never arrested or charged. How ironic that I got investigated for statutory rape for a girl I never touched and had no legal consequences for the girls I did touch inappropriately.

Today, we would call what I was doing grooming. No, I did not touch Tara, but I was moving in that direction and would have if they hadn't thwarted things. They were right, and it was lucky for Tara that The Groomer was caught before he did more harm.

The Other Dirty Little Secret of Campus Terrace Apartments

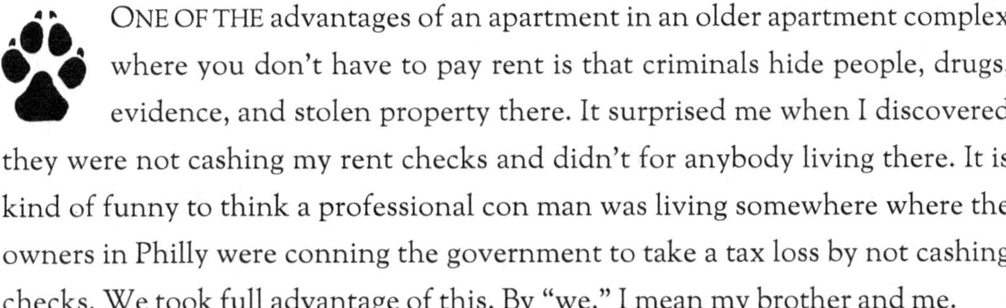

ONE OF THE advantages of an apartment in an older apartment complex where you don't have to pay rent is that criminals hide people, drugs, evidence, and stolen property there. It surprised me when I discovered they were not cashing my rent checks and didn't for anybody living there. It is kind of funny to think a professional con man was living somewhere where the owners in Philly were conning the government to take a tax loss by not cashing checks. We took full advantage of this. By "we," I mean my brother and me.

Because I looked more clean-cut and wholesome than the rest of the crew, I was ideal for ripping off and hustling other criminals, which I gladly did. I stole a $32,000 brick of pure pink Peruvian cocaine from a local cartel. When they returned for retribution, I hopped into the gold Corvette, going to Glassboro and the old Campus Terrace Apartments.

The problem was that I had changed. I didn't look like a student if I ever had. Now, I looked like what I was: an urban drug dealer. There wasn't anybody else on the Glassboro Campus driving a brand-new gold Corvette or wearing a big fat gold chain with a pendant shaped like a gold record album, a $2,200 gold and onyx watch, speaking like a guy out of a mediocre, late-night movie about low-level Mafia losers.

Gus, a friend from the apartment complex, still did some business with me. We used codes through our beepers to call from certain pay phones and meet at specific rest areas on the New Jersey Turnpike.

A few days later, there was a sit-down with the bosses, who determined that they would play nice if I gave them back the cocaine. One slight problem: there was no cocaine left to give back. Plenty of it went up my nose. The rest, Joey, my drug-addicted sidekick, and I sold on the street since it was high quality.

Joey and I figured our best move was to rob somebody else of drugs or money and not piss off the bosses. Gus from Campus Terrace seemed the best target or, at least, the easiest.

We had set up everything in advance. Joey, the drug addict, and I would drive to South Jersey. We would sneak into my unused apartment. We parked a few blocks away, and we took a shitty car instead of the Corvette not to draw attention. Glassboro is a long drive; we wanted to get ourselves cleaned up and ready to execute the plan. And getting ourselves "ready" meant doing a bunch of lines before.

When ready, we went to a payphone and dialed Gus's pager, telling him when to meet us. We chose behind a Friendly's restaurant because of the wooden fence in the back of the parking lot, which blocked the view of neighbors. Joey hid on the back seat floor with blankets and pillows covering him. We made sure we got there first. When Gus pulled up, I got out and went to his car. The plan only works if I was in Gus's car. We had a big fat roll of single dollar bills with a $100 bill on top wrapped in a rubber band that was supposed to be $10,000 to purchase the cocaine.

While I sat in Gus's car, working out the deal, Joey snuck out the back door on the far side of the vehicle, which I had left open just enough for him to crawl through. He quietly walked around the back of the car and snuck up to Gus's side. I kept Gus focused on the money, drugs, and the transaction.

He stuck the .22 pistol on the side of Gus's face, "If you even breathe, I'm

     Raised by Wolves, Possibly Monsters

going to pull this trigger three times. There will be so much blood all over Mikey that we're going to have to leave his fucking clothes in the dumpster and drive home naked. Do you understand?"

Gus nodded his head, then a second time out of fear of freaking Joey out. Freaking Joey out was easy because even when he had no cocaine or speed, he was the most nervous and agitated person I had ever met. When he was on cocaine and speed with a gun, he looked like the crazed maniac he was.

"Good. Mikey will slowly open the door and leave with the drugs and money. I will stay here with this .22 shoved in your face until he's in the car and ready to go. Do you understand?" Gus did the same two nods again. I got out of the car and looked around, ensuring there were no cops, detectives, or anybody else hanging around. I made my way to the shitty red Mercury Lynx. I turned the car on and nodded to Joey.

"I'm going to pull this gun away from your head slowly. You will not move except to hand me the keys to the car slowly. If you suddenly move, it will paint your gray interior red. You'll put the keys on top of the dashboard and then lock your fingers together." Gus did as instructed, and Joey took his keys, holding the gun while walking backward into the car through the front passenger door. I had already opened the door for him. He was still pointing the gun at him when I put the car in reverse, threw it in first gear, and pulled out of the lot.

We didn't plan for Gus to have a spare set of keys with him.

As I pulled out of the Friendly's parking lot, turning right on Delsea Drive, Gus screeched his tires and came after us. The other thing we didn't plan on was Gus also carrying a loaded .22 pistol, which he started shooting at us from behind. I was swerving to my left and right, just like they do in the movies. He accelerated his car into the oncoming traffic lane when no vehicles approached. When Gus pulled almost next to us, he continued shooting at us. Fortunately, there was so much going on he couldn't get a good look or aim. He knocked out a window, put a hole in the trunk, and missed another few shots.

I accelerated as fast as that piece of shit car could go, which probably was about 82 on the road with a speed limit of 35. It's a fine line between protecting your life and not wanting to have a cop pull you over with a rifle. After about seven miles of Gus chasing us and banging into the back bumper a few times, I squeaked through a yellow light about to turn red, knowing there would be cross traffic and Gus couldn't get through. It worked.

We drove another ten minutes on Delsea Drive. We pulled over to catch our breath, piss, and do a few lines before we headed home. We sent somebody to pick up the Vette two days later.

The End of the Dirty Little Secret
at Campus Terrace Apartments

ABOUT A YEAR after Emelie, Jacob, Gus, Smooth, Kevin, and everybody else hated me, I received a phone call from Smooth. "Hi Mike, I just wanted to let you know that Louis, the superintendent, has put police 'Do not cross line' tape in front of your apartment and an eviction notice of Friday."

It startled me to hear Smooth's voice. The flat tone in which he shared this information and information caught me off guard.

"Listen, Man. I'm doing you a favor by calling. I don't want to connect or discuss the weather with you; I just wanted to let you know the eviction date is Friday, and today is Tuesday. Do what you want." I heard the phone click, followed by a dial tone. On Thursday, we went down with a U-Haul to pick up everything. Louis, the superintendent, told people, specifically Tara's Aunt Linda to keep an eye out if I showed up. We went to the top of the steps and ripped down the police tape, but my key didn't fit the lock. He changed the locks in case we showed up to take my stuff and leave the place a mess.

One of the benefits of having David around was that he had no fear of physical pain. He cocked his arm back, put his hand through the hollow wooden door, and opened it from the inside. As usual, we had cocaine that needed to be refrigerated; that was first. As soon as we closed the door to the fridge, we heard what we assumed was Louis stomping up the steps with a cigarette in his mouth, complaining out loud to nobody. He came barreling in the door, threatening to call the police for rent.

David did what he always did in these situations. "Hey, Louis, I'm David,

Raised by Wolves, Possibly Monsters

Mike's uncle. I think we can take care of this without the police." He reached into his pocket and gave Louis four crisp $50 bills. "Does that cover it?"

Louis answered in his heavy smoker's voice, "I don't think that's going to cover the damage to the door; that's going to be extra."

David gave him three more $50 bills. Then, he gave him another and thanked him for keeping an eye on the place. "Young kids today don't know how to do things correctly. Mike keeps getting himself in trouble, and I must keep cleaning it up. Glad we have guys like you around to make sure he doesn't do anything stupider than the stupid shit he already pulls!"

David reached out, shook Louis's hand firmly, and tapped him on the shoulder with his left hand. He gently turned Louis around, facing the door, and told him we needed about two hours to get everything out. Louis thanked David for being such a good uncle and left happy.

About twenty minutes later, we took everything that seemed worth the effort, crushed the cocaine in the fridge, and left before anything else happened. That was the last time I set foot in Campus Terrace Apartments, where I lived for four years rent-free.

Collecting More Lisas

YEARS LATER, AFTER David, now in his twenties, was released from serving three years at Annandale Minimum Security Prison for six counts of armed robbery, we opened several small little outlet "stores" in trendy indoor marketplaces. These marketplaces felt like flea markets, but most of the vendors sold brand-new merchandise, not used pictures from their grandmother's attic. The shop in Staten Island was the most prominent. In case it's not apparent, Staten Island, New York, New Brunswick, and Rockaway in New Jersey were storefronts for processing fraudulent credit cards.

David and I spent most of our time at the jewelry shop in Staten Island because it generated enough business to justify us both at that location. David had a steady girlfriend, Gina, who eventually became his wife and the mother of their kids, Carlo and Anthony. That did not prevent him from collecting girls named Lisa. I am intentionally using the word "girls" since all of them were in high school. At one point, I think he was dating and having sex with five girls named Lisa; some knew each other and were friends. He took pleasure in witnessing the drama between them.

He liked exploiting attractive, popular, sexy adolescent girls who liked trouble but who, underneath their exteriors, were sweet, innocent girls wanting attention and being desirable. I remember him saying, "I like fucking the innocence right out of them and coming inside their virginal pussies." Every time he said this, I felt terrible, disgusted, ashamed, and an erection built inside my pants. I was experiencing lust and desire for physically and personally attractive young girls who were too young for me and way too young for him. I knew what he was doing was wrong; therefore, I felt shame and disgust. His monster woke up mine.

I could never discern which of these fourteen, fifteen, and sixteen-year-old girls had sex before my brother pulled up with his thick gold chains and brand-new gold Corvette. Part of me wanted to know who he had ruined; most of me did not want to know anything about it.

What Was It Like to Be You Back Then?

OVER THE YEARS, when I mention to people that I used to be a drug dealer, a low-level mob guy, and a drug addict, they laugh as if I am kidding. Then they ask me if I was really a drug dealer, mob guy, and drug addict. I get it; I don't act the part or carry myself like what we understand a drug addict/dealer looks like. They think I am exaggerating or outright lying. To show them who I was and how I lived, I share this experience with them about being me in 1985/1986.

I had just robbed a group of drug dealers of about $25,000 worth of pristine pink Peruvian cocaine. It was still in a block, uncut. I knew they were looking for me, as were the local police and possibly the Feds. David was not part of this heist but joined me in what to do next, meaning he wanted to use the highest quality cocaine available in an abundant quantity. His plan was for us to hide in his apartment, but not much of a plan. So, we stocked up on alcohol, weed, lots of takeout food, and ammunition for his .357 Magnum.

We did not stock up on toilet paper. About four or five days in, we ran out and started using whatever paper supplies we had available, then moved to rags and towels. A week later, we knew we needed more supplies. But first we had to shower. And because we were on high alert, while one of us was showering, the other person would stand at the door with the loaded .357 in hand if anything happened. David said I should shower first, so I did. When I came out with my glasses off, high, drunk, hungry, and a week without sleep, I grabbed one of the towels to dry myself off. After finishing, I went to the mirror to groom myself for going out when I noticed brown lines around my face and upper body! I jumped back in the shower to clean the dried shit now all over my body.

This is what it was like to be me then. This was my bottom, except it was not bad enough yet to get me to change. That wouldn't happen for several more years. I wasn't done yet.

The Secret Service Building in East Orange, NJ

 MY MOBSTER LIFE was about to change. That year, seventy-five of us, including myself, were picked up, held, and interrogated by the Secret Service.

Joey, my "business partner" in the mob, was "the family's" youngest brother, with his older brother being a lower-level mob boss and the oldest brother being a mob boss. We were partners in many things, including moving truckloads of stolen merchandise, drug distribution, and turning a local recording studio into a fine-tuned mob business where we stole young musicians' parent's money and dreams, hustling tens of thousands from upper-middle-class white families. We ended up with three recording studios in New Jersey and Brooklyn Heights, New York.

However, the biggest thing that Joey and I did was part of an extended organizational system of creating copies of credit cards with balances of $10,000 or more in the early and mid-80s. We would sell those duplicate cards and make arrangements/partnerships with small local businesses to "sell" tens of thousands of dollars in "merchandise" without them needing to have or lose any of their merchandise in inventory. They would pay for this service we did for them in exchange for getting a clean profit for months. The recording studio, the drug business, and the fraudulent credit card distribution and sales were my primary work for the organization.

I did not know until that first morning when I was picked up in Morristown and brought down to the Secret Service building in East Orange that the Secret Service's other job besides protecting the president was counterfeiting and fraud, which are federal offenses.

It was literally like a scene in a bad movie. It was a small room with all-white walls and ceilings with nothing on them and a rectangular table with four chairs. Four Secret Service agents were cramped into that room with me. There were threats, deals offered, pressure, and everything else you see on TV and in movies. At first, it was easy as pie because I was still full of alcohol and cocaine from the night before. As I lost the cocaine high, my cockiness went with it. The first time, they held me for about four hours. I did not think I was going home that day. In retrospect, it's comical to believe that I was so clueless and arrogant that I didn't realize how problematic it was to have driven my car between their two vehicles to the Secret Service office with my revoked driver's license. I was on probation for possession and distribution of cocaine. There was cocaine in my car, and the car did not have registration or insurance. Meaning they let me go. I was aware that they knew all of this information because they tried to use it as leverage and that they would probably pick me up as soon as my car left their guarded parking lot. I have no clue why, but they both let me leave the interview and left in that car with me driving it!

I received a subpoena the following month to come down for more interviews. I arrived prepared this time. We had a mob lawyer get everything ready. I arrived clean-shaven, showered, and mostly sober. I had been instructed on what to answer and what not to answer and knew a support system was behind me. Additionally, I was going inside with thousands of Secret Service agents on purpose this time. My chest hurt when I walked into the building, and my heart was pounding fearlessly.

 Raised by Wolves, Possibly Monsters

They were more focused on getting information about other higher-ranking people than me, which was everybody. They showed me pictures and asked me if I knew people. They gave me the names of people and asked me if I knew them. They did the standard, "So and so is coming clean about you; you better save yourself while you still can" routine. They also did what the attorney counted on in advance: they made me write the names of people I was conducting business with. After that, they gave me a list of about thirty or forty names of people to whom we sold fraudulent credit cards. They wanted me to sign those names as well. What they wanted was to have a signature match that my handwriting matched the signature of one of the cards, if not many of them. They were looking for evidence and didn't get it for whatever reason. The attorney told me to practice using a different script handwriting the week before the appointment, which was helpful.

About two weeks later, my brother and sixty-two others were arrested for some combination of the RICO statute for participating in organized crime or committing fraud and counterfeiting. I was not one of those people. I thought it was because I was more intelligent and sharper than them. In my mind, they were all a bunch of "Dumb Guineas who couldn't do anything but be street thugs and criminals," whereas I was somebody with an exceptionally high IQ and went to three colleges. Yeah, I know, I got kicked out of them, but somehow, my going meant I was more intelligent and better than them. Many years later, in an AA meeting, I realized it wasn't because I was brighter and sharper. I wasn't worth the federal government's time and money! I was furious when I figured this out.

With these new counterfeiting and fraud charges, my brother was found guilty and served one and a half years in a federal penitentiary in Upstate New York, Ray Brook, near Lake Placid. I only had to visit him once.

The One That Didn't Get Away

 LEIGHTON AND I didn't like each other much when we first met. We didn't like each other very much after seeing each other at work every day. She wasn't my type, and I wasn't hers. I was an Italian-Jewish guy

working part-time at Radio Shack, hiding from the Feds and the people I had robbed along the way. She was a German-Irish Catholic girl who graduated from a Catholic high school. We tried to avoid each other at work so we wouldn't fight. For the most part, that strategy was effective.

The store manager, Cliff, was an annoying twenty-six-year-old guy. I didn't like him very much either. He was having a big party with his roommates on New Year's Eve. I had met one of his roommates, and he seemed fun to hang out with, specifically to do cocaine together. So, I said yes. It was a condo full of people in their twenties, drunk, high, and obnoxious. It was easy to hide in plain sight there. Both of Cliff's roommates were handsome guys, charismatic, and had many friends. I had invited two of my ridiculously gorgeous friends, Marissa and Selah, to stop by since they would see a friend in the neighborhood.

By the time it got close to midnight, people were even more high and drunk than they had been earlier. I don't remember exactly how it happened, but we had the TV on to do the countdown, watching the ball drop at midnight in Times Square. Ten, nine, eight, seven, six, five, four, three, two, one, Happy New Year! Somehow, Leighton and I kissed each other as the ball dropped, and a minute later, Leighton and I fell to the floor with me on top of her. We made out in the middle of the dance floor while everybody was screaming, shouting, and jumping up and down. Right there on the dance floor, I started playing with her 36D breasts over her white button-down shirt. Two minutes later, my hand was up her skirt, pushing aside her underwear, while our supervisor, Cliff, was ten feet away.

We hung out on the floor for what seemed like quite a while. Leighton was turned on and excited. She was trying to conceal her moans and groans, but her writhing body and well-lubricated genitals let me know what everybody else couldn't hear amongst the chaos. "Michael, let's find a room upstairs." It was the first time either one of us spoke since 11:59:59 seconds. I took my fingers out from inside of her, rubbed them on her lips, laughed, and pulled her up with me as I was standing. The whole room seemed utterly different than it had been just moments before. We went upstairs to the mostly empty bedroom that Leighton would be moving into the following month. There was furniture that wasn't hers presently in there, including a bed, a coffee table, and a TV. Some people were

   Raised by Wolves, Possibly Monsters

hanging out in bed, watching TV and talking. Neither one of us knew any of them. It did not stop us from getting on the bed and continuing where we were.

This time, I just went ahead and took her underwear off, put it on the bed to get it out of the way, and silently communicated to the people in the room to get out of it. They laughed and started tossing around her underwear. Leighton did not care. She was drunk and horny and just wanted to get fucked. I unbuttoned her shirt, unhooked her bra, and was amazed at these beautiful, large, naked, and round breasts. I needed to pause for a minute to take in the moment and the beauty of these female-bodied objects called breasts. Leighton was nineteen, and I was twenty-five. She was a lost teenager who was a total mess. I was a lost young adult who was a bigger mess. I knew how to hide my mess and pretend I had my shit together; Leighton had not learned that skill yet. While I was licking and sucking her breasts and playing with her labia, clitoris, and vagina, Leighton lost her patience. "Can all of you just get the fuck out of here and let us fuck in peace?!?" They all laughed and made some side remarks, and one of the guys mumbled something about a train and group fuck. I stopped what I was doing, grabbed his shirt, and pulled him closer to me; "You have about ten seconds before your mother doesn't recognize you again." They were gone in about seven seconds.

Now we had the room to ourselves less than an hour into 1986, and the big shot, low-level gangster, drug dealer DJ was about to put his penis inside a woman's vagina for the first time. Leighton had my penis in her hands, stroking it. At that moment, one of the other guys who lived there, Matt, who we all called Matteo, knocked on the door, "Yo Mikey, these two gorgeous girls named Marissa and Selah are downstairs looking for you. They said they drove all the way here to hang out with you. Glenn said you were in this room and just threatened to beat the shit out of some other guys so that you could fuck some girl." Matt started laughing. "Yo Mikey, I know you're in there." Leighton and I didn't move beside my fingers inside of her.

A moment passed, and Matt opened the door and barged in. "Holy shit! Leighton, I didn't know you were the girl in here with Mike."

"I am. Have you ever heard of privacy? I will be the only girl living here in a month. You think you could check before you walk in!"

"I did, you didn't answer. Mikey, are you playing with her pussy while having a conversation?" It did not occur to me that he could see me even though he was standing five feet away, and there was no way not to see me. When he had barged the door open, Leighton covered her breasts with her shirt, holding them from being exposed. I think both of us forgot that my hand was in her genitals. At that moment, I knew the right thing would have been to take my hand out and pull her skirt down. "Aren't you at least going to go see your friends downstairs? They arrived right after midnight and have been waiting for you, asking everybody where you were."

"Fuck!" I removed my hand from Leighton, pulled her skirt down, stuffed my penis back in my underwear, and zipped up my tight Calvin Klein jeans. "I'll be right back, Leighton. Let me say hi to them and tell them I'm busy. I'll be back in five minutes."

"Are you fucking kidding me? Are Selah and Marissa the two girls I always hear you talking to on the phone at the store and telling everybody how much you want to fuck them? Are you out of your mind? What's wrong with you?" She buttons her shirt, grabs her bra off the bed, and tells Matt to leave. She looked at me with a red face, eyes ordinarily light brown, but now dark brown, almost black, and everything in her body clenched, "You're an asshole. I always knew you were an asshole. I don't know why I decided to kiss you at midnight and come in here to fuck you. Go see Marissa and Selah and go fuck yourself!"

I met Selah when I was in high school. She was one of Richie's ex-girlfriends, and his current girlfriend at the time was Selah's best friend, Cathy. My jealousy, resentment, and envy grew with each fantastic, fun, intelligent, and gorgeous current or former girlfriend of Richie's that I met. She was at the top of that list. There was something different about my experience with Selah. Yes, she had physical features that attracted me to her, but Selah, being intelligent, faithful, joyful, fun, and full of curiosity and life, was what I came to love about her. Selah was also fashionable, but not as a full-time job, oozing with sexuality without making that the first thing you recognize or notice. Selah possessed those attributes, plus strength, courage, and warmth.

She was all these things, yet with clear, firm boundaries. I would not know how to describe it back then as a pot-smoking adolescent boy, but somehow, I

Raised by Wolves, Possibly Monsters

knew what was allowed and what wasn't when it came to Selah without her ever saying anything about it.

Way before I met Leighton, I had met Marissa at a club where I was a DJ sometimes and a guy doing cocaine in the backroom more often. The name of the club was Creations. I had become friends with a woman named Amy, who trained figure skaters. I found her attractive in some weird way, even though none of her physical or personality characteristics appealed to me. She played so many games and tried to manipulate people so much that she felt like an acceptable opponent to match wits. Occasionally, late at night, we would make out, and I would play with her breasts and sometimes grab her genitals over her pants, once up her skirt and inside her. It felt like a victory even though the experience wasn't all that enjoyable since Amy was performing, too.

Marissa was one of those people who made everything fun and playful when she walked into the room. She loved to talk and listen and was incredibly curious and intelligent. When Marissa finished college, she got a job working in Manhattan, and a year later, she moved to Manhattan. Marissa continued to move forward professionally and, by age twenty-five, was earning a substantial income, possibly more than I was as a low-level organized crime member.

Marissa loved to hear stories about what gangs we robbed, which drug deal went down for $30,000, which family we robbed of $12,000 and their kids dream at the recording studio, or which police department arrested me, and I got released an hour later. She loved all of it. I do not recall ever meeting a man who did not want to have sex with Marissa and was willing to go to any lengths and ruin their life in the process of doing so. She knew this, and it was part of her confidence that she brought to everything.

As intelligent, successful, and confident as Marissa was and still is, her blind spot was meeting accomplished, successful, good-looking, and dynamic men. They would fall in love with her; she would eventually fall in love with them, and they would get engaged. Somewhere along the way, "he" would wake up one day and recognize that Marissa was a real human being, not just a manifestation of every fantasy. This realization crushed them. And then Marissa was devastated.

"I'll be back in five minutes!" I put my shoes back on and followed Matt downstairs to Marissa and Selah. Leighton was right. I did have a crush, possibly even in love with both of them, whom I met separately years before and who had recently become friends. The idea of fulfilling a fantasy of being with them simultaneously on New Year's was too seductive to pass up. Besides, they were about as attractive, exciting, and fun as any girls/women I had ever met, which would give me excellent credibility.

Five minutes became 10 minutes, which became fifteen minutes. They both started asking me if I had any cocaine on me, which I did. We were trying to find a place where we could be private that would be just the three of us, and Matteo followed behind, hoping to get some version of cocaine, Marissa or Selah. We couldn't find a place to hide. Marissa said her friend lived in the same condo complex. He said they could stop by briefly on their way to the party. She said we could go over to his house. I knew this was going to make things even worse with Leighton. I knew this was going to be awful. I knew that my chance of starting the New Year's inside of a woman evaporated by the moment. It was a fantasy come true to be with either Marissa or Selah and probably the most significant fantasy in my life; being with both completely overrode my system's ability to think.

We walked over to their friend's house, and he was an annoying, whiny, nervous, coked-up guy. We did lines upon lines upon lines. Not only had more than five or fifteen minutes gone by, but when I checked the clock, it was now 2:45 a.m. At that point, I submitted to what was happening.

For the record, I did not "get" Marissa or Selah then or ever. At 4:30 a.m., I returned to the condo where the party was to see what was happening with Leighton. Matt and I were laughing while walking back without Marissa and Selah. Most people were gone, but some crashed on couches, chairs, and floors. Some new and old couples played and possibly had sex in random corners. I walked upstairs to the room that Leighton would be moving into, and she must have locked the door. I knocked on the door quietly a few times. I heard some movement, but nobody responded. I knocked on the door a little louder. Leighton's best friend Martha replied with a lot of energy, "Mike if that's you, you have a lot of nerve showing up again after what you did! So go fuck yourself, get out of here, and leave Leighton alone!"

I went into some bullshit pitch and story with a bunch of drama, trying to

     Raised by Wolves, Possibly Monsters

convince Martha or Leighton to let me in. There was a lot of whispering. Martha whispered things like, "Don't talk to him; he's an asshole," "Mike is too stupid to know what he had, "and finally, "He is not worth wasting your tears." Leighton was full-on crying now.

"I am so sorry, Leighton. I can explain the whole thing and what happened."

For the record, I never once had sex with Marissa or Selah. They always saw me as a safe and trusted friend. Although few people saw me that way, and they did, which I appreciated, I would often feel rejected because they didn't want to be with me physically. But Leighton wasn't having any of it. She yelled, her voice cracking, "I don't care about your bullshit story. You're an asshole, and I hate you all over again!"

Leighton and I were scheduled to work together on January 2nd. I opened up the store that morning. I got there early to get myself settled. I prepared for what I knew was going to be an awful experience. I was right. It sucked.

"Okay, Mike, let's get this out of the way before we open the store. You're an asshole, and I hate you, and I knew I was right about you that you were an asshole and didn't care about anybody but yourself, but we have to work together, so let's just put up with it and not talk to each other except when we have to. Deal?"

"Deal. and I want to apologize . . ."

"Stop right there and shut up! I don't care what you think or if you're sorry, you're an asshole, and I hate you. Let's do the best we can to deal with having to be around each other." And she walked away.

Six weeks later, I orgasmed inside Leighton in the same room she now occupied as a roommate of Glen and Matt. I was no longer a virgin. It's sad; even though I had not had intercourse before that particular night, just because I was Bernie's son and David's younger brother, I don't think I qualified to be a virgin after I turned age eight.

There was nothing unique or exciting about that moment and that night besides no longer having to lie about being a virgin. It was fun, and the orgasm was incredible. Leighton was passionate and satisfied. Since I couldn't talk to anybody and ruin all of the lies I had been telling for years, a colossal thing happened, and nobody knew about it but me. It's sad to think that anybody would have a rite of passage like that and be unable to share it because they were such liars. My reputation had everyone believe I had sex with dozens of women.

Leighton and I spent much time together over the next few months. In the three and a half years that we were together, I don't know that we ever liked each other, but we did grow to love each other and become dependent on each other. There were moments of intimacy and connection; they were not the norm. The bulk of our relationship was focused on what I wanted.

She came from a family with three recovering alcoholics and spent her high school years attending Alateen meetings. She was well trained in caring for others and ensuring other people's needs were met, but not hers. I was very well trained in ensuring my needs were fulfilled at any cost, and the only time other people's needs were met was when it ultimately served my needs. This created a situation where everything was fine as long as we were both focused on meeting my needs. When Leighton wanted or needed something, I would verbally and emotionally attack her into submission of what an awful, rotten person she was. She would beg me to be nice to her and not break up with her. I learned early on that Leighton would do anything if I threatened to break up with her.

The first time I broke up with Leighton was because I didn't like the way her breath smelled from smoking two or three cigarettes a week; she stopped smoking cigarettes. She went a week without eating because I told her she was too fat. She stopped talking to her best friend because I complained that her best friend was too involved in our lives, which was code for her challenging how much power and authority I had in our relationship. She started jogging every morning at 7 a.m. the second time I told her she was gaining weight. I remember joking with my friends that some people have pet cats, some have pet dogs, and some have gerbils, and I had a pet Leighton.

Leighton continued not to smoke, barely eat, spend less time with Martha, and jog regularly, and I agreed not to break up with her. I was also not allowed to fuck Marissa or Selah, which was easy since they weren't interested. I had promised Leighton that if she lost another fifteen pounds and continued not to smoke, we would get an apartment together. Three months later, Leighton had a flat stomach, a firm ass, and long tight legs with huge breasts. We got a lovely apartment in Morris Plains just outside of Morristown. The space had beautiful wood floors, large windows, and a huge bedroom. We purchased all new furni-

Raised by Wolves, Possibly Monsters

ture and kitchen supplies for our new home. Both of us were excited about the possibilities. There was even talk about marriage, but deep down in the back of my head, I knew it was predominantly bullshit.

The first few months were fun. We would go out with our separate friends on Friday nights. Saturday nights were date nights, either just the two of us or with other friends, and on Sundays, we did brunch. I would read the sports section, and Leighton would do crossword puzzles. We would spend Sunday afternoon cleaning, meaning she would spend Sunday afternoon cleaning, and I would watch sports on TV and take naps because I had such a hard week at work. She may have had a more challenging week but was never considered.

The primary obstacle to our living together was that I was a neat freak, and Leighton made a mess everywhere she went. One of the "strategies" we employed was putting masking tape across the bedroom floor, defining which side of the room was hers and which was mine. Mine looked as tidy as a museum, and hers looked like somebody was trying to hide the hardwood floors. I don't remember ever being so motivated to keep everything clean and neat as then because I could continue to prove to Leighton how much better I was at taking care of our home and life. The shame was debilitating for Leighton.

We fought about mess and cleanliness all the time. Eventually, "we decided" that Leighton would move out and I would keep the apartment and all the furniture. It's funny to think about if it wasn't so awful. My idea was for her to move out so that we could work on our relationship and live together again after we improved our skills. The skills that "we" needed to work on were Leighton being cleaner and me not yelling for her to do so.

One of the things I had not considered when convincing Leighton to lose weight and stop smoking was that she would receive more male attention when she was out in the world, especially when she was out partying with her friends. That was the microcosm of my view on relationships and life. Everything was about meeting my immediate needs and instant gratification without recognizing the potential problems and obstacles the process created. In this case, in response to my criticism of her body, Leighton became more physically attractive, which is what I thought I wanted, to be with a hot girlfriend. But now, I had to deal with my feelings of jealousy, resentment, and betrayal, which I did not want to face.

When Leighton's grandmother died, Leighton became lost and depressed. She started spending more time with an ex-boyfriend who had also lost his grandmother earlier that year. I did not know it then, but Leighton and Henry began to kiss and eventually had sex. All this came out later when I caught her cheating on me with some guy she met at a club. I instantaneously broke up with Leighton and told her she was a total whore and a slut and would never be anything better. Leighton begged and pleaded with me to give her another chance. She did a good job convincing me; I told her I would meet her in a public place like the local Arboretum to talk.

When we both arrived, I pushed Leighton to tell me everything she did that would qualify as cheating. I forced her to describe all the intimate details while she was falling in tears onto her knees in a public place, begging and pleading with me to take her back and forgive her. The freshly cut grass stained Leighton's white stockings and her gray business suit. I continued to rip her to shreds, just like her stained stockings. She had no idea I would never take her back as a girl-friend but would "allow her" to give me sex. That was the narrative in my head. We argued, screamed, and cried for three and a half hours, ending with her getting back on her knees and swallowing my semen in public. I had succeeded in completely humiliating her whole being. I was satisfied enough to go about my day. Leighton was on her knees in her professional attire with semen on her face in an open field, sobbing by herself.

Leighton didn't know about my stuff. I had made out with her next-door neighbor, one year younger than her, played with the breasts and butt of her German cousin while visiting for a week, and eventually had sex with her best friend, Martha, out of spite. That doesn't include the other girls in clubs that I made out with and received oral sex. I never mentioned this to Leighton because it didn't fit my needs.

Leighton had been in therapy with the woman who had worked with her stepmother when she first got sober and her older brother when he first got sober. She was a drug and alcohol counselor. Leighton felt safe with her. Her name was Leighton as well. I learned later that they were working on empowering Leighton. Leighton felt empowered by gaining her voice and embracing her newfound attention from good-looking and successful guys. She was not falling

Raised by Wolves, Possibly Monsters

for my games and manipulations any longer.

About a month and a half later, Leighton and I got back together. We were dating, but I could date other people, and she couldn't. A week after we made this arrangement, she informed me that if I were going to see other people, she would also. I was so pissed off. I wanted to ask Leighton's therapist whether this was her idea. My solution was to see Leighton, the therapist because she ruined my relationship. I intended to convince her that I was a fantastic boyfriend, Leighton was an awful girlfriend, and I didn't need any help. I laugh every time I reflect on the fact that I thought that this strategy was bulletproof!

It was my third or fourth session with Leighton when she interrupted me as I spoke, "Mike, I want to take a minute and share a conversation I had with my supervisor this week. We discussed this without disclosing your name or anything like that. She brought it to my attention that everything you talk about starts with 'I was high,' or 'I was drunk,' or 'I was high and drunk,' and you launch into the story of what happened. It occurred to me we should talk about this. Is that okay with you?"

"Yeah, sure."

"Mike, do you think you have a problem with chemicals?"

"I've always thought I had a chemical imbalance." I was excited and full of energy for the first time in any of our sessions. Somebody figured out what was wrong with me, and it wasn't that I was fucked up and insane!

Leighton broke out laughing and quickly apologized. "I'm sorry, that was highly unprofessional of me. You seem to bring that out in me. Mike. That's not what I meant. Do you think you have a problem with chemicals like alcohol, marijuana, and cocaine?"

I took a minute to assess and rethink my strategy before answering. What answer will help me to convince this Leighton that the other Leighton is the problem and not me? "Yeah, maybe that makes sense. I mean, the problems I've had with Leighton and lying and cheating, crying, and all of her emotional temper tantrums have fucked me up. Getting drunk and getting high is how I'm dealing with it. I can't imagine what I would do to her if drugs and alcohol weren't calming me down." As a professional counselor for more than thirty years, it is hysterical that I thought this was an effective and well-thought-out strategy to employ with a full-time professional therapist!

"Thank you for sharing, Mike. I appreciate your honesty." Leighton started reading snippets from her notes of various stories that I had shared with her that started with me using alcohol and drugs, and most of them took place before I met Leighton. I remember thinking in my head at the time. Inside my head, my response was, "Fuck! I screwed up my plan!"

Leighton launched into a long, carefully thought-out intervention to educate me about drug and alcohol abuse. She had been a drug and alcohol counselor for many years. Leighton "encouraged" me to get an addiction assessment from the drug and alcohol counselor who used to be her professional partner.

While she was talking, I hatched a new plan. I would go to the alcohol and drug assessment and convince them that I was not a drug addict and that I just needed my girlfriend to be a better person by stopping cheating and lying to me, and then everything would be fine.

When I got home that day, I called the phone number on the business card Leighton had handed me. "Hi, is this Linn?"

I was expecting Linn to be a woman, not a man. Even though it was spelled Linn. "Yes, this is Linn. How can I help you?"

"My name is Mike Swerdloff, and my therapist Leighton recommended I call you about scheduling something called an alcohol and drug assessment."

"Yes. Leighton left a message on my answering machine telling me you might call. That's great that you made the phone call so quickly. Good for you!"

I rolled my eyes that in his silly therapist mind, he thought I was making some big step forward in life. Little did he know, I was about to bullshit him into making my plan work. "Yes, I'm always trying to better myself." I had to contain my laughter. The rest of the conversation was about scheduling an appointment for the following Thursday at 11 a.m. He gave me the address, which I already had on his business card, and gave me directions even though I already knew the way. I didn't listen to anything he said. We said our goodbyes, and he again wanted to tell me how great it was that I was taking this step in life. I did a great job of not telling him to fuck off and just said goodbye.

     Raised by Wolves, Possibly Monsters

PART II
What Happened

"Trauma is not your fault, but healing is your responsibility."

Brianna Wiest

The First Day of One Day at a Time

 ON MONDAY NIGHT, September 10th of 1989, I was watching Monday Night Football on TV with the Washington Redskins and the New York Giants. My roommates were Giants fans, and I was a Redskins fan. When the game got out of hand and Washington was far ahead, they went to sleep early. I stayed up to watch the game and to drink beer. I even watched the post-game interviews for a regular season game; that didn't matter. I stayed up to drink beer. There was no other reason. The last part of my strategy to prove to this guy that I was not an alcoholic was to stop on my own on Monday in advance after the assessment on Thursday. Tuesday morning was September 11th, 1989.

I drank three cups of coffee Thursday morning before getting into my Mitsubishi Starion for the appointment. To say I was distracted would be an understatement. I took I-78 West out of Basking Ridge to head to Summit, the Outpatient Center of Fair Oaks Hospital. I was about fifteen miles into my journey, going 80-something miles per hour, when I realized I was going the wrong way. Summit is East, and I'm traveling west. "Fuck!"

I turned around at the next exit and headed Eastbound towards Summit at a speed of under 100 since I needed to go about twenty miles in twelve minutes. Because I didn't listen to his directions, I got off I-78 the wrong way in Summit and added another six minutes to my drive. "Fuck!"

My heart was racing, my hands were shaking, and my eyes were darting all over the room as I entered, looking for a guy named Linn. I waited a few minutes before he came out to find me, and we went to his "office," which was more like a cubicle. He looked like one of those old-school alcoholics in movies with the hair parted in the middle, a little bit long in the back, and a big handlebar mustache. He was wearing a checked shirt with shiny buttons, similar to cowboys going to Sunday church in movies.

"Mike, why don't you tell me a little about yourself and why you want an assessment?"

"Well, as I said on the phone, that lady Leighton said that she thought we were treating a stomachache with aspirin and wanted me to get an assessment from you, so we don't waste each other's time. It couldn't hurt to know. So, here I am."

He chuckled. "Okay, let's get to the test then. There are twenty questions that a bunch of smarty pants up in Boston at Harvard came up with that they think determine whether somebody's an alcoholic or not. It's not perfect, but it gives us something to go on and start the conversation. They are all yes or no questions; try to answer them as best you can. Are you ready to dive in?" I nodded my head. "OK, let's get to it!"

He proceeded to ask me twenty questions. He spoke slowly like I was stupid or English was my third language. I strategized in my head that if there were twenty questions, at eighteen, you probably have alcoholism, and at sixteen, you're too close for comfort. In total, I answered nine questions no, which left me with eleven yes. I felt safe that I was in the clear and not an alcoholic. When we completed the test, he told me that at six, you're someone who abuses alcohol, and at eight, you're considered an alcoholic. I initially thought I had screwed up my analysis in advance and wanted to retake the test. Linn started going on and on for the next five minutes. The test is new, and they're still learning things about it. It's not perfect, but we use it as a guideline. I was quickly pivoting my strategy.

"Anybody above seven, we recommend they consider going to rehab if they can. If they're not, we offer an outpatient program four nights a week, and we encourage you to go to AA or NA the other three days of the week." He stopped talking, and his voice trailed off as if he was asking a question, but there wasn't any question. He was waiting for me to respond. I held steady and didn't say a word. I was staring him down. He started chuckling again. "What do you think about that recommendation there, Mike?"

I think I want to beat the shit out of you, is what I think, you fucking old drunk. I verbalized this out loud, "So you want me to go to an outpatient program four nights a week after I work all day and then go to these meetings the other three days of the week? Did I get that right?"

"Unless you think you should go inpatient instead?"

"I can't lose my job because I'm at rehab. How long would I have to do this outpatient thing?"

      Raised by Wolves, Possibly Monsters

"That depends."

Okay, I can play this game too. "Depends on what?"

"Depends on you and your progress. For some people, it's six weeks; for others, it's three months."

"Three months? I can't take off five nights a week for three months."

"There's a saying in AA, "Anything you put before your sobriety you will lose."

There's a saying in Newark, anything else you say stupid; you will lose your ability to talk, fuckhead. "How much does this shit cost?"

"They ran your insurance, and it will cover the whole thing. Shouldn't cost you anything out of pocket."

"And how much does AA cost?"

"AA doesn't cost anything. They pass the hat around for donations. Most people put a couple of bucks in the hat."

I knew that if I said no, he would tell Leighton, the therapist, that I wasn't willing to accept treatment, who would tell Leighton, the ex-girlfriend. That was going to ruin my plan. "Okay, I'll do it. When do I start?"

He looked surprised. A big shit-eating grin came across his face. I am entirely sure his mustache even jumped. I also considered reaching across his desk and grabbing him by his mustache till he screamed. "We can set you to start tomorrow night in Morristown. Bill and Amy are great counselors who run that group, and it's a smaller group. You'll fit right in." My mind wrote this narrative, "You mean you'll fit right in because you're one of them assholes." He interrupted my thoughts, blurting out. "I'm excited for you, Mike. Let's get the paperwork set up so all you have to do is show up. One more thing, you have to show up sober tomorrow night."

"That's no problem. I quit drinking on Monday." He had that same shit-eating grin on his face. I thought about reaching over, grabbing his mustache, and yanking on it again. "That's great, Mike. You're just full of surprises!"

He was just a little too happy and excited for my comfort. We filled out the paperwork, including six different initials or signatures. I was waiting till they were going to ask for blood, semen, or both. When we finished, he got excited again, shook my hand, and muttered, "One day at a time." I shook his hand, leaving with a handful of everything I agreed to without reading. When I got in my silver Starion, the only thought in my head was, "What the fuck did I just agree to do?" I did not get lost on my way home. That was the best part of that day.

I don't remember much about those first few meetings; they all sounded like alcoholics and drug addicts. However, I remember a cute girl about nineteen years old that I saw at my third AA meeting on a Friday night, which kept me returning to that meeting to find her. She shared, "I always get sober for a few months and then find a hot guy at a meeting, fuck his brains out for the next few days, and end up back in rehab." I don't know anything that was said after that. All I could think about was that I was going to be the next guy she fucks for the next few days before she landed in rehab. As soon as the meeting ended, all the women swarmed her to keep her from the guys in the meeting like me. Foiled!

I never saw her again, but I attended that meeting four times.

In those days, AA was made up mostly of older people. Some young people's meetings consisted of weird people in their twenties trying to impress each other and get laid. They both had value in my life. This was my routine: work during the day, groups at night, AA meetings on Wednesday and Saturday, and an NA meeting on Sunday night at Saint Barnabas Hospital, yep, the hospital I lived across from in high school. I kept my distance from everybody and didn't engage. I shared a little more in my outpatient program. The overriding feeling I experienced then was that I didn't belong in any of these places; these people were losers. I was playing the long game and wanted to prove that I was acceptable to the Leightons.

Leighton, the ex-girlfriend, and I had little contact. We went out on some solo dates and double dates. They felt awkward for both of us; Leighton and the people we were with were drinking, and I was not. They were having fun and laughing, and I was not. They wanted to be there, but I did not.

Leighton and I had a fierce fight that ended in her living room, telling me we needed to take a break for a few weeks until I got more solid. She wanted to adapt to my new lifestyle. I understood what she meant; she wanted to party, play, have fun, and fuck, and I was not part of that now.

I hit a new low, and I started to experience depression; nobody knew how

        Raised by Wolves, Possibly Monsters

bad I felt but me.

The night I fought with Leighton, I felt like my life was slipping away from me. I decided to go to a midnight meeting in Verona because I was losing my mind and wanted to get drunk. On the way, a cop pulled me over, driving 103 mph on Route 280. The cop approached my car with his rifle pointed at my head. He asked me if I was drunk, and I said, "Not only am I not drunk, but I'm also sober six weeks, and I'm trying to go to an AA meeting." He wanted me to do a breathalyzer anyway, so I did. He asked me if I knew I was going 100 mph. I was about to answer sarcastically and say, "Well, actually, I was going 103." Instead, I said yes. "I was having a tough night and wanted to get to a meeting because I was afraid I would drink, get high, and ruin everything."

He wrote me a ticket for speeding but not for reckless driving and offered to escort me so I could get to the meeting quickly and easily since I didn't know where I was going. I sat through the meeting in a dark and musty basement, listening to some guy go on and on about his misery and awful recovery. I did one important thing during that hour: I went to sleep without any drugs or alcohol in my body. However, I now had a $120 ticket and four points added to my driver's license, which probably meant I would lose it again for the fourth time. I already had twenty-one points on my driver's license; in New Jersey, you lost your license at twelve points.

I went to bed around 1:00 a.m. feeling defeated and demoralized. A couple of hours later, one of my housemates, Jared, who ran a club inside a Hilton Hotel, was drinking and partying in the living room with two girls. They sounded like they were having a good time. I woke up even more miserable.

Since I was still in bed and didn't turn my lights on, hoping that I was going to fall back asleep soon, I had no idea if it was ten minutes or thirty minutes, but I heard Jared say to one of the girls, "We'll be right back. I want to show Mandy our big backyard." Jared and "Mandy" left through the front door, and a minute later, I heard his car pulling out of the driveway, and Mandy laughed loudly. The girl in the living room chased them, but they were already out of their driveway, turning right on Lyons Road before she descended the front steps. The girl returned to the house and was alone in the living room. I was curious about what she was going to do.

A little while later, guessing fifteen minutes, I heard footsteps walking around the living room, dining room, and kitchen.

She tapped on my door. I remained still. She knocked again three more times with a little more pressure, "I know you're in there. Jared said you're home; this was your room, so we had to be quiet. I know you're in there. Jared left with my sister, and I'm stuck here. I don't know where I am or how to get home." Her voice cracked more with each sentence. "Please help me." Her voice was soft and gentle. "I'm scared." That was my cue that she was vulnerable to being manipulated. I could exploit her at 2:30 in the morning and theoretically still be "in recovery."

"You can come in. I'm up now."

She opened the door slowly as if she didn't want to disturb me, herself, or the silence. My room was dark, and the hallway was bright. I only saw a silhouette of her figure, which looked more like an hourglass than an apple. It appeared she had blond hair, but I wasn't sure. I smelled perfume and vodka emanating from her body. My penis instantaneously woke up.

"Hi, I'm Harley. My sister left with Jared, and I don't know where I am or how to get home. I'm drunk and lost and don't know what to do." She stood halfway between the door and my bed. At this point, I could tell she had blond hair mixed with light brown streaks. Her blue blouse was showing cleavage. Her jeans were tight; I could see part of her butt from where she stood.

"Hi, I'm Mike. You can sit down if you want." I pointed to the edge of my bed, where she hesitantly moved forward, stopped right before she was about to sit down, and looked around as if waiting for another better solution. It didn't. She began crying about being lost and left behind by her sister. A minute later, she was in her underwear under the covers. We kissed, and I was touching her body. Another minute later, Harley was naked, as was I. Although, I didn't have far to go since I only wore my dark blue boxers.

I don't know how to describe what happened next, but somehow, we started to have intercourse, but we didn't, or maybe we did for like ten seconds. We both had orgasms somehow without intercourse. The stranger in my bed fell asleep with my penis between her legs and my tongue between her breasts. We woke in the morning hearing Jared and her sister Mandy laughing in the kitchen.

　　　　　Raised by Wolves, Possibly Monsters

Harley freaked out when she realized the situation, as she should, and she was getting ready to jump out of bed. I grabbed her arm, kissed her, and told her it was okay. I'm not sure why, but that comforted her. She leaned in and kissed me. This was the first time I saw what she looked like. She was probably about twenty-one years old, possibly younger. She was shy at first; the alcohol had dissipated. When I started licking her nipples, this cute little white girl started breathing heavily. When I rubbed her between her legs, she breathed even heavier. Harley began to play with my erection. I rubbed it against her thigh, and she went wild. Just like in the middle of the night, somehow, we started to have intercourse, but something else happened, with both of us having an orgasm again. Mine was in her mouth, and hers with my fingers inside her. We dressed and entered the kitchen to see what Jared and Mandy were doing.

The four of us had brunch together. Jared offered to drive the girls home since he had to go to work anyway. I kissed Harley goodbye and grabbed her butt. She got out her purse and wrote her phone number on a scrap of paper, handing it to me with her name on it in case I didn't remember her name as they left. I did the only logical thing I could think of, which was to go back to bed, attempting to get the sleep that kept getting interrupted the night before.

I fell asleep with a smile but spent the bulk of the day trying to get my shit together between lack of sleep and an emotional hangover. I spent the afternoon alternating between naps, watching football, and drinking fluids. I have no idea why I was drinking fluids since I didn't have any alcohol in my system, but I felt hungover, so I drank lots of water and orange juice.

During one of those naps, the phone rang at 5:37 p.m. on my large red LED alarm clock. I thought about not answering the phone but went ahead and answered. It was Leighton. My heart and body sank. We were not supposed to speak for a month; it had only been a day. I was not prepared to tell Leighton about the night before.

"Why are you calling me? You told me last night that you didn't want to talk to me for a month, and now you're calling. Why are you doing this to me?"

"I woke in the middle of the night and had a bad feeling that something terrible had happened to you. And I got terrified and wanted to make sure you were okay. I know I wasn't supposed to call, but I didn't know what else to do.

Are you okay?"

"Leighton, you shouldn't have called. Now you call me, and I have to restart all over again. I'm fine. Do you want anything else? I want to go back to sleep because I'm tired!" I wasn't asking a question; it was more of a demand.

I could hear her crying.

Her tears rattled me. I lost my composure. I told her everything.

Leighton's reply was firm and to the point. "You have twenty minutes to get here, and if you're not here by then, I'll never talk to you again. I can't believe you pulled all that shit last night while you're supposed to be in recovery, and I'm up all night worried about you. You have twenty minutes to get here or forget everything!"

I threw on some sweats quickly and was out the door in about ninety seconds. I was back on Route 287 on my way to Route 24 East to her home in Madison, by Drew University. I pulled in front of her house; Leighton was standing in the street. I almost didn't slow down in time. My tires screeched, but everything was fine. I got out of the car with my keys still in the car. She came charging at me, yelling and pushing me in the chest and pounding on my chest and yelling at me and crying and screaming and hitting my chest again and more crying and more screaming and more tears. I could barely hear what she was saying. My mind was racing and confused. My brain was flooded.

I looked over her shoulder and saw a massive old oak tree. I had a fantasy in my head that I would get back in my car, rev up the engine, throw it in gear, run over Leighton, drive into the tree, kill myself, and put both of us out of our misery. I hated life with drugs and alcohol and hated it even more without drugs. I hated being with Leighton, and I hated being without Leighton even more. I stared at the tree; Leighton stopped pounding on my chest and yelling or crying. She charged the four steps towards the driver's side door and got inside. I thought she would turn the car on and run me over. Terror filled my body, and maybe even a little relief. What she did instead totally caught me off guard. Leighton grabbed the keys to my car, ran inside the door to her home, and locked it. She closed all the windows. She made sure there was no way for me to get in. I landed on the stoop to her front door, yelling, threatening, and eventually crying until I gave up, ran out of energy, and flopped. I kept pleading with her

     Raised by Wolves, Possibly Monsters

and crying. At some point, I fell asleep, leaning against her front door.

When I woke up, it was light out, and the front door was unlocked, so I went in quietly. I entered Leighton's room. She was in bed, and my entering woke her. I sat on the floor next to her bed and started crying. I fell back asleep on the white carpet next to her bed. I woke up with Leighton on the phone the second time, whispering in her kitchen.

"He's sleeping on the floor in my room right now. Yes, he says he didn't relapse. Yeah, that's what he said. And he got pulled over by a cop doing 103 on the way to a meeting." There was a long pause; whoever was on the other end spoke for a while. I could hear Leighton pacing around in the kitchen anxiously. I could hear her breathing heightened and rapid. "Are you kidding me? He'll never agree to that. Leighton, I know you're a therapist, but you don't know him like I do. I never saw him like he was last night. He had this look in his eyes like he was ready to kill me and himself." Another pause. I did not like her talking to Leighton, the therapist, on the phone about me. I stayed perfectly still so she would not know I was listening to every word she said. "Okay, I'll try. But I need you to stay by the phone because I will call you if this doesn't work. I hope he doesn't lose it. I was terrified last night. Thanks, I appreciate it. Okay, I'll call you back. Thanks again for talking on a Sunday morning. Okay, I'll let you know how it goes. Bye."

I heard Leighton let out a big exhale. The second one was bigger and more profound. She walked into her room wearing a pair of gray sweatpants with a blue stripe on the side and her Saint Elizabeth Catholic School T-shirt without a bra. I could see her nipples poking through, and for a brief second, it excited me. Her face looked like she had been through hell: pale skin, bloodshot eyes, and messy hair with rings around her eyes. There were fresh tears on her cheeks.

"We need to talk. I just got off the phone with Leighton, and she devised a plan. She gave you a choice: either to go into Fair Oaks Inpatient Rehab right now, and I can take you, or if I don't call her back, she will call the police and have you picked up. It took me almost a half hour to convince her to give you a choice. She wanted me to call the police. Please say yes, Mike. I don't want to see you taken away by the police. You're finally starting to get your shit together. Please! They have a bed ready for you, and your counselor from the outpatient program said he would meet you there and get everything squared away for you. Please say yes, Mike. Please don't make me call the police or have Leighton call the police on you. Please!"

I could feel Leighton's pain and sadness, fear and shame, surrounding me with her chest and arms. "OK. I'll go." She hugged me tighter and lovingly. We held each other quietly for just a moment. Leighton released and held my shoulders, looking directly into my eyes, "Okay, I swear it will get better. It will get better, Mike; let's go to Dunkin Donuts. I'll buy us coffee and donuts; we'll go to Fair Oaks to meet your counselor. He'll make sure you're taken care of." She took a breath, "I do love you. I always have, and I always will. I'll be here when you get out. Please know how much I love you!" Leighton kissed me on the lips gently and tenderly. I kissed her back. More tears, another kiss, and we got up and went to the door. We walked down the steps, and she took my right arm, "Let's go in my car."

Leighton drove me to the mental hospital. I entered the intake unit one hour later with metal doors locked behind me. I didn't resist. Life had beaten me, and I knew it.

Fair Oaks Mental Hospital

IT WOULD PROBABLY be a lot more interesting to start this section with a statement like, "This is where my new life began" or "Being in rehab changed my life." But anything like that would be a lie. However, here are a few things about my experience in Fair Oaks that seemed important.

When I woke up the following day, I had several genuine moments of gratitude for probably the first time. I was aware of how close I came to not being alive anymore. In addition, I was also grateful for Leighton's instinct to steal my car keys and not let me into her home.

They decided to put me in the mental health unit instead of the drug and alcohol unit. This was my first experience with people with clinical depression, bipolar disorder, panic attacks, and other mental health challenges. One young woman on the unit was beautiful, seductive, and flirtatious. She was also an alcoholic and addict like me. Lilliana wore her sexuality like a bracelet. Whenever we would go around and introduce ourselves before every group, Lilliana would introduce herself like this, "My name is Lilliana, and I'm a drug addict and alcoholic and a sex addict, and if somebody doesn't fuck me soon, I'm going to have to kill somebody or myself." From my first day in that unit, she always ended her introduction by staring me down. I never knew if that was an invitation, a challenge, or a boundary. I took it as all of the above.

I also met the psychologist I worked with regularly for the next five years at Fair Oaks. Dr. Lauraine Hollyer showed commitment and concern, which caught my attention. I will get back to her later.

The most impactful experience at Fair Oaks was knowing I never wanted to be inside a locked mental hospital again. I would do anything to avoid ever having a doctor, psychiatrist, court, or judge be able to control where I go, where I don't go, and when for the rest of my life.

One morning, I woke up and decided that starting that day, I would tell everyone to call me Michael. I had been Mike, Mikey, or Squirrel my whole life and couldn't stand any of those names. I always thought Michael was a beautiful name. My name was now Michael, and it still is today.

I had one other "interesting" experience at Fair Oaks. On my third day there, just after dinner time, we were in our evening group. A couple of team members came in and whispered in Lauraine's ear. She looked startled by whatever they were whispering. She looked directly at me, as did both mental health support staff members. A minute later, Gina, the head nurse during the evenings, entered the room with a sense of urgency. Lauraine announced that Gina would take over the group. And then, "Michael, can you come with me for a moment?"

My brother and one of his buddies, a big goon that hung around him a lot, were at the reception office with guns, threatening the staff to release me. Lauraine wanted to know what I think they should do. I didn't understand the question, and then a nurse clarified.

"Michael, they have threatened both of our security guards, the staff in the reception area, and a nurse at gunpoint. They're trying to break you out because they think you're being held here against your will. Should we call the police or the fire department? Should I go down and talk to them? Do you want to talk to them? What should we do?"

I couldn't believe they asked a new mental health patient who was a drug addict and alcoholic about killing his girlfriend and himself seventy-two hours before what they should do with his sociopathic brother, a strong arm in the Mob.

"Please don't call the police. David has a record, two kids, and their mother is going through a lot. Please don't leave my nephews without their father again."

"Well, we can't just do nothing. Somebody can't just show up at a mental hospital with a gun and threaten people. Do you think he would harm somebody?"

"Is there any way I can talk to him and tell him that I'm okay and that you're not holding me here against my will?"

"We can't let you go down there. By law, we can't let you leave the unit until we have finished evaluating you because you entered with homicidal and suicidal tendencies. Let me check and see if they'll let you talk to him on the phone. Can you wait right here, please?" I learned that if people think you are going to kill your girlfriend and yourself, they suddenly start using the word "please" frequently.

I nodded yes, and Lauraine hurried away behind the main desk and called the reception area downstairs with the perfectly vacuumed lush, forest green carpet. A minute later, Lauraine returned and said we could call the front desk and come with her to her office. Lauraine dialed the front welcome area and asked the woman to hand the phone to David, and then Lauraine handed her phone to me.

"Hi, Dave. What the hell are you doing? Did you come to a mental hospital with a gun? How did you think this was going to go?"

"Well, I don't give a fuck about how they think it's going to go down. If they're holding my younger brother, I'll break the fucking walls down and blow the place up to get you out! They don't know who the fuck they're dealing with!"

"You don't have to break me out. They didn't come and get me and take me away against my will. I came in on my own."

"Well, you must be fucking crazy if, on purpose, you go somewhere where you got locked up, and they drug you and keep you against your will. What the fuck is wrong with you?"

     Raised by Wolves, Possibly Monsters

"A whole bunch of shit went down, and I had a choice of either going here or the police would come and get me. I chose here on my own. I'm having many problems these days and need help." I was working hard not to break down in tears.

"How come I didn't know about any of this? What kind of shit happened? Are the Feds or the Secret Service after you again?"

"No legal problems going on. Look, Dave, I don't want to get into it right now; I need you to leave. You being here is just making it worse for me. It's proving to them how fucked up my family and I are. Please leave. I promise you they're not keeping me against my will."

"If you promise me, they didn't come and take you away in handcuffs or anything like that, I'll leave. But you better not be bullshitting me. Otherwise, I'll be back and bring the whole crew!"

"You realize if you do that, then they will keep me here against my will because I'd have to be crazy to come from a family that breaks into a mental hospital. Please leave."

"Okay, we'll leave. I'm taking your word that you're not here against your will. Just know I love you, and I'm out here if you need help with anything or if I need to get you out of here."

"Thanks, Dave, I love you too." I hung up the phone and broke into tears. I knew Lauraine was talking to me, but I couldn't hear anything she was saying. At some point, I faintly heard her voice repeating, "Michael, are you okay? Are you okay?"

"No, I'm not okay! They didn't believe me in my outpatient program, and now nobody believes me here. This is my world and my family. They're all nuts. My mother tells the staff she's bringing dinner for me every night. My father says he will have his lawyer sue the hospital for keeping me against my will. And he comes to visit with his wife, who shows up drunk. Then, my brother and his asshole friend tried to break me out with guns the next day. This is my family. Do you believe me now?"

"Yes, I believe you, Michael." Those words and the authenticity of her voice meant a great deal to me—the story. My story, hidden from everybody, was shared with somebody else, a professional, and they believed me.

Two months later, when my insurance had run out, magically, the next day, I was "ready to go home." It blows my mind more than thirty years later that a mental hospital would let a drug addict go home the week before Christmas and New Year's!

More Than Just Body Parts

 I REMEMBER CELEBRATING one year sober and thinking, "They made me sign an agreement when I left Fair Oaks. While I went to their daytime outpatient program, I would not have any contact with Leighton till I had one year sober. I was now one year sober. They argued with me, pleaded with me, that it was a bad idea, and I was going to relapse. I was going to get back into my old patterns. We were terrible for each other, and nothing good could come from it." Each additional reason they listed for why I couldn't do it increased my motivation to do it.

"Well, this was the agreement, and I did my part. I will call Leighton and get together with her, with or without your support." The next day, I called Leighton.

We met for lunch on a Friday afternoon. We discussed each other's jobs, living situations, roommates, family members, and friends. Leighton asked about my recovery, and I asked her about her new car. After we finished the basics, we had nothing to say. We talked more about recovery in twelve-step programs and alcoholics. We looked at each other when that ran its course, not knowing how to connect.

"I can't wait to share how ridiculously dramatic they were about their fears of us getting together again." We laughed for the first time together in a year. And it would be the last time for several years. Eventually, Leighton and I became casual friends and met a few times a year to share a meal and catch up.

With Leighton in my rearview mirror, I felt ready to start dating in recovery. Let me translate English into English here. I wanted to have sex with a woman. Soon. The options in the local AA community were not thrilling, but there were a few. For one reason or another, it never worked with them more than just

          Raised by Wolves, Possibly Monsters

flirting or a couple of dates.

However, I noticed a woman who worked at a health food shop in the Mall of the Radio Shack where I worked. I used to go there every few days to get some natural juice, a hummus sandwich, or a nice salad with fresh greens and sprouts before there was a movement or lifestyle or the phrase "crunchy granola type." Her name was Marissa, and she was a student at Rutgers University. She was intelligent, thoughtful, creative, attractive, and completely natural in her presentation of self, with no makeup, perfumes, fancy clothes, or jewelry, and it looked like she barely combed her hair when she left to go to work for the day. These traits were divergent from the pre-recovery days of the hot chicks in clubs who spent the bulk of their time focusing on how to get and keep the attention of guys like me who were trouble.

Marissa and I became friends and had great conversations. Since I drank only apple-strawberry juice, she called me "Apple-Strawberry Man." Soon, the rest of the staff did as well. As Marissa and the Apple-Strawberry Man were becoming friendlier, the Apple-Strawberry Man wanted to ask Marissa on a date. I wanted to consult with Lauraine before doing so.

"Michael, what do you like about Marissa?"

"She's intelligent, interesting, nice, fun to talk to, and has a good personality."

"What's your favorite thing about Marissa?"

"She has a great ass!" I could feel the energy and excitement within myself pouring out.

She snapped back at me, "Michael, women are more than just body parts!" This was the first, and possibly the only, time that I saw Lauraine lose her composure during one of our sessions.

I know this sounds funny, but somehow, I had made it to thirty years old, and this thought had never crossed my mind. I was puzzled by the statement. I honestly did not understand what Lauraine was saying, and she said it with such force I was embarrassed to ask her what it meant. She said it like she was reminding me that one plus one equals two, and how did I not know this if I went to grammar school?

I couldn't get that statement out of my head the whole ride home, an hour and 10 minutes. While having dinner with my buddy Chris before the meeting that night, and while I was trying to fall asleep at night, the statement kept coming up, "Michael, women are more than just body parts." When I woke up in the morning, "Women are more than just body parts" while driving from Bernardsville down to South Plainfield for work. "Women are more than just body parts." I could feel it in my bones that there was something vital for me to understand, and I could not figure it out for my life. I asked a few of my guy friends, and they took some random guesses, but none knew. They were all speculating.

My friend Victoria and I often hung out on Saturday afternoons, listened to music, and caught up. Victoria was one of my closest friends. Victoria was brilliant, educated, and probably the only woman I knew who identified as "a feminist" then. I planned on bringing this up when we were together, knowing full well that I would get a lecture on how stupid men and I were, but she would teach me something valuable. I knew I could count on Victoria for being honest and straightforward and for her genuine concern for my well-being and development as a man and a friend.

"What do you mean you don't understand the sentence? You're not an idiot, Michael; you're an intelligent man. What part don't you understand?"

I carefully considered my response based on Victoria's red face, which was like her hair, as were her eyes. She looked like she was ready to pop. History had taught me that when Victoria popped, run for cover. For some reason, I decided to come clean instead and tell her I didn't understand anything about the sentence and that I felt foolish.

"Well, that part you're right about. I'm going to pretend that you're a ten-year-old boy and not a grown man who's an idiot." Victoria slowly explained to me while shaking her head back and forth, "What's wrong is that guys like you only notice and care about a woman's looks. Women have feelings, thoughts, ideas, desires, a personality, and character. Michael, we are whole people! We're not just here for you and your needs and sex. Liking our breasts or our ass or legs or eyes doesn't mean you like us. We are more than the parts of our body that you find hot or attractive and want to touch and have sex with. We are whole people, Michael! The sooner you understand this, the better chance you'll have

    Raised by Wolves, Possibly Monsters

of meeting a good girlfriend and being in a decent relationship." Victoria hesitated. "Michael, if guys like you don't get this because you're one of the good ones, there's no hope for things ever getting better. It's imperative to me that you understand this and that you understand how important it is. If you can't get it, how are all of the fucking idiots in between jobs living with their mothers going to?"

It became my mission for the next few months to understand this statement, "Michael, women are more than body parts!" It took a while, but I started to get it in bits and pieces. More than anything, it was my female friends in AA that I built solid and caring friendships with, and the love, compassion, and understanding that they offered me even though I was predominantly still a jerk. The fact that I was less of a jerk than many other men didn't change the fact that I was still a jerk.

In retrospect, as my mind scans through me trying to learn this important lesson, I can see how patient and supportive the women in my life were. They saw how important it was for me to understand this basic principle of knowing and respecting women. They put up with a lot of crap because, for them, it felt worth the investment. Me "getting it" would create opportunities to help other men get it, too. If this is correct, they were right.

I'm writing this right now because of those women! I want to thank them for their time, energy, patience, and investment in me. I get it now!

This was the beginning of me shifting from a guy who solely saw women for his own needs and desires to a man wanting to learn how to be a friend and boyfriend to women who were working on their lives and had been through hell. Compassion and empathy came soon after, and respect was not far behind. What I didn't get from Victoria and my other AA friends got hammered into my head on a snowy night in Mendham, where my brother had beaten six boys on the football team to a pulp years before.

Thank You for Not

 I MET SELENA at the Bernardsville Sunday night speaker meeting. It was one of those meetings where everyone was 150 years old. They shared, starting with, "I remember when AA was for real alcoholics."

They'd launch into a twenty-minute rant about how great the program used to be and how people didn't go to meetings from rehabs, Division of Motor Vehicles, or use cocaine. You know, back in the good old days of AA: "You don't drink and go to meetings" and stay miserable, full of caffeine, nicotine, and sugar for the rest of your life. You know those good old days.

At one of their celebration meetings, I noticed somebody sitting in the back row who looked young enough to be born in the twentieth century. The woman had olive skin, brown eyes, and long black hair parted in the middle. We glanced back and forth at each other a couple of times. After the meeting, while grabbing a piece of cake from the celebration, she made her way over and introduced herself.

"Hi, I'm Selena." She reached out cleanly, clearly, and straightforwardly, and I shook her hand. We started chatting, and I found out Selena had been sober for six years and was sponsoring the woman who celebrated one year. She pointed to the woman, and I made an association in my head. Her sponsee Susie and I had flirted a couple of times. We both had attended an AA dance. I had started flirting with Susie and thought she was flirting with me. She was not; she got pissed off and told me I didn't know how to treat a lady respectfully and not talk to her again. Fortunately for me, when I spoke with Selena, she conversed with the three older women. I moved my body to be on the other side of Selena, avoiding facing Susie.

The conversation was pretty simple, without flirting or any sexual energy between us. It was not much different than if I was talking to one of the older men born in the 19th century, except she was more attractive. Sometimes Selena's eyes would be excited when sharing. I was about to give up and walk away because we weren't hitting it off.

Selena said, "I'm enjoying talking to you, Michael, and I would like to know if you would like to go on a date with me this Saturday night."

I was astonished and flattered. I said yes. Selena looked excited and possibly proud. We exchanged phone numbers. Selena continued, "Since I initiated asking you out, it's your job to make plans for us." I was intrigued and interested. This kind of interaction was new territory for me; she had been sober for six years, so I felt safe with her. By the way, I didn't know that she was Mexican at this point. That's relevant to what transpired.

In my ignorant, bigoted mind, assuming she was Puerto Rican, I thought I would take her to my favorite Mexican restaurant in Morristown. When I called, Freddie, a young guy who was one of the owners, told me they closed their doors for the last time.

Staying with the assumption that I should take her out for Mexican food because that's what you do with a Puerto Rican woman, I found a place about twenty minutes away in Stanhope. We set our time to meet at the church parking lot at the Mendham Archdiocese. I picked up Selena about five minutes late because my sports car was made for dry roads, not five inches of snow during heavy snowfall.

Selena got in my car and put on her seatbelt, checking it twice to ensure she snapped it. Shen placed her bag on her legs instead of the floor. She had one hand inside the pocketbook for the entire forty-minute drive. Because of the snow, we were only going twenty miles per hour. There needed to be more conversation. I was intent on making it there without sliding into a snowdrift on the side of the road.

When we finally pulled into "La Fiesta," I got out quickly, getting ready to open the door for Selena. She almost jumped out to ensure she got out before I could do it.

"I'm capable of opening the door myself. Thank you." She continued surprising me by saying things women didn't say to men in those situations. I felt both confused and curious. In the early 90s, most of the young women I met who were "feminists" dressed and presented them differently than other women. Selena was understated and seemed not to want to be noticed at all. She walked ahead of me so that I wouldn't open the door to the restaurant for her. I was trying to figure out what was happening, so I decided not to pull the chair out for her when the host brought us to our seats. I was embarrassed when I told Selena after the server brought us chips and salsa while we looked at the menu, "This is common in Mexican restaurants." She gave me a fake smile. I didn't know what to do with it until Selena spoke with the server in fluent Spanish when the server returned.

Dinner was fine. At times, we engaged in conversation; at other times, we didn't. At times, it was awkward, and at different points, it wasn't. The food was acceptable, and I did not make any comments about it. Selena shared that she was Mexican and was born in Monterey. After we finished dinner and flan, I asked Selena if she wanted to go somewhere else on the way home.

"No, thank you. I'm glad we came here tonight. It has been a nice night, Michael. I think I'm ready to go home if that's okay with you."

"Yes, of course." I raised my arm to wave over the server. When she didn't come, I lifted my arm until she saw me. As she came in our direction, for the first time, I saw an expression on Selena's face that I interpreted as distaste. At the time, I didn't understand why a young Mexican woman needed to stop everything to come over because the white male was waving his hand at her like she was a dog. Selena did not say anything about it.

The way back to the church parking lot was not as long since it was a couple of degrees warmer, the snow was wetter, and the plows were out and moving snow. There was some conversation on the ride home, but we had now spent almost two hours together and had not had one fluid or passionate conversation yet about anything.

When we pulled into the Catholic Church lot in Mendham, part of me was relieved that I would drop her off. My inner voice was curious and intrigued, and I wanted to kiss her goodnight. I pulled up next to her car, "Selena, if you'd like to turn your car on, let it warm up and stay warm here; we could say goodbye then."

"That's thoughtful, Michael; thank you!" She smiled warmly at me, and it was the first time I felt like she smiled with ease and the intention of making a connection with me. I felt warm all over. When she got out of the car, my mind started racing about initiating a kiss or asking her first. When she returned to the car, I could see something was happening with her that I had not seen previously. "Michael, I enjoyed our date tonight. I will consider if I would like to go out with

 Raised by Wolves, Possibly Monsters

you again. If so, I will call you. This time, it would be my idea of where to go for a date." Selena hesitated momentarily, gathering herself for what I thought would be her leaning over to give me a goodnight kiss. My heart was racing; I was steadying myself and preparing my lips.

"Thank you again for being willing to drive in the snow. I appreciate it." She leaned towards me slightly, "And thank you for not raping or beating me." Selena opened her arms and asked if I would like a hug; I answered yes. We shared a brief but full hug. "Thank you again, Michael, and have a good night." She unlocked her seatbelt and left the car methodically as if this was how most dates ended and that it was a regular interaction.

When I got home, I called one of my AA buddies and gave him a brief overview of the date and, more importantly, our interaction in the parking lot. "Wow! Mike, you sure do know how to pick the crazy ones." We laughed nervously since neither of us knew how to talk about this. I then called Victoria because Victoria identified herself as a feminist. She would know what happened and tell me how to deal with it.

"Good for her. You have no idea, Michael; what a relief it is after a date when you go out with a guy you don't know and get home in one piece. I'll bet you she truly was grateful. And I also want to say that I'm proud of you for not making some wise-ass remark or trying to make a joke. I'm sure she's had some awful experiences for her to say that, and it must have taken a lot of courage to go on a date with you and share that with you at the end. Amazingly, she was strong enough to approach you at the meeting and ask you out on a date and get in the car with someone she barely knows to drive to some hillbilly town in the middle of nowhere during a snowstorm."

As I was lying in bed that night, trying to process things, an exciting and ironic thought came across. After all of the physical and emotional harm I had done to girls and women, now that I was sober and was not doing something wrong, this was one of the first times I had to deal with the consequences of rape and violence toward women. Another exciting thought followed this. Maybe Selena said this to me because I wasn't the guy who would do those things now!

Today, I interpret it as creating a safe enough space for her not to be afraid the whole time. She could share something as vulnerable as she did because I was a safe enough male to be in the presence of.

I've thought of Selena many times over the years. Selena never called me for a date, which I mostly assumed. I was curious: if she had called me back, what would have happened? When I think of Selena, I reflect on what it must be like for Selena and other women like Selena. They've had multiple experiences of male violence and don't feel safe in the presence of a man alone in a car.

What must it feel like to go through the internal dialogue, to wonder if it is worth navigating through all of these fears to just go on a fucking date? Or should I get a quart of Ben & Jerry's ice cream and watch a movie at home?

I never ever, ever have to go through that conversation in my head when shaving to prepare for a date. I never have to think about her wanting to kidnap me, or rape me, or beat me, or even possibly murder me.

As horrific as it was for me to hear those words come out of Selena's mouth, "Thank you for not raping or beating me, Michael," I am so grateful she had the courage and felt safe enough to share it with me. It is one of the most impactful statements anybody has told me. That sentence, then and now, inspires me to be a better man. To be a man who is willing to step up and raise my voice when men speak about or to women in a condescending or hurtful manner. I want to be patient and empathetic when my female friends and clients share about feeling a lack of safety and trust with me or men in general. Selena is part of why creating safe spaces for women is one of my missions. Little did she know when sharing that statement with me in the passenger seat of my silver Mitsubishi what would take place next year as part of my twelve-step program of making amends.

Step Nine: Made Direct Amends

HAVING GONE THROUGH the arduous and brutal process of taking a moral inventory of myself, I created a list of all the people I had harmed and got ready to make amends to them. I started with the easy people, like a couple of my cousins and old friends who weren't part of my life anymore. I made amends to Leighton, which felt like an emotionally big deal, but she took it very casually because she grew up in a family of twelve-step recovery. More

    Raised by Wolves, Possibly Monsters

importantly, she realized everything I had ever said to her was a lie in some shape or form; hearing how I lied to her was not news.

I moved to the next level of amends, including people like my brother and my parents. In some ways, they were more arduous and manageable than others. Deep down inside, I knew no matter what I did to them, they did worse to me, so I didn't feel exposed.

The following people I wanted to make amends to were women, especially those I physically or emotionally harmed, including putting my hands on their bodies without their consent. When I was preparing to make my amends, my first sponsor, Rob, explained he didn't feel prepared to guide me through the amends process. He recommended asking a guy named Mike to be my new sponsor. I asked Mike, and he said yes. I was nervous about asking him because I would have to start making amends if he said yes.

"I'm struggling with guilt and remorse, primarily about Deborah, Jasmine, and Emelie. There are other girls and women too, but those three are high on my list, and also, I'm petrified of doing it."

"Well, I've been thinking about that, Michael. In all three cases, making amends would harm them since they haven't been in your life in many years. I don't see how you showing up now will help them."

Through the lens of what we know today, what my sponsor Mike shared with me seems somewhat simplistic. We didn't have a great understanding of the impact of sexual trauma on girls and women like we do today. If I randomly reached out to them, it could have caused them harm. Still, I think the benefit would have been more significant than the harm, knowing that someone who caused them great harm understood he did this and wanted them to know he wanted to make things right and take responsibility for his actions. And that men can change; even former monsters like me. But what came out of this was extra-ordinary.

"I don't understand. What are you saying? That I shouldn't make amends? How will I move forward and feel better about myself and my relationships with women whenever I have a girlfriend again? This stuff keeps hanging over me, and I want to feel better and be better!"

"Nice try, Michael. I don't remember ever saying that you wouldn't do something. I'm just suggesting in my experience and reminding you that Bill is my sponsor, and that's who I learned all this from." Big Bill was a guy who was incredibly unique to the recovery community. To begin with, he was sober for over forty years, which was scarce and exceptional back then. Bill was among the most loving and generous people I have ever met. When I think about Bill, I think about this old guy who stood at the door to greet people in meetings, and if they approached, he would open up his arms for them to receive a hug if they were willing and interested. If not, Big Bill would put his left hand over his heart and his right hand out so they could shake it. He was a significant figure and some-body who I trusted and respected.

"Bill is pretty clear about not going back to women that aren't in your life anymore, that to just show up with the things we did to them while we were drunk is harmful. However, before you think you're getting a get-out-of-jail-free card, we can make amends by working in the community that improves the lives of the people we have harmed. In this case, you find a volunteer position at a rape crisis center would be your form of amends."

"Me at a rape crisis center? What the fuck could I do?"

"Who knows? Maybe you can help them with marketing, clean the bath-rooms, or be a security guy who sits outside the door to ensure women are safe. Maybe you can mail flyers. It's not about what you do; it's about doing it."

At that moment, I was in my early thirties and had never offered to volunteer anywhere without getting some immediate benefits, like impressing a girl. Not once. I was aware that people volunteered as a regular part of going to church or temple. Still, whenever I saw volunteers, I thought of old white people in plaid shirts having a bake sale and trying to convert people to Christianity.

"Volunteer? I've never volunteered anywhere and don't know how someone would do this. Are you sure that I shouldn't make direct amends?"

"Michael, it's your choice; it's your recovery. You have to make your own decisions. I'm giving you a recommendation based on what Bill has taught me. I won't get in the way or try to stop you if you think you need to make direct amends, and it won't harm them. If any part of you thinks you will harm them or their family or friends, I would take this into meditation before doing so. Some of these women may be married or have children or both. How are they going to

     Raised by Wolves, Possibly Monsters

explain this to their children or husbands? What if you reach out to them and they are not interested in meeting or talking to you? Then you stir shit up in their life, and they don't even get the benefit from the amends? Remember, all of this is about being of service."

"Okay, I get it. It makes sense even if I don't like it. Can I take a couple of days to think about it?"

"Absolutely! Let's schedule a time to talk on the phone next Saturday afternoon."

"Thanks, Mike. I appreciate your help and support. As much as I hate this shit, it feels important."

I got out of Mike's car, hopped into my car, and drove home. I'm glad I only had to go a mile and a half because I wasn't paying attention to anything I was doing in the car; all I could think about was being a volunteer at a Rape Crisis Center and how I would be the worst person in the world to be there. Shit, chances are good that I go there to help and try to pick up all the teenage girls hanging around there. Why did I think adolescent girls would be hanging around there anyway? Have I learned anything yet? Fortunately, I made it home without running anybody over.

I called Mike the next day and asked him if we could have a fifteen-minute conversation. He said yes. "Here's the thing, Mike. As I mentioned yesterday, I've never volunteered anywhere, and I don't know how. What do you do? How do you know where to go? Do I have to type up a resume or something like that?"

Mike burst out laughing. "Slow down there, Michael. First, you have to decide that you're going to do it. Have you made that decision yet?"

The answer was yes, but I hesitated before answering. I let out a big sigh, "Yes. I need to make amends, and if this is how I am guided, then I will do it."

"I would start by looking in the phone book for rape crisis centers. Call each one, letting them know you want to volunteer. Most of them are going to say no to you. Keep calling till you find one. And if you can't find any, let's meet again and devise another plan."

"There are rape crisis centers in the phone book? Okay. Let me see if I got this straight. I keep calling and telling them I want to volunteer. And if they ask why I want to volunteer, what should I say?"

"Michael, I know you don't know this, but millions of people volunteer daily to help and do service work in the community. But they might ask you because you're a guy. You can tell them it's part of your amends in AA, and they will understand."

"Okay, thanks, Mike. I have the rest of the day off; I will start today before I talk myself out of it."

I called all the domestic violence, women's resource centers and rape crisis centers I could find in the county phone book. All of them said no, and one had an answering machine. I left a message. A woman somewhere was going to listen to my voicemail message saying that I wanted to volunteer as part of my amends process in AA kept me up at night. Three days later, I got a phone call.

"Hello, is this Michael Swerdloff?"

Somehow, I knew by her voice this was the lady from the rape crisis center. I felt my body tighten. I could barely squeak out anything through my mouth, "Yes, this is Michael."

"My name is Denise, and I work at the rape crisis center in Somerville. We received your message, and I would like to talk to you for a few minutes first. Is now an okay time?"

Now is a bad time, and every time will be bad. "Yes, I have time now."

We talked for twenty minutes. Denise asked basic questions to understand who I was and what I was doing. She was nice and friendly, which I didn't expect. I expected a woman who hates men. She did not fit that mold at all. Denise was casual and even made a few jokes along the way. After she had asked her about my intentions, background, and motivations, I asked her what they do and what possible volunteer positions might be available.

Some of the possible tasks she said I could help with were mailings and organizing filing cabinets. Denise hesitated for a moment. She came up with an interesting idea that maybe I could go with her to public speaking events to talk about date and acquaintance rape. Denise said she would speak to the Director and call me back next week.

A week later, Denise called. She and the director, Katherine, wanted to meet to see if I was a good fit. I was able to read between the lines. They needed to figure out if I was a psycho who would blow the place up or worse. We scheduled

Raised by Wolves, Possibly Monsters

an appointment for the following Tuesday afternoon.

I was working late that day at my job at Radio Shack. I had been promoted to store manager and then to a higher volume store in a mall. This change becomes relevant later on. The whole week I was freaking out, remembering the horrible things I had done to girls and women over the years and realizing that my day of reckoning was coming on Tuesday.

I drove there slowly in my silver Mitsubishi, so I didn't get a speeding ticket. I followed the instructions she gave me over the phone for where to park. Before I exited the car, I said the Serenity Prayer six times, then headed to the third floor.

They were both nice women, but Denise was warmer and friendlier than Katherine. In my mind, Katherine was the director because she was the watchdog. They grilled me for about an hour and a half. They weren't angry at men or anything like that. They were asking me questions that were hard to answer. Some, I didn't know how to respond, "Why did I do what I had done?" They asked me if I understood the impact of rape on girls and women. I didn't. They asked me if I had a criminal record, and I told them I didn't, but I should have one. They asked me if I had three personal references and one professional reference. They wouldn't tell the professional reference why they were calling or what I wanted to do, and they would tell the personal contacts. I agreed to give them the references so they could tell the three personal references why they were calling.

They told me about a public speaking program they had received a grant for the previous year but had never started. They wanted a man like me to go with Denise to high schools, colleges, and possibly businesses to discuss date and acquaintance rape. They wanted me to share my story and experiences in public.

Of course, one part of me was excited about this kind of work. But the loudest voice inside of me wanted to scream. And a third part of me thought how easy it would be to meet hot girls and women by showing what a great guy I am now. I felt shame and embarrassment for the third part.

Denise brought me to the other room to complete the volunteer application when we finished. I completed the whole thing, plus the professional and three personal references. I had to sign and permit them to make these calls. I paused. A little voice in my head whispered, "Willing to make amends wherever possible." I signed the application. Denise thanked me for coming in, putting up with them, and grilling me hard. They wanted to ensure I was serious. She shook my hand and told me she would call soon.

Four days later, Denise called me and said she had processed my application and contacted my references. They would like to schedule a time to train me for the public speaking program. My heart almost stopped out of excitement and fear. After we got off the phone, I remember the tears coming out of my eyes against my will. I qualified as a good enough person to be allowed to do this. I was grateful, went into my room, knelt, and prayed.

I Don't Condone What You've Done

MY FIRST PUBLIC speaking assignment was at Raritan Valley Community College as part of their incoming transfer student's orientation process. We were going to speak on date and acquaintance rape. Denise started with the introduction. She went over the basics of date or acquaintance rape, the law, campus policy, and how to report it. She did a quick Q&A after she had completed her content.

"At this time, I would like to introduce to you a volunteer at the Somerset County Rape Crisis Center. Michael contacted us recently about sharing his experiences, and you get to be the first audience that Michael will speak with. We are so excited to have Michael be part of our public education program. Please welcome Michael!"

About thirty students crammed into a classroom built to hold twenty. They clapped heartily. A couple of boys in the back looked like they wanted to roll their eyes and growl but did a half-hearted clap not be noticed.

Deep breath, pause, deep breath, pause, a quick Serenity Prayer. "Hi, my name is Michael, I'm here to tell my story. Before I dive in, I want to mention that I am a recovering alcoholic and drug addict with a little over two years clean and sober." There was another round of applause. I waved my hands for them to stop. "No reason for applause. Being sober is what I should have been all along, so I'm only doing what I should have been doing. My abuse of girls started in seventh grade in Mr. Sobieski's science class. A girl named Deborah sat in front of me based on the alphabetical order of our last names." I went on and spoke for about twenty minutes. I included Deborah, Jasmine, Emelie, Evie, and some of the more generic offenses along the way. I talked about lost friendships, self-esteem, self-respect, and the lost respect of girls and women that I harmed.

As I shared my experiences, I heard sniffles, tears, and then crying, and a couple of students got up and left the classroom. Denise followed them out each time. I was not prepared for this. I volunteered to educate boys and young men. It did not occur to me how much it would affect the girls and women in the audience. Some versions of this happened in every speaking engagement, including colleges, universities, high schools, Vo-Tech schools, and corporate presentations.

I did not expect girls and women to come up after the presentations and thank me, hug me, and even cry in my arms without saying a word. In general, even the girls and women triggered by my experiences were grateful that somebody who had done what I had done was willing to go out and speak about it. They told me how important it was for a man to be sharing these experiences, not just the women who had been violated and abused.

During the question-and-answer session at one high school program, two girls spoke: the first was grateful I was talking about rape so the boys could hear about it and know that the girls aren't making it up. The second girl shared for the first time publicly that she had been raped by one of her friends the week before. She was in tears and experiencing pain, sadness, and shame. Denise asked if she would like to speak outside, and she said she wanted to stay present for the rest of the class.

After she had agreed to stay, a young man raised his hand, and I called on him. "I appreciate your courage and sharing your experiences with our class. It's brave, and so is your honesty. As the son of a Christian minister, I also have to say that I do not condone what you have done in any shape or form. You have changed your life, got sober, and you're doing this service work, which is great, but what you've done is not okay, and I will never condone it."

The room went silent. I didn't know what to say or do. I was emotionally shaken. Nobody had spoken to me in this way at the previous presentations.

What he said was true, and he shared it respectfully. I thanked him for sharing as tears started to form in my eyes, and my voice cracked. Denise asked me before the group if I wanted to take a break or let her take over.

"No. I don't need to take a break, and I don't need you to take over. The young man is correct. As hard as it is for me to hear him say it, everything he said is true. If the young lady who just shared about being assaulted can stay in class, I can stay in front of the room. And for the boys in the class, I beg you to listen to your classmate and what he said. No matter what your friends, family members, or TV shows say, sexual assault and rape are not okay, and none of us should condone it."

I took a breath and paused to regain my composure. We continued with the question-and-answer section. The girl who had shared about being raped recently mouthed to me silently, "Thank you." I asked if there were any other questions, and there were a bunch of them. Our process for answering questions was simple. I would respond if it were about my experiences, about the girls/women I harmed, or what it was like for me now. Anything that was about sexual assault and rape, Denise answered. After we were done and walking out to our cars, Denise asked me if I would like to go to lunch to discuss what had happened. We went to lunch at a local diner and discussed our experiences. I felt respected and supported by her.

These programs took place in 1992; as a primarily clueless recovering addict, I was startled and surprised by how many girls and women were sexually assaulted and raped. I had no clue about this, which is hard to believe since I was the perpetrator of the crime; I didn't think it happened often. It scared me that so many girls and women had to deal with this. It wasn't until decades later that I truly understood how prevalent sexual assault and rape are in American culture.

As I accepted these presentations, my self-respect grew, and my shame and embarrassment decreased minimally. Still, it was happening, and I was aware of it. I was starting to respect girls and women and their strength and courage. This perspective was new to me. Seeing the challenges they experienced as a girl or woman was startling. Why was I, and so many other men, ignorant about the prevalence of assault? What was it like to carry these pains and scars without

Raised by Wolves, Possibly Monsters

being able to share them with the men in your life without being shamed, blamed, or dismissed? Again, how did I, of all people, not know this was such a thing with Bernie being my father, David being my brother, and me being the guy I saw in the mirror every day?

Another aspect of this that surprised me was my arousal when women shared that they had been sexually assaulted or raped. This experience happened almost without exception, especially during the year and a half I volunteered. The first couple of times, it caught me off guard. I spoke to Lauraine, my therapist, about it, and she explained how I had been programmed within my family and our culture to be aroused by sexual assault and rape. Lauraine asked me to pay attention to TV shows and movies and how they portray girls and women being raped. She expressed that they had their hair done perfectly, their makeup perfect, and they wore sexy clothes and underwear. How could I not be turned on by rape since they portrayed rape as sexually attractive? This scared and infuriated me. How could we as a culture be like this? What does it feel like to be a teenage girl seeing an actress raped on your TV, and while being raped, she looks hot and sexually appealing? What message will she walk away with after viewing this?

I wanted my body to change in response to the way my mind was, but that's not what happened, at least not at that point. At times, I would feel rage at my own body for its reaction to hearing tragic and brutal violent experiences retold by victims. I hated that it would create a full erection without my consent! I hated myself for these experiences and how powerless I felt when it happened. The shame was crushing, especially if I was watching a movie with a female friend or friends and they were trembling and/or in tears, and I had to hide this thing growing in my pants. There were times I felt like I would never be normal again or able to be a true friend or boyfriend, no matter how much work I did. The fantasy of the man I was or wanted to be did not yet match what my body told me. I wanted to be better for the women in my life, all women, men, and most of all, myself. Fortunately, I didn't give up. The combination of therapy with Lauraine, staying sober, my friends in AA, meditation, and Reiki had enough impact to help me change. I tried to accept and forgive myself for who I was now as I waited for something different to emerge. When it did, the women in my life recognized this before I did.

For men who may experience similar challenges, my message for you is, please, don't give up. The women in our lives need us to be more than our shame, self-hatred, and violence. They need us to step out of our pain, trauma, and numbness and step into being the men we were born to be before toxic masculinity squashed it out of us. We control when and where we let the wolf and monster loose. We control those impulses and create a safe place in ourselves to hold them so that those impulses no longer terrorize women, children, other men, and ourselves. Creating safe spaces is one way we protect women; it doesn't happen in the gym, the shooting range, or the military. It happens right here in our minds, bodies, and spirits.

The final surprise experience for me in this process with Somerset County Rape Crisis Center manifested during a call with Denise. She told me that she was leaving her job, that she was moving, and that the federal government had not renewed the program's funding. I experienced sadness that Denise was leaving and a mixture of sadness and relief at not doing this work anymore.

While talking, I mentioned to Denise that I was taking an Introduction to Social Work class at William Paterson University because I was considering becoming a social worker. She expressed her support and enthusiasm for me. I told her I received my acceptance letter into the Social Work Program at Ramapo College.

Denise laughed. "Michael, I have a friend whose sister used to date a guy who runs an outstanding program for teens and families in crisis all over the tri-state area, and his office is in Newark. His name is Jared. I've met him twice; he's pretty amazing. Would you like me to call my friend and see if I can get his phone number for you?"

I was so excited I could feel my heart thumping. "Yes! That would be amazing! Thank you so much!"

"Well, we'll have at least one more phone conversation before we say good-bye. If I don't get the chance to tell you this during our next conversation, I have appreciated working with you and have seen you grow and develop as a man and a person during this process. It's been wonderful to witness. I am so proud of you. The work that you have done in the community is so important! We didn't want to tell you this then, but we were getting ready to send back our grant money because we never thought we'd find a man who could do this and do it well, with integrity. Thank you from the bottom of my heart for showing up when you did. You've heard my story and know what I've been through; being your friend and partner in this project has been healing for me."

Denise started crying before me, but not by much. I felt moved by her profound respect for me. I thanked Denise for letting me be part of this program and for her support and guidance all along the way.

One of my staff members came into the back room, heard me sniffling, and saw me wiping tears off my face. She was surprised. "Never mind. I didn't know you were in the middle of something. I can take care of it." She hurried back into the store, closing the door behind her.

About a week later, Denise called me and gave me Jeff Fleisher's phone number. It took me a few days to get the courage to call Jeff, but that call initiated another list of surprises in my life.

Can I Put My Hands on Your Head?

BEFORE ENTERING THE social work program, I met three friends essential to my spiritual education. It started at Radio Shack, as many things did for me in the early 1990s. Charles was a Manager Trainee and a great guy. We became friends. Soon after that, I became friends with his wife, Karla, the manager of a different store in the mall. They lived on a farm, like a real farm. I was often invited to their home and started hanging out with them regularly. They were the beginning of my making friends outside of AA, and they were excellent role models for me. I liked having friends who were more wholesome than me and the folks in AA. They also supported my desire to learn more about spirituality beyond the Twelve Steps. They were a breath of fresh air for me, their playfulness, romantic interactions, their home on a 105-acre tree farm with two ponds, and the stone house built in the 1600s.

Karla introduced me to her sister, Adriana, who everybody called Adri. Unbeknownst to Adriana or me, Karla set us up because we were both single and thought we were a good match. We never officially dated, although we went to dinner a few times and flirted pitifully. We weren't a good match because we were both beginning our transitions from what we had been to what we wanted to be. Adriana and I became close friends with a few mishaps along the way.

Since the first week I met Charles and Karla, they frequently talked about Betsy, Karla's mother. They kept saying, "Mom is in retreat." I had no idea what being in retreat meant. My only knowledge of retreats was that Catholic Nuns would have retreats around Easter every year, according to the sign in front of the Catholic Convent I passed near Morristown, NJ. New Age spirituality was still far from mainstream, unlike today. I never asked them what "being in retreat" meant because I didn't want to seem stupid.

Betsy was apparently "out of retreat" and visiting the farm to see her daughters for the first time in over a year. They invited me to dinner to meet her and Granny, Betsy's mother. I said yes, less than enthusiastically.

Charles and I finished closing the day's books in the backroom. The store was closed, and we were the only people there.

"Michael, I promised Karla I wasn't going to say anything. But I can't in good conscience keep this a secret from you without consequences." He took a deep breath and let out a big sigh. "Betsy, Karla's mother, is a faith healer."

"What?"

"Karla made me promise that I would not say anything to you about her because you were skeptical about her anyway for living in the desert and being in retreat since you are coming to dinner to meet her tomorrow night. Betsy is excited to meet you, and I can't let you show up without knowing she's a faith healer."

"What the hell is a faith healer? Is she one of those Southern Baptist creatures with white hair on cable TV that push people over, and they get 'healed'? And keep talking about Jee-sus?"

"I'm going to end up on the couch for this one anyway, so I might as well come clean. Betsy is nothing like that. She shows up, and things happen. She doesn't talk about Jesus or anything like that. Just weird shit happens when she's around."

"What kind of weird shit happens when she's around? You have me very

     Raised by Wolves, Possibly Monsters

concerned right now, Charles."

"Things like microwaves and toaster ovens won't work when she's in the room, or light bulbs start smoking. Sometimes, broken audio equipment piled in closets for years works fine as if nothing happened. One year, the chicken eggs' shells were light blue instead of their usual brown. There have been times when people with cancer and addictions have come to see Betsy out on the farm, or once an old lady who had recently lost vision in her left eye due to a stroke came over. Betsy did some things with her hands, and the woman could see again. And the chickens get weird when she's around. I don't know how to describe it, but they get weird. This is the weird shit I'm talking about!"

"You are out of your fucking mind if you think I'm coming there to meet her or ever getting in the same room as her. I would have to be nuts."

"Here's the thing, Michael, all kinds of weird shit happen, but she's an amazing lady. She can help with things you've been struggling with."

"I am not having dinner with a faith healer who stops microwaves and toaster ovens from working and lights to flicker and smoke! No way!" I called Karla from the speakerphone.

Karla answered, "Are you getting ready to leave to come home?"

"It's not Charles, it's Michael."

"Hey, Michael! We are so excited to have you over for dinner tomorrow night. Mom can't stop talking about it! Adri is even going to make Upside Down Lasagna for the situation. I made an apple pie and picked up organic vanilla ice cream for everybody else and organic coffee ice cream just for you!"

"About tomorrow night. It turns out I will have to work late because…"

Karla interrupted me by screaming through the speakerphone, "Charles!"

Charles took an even deeper breath than he had a few minutes before. He reached over to take the handset out of the cradle with his left hand and pushed the speakerphone button off in his right hand. Even though Charles held the phone up to his left ear, I could hear Karla word for word. "You promised that you were not going to tell Michael. How can you do this to Mom? What were you thinking? Be prepared to sleep on the couch. I can't believe you did this after you promised."

"I'll leave now." I could hear the click and the dial tone before Charles could hang up the phone. He looked depleted, as if he were preparing to go to court for a sentencing hearing. Charles was gone about ninety seconds later. As soon as the back door closed behind him, the phone rang, and I saw it was Karla.

"Michael! You're coming tomorrow night! I don't care what Charles told you; Mom wants to meet you, and we're all looking forward to you being here, including Granny, and don't give me a bunch of bullshit about you having to work. Charles made the schedule this week so you could be here. He paid Paul twenty bucks to promise he would work no matter what tomorrow night. So, you're coming, and that's the end of that!"

"I'm not coming. No matter what you say, you can't make me come. You can't even use Adriana as bait."

"Do you think I would use my sister as bait? But since you brought it up, will it work?"

"Like I said, there is nothing you can say; not even Adriana wanting to have sex with me will convince me otherwise!"

I heard Karla yelling in the background, "Adri? Michael said he won't come tomorrow night to meet Mom unless you have sex with him. Will you have sex with Michael tomorrow night so that he'll come and meet Mom?"

"Karla! Did you really tell Michael that I'd have sex with him so that he would come to dinner to meet Mom? I know sometimes I make some bad choices with sex partners, but I'm not a prostitute that you can sell to Michael! I decide if and when I want to have sex with somebody, including Michael! Did you promise him that I would have sex with him?"

I yelled at the top of my lungs so everybody could hear me. "I'm not coming! Adriana, I would never make your sister promise you to have sex with me so I can meet your mother. I didn't say any of that; I said the opposite. I said that even if you did promise to have sex with me, I was still not coming!"

Adriana grabbed the phone from Karla. "Am I that awful a person that you don't even want to have sex with me?"

"All I said was that I'm not coming to see your mother in exchange for you having sex with me. I don't want to come there tomorrow night because Charles told me your mom is a faith healer, and I'm scared to show up. I told Karla I'm not coming, and she won't listen, so she has brought you into this mess. I'm sorry

 Raised by Wolves, Possibly Monsters

that I said something that hurt you. I didn't mean to hurt or insult you."

"It sounds like my mother is crazy, but my mom is cool, and I think you'll like her. And I'm making Upside Down Lasagna specifically because you are coming, and it's the only thing I make that tastes good. Please come, and I'll make sure Mom doesn't do anything weird. Okay, I'll take that back. I'm sure Mom will do something weird, but if she does, I'll ask her to stop. Will you come tomorrow night?"

"Okay, I'll come as long as I don't have to do any weird faith healing or give my soul to Jeee-sus or whatever faith healers do. Promise?"

"I promise to watch Mom for you, Michael."

"Goodbye," I replied as I hung up the phone. The whole ride home, I was freaked out about meeting Betsy. My mind kept seeing visions of smoke and fire coming out of the toaster oven.

Dinner was at 6:00, and I arrived at 6:15, almost 6:20. I was incredibly nervous and anxious the whole ride there. Adriana, David, Charles, Karla, and Betsy were in the kitchen, fussing and talking. Granny was lying on a hospital-type bed with wheels. Everybody stopped what they were doing when I came in. They were afraid if they didn't come and greet me, I might have turned around and left. They were partially correct.

When we made eye contact upon introduction, Betsy reached out her right hand to shake mine. Her grip was firm, solid, and warm. She held contact longer than one would typically do with a stranger. Everybody else hugged me. Karla ushered me over to meet Granny, who looked like she was fighting to stay awake. I was grateful for the distraction.

Betsy looked different from the images I created. She was tall, about six feet, powerfully built, with high cheekbones, black hair, and brown eyes like her daughters. Her hair was simpler than theirs, short and neatly kept. I assumed it was neat and short for convenience, not fashion or style. She was wearing a gray and navy-blue dress that appeared to be handmade. It was simple and attractive. During dinner conversation, I learned that The Faith Healer was a textile professor at multiple universities. This information did not match my narrative either.

About five minutes into me getting to know Granny, Adriana yelled from the kitchen, "I'm about to take out the Upside Down Lasagna. Everybody get out of my way, so I don't drop it on the floor." We all crowded into the kitchen to watch this vital ritual.

Adriana safely made it eight feet from the oven to the kitchen table. The Upside Down Lasagna was not upside down after all.

The conversation was light and relaxed. I enjoyed the lasagna, the steamed broccoli with lemon, the vegetable salad, and Karla's apple pie for dessert. I was grateful she made the apple pie and purchased coffee ice cream for me. Of course, this became the topic of conversation during dessert: "Why does Michael get his ice cream? I'm your husband, and I don't."

David said, "And I've been your best friend for ten years, and you have never purchased special ice cream for me either."

"I'm your sister! Where's the chocolate ice cream that I asked for?"

Betsy couldn't stop laughing, "Well, I'm glad you made apple pie."

One by one, as we finished coffee, tea, and dessert, I realized I was alone, sitting across from Betsy. I was about to yell out for Adriana to stay and protect me, but I didn't have the guts to say it. Our light conversation continued until it didn't. Betsy said she had heard that I was in recovery. She shared that an older couple was in one of the other houses on the property. The man had been in recovery for thirteen years and remembered when he first got sober. She spoke about Alcoholics Anonymous, the twelve-step program, and its recovery value. I could feel the tension and energy shift as she slowly eased into deeper conversation. I was doing my best to keep my answers short and simple. I kept thinking that at any moment, she would reach out her right hand, push me over by my forehead, and start ranting about "Jee-sus!" but she never did. It was worse.

I was talking again about making my amends and the process of the ninth step in recovery. The Faith Healer waited till I hesitated between sentences and casually, with no affect, asked, "Michael, is it okay for me to put my hands on your shoulders for a few minutes?"

I stopped breathing. I froze. My spine was stiff, and my hands gripped the kitchen chair's wooden armrests. I wanted to scream, "No!" and run home, a forty-five-minute car ride even in my Mitsubishi.

Without my consent, my mouth opened, "Yes." Betsy had a broad, beaming

Raised by Wolves, Possibly Monsters

smile and slowly stood, gliding until she stood behind me. I was still contemplating running, screaming, or both. I did neither. I silently recited the Serenity Prayer. And a second time. And a third time.

I felt the warmth of her hands above my head, even though I didn't feel her hands on my head. My internal dialogue was trying to figure out why on earth I said yes. More importantly, she asked if she could put her hands on my shoulders, not my head. What were her hands doing near my head? Was she reprogramming my brain or some kind of mind control?

All of this activity was going on internally. At some point, Betsy's hands landed on my shoulders like a bird's wings, landing gently after flight. My whole being shifted its focus to my shoulders and her hands. Her hands felt hot. It's not the kind of warmth one gets when holding something hot. It was a different form of heat. It felt more like the warmth of your favorite blanket when you were home from school sick. My shoulder started getting warmer, which freaked me out, but it felt gentle and supportive. My head, chest, and trunk were warm with this unique, almost tingly feeling. Her hands had not moved, but now my hips, thighs, calves, and feet were warm. All of me was warm with that strange, tingly feeling.

It was almost as if my body was vibrating, although I certainly would not have used that word then. Then, a peaceful feeling came over me. It felt beautiful as if this warmth was covering me. I felt relaxed, and the peace moved deeper within me. I was now at peace. I was thirty-two years old and experiencing peace for the first time. At that moment, I felt like I was experiencing the presence of God! I had no other explanation or description besides that there was warmth and peace and what felt like the presence of God.

I had a thought in my head. If this is what all of the holy rollers on cable TV are always preaching about, then I get it. It makes complete sense now. I don't remember doing so, but I remember noticing my eyes were closed. I did not remember closing them. When I thought about the preachers on TV, I shifted out of the peace and warmth and returned to being regular old Michael. It felt jarring when I opened my eyes. You can imagine my surprise when Betsy sat across from me on the other side of the table, smiling with her hands folded on her lap!

I remember turning my head to the right to look at my shoulders because it felt like she was still behind me with her hands on my shoulders.

I still felt the warm and tingly feeling in parts of my body, specifically my shoulders.

As if all of this wasn't weird enough, a slow drip of warm, salt water rolled out of my nostrils onto my lips. There was no mucus or anything else, just warm, salt water.

Betsy looked like something from a science fiction movie. She was sitting there; I could see her body and smile, her gold and blue scarf around her neck. She looked like she had golden, white light around her body. I closed my eyes and reopened them to make sure what I was seeing was what I was seeing. When I opened them again, I hoped she would look like the woman I was eating apple pie and coffee ice cream with just a few minutes before. In the right-hand corner of my eye, it was now 8:20. Everybody else left the table at around 7:45. What felt like two or three minutes of her putting her hands on my shoulders was close to thirty minutes. I felt confused and disoriented, and this little drip from my nostrils continued.

"How are you, Michael?" Her smile and voice penetrated me. Another wave of warmth and peace came over me.

"Good." I jumped to my feet and proclaimed I had to leave. I started saying goodbye to everybody in the living room, grabbed my full-length gray leather coat, and somehow, without even seeing her get up, Betsy was standing at the front door waiting for me when I arrived there to leave!

She handed me a piece of paper with her name and phone number. "Thank you, Michael. Call me when you're ready."

I hurried to my car, and before putting on my seat belt, I pulled out of their driveway. I raced down the road, hoping to outrun the energy or the warm salt water gently dripping down my face and chin. It continued to drip the entire forty-minute ride home. I didn't say hello to my roommates and went directly to my bedroom.

I locked my door behind me. I sat on the floor next to my bed, where I prayed and meditated every morning and night. Like children in movies, I prayed with my hands tightly together, desperately hoping God would save them. The

   Raised by Wolves, Possibly Monsters

dripping continued for another minute or two and stopped.

For the next few weeks, Betsy started showing up regularly in my meditations and dreams. I kept hoping that she would somehow disappear and go away, but she didn't. Weekly became daily, and weeks became months. I felt like she had haunted me.

Finally, while meditating on the floor next to my bed one morning nine months later, I said out loud to nobody, "Okay. I'll call you!" I reached into the drawer of my dark wood night table, fishing until I found that piece of paper with her name and phone number. I lifted my Radio Shack cordless telephone and dialed her number in New Mexico. Betsy picked up between the first and second ring before I could say anything, "Good morning, Michael. I've been waiting for your call."

And that was the beginning of my relationship with Reverend Betsy Browder.

A Stroll Through Phillipsburg Mall

 IT WAS GOING to be a simple task. Simple, because I was going to be able to prove Betsy wrong in five minutes, seven tops. Betsy had given me "an experiment" to understand myself better.

My mission was simple. Every time I walked down the halls of Phillipsburg Mall, I was supposed to do what I always did: look at all the attractive women in the stores. Simple, right?

Betsy added another step to my daily practice of staring at girls in their late teens and early twenties. I was to notice them while I was staring at them, particularly which body part I was staring at, to see how the girl/woman and her body responded to my gaze.

If I looked at her butt and she was facing in the other direction, did anything happen?

My first target, only because she was two doors down from Radio Shack, was Catherine at Cinnabon. Yeah, I know, the fact that my first target had "buns" in the title of the establishment is priceless, but since I couldn't see her "buns" behind the white counter with the glass cases, I was able to see Catherine's "rack" that the buns we're sitting on. Okay, enough with the bad jokes. Although I did see Catherine's breasts from a profile view as I was slowly walking past the shop, I needed to resist saying hello to her so that she wouldn't know I was there. I walked slowly and quietly so she wouldn't know anybody was walking by before the mall opened to the public. While I looked at Catherine's breasts, she pulled her white sweater with a zipper closer together, covering them. Again, she didn't know I was there.

It could've been a coincidence, and the mall is always quite cold in the morning, so maybe she was cold.

As I continued walking, I noticed Mandy at The Limited wearing her tight white cotton dress that I'd seen her in previously, that barely covered her butt, straightening out the racks of jeans. For a brief moment, I forgot that I was conducting an experiment and got lost in staring at her butt. That is until she stopped straightening the jeans, pulled her white shirt down slightly lower rather abruptly, and then turned around and gave me a fake smile. It didn't feel like a smile. "Good morning, Michael."

"Good morning, Mandy." Her dark brown eyes looked hardened while attempting to smile at me politely.

A few doors down, a new girl was working at the toy store wearing tight, dark blue jeans. I first noticed her butt, and while looking at it, she reached behind her back without paying attention and pulled up her jeans. I shifted my gaze to her breasts, and about two seconds later, she crossed her arms in front of her chest, staring at the box she was unpacking. As I walked past, shifting my gaze in front of me, she relaxed her arms at her side. Curious, I twisted my head towards her breasts again, and her arms crossed her chest again.

Instead of getting coffee in the food court, I wanted to first take a detour past the Merry-Go-Round store, where, at any given moment, there were somewhere between two and five gorgeous girls and young women all dressed and ready to go hunting in a club. Three of them were talking in a semicircle, assessing the display of halter tops, which two were wearing. Quite truthfully, between the six legs, six butt-cheeks, six breasts, and all of the hair and makeup, my eyes darted from body part to body part to body part enough for me to get excited. I stood off

Raised by Wolves, Possibly Monsters

in the distance, partially obscured by the escalators so I wouldn't be seen unless somebody was looking from behind me and discovered I was a creepy guy gawking at women in the shadows. While staring at them, precisely their asses, two of the three women pulled their miniskirts down from behind. I shifted my gaze to the three girls' breasts, specifically the two wearing halter tops, and their hands went from their dresses to crossing their chests. It looked choreographed.

I became uncomfortable with how excited I was objectifying their bodies. I stood staring at their body parts without them knowing I was there. And their responsiveness to my gaze was a turn-on. I was uncomfortable enough to stop the exercise for now.

I went to the coffee shop to get my regular medium-sized coffee with one sugar and cream. The woman was working in the coffee shop, and I had a date about two months before. She had asked me out two or three times, and I finally said yes. Although I mostly found her attractive with a soft smile, nice full light brown hair, and pretty average but still attractive body, she didn't turn me on. She was in a tank top without a bra, and since the mall wasn't open yet, she didn't have her uniform on. Before I said hello to her, I noticed her nipples pointing through her baby blue shirt. Even though the mall was about fifteen minutes from opening, she stopped what she was doing with the croissants and walked to the other side of the counter to get her uniform, a red button-down shirt.

I was getting irritated with this trend.

When Carolyn noticed me, she stared at me with a similar stern glance as Mandy from The Limited had given me moments before. It was not a warm, friendly gaze. Carolyn had anger emanating from her eyes. I went there every morning before the store opened. It started about two weeks after I started working there when Carolyn told me I could go there before the mall opened if I needed coffee to start my day. It was a sweet invitation and initiated us becoming friends, flirting, going out on a date, and then not flirting and barely being friends. In addition to the stare with fire in her eyes this morning, she said, "My boss told me I can't give coffee before opening anymore. Sorry, come back when we're open, like everybody else." Carolyn spoke without a facial expression

I walked away nervously, a bit confused and a little startled. That was until I saw Daryl arrive; I think that's his name. I wasn't good at remembering men's names because they weren't potential sex partners for me. As Daryl approached the counter, Carolyn smiled, said hello, and poured him a coffee.

I was beyond hearing distance, but I saw their friendly banter. Carolyn gave him a coffee before opening, after telling me she wasn't allowed.

I headed back to Radio Shack without coffee but with irritation, frustration, and confusion. As I approached the infant and toddler store on my way back, I smiled, seeing Bethany in her white sweater and tiny black skirt she wore once a week. That was often one of the highlights of my day. While looking at her legs and ass, she pulled her skirt down, turned around, and said hello. Bethany and I were friends who sometimes flirted, along with social and intellectual conversation. Bethany was bright, fun, engaging, gorgeous, and studying at a university in Pennsylvania, preparing students for Christian missions in third-world countries. I had fantasies of my penis in Bethany's body and releasing semen all over her perfect virginal Christian body more than once. Part of me saw her for who she was, saw her commitment, and I wanted to honor that, too.

My desire to honor her commitment was a new experience for me. When talking with Bethany, I would vacillate between lusting after her and wanting to protect her from other men like me. I appreciated her warmth and authenticity and enjoyed how smart and wonderful she was. I was relieved that she responded to me as she always did. I walked over to her, and we engaged in a friendly conversation.

I was always aware that Bethany was attracted to me and that it made her uncomfortable. I could see it from how she responded. While she was talking, I gazed at her breasts, noticing the outline of her bra underneath her thin, white sweater. I was barely listening. When she noticed, she spoke louder and firmer to return my attention to her face. I made eye contact with Bethany, and I saw her eyes were red and watery, and her voice was cracking.

"Bethany, are you okay?"

Her right eye became even more watery, and her mascara dropped. "I like you, Michael, and I like talking to you. But you make me nervous sometimes the way you look at me, especially since you know that I don't date boys, and I won't have sex until I'm married. But you still look at me that way." Her mascara dropped more. Bethany shifted her body several times and wiped the tear from

    Raised by Wolves, Possibly Monsters

her eye. "And now you made me cry, and I must fix my makeup. Why do you always have to look at me that way?"

She didn't wait for an answer. Bethany hurried, almost running to the back room. I stood there trying to digest Bethany's response to me gawking at her body. Every part of me wanted to follow her and apologize. But I didn't. I made a note to apologize later when she had had a chance to gather herself.

I returned to Radio Shack, where my staff had prepared the store for the day. I went to the back room, put on my navy blue sports coat, fixed my red tie, and took a second to look at myself. I was on the verge of tears.

I continued this experiment daily for the next two weeks as Betsy instructed.

I felt worse and worse about myself every morning when I went for coffee after the mall opened, every time I went to the food court or walked down the hall to take a break or shop. Leaving my store had become unsafe territory for me. It was dangerous for me because I knew how unsafe it was for the girls and women I was attracted to.

That weekend, two friends, Diane and Victoria, and I went out to the diner after the AA meeting. I told them about the experiment and the data I was collecting. They couldn't respond quickly enough, talking over each other and how happy they were that this lady, Betsy, whoever she was, was making me do this. They took turns telling me how many times they've experienced this kind of predatory energy from me, but more importantly, how every new girl or woman who came to AA did as well. They were uncomfortable in my presence.

I was stunned and started defending myself, even though I knew they were probably correct. I pointed out how they all flirted with me and would laugh and play with me.

"What else are they supposed to do, Michael? You've been sober for a couple of years. Everybody respects and is friends with you; they're new, scared, and want to belong. They're a fucking mess because they just got sober, and their life sucks. So, what would they say? Stop looking at my tits so I can pay attention in the meeting and not worry about you ogling me the whole time?"

Victoria hesitated momentarily and gave me that disapproving look that was her trademark expression, then downed some of her black coffee. Her voice softened, "What else are we supposed to do, Michael? We laugh because we're nervous and uncomfortable, not because you're funny and we're enjoying you. I don't mean that you're not funny and we don't enjoy you. I do, and I think Diane does, too, as do most of us. But we often laugh and giggle because we don't know what else to do when you or any other guy makes us uncomfortable."

Diane "coded" what Victoria had said for me in more simplistic language. The message was the same, "Stop gawking at our bodies. Stop thinking we're flirting with you whenever we laugh and giggle because we're probably uncomfortable. Keep listening to this Betsy lady and do whatever she tells you."

When I met with Betsy the following week at a local coffee shop in Hackettstown, her reply to my data collection and conversation with my friends was straightforward. "Good."

"That's it? Just good?"

"You're an intelligent man, Michael. I don't have to tell you what needs to shift, do I?"

I shook my head.

"If you would like, I can give you another assignment. But you probably won't like it."

I remember thinking, well, I didn't like this one, so who cares if I like it? "That would be helpful."

"Every morning in meditation, I want you to start asking God to help you with this. Second, every night before you go to bed, I want you to write in a journal about every girl or woman whom you stared at and objectified, taking a nightly inventory like you do in the tenth step in AA. And continue to notice how women respond to your gaze, not just at the mall, but in AA meetings and restaurants, volleyball, and anywhere else you go. Pay attention! Their responses will teach you everything you need to know. Like everything else on the spiritual awareness and development journey, we always return to the same thing, be present and pay attention. Your Higher Self will instruct you on what to do with that information when you pay attention while present."

I learned many new concepts from these experiments.

I learned that women respond to people staring at them without even knowing someone is staring at them.

I learned that my "stare," which I now know is energy, affects people,

        Raised by Wolves, Possibly Monsters

especially women I am attracted to.

I learned that Betsy is tapped into something way beyond what I had experienced in my life at that point.

I learned how powerful I was, and I needed to pay attention to that power and find ways to use it for good.

I learned that women sometimes laugh to cover up uncomfortable emotions and being sexualized by men, and me specifically.

I learned that I needed to learn a lot more about energetic vibrations and their meaning. This awareness was, without my knowing it, setting me up to become a Reiki Practitioner in the near future.

I learned that my spiritual awakening had a lot more to it than I thought, and I was just starting, which my ego did not appreciate.

A Look in the Mirror

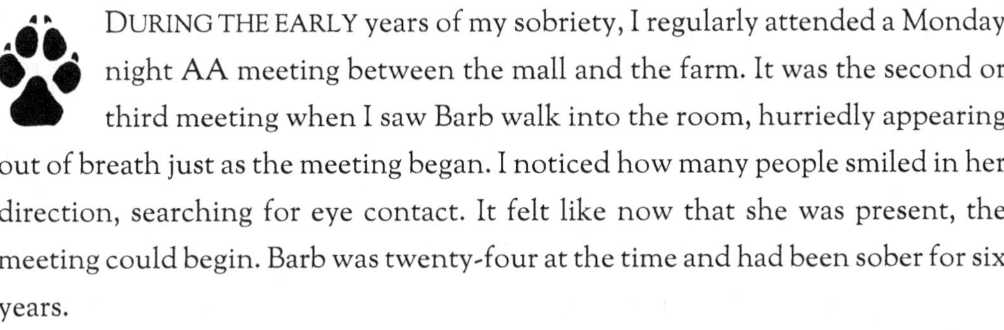

DURING THE EARLY years of my sobriety, I regularly attended a Monday night AA meeting between the mall and the farm. It was the second or third meeting when I saw Barb walk into the room, hurriedly appearing out of breath just as the meeting began. I noticed how many people smiled in her direction, searching for eye contact. It felt like now that she was present, the meeting could begin. Barb was twenty-four at the time and had been sober for six years.

Barb was not my regular "type." Her clothes were beaten up and worn down; her sneakers were dirty; she had long dark brown hair that was wavy and pretty unattended, and she didn't wear any makeup. What struck me about Barb upon her arrival was that she was gorgeous, beautiful, and authentic without doing anything. She was utterly Barb. When she shared later in the meeting, every set of eyes and ears in the room were attentive. Her voice, smile, sadness, warmth, playfulness, and intelligence hijacked whatever random thought or feeling I was obsessing about at the time.

Over the next few weeks, I listened to Barb share in meetings and joined the group of people huddled around her afterward. One night, at the end of the meeting, when the leader asked for volunteers for cleanup, Barb raised her hand, and then I raised my arm high without choosing to do so. The two of us cleaned up the kitchen and made small talk.

Barb introduced herself. I told her I knew who she was already, and she waited for me to say who I was. When I recognized that Barb was waiting for me to say something, I remembered that she had told me her name, but I had not said mine. Barb laughed at how startled I was; I did as well. Something happened at that moment, and we both knew it. We looked at each other, waiting for the other to say or do something. When neither of us did anything, we let out a belly laugh, acknowledging our nervousness and awkwardness. We continued cleaning cups, mugs, and the coffee machine—lots of small talk, nervous laughter, and connection.

Over the next few months, we became regular volunteers to clean the kitchen on Monday nights. Barb had become my first full-blown crush in sobriety! During our random conversations, I learned that she worked part-time at her family's hardware store in town and was finishing her degree at Centenary College. And that Barb had an eating disorder, and that's why she initially went into rehab in high school. I told her about my breakdown and that when I was in rehab several times, I spent the whole day in "the quiet room," better known as the rubber room, punching and kicking the walls till my hands were full of blood. Barb and I had both been through painful life lessons. I saw her brilliance as she reflected on all she had been through. She discovered that despite my checkered educational path, I, too, was intelligent and loved to question and figure everything out. Soon, I lost the ability to talk about anything but Barb. One night, a bunch of my friends and I were at a diner after a meeting when Chris, in his deadpan conversational style, stated, "Mike, we're kind of sick of listening to you talk about Barb. We discussed it behind your back the other day and decided you have two weeks to ask Barb out. If you don't, you can no longer talk about her when we're together. And can you pass me the ketchup?" I passed the ketchup and froze. I did not know there was an expiration date for crushing on Barb, nor did I like that my best friends collectively decided something about my life without me present. I disliked having to do something about my crush on Barb!

The following Monday, Barb and I cleaned the coffee machine in the kitchen.

    Raised by Wolves, Possibly Monsters

We talked about our plans for Thanksgiving and how much we dreaded being with our families. There was a brief pause, and I blurted out, "Barb, I want to ask you out on a date."

"Okay. That sounds cool. Where would you like to go on our date?"

Holy fuck! I was so engrossed in the first part of the process I completely forgot to have a plan for what to do.

"Honestly, Barb, I didn't think you would say yes, so I never devised a plan!" We laughed.

She reached into her blue denim purse and pulled out a pad printed across the top in bright red, "Miracles happen." She wrote her first and last name and phone number on it and handed it to me. "That's cool. I'm going away this weekend. How about you call me at the beginning of next week, and we'll make plans for the following weekend?"

It was that simple. I had asked Barb out on a date, and she said yes, and we were making plans to go on a date.

The following Monday night, after the meeting, she approached me and said, "Since we're both here and going to clean up the kitchen, how about instead of waiting until the weekend, we just go to the diner and scoff down food together?"

Fuck. I was not prepared to go on a date with Barb tonight. But it seemed completely stupid to say no. So, I said yes, and we finished cleaning the kitchen. There was sexual tension in the air. She wanted to go to a different diner than the one that everybody else already was. I followed her on that cold, snowy night to the restaurant. The bright lights startled me as we entered. The diner was large, and there were only four other people besides the servers in the whole place.

After we both ordered our food and made fun of the fact that the menu was eleven pages long, Barb started sharing, and I faded out of the conversation. This was the narrative going on in my head. "I can't believe I'm on a date with Barb. She's smart and getting her life back together. Barb has a good family, goes back to school, is pretty, fun, popular, and well-respected, and she's out with me. I have finally arrived. I have recovered enough to be out on a date with an amazing woman who likes me even though she actually knows me." I remember having a quick moment of thanking God for my recovery, growth in sobriety, and for Barb. And then I remembered that Barb was sitting across from me talking. At this point, I mentally returned to the conversation.

"I have no friends. Nobody likes me. I have no future. I am ugly and fat. I have fucked up everything that you can fuck up in life. I've been thinking about quitting school and being a full-time clerk at the hardware shop because hanging parts on a peg is the only thing I can do well in life. And for the first time in about three years, I don't know if I want to live any longer. I haven't made a suicide plan yet, but I just feel like it's not worth it any longer." Tears ran down Barb's cheeks. All of her life, love, vitality, and joy left with those tears. There was only pain and sadness. I felt like I had just fallen off of a bicycle into a frozen pond. Fortunately for both of us, my Higher Self took over, and I supported Brynn in all ways a friend would do. At the night's end, I walked her to her car; she leaned into my arms and cried and cried and cried.

A strange thought entered my mind as I drove down the hill on the S-turns in the snow and ice, headed towards home on the other side of Hackettstown. If Barb, who is gorgeous, tall, and incredibly thin, thinks she is fat and ugly, maybe I have been wrong about my issues around what I look like, too. At this point, I had made it to the bottom of the hill, driving on Main Street. I looked at myself in the rearview mirror, and what I saw startled me. I wasn't ugly. Six minutes later, I was home. I barged in the front door, ignored everybody in the living room, and went directly to my bedroom. I closed and locked the door behind me. For reasons I do not know of, I stripped till naked and stood in front of the full-length mirror on the wall between the two closet doors.

There I was. I was thirty-one years old and not an ugly, awkward adolescent boy with pimples and a scrawny body. I had a firm, athletic body, beautiful brown eyes, soft cheeks full of life, and thick, wavy hair. I was not only not ugly, but for a brief moment, I considered that I might qualify as good-looking. I had made it to age thirty-one without ever considering myself a handsome guy. Since I was already naked, I went and took a hot shower and used all of the hot water. I put on my bathrobe, sat on my bed, and reflected on all of the times that amazing and attractive women in the last couple of years have flirted with, played with, and flooded me with attention to make sure I would notice them, and I talked myself out of it. All those times that she (whoever she was at the moment) wanted to date or go out with me? As I reflected on that possibility, another thought popped

Raised by Wolves, Possibly Monsters

into my head. What do I do with this information if I'm not ugly and might even be good-looking?

You Quit Your Job and Become a Social Worker

ONE MORNING AT Radio Shack, a well-tended-to suburban white woman, a living *Vogue* magazine cover, strolled in. Her son, browsing like most boys between eight and twelve, wanted to try remote-controlled cars, police scanners, audio equipment, and computers. She grabbed his hand and yanked him away each time he touched something. Her tone and words had bite and bark. When he felt the keyboard of one of the fledgling home computers made by Tandy, she even slapped him across the face! She grabbed his arm, dragged him to the counter, handed me a calculator, and told me to replace the battery. It was not a question; it was a command.

My heart ached for that little boy, and I was furious. I replaced the batteries quickly so that she would leave the store.

It was a Wednesday afternoon in 1993, and that night, I had to be at a class, Introduction to Social Work. It was a new direction for me, one I felt very ready to take. While I enjoyed sales and my work at Radio Shack, something inside told me I could do more with my life than help suburban ladies buy the correct battery. So, in the spirit of a question, I signed up for a one-semester intro to the field of social work at William Paterson University. It didn't hurt that Professor Stacey Block taught the class; I had a crush on Stacey and was impressed with everything she did.

At the beginning of every class, Stacey asked if anybody had questions or experiences, they wanted to share with the class. I raised my hand and shared what I had experienced at work earlier. When I finished sharing, I said, "I was so upset by what happened I didn't know what to do. So that's my question: What do I do?"

Stacey looked at me and hesitated. She placed the white chalk in the chalk holder on the bottom of the green chalkboard and slowly walked towards me. When my instructor got to my desk in the third row, she sat on my desk, leaning toward me and looking directly into my eyes.

"Michael, what you do is you quit your job at Radio Shack tomorrow, and you become a social worker!"

I was stunned. I was thrilled that what I had shared moved the instructor enough to stop what she was doing and give me a direct call to action. And I was inspired in a way that I had not experienced previously in my thirty-something years of life. During my ride home that night, I decided that when I got to my store in the morning, I would call the District Manager and resign, which I did. In the morning, I quit my full-time job at Radio Shack after eight years, giving them two months' notice without knowing how I would support myself after that. Quitting Radio Shack was my first giant leap of faith in sobriety.

After formally resigning, I told the staff I was leaving during our Saturday morning meeting. A guy named Harold worked part-time, two evenings a week. He was a retired business owner of an electronics sales and repair shop that he ran for thirty years. I told him individually about leaving Radio Shack. That night, Harold caught me off guard with his response.

"Let me tell you something, Mr. Swerdloff. You're a good guy, and I like working with you. I hesitated to work part-time for a young white guy, but you're alright. Here's the thing, Mr. Swerdloff: you're not as far along in becoming a great man as you think. Yeah, you heard that right. More importantly, the retail industry, especially retail electronics, loses its good people who have integrity to other industries. There have to be some people with integrity in retail. We can't be stuck with all the sleaze bags and dirtbags. Retail needs good people, too!"

I've always remembered what Harold said and the clarity, honesty, and humility with which he shared it. Between Stacey and Harold, I became a social worker, and then, between Jeff and Dorienne, I became a social worker, community organizer, and alternative counselor.

But I still needed to call Jeff Fleischer.

 Raised by Wolves, Possibly Monsters

Let's Meet Today!

 WHEN I FINALLY got up the nerve to call Jeff, I was surprised by how casual and friendly he was. It was a Tuesday morning, and he wanted to meet with me on Friday afternoon at his office in Newark, near where I was born and even closer to the neighborhoods where I used to run around with mob guys, trained and organized monsters and wolves. He asked me to call him on Friday morning to discuss the details of our getting together.

I called him a few times on Friday morning and left voice messages. Since this was in a different era, once I left my home, I didn't have a way of seeing or knowing if he called me back. I decided I would be a pain in the ass and keep calling, even though I was hanging out at my friend's house, swimming in the pool in his backyard.

When I called Jeff at his office, he could talk briefly.

"Hi, Michael! Thanks for persisting. I've been swamped all day."

"Thanks for squeezing me in, Jeff. Since you're so busy, do you want to try another day?"

"What are you doing right now?"

"I'm at one of my friend's houses swimming."

"Will your friend be distraught if you came down to meet with me now?"

"I'm sure he would be fine, but I'm gross and sweaty in shorts and a tank top.

"Perfect! It will be like we planned our attire since I'm wearing about the same. Let's meet at my office here on Broad Street. I can show you around, and then we can talk next door at my favorite Bodega?"

"Okay. Why not."

A short while later, Jeff showed me around the offices and introduced me. I became more embarrassed about how I was dressed with each person he introduced me to. Most of them were well-groomed and in either professional or semi-professional clothing.

The first thing I noticed about the various staff members and directors I met was that they were an incredibly diverse group. Everybody was focused, intense, warm, and friendly, regardless of position.

Jeff declared he was hungry and had yet to eat lunch. He asked if we could continue our conversation at the Bodega next door.

Jeff and I talked for about thirty minutes. He told me about the Youth Advocate Programs, what they were doing, and what it was like to do the work. He asked me about myself and what my strengths and interests were. I don't think anybody had ever asked me that before. We continued our conversation in his office for a little longer. I was impressed by listening to his conversations on speakerphone. Program Directors from their programs all over the country were calling for support and guidance on everything, from a father killing the mother of a kid in Fort Worth, Texas, to a fourteen-year-old girl who ran away from home in rural Pennsylvania and showed up at the home of the family's team worker, to a gang member in Trenton, New Jersey who wouldn't go to a family team meeting unless his gang boss and two gangster brothers were present at the meeting to protect him. Jeff moved from one subject and conversation to the next casually, focused, and passionately; I felt inspired and petrified but mostly inspired.

"So, what do you think, Michael? Are you one of us?"

"I'd love to do this kind of work someday. I'd be good at it and would enjoy the challenges of working with the teens and their families in the community."

"We've talked about opening a new office in Warren County where you live, but we're not there yet. But we do have an office in Newton covering Sussex and Morris Counties. Robin is the Director up there. Do you want me to set up an interview for you?"

I did not think we were having this kind of conversation. I thought we were just having a conversion, and Jeff was letting me know what they did. In case I ever wanted to apply for a job down the road. I did not think we were talking about doing that right now. "I didn't know this was an interview or anything like that today. I thought we were just talking."

"I didn't either, but I like you, Michael. You would work effectively with our kids, which would be great for you. Robin's programs are expanding, and she could probably use the help, especially since it's hard to find good young men in many of our programs. Besides, I've already pre-screened you; why waste the information gathering I've already done?"

"Okay. Let's do it!"

     Raised by Wolves, Possibly Monsters

This incredible man I had just met stood and walked around to give me an enthusiastic handshake.

I remember how excited and honored I felt conversing and shaking hands with Jeff. He grabbed the phone, stood, and dialed Newton's Youth Advocate Programs office. When Robin answered, he informed Robin he had met a young man who would do great work there, and I was present on the speakerphone. As dynamic and larger than life as Jeff was, Robin was equally straightforward, understated, and gentle. We scheduled an interview for 2:30 the following Thursday afternoon at her office. I could barely contain my excitement and enthusiasm.

In January 1994, I started working part-time at Youth Advocate Programs and started the Social Work Program at Ramapo College. The identified client of the first family I was working with was a twelve-year-old boy who lived with his mother, stepfather, older brother, sister, and newborn baby brother. Four children were in the family, each with a different father from a different culture. I loved working with this family. I could not stop talking about being part of this process to everyone in my life. Months later, Robin gave me another case, working with a fourteen-year-old boy returning home after running away for the seventh time in two years. A month after that, my caseload included a third case, working with a thirteen-year-old boy who was having intercourse with three different girls and got kicked out of school.

Between the classes at Ramapo College and my work with the Youth Advocate Programs, my world was full of life, learning, passion, and inspiration. I felt like a new human being.

I was at the Youth Advocate Programs for over seven months when Robin informed me that she was resigning and would leave the program to work with legal aid. She was a lawyer and missed the work. She asked me if I would be interested in applying to be her replacement. I was startled. I still felt like the new kid on the block and didn't have a clue what I was doing. Robin saw things otherwise. We talked briefly about the work and that I was still attending school. She encouraged me to think about it and told me that during our weekly supervision the following Monday, I should let her know what I thought.

I brought it into meditation and asked all the essential people in my life.

Across the board, the responses were almost identical. I should apply and do everything I can to get the job, and my life will be complete chaos doing this new work, a full-time job that will be fifty hours a week, plus going to school to be a social worker. Ten days later, I was back in Jeff's office on Broad Street in Newark, interviewing for Program Director at Youth Advocate Programs in the Sussex and Morris office.

A few weeks later, they promoted me to Program Director at the Morris-Sussex Office of Youth Advocate Programs.

This new version of my life was full of juicy, intense, and powerful experiences. I made many awful mistakes at work, and the program doubled in my first year! The School of Social Work decided to allow me to use my new job as my internship since they knew it was not possible, on top of what I was already doing, to do an internship as a volunteer sixteen hours a week somewhere else. And I was still very involved in AA.

Mom Wants to Teach Us Reiki

IT WAS 1994, and I lived with Charles, Karla, their daughter Alia, and David on their farm. Karla was pregnant with their second child, and the time had come for me to be out on my own. I felt strong enough, stable enough, and sober enough. I decided to move to a loft across town on a property with a brook in the back, a pool on the side, and beautiful cherry wood paneling inside.

I had not yet moved. One night, after finishing a big bowl of Cheese Glop, a thick pot of cheese with whatever vegetables and leftovers available in the fridge that Karla had made the day before, she came barreling into the kitchen out of breath, her face full of life and energy. "Michael, I spoke to Mom this morning, and she wants to come to New Jersey to teach us Reiki! She said that if the training were for you, me, and two other people, she would be able to fly here. I am so excited! Isn't this great?"

I froze and forgot to breathe for a moment. I had experienced Reiki a few times since the night I met Betsy and encountered God. Reiki was interesting,

 Raised by Wolves, Possibly Monsters

and it felt nice when I received it, but I was not sure I wanted to be trained in it or be responsible for it, whatever "it" was. I was not sure yet if I even believed in it. And my life was loaded with commitments already.

"Do you know when she wants to come? I'm busy with work and school these days."

"Why are you not excited? You get excited about everything, Michael." She looked down at the empty bowl with her face scrunched up. "You even get excited with day-old Cheese Glop for dinner. We may never get this chance again for Mom to teach us Reiki." At this point, there were less than one hundred Reiki Masters in the country.

I didn't know what to say or do. What if Reiki really was satanic? Would I still be able to stay sober?

"And besides work and school, I'm getting ready to move. There's just so much going on right now. We're considering opening a program in Warren County, adding to my other programs, along with Morris and Sussex."

"Michael, what is up with you? I haven't seen you this scared and uncomfortable since that woman kissed you at the sober dance last year." Karla started laughing, but she noticed that I wasn't laughing. "Don't you want to receive Reiki training and attunements?"

"I'm not sure. I need to think about it first."

Karla looked me over from head to toe and studied my expressions and energy. Her gaze was intense and focused. She lowered her voice slowly and gently, "I'm sorry if it feels like I was pushing this on you. I thought you would be excited, and so did Mom. I didn't know this would make you uncomfortable. Just so that you know, Mom wants to be here in February. You have a few months to think about it, but we'd have to find other people to participate so Mom can afford to come here."

"Thanks, Karla. I'll think about it and get back to you soon."

As I did my nightly meditations and prayers before bed, the question of why I was responding so forcefully hijacked whatever else I wanted to think about or do during those ten minutes. I had not yet learned about the process of spiritual resistance.

Spiritual resistance was a new concept for me. In recovery, I'd go 100% to anything that interested me as long as it wouldn't risk my sobriety. Reiki would not threaten my sobriety; if anything, it would enhance and strengthen it. I was confused and disoriented, but more than anything, I felt scared. I was frightened of saying no, of saying yes, and of being scared. I asked God for help with my fear. I woke during the night with a vision of Betsy from the first night I met her. Her smile was fierce. I had a similar vision of Betsy during morning meditation and prayers, later that night, the following day, and so on.

I tried my best to bury myself in work and school. I started going out with Lilith, my first official girlfriend in recovery. Lilith and I had met at a Social Work Practicum class at Ramapo College. One day, while walking down the hill to the parking lot after class, she approached me and said that she liked what I shared in class. Anyone who stroked my ego was utilizing an effective strategy to get my attention; this case was no different.

What was different was that I didn't know that Lilith was flirting with me. All of my experiences in my teens and twenties, and with women in recovery except Selena, were generally with them acting like women on TV and in movies that were flirting blatantly and doing all of the sexual seduction things with their hips, hair, and chest. Lilith didn't do any of that. She talked to me like she was a human being, and I was a human being. I didn't understand this form of female courting.

The sun was bright, the sky was blue, and there was a freshness in the air. Lilith walked with me to my car.

"Michael, do you have plans tomorrow night?"

"Well, I was thinking of attending my regular Friday night meeting; it's our monthly celebration meeting." I was still clueless about the situation.

"I have tickets to this guy's performance. I like that he's part musician, part comedian, and part philosophical waxing. I have an extra ticket. Would you like to come with me so we can go together?"

I took a moment to think about it, still clueless that she was asking me out on a date. I asked about the musician, the atmosphere, and who would be there. She answered all of my questions patiently. I remember thinking she would become a good therapist after graduating from Ramapo. I was correct about that part. I eventually said yes for no reason other than I couldn't find a good reason to say

     Raised by Wolves, Possibly Monsters

no, and my therapist Lauraine had encouraged me to expand my friendships to include people not in AA, so this would meet that need.

We planned to meet at the coffeehouse where the performance would take place. My new friend handed me my ticket. As she did, Lilith held my hand for two seconds longer than necessary. I almost jumped but was able to keep my composure. When I got home that night, I shared with Karla, Charles, and David that I was going to a show with Lilith the next night. As soon as I finished speaking, they all looked at each other and laughed.

Karla exclaimed, "You know you're going on a date, right? Please don't tell me you're so clueless that you didn't figure that part out?" All three laughed heartily again, exchanging glances at each other and then back to me, waiting for my response.

My initial response was to run and hide in my bedroom. I sheepishly let the word "No" escape my mouth. The four of them laughed again. "Do you really think that Lilith was asking me out on a date? Why would you think that?"

Karla reached across the table, put her hand on my wrist, and held it. "Because she walks you to the parking lot every day, you're in class together, she initiates conversations, and now you're going with her to an event where many of her friends will be present. She gave you the ticket that she paid for. Isn't that what somebody does when they want to ask someone on a date?"

I had no way to refute her statements. I was reflecting on various exchanges Lilith and I had walked down the hill, and not once did she do any of those things that women do to seduce you or show you that they want to be with you. I muttered this thought to the three of them, and they all smiled warmly and affectionately at me. Their doing so made me uncomfortable.

Charles had a big smile on his face. "This is exciting, Michael. You've met a woman who likes you, who doesn't want to seduce you with sex and her body. Do you think she's pretty?"

I didn't think Lilith was pretty or not pretty, sexy or not sexy, cute or not cute. I had not thought of Lilith that way, even though she had a beautiful smile, long black hair, typical Italian cheekbones, brown eyes, and a full chest. How did I not notice that there was an attractive Italian woman with large breasts in my class, and we were friends and talked regularly? I did not know how to process this information. We continued our conversation till they helped me understand that not all women use sex to meet and date men. And more importantly, my brain only notices women if their face, hair, and body are presented as sexy or seductive, if not downright provocative. I was taking it all in intellectually, but it hadn't landed yet.

I was nervous going out on that first date with Lilith because I didn't even know if I was attracted to her or interested in her yet. I had never considered it. I arrived a few minutes late, just as the performance began. People were seated in all the seats up front where Lilith was sitting; we exchanged a smile as I came in and took a seat in the back row. After the performance, which I liked, there was a ten-minute break, after which the musician would take questions.

Lilith waved for me to join her up front next to her. As I got close to her, she jumped up and hugged me, not something we had done previously. I liked the gentleness with which she embraced me and my body, but I was caught off guard. I noticed her breasts pressed against me. We sat down, and when the performer returned to answer questions, she reached over, took my hand, and placed it on her leg as she held it. I got excited but nervous. When she noticed that I didn't take my hand away, she pulled it against her abdomen and lightly brushed it against the bottom of her breasts, which felt incidental.

All I could think about was the light on her face. Now and then, Lilith turned to look at me with this radiant smile and joy while rubbing my hand. I was excited and desired this woman I had not noticed as a potential romantic option.

Afterward, we talked in the dark parking lot for a few minutes. It was my first time seeing Lilith at night; the moon was doing its magic on her face and smile. She reached across and retook my hand. There was the same nervousness and excitement as earlier, but this time, there was less anxiety and more excitement.

"Do you remember that I just moved to a new house?"

At first, I didn't know what she was talking about. I then remembered that she and her two sons moved into a house. She was excited about the home; it was the first time she would live with her two sons since she had moved out from her ex-husband. She had stayed in a friend's house previously with the boys. "Yes, I do remember. It's in Clifton. I mean, Wayne?"

She smiled. "Yes, Wayne, you were listening. Well, I'm having a house-

              Raised by Wolves, Possibly Monsters

warming party in my backyard tomorrow night. I know you like volleyball, and I will set up a volleyball net in the backyard. We are just going to hit the ball around. And it's going to be a potluck. I'd like you to come. Are you interested?" Lilith took my other hand and held both while making eye contact. She did nothing to seduce me, yet I noticed that I was attracted to her.

I hesitated for a moment and wanted to pull my hands back. Lilith must have noticed my flinch because she took my hands and gripped them a little bit fuller without being forceful. It felt nice and sweet. My heart was beating louder than usual, and my breath was erratic, but I was at least breathing. While trying to decide the answer to Lilith's question, my mouth opened and said, "Yes," without really checking with myself to see if I wanted to go.

Lilith's face lit up; her response was to hug me. She hugged me with a warmth and intimacy I had not experienced previously. As if I could feel her arms around me, her breasts on my chest, I felt that my whole being was embraced by Lilith, even the parts of me that had no contact with her physically. I felt like I was being enveloped in her energy, although I would not have used those words then. She wrote her name, phone number, and address on a piece of paper under the almost full moon in the parking lot. This time, she offered me a hug instead of just hugging me. I was invited into the process, which felt nice.

When I got home that night, everybody, including Adriana, was in the living room. David asked me to come sit down and tell them about my date. He exited the big brown leather armchair and motioned for me to sit there. I felt like I was being put on the hot seat since they all sat and squatted around me.

Karla was first, "Well, how was your date?"

"It was nice. I had a good time. Lilith hugged me twice and invited me to a party at her home tomorrow night."

It was Charles this time. "So, are you going?"

"I said yes but left an escape route if I changed my mind. But I'm pretty sure I'm going."

Adriana elbowed her way between Charles and Karla. "Is she hot?"

My initial thought was not as hot as you, Adriana. "No, she's not hot." They all groaned and sounded disappointed. "I don't mean that in a bad way. She's just not hot; that's not her personality. She doesn't wear makeup or do anything fancy with her hair, and there was no cleavage or tight pants that you could see her ass or anything like that."

Adriana changed her expression, "I'm sorry, Michael. I didn't mean hot like that. I meant, "Do you like her and want to go out with her again?"

"I do. I like Lilith in a different way than I've ever liked women before. Like she's pretty, but she's smart and interesting, and she doesn't play games, and I like talking with her. Yeah, I guess I am going to go tomorrow night."

Now, they were excited. We had fun discussing the date, what I would wear the next night, and everything else. When I was talking about the fact that she took my hand and was holding it right on the bottom of her breasts, they all got excited. They continued to keep telling me that she really liked me and that it was really a date, and I was going on a date with her at her home with her friends present tomorrow night. I was still having trouble wrapping my brain around a woman who found me attractive and wanted to date me. She wasn't using typical ways women let you know they are interested in you, at least based on my experience.

More Cinnabons

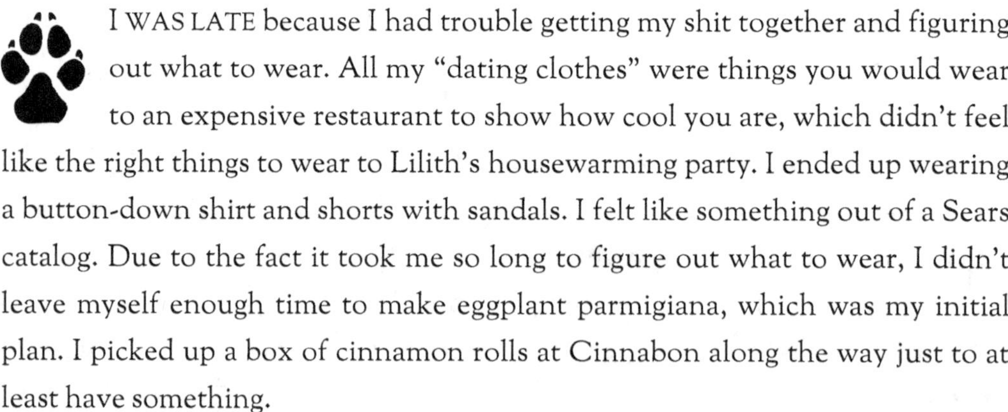I WAS LATE because I had trouble getting my shit together and figuring out what to wear. All my "dating clothes" were things you would wear to an expensive restaurant to show how cool you are, which didn't feel like the right things to wear to Lilith's housewarming party. I ended up wearing a button-down shirt and shorts with sandals. I felt like something out of a Sears catalog. Due to the fact it took me so long to figure out what to wear, I didn't leave myself enough time to make eggplant parmigiana, which was my initial plan. I picked up a box of cinnamon rolls at Cinnabon along the way just to at least have something.

Everybody was nice. All of Lilith's friends were wholesome people. There was alcohol, and most people had either a beer or a wine in their hand, but they barely drank. The people were friendly and warm, and they laughed and shared stories. I felt out of my environment. I was able to enjoy myself after we started playing volleyball since I was better than everybody else. I made a mental note of not showing off or spiking the ball into anybody's face. I was grateful I made that decision.

When the sun went down, it got slightly cooler outside, and we all moved inside to the living room to hang out. Lilith's new home was simple, with light wooden floors, white walls, lovely wooden counters in the kitchen, and a fireplace in the living room. It suited her from the little bit I knew about her. I felt happy for my new friend, who I was theoretically on a date with. When we were all inside, Lilith took my hand and led me to sit beside her on the couch. I was a little uncomfortable, but I went along with it. Having her hold my hand felt nice since I still felt nervous and awkward.

We drank coffee and tea and ate desserts. The cinnamon rolls were a hit and became a topic of conversation. We laughed and made jokes about replacing the word Cinnabon with other nouns in sentences. It was good, clean, and fun, and I liked it even if it was a little foreign to me. Eventually, Lilith's two best friends, Katherine and Todd, were the only ones left. The four of us laughed and drank coffee until they were ready to go home. They lived close and were going to walk. Lilith hugged them goodbye, and they shook my hand and left. Lilith and I were alone in her living room, just the two of us. Since this was new, I had no idea what to do or what would happen next. I was pretty sure that we were not going to go upstairs to her room and fuck. I was sure we would not fool around on the couch since the lady who owned the house was home, and her bedroom was on the first floor. I did the only thing I could think of. I said, "It's getting late, and I'm playing volleyball tomorrow morning."

Lilith said okay and retook my hand to walk me towards the door. She let go of my hand and ran over to get the half-eaten box of Cinnabons. She put them in a bag so I could take them.

We walked outside the door with Lilith in front of me. Lilith kissed me when I was about to step from the top stoop to the ground. We were making out like two teenagers under the full moon with crickets in the background. About a minute later, without me realizing it, I forgot that the bag of cinnamon buns was in my hand, and I dropped them. They made a thump.

We broke out laughing and started making out again. This time more passionately. It may have been the most beautiful kiss I had experienced yet. It felt beautiful; there was no other word to describe it. I felt soft, open, and connected with Lilith. Much to my surprise, my penis suddenly woke up. We both laughed at that and then returned to it again. While driving home to Independence, where I lived, I was so excited to tell everybody about my date, kiss, and Cinnabons that I went even faster than usual in my silver sports car.

The First of Two Really Bad Flinches

LILITH AND I continued to date and get to know each other over the next few months. Everything we did was new territory for me. When we got up in the morning, we would sit across from each other naked on the floor cross-legged, praying and meditating together. Before meals, we would hold hands and share what we were most grateful for. Her older son John, who was twelve, began paying attention to me. Initially, I was the only person he could talk to about sports in the household. It grew to something more, and I was the only person invited into his room with whom he did not share DNA. Her younger son Daniel, who had just turned eight, used to lie on the couch with me, and we would give each other nose kisses and rub each other's noses together. Lilith was expanding my horizons in a multitude of ways. The wolf was becoming less and less in charge.

"Honey, I have a question for you. Since we've spent time together, you have stopped eating meat. Do you eat meat every time we're not together, and you just don't need it when we're together because you're respecting the fact that I'm a vegetarian?"

I hesitated for a second to reflect on what Lilith was asking me. I had chosen not to eat meat when Lilith and I were together. Had my omnivorous habits also changed when we were not together? I thought about it. I only ate one or two servings of meat a week without choosing to do that. "I hadn't given it much thought, but I only eat meat once or twice a week tops these days. Initially, it was to support you, but it seems it has expanded even when we're not together."

Lilith smiled. She had such a wonderful smile. Her face would become soft and glow. I did not have terminology or awareness about these things then, but Lilith's energy was clean and bright. She didn't lie or manipulate; she worked hard at being centered and grounded. As strange as it sounds, watching her mothering the boys used to turn me on. She was firm and respectful, which felt solid and feminine to me.

"Since you don't eat meat, anyway, why don't you decide to be a vegetarian and hold that intention moving forward?"

I sat with it momentarily and couldn't find a good reason to say no. "Okay." And that was that. That was when I decided to become a vegetarian, which became my lifestyle for the next decade and a half. That was not the big flinch.

She had invited her mother to her home for dinner with her and the boys and included me a couple of times. Her mom and I hit it off and had lots of fun together. Lilith seemed wary of the two of us connecting so quickly, which made it even more fun. That was not the big flinch, either.

Lilith had a friend named Jennifer who had once been to a Tibetan monastery in Washington Township, about twenty minutes west of where I lived in Independence. Lilith arranged for the three of us to go to the Tibetan Buddhist Learning Center to check it out since they had a big event on the upcoming Sunday. I had gotten rid of my Mitsubishi sports car, and now I am driving a Suzuki Samurai. I liked having this tiny, little four-wheel drive vehicle that I could take the roof off whenever I felt like it. The three of us went out to the middle of nowhere without accurate directions or a map, hoping that Jennifer would remember how to get there or that we would intuitively figure it out.

We eventually found our way to the Tibetan Buddhist Learning Center, which I discovered was initially started by His Holiness the Dalai Lama. That made it even more appealing to me. The ceremonies, chanting, and marching inspired me, even if it felt weird and foreign. When we went to the bathroom inside the public building, Lilith noticed a flier for a New Year's Eve event. It would start on New Year's Eve and end on January 2nd. We looked at each other, smiled, and nodded our heads, and we signed up. This was not the big flinch either.

I want to share two relevant New Year's retreat elements. The first experience happened during lunch. The retreat started the night before, and everybody stayed over, had breakfast together, and went to teachings all morning. I understood about five percent, and that's being optimistic. I was hungry and ready to eat the lunch they served.

The meal itself did not stand out to me. What caught my attention was an older man wearing gray pants and a gray shirt, resembling what many American janitors would wear. All of the monks were wearing traditional Tibetan burgundy and gold robes. It was extraordinary how he knew what was happening and what was needed all the time without appearing to be paying attention. He was talking to the monks and eating his meal. If something spilled on the floor somehow, he knew about it and would just casually be there to clean it up. It was like he floated or glided. He did nothing fast but moved from one space to another almost instantaneously. When the salad bowl was empty, he casually walked to the kitchen and walked out with another bowl even though his chair was facing the other direction. I was talking to a young man with dark brown hair and a beard. One of the people at the table that we were sitting at had come back from the bathroom and had muttered there weren't any paper towels in the bathroom, only loud enough for the two of us to hear it. I noticed in the background that the guy in the gray pants and shirt just casually got up, headed to the bathroom, and pulled out rolls of paper towels from a storage closet.

While he was in the bathroom with the paper towels, I cautiously asked the guy I was eating with who the man in the gray clothes was and where they found such a fantastic janitor who just glided around the room as if on ice skates.

The young man laughed and shook his head from left to right. "He's not a janitor. He used to be a monk. He was one of the monks who led the Dalai Lama out of Tibet into India for safety. He figured since he saved Tibetan Buddhism from the Dalai Lama being kidnapped or killed, he didn't need to wear a robe anymore. So, he stopped wearing the robe and started wearing these gray pants and shirts constantly." I was embarrassed for a split second but replaced my embarrassment with laughter. We both enjoyed my innocence and ignorance.

The other occurrence demonstrated even more ignorance but not innocence. Two young women in their early twenties were cute, bubbly, and enthusiastic. They were helpers during parts of the event, but for the most part, they sat

     Raised by Wolves, Possibly Monsters

directly in front of me during all the teachings and practices. I gawked at them the whole weekend because I needed something to focus on. Besides that, I had yet to learn what the teachers were teaching. I was new to Buddhism, and as one student mentioned, "Basically, you're coming to a kindergarten class designed for doctoral students." That about summed it up for me. Lilith and I fought intensely on the ride home about me looking at and flirting with the two young women. She had decided that if we were going to be together in the future, she would have to sit in front of me and walk in front of me so she wouldn't have to watch me ogle at women. I was glad that we were staying together and that she didn't break up with me, and I felt miserable about the pain and anger I had caused her. I was filled with shame.

About a month later, I received a call from Philip, one of the caretakers and directors of the Center, asking if I was going to a talk that the monk I had received weekly teachings from was giving at a new-age church. I told him that Lilith and I had not decided yet and asked him why he wanted to know. He wanted to see if we could give Lobsang Setan, the head teacher at the Tibetan Center, a ride home after his Teaching. I said yes on the spot, stating that I would drive him home if Lilith did not want to come. I called Lilith as soon as I got off the phone with Phillip, and she was even more excited and enthusiastic than I was.

We went to the teaching and enjoyed ourselves. The monk was more animated and playful than usual, which is saying something. He was sweet, intelligent, and full of heart and love. Lilith and I noticed he wore sandals on a cold winter night with about four inches of snow. He stuck around afterward to answer people's questions, and then the three of us piled into my Samurai.

We talked and laughed the whole way, heading west to the Tibetan Buddhist Learning Center. Lilith held my hand next to her belly like on our first date. She was wearing a heavy sweater of earth tones with a full-length brown wool coat on top. For some reason, she was wearing a skirt that night, which was unusual for her now that it was cold out. While he was telling a story, I played with Lilith's skirt to see her response. She grinned and moved my fingers two inches up a little bit higher. That was the cue I needed. The idea of sliding my fingers below her underwear and inside of her while driving a monk from the Tibetan Center founded by the Dalai Lama turned me on intensely and fiercely.

I played with her genitals while the three of us were conversing. Eventually, Lilith dropped out of the conversation as she approached climax. She gripped my wrist with all her might so she wouldn't scream or make noises during her orgasm. When Lilith relaxed, I casually took my hand back and drove through the mountains with both hands on the wheel. It never occurred to me that he may have figured something out since my left hand was in a heavy black leather glove, and my right hand was bare. After we pulled in the gates to the Tibetan Buddhist Learning Center, Geshe, known informally, kept thanking me for going so far out of my way to get him home. I tried to explain how I was honored to be in the same car with him and grateful to drive him home. As we left, we watched him walk through the snow in sandals without socks effortlessly.

Before our rendezvous with Setan Lobsang, I will remember the first week of November for the rest of my life. Three very impactful events all happened in the same week. The first occurred during a visit to the Morris County Child Protective Services Agency and a meeting with one of the casework supervisors, Judy. We met at her office every other week to review the cases we worked on and assign new referrals. She had referred two new cases, both of teenage boys with histories of violence, drugs, and theft. The third case created a mess of ripples in my life— which I still experience sometimes today.

Judy handed me a new case involving a twelve-year-old girl. As soon as it reached my hands, her beeper went off, and she informed me that it was the code for emergencies. Judy put up her right index finger, gesturing to me to wait for her. She picked up the phone and called the caseworker. I didn't hear one word of what was happening.

The referral's description included how this girl snuck into her eight-year-old brother's room several nights a week to play with his penis and anus. I froze. I trembled. My spine and neck stiffened. I stopped breathing for several breaths. I reread the same sentence two or three times, and for the first time in my life, I had a flashback of being molested by my older brother, David. Every counselor and therapist I had met individually or in a group had suggested to me that I had all the symptoms of somebody who was sexually molested. I forcefully maintained that I had no recollection of this, and it didn't make sense. But at that moment, it was as clear as could be. They were all right.

          Raised by Wolves, Possibly Monsters

Fortunately, Judy was engaged in her phone call. I was grateful she was busy while I was trying to get grounded and not fall apart right then and there at Child Protective Services.

By the time Judy got off the phone and joined me, I acted solid enough to complete our work together, and I left the building with all three files in my briefcase. But that third one with the twelve-year-old girl and the eight-year-old boy captured my attention and focus. I got into my Suzuki and just sat there crying for who knows how long. I didn't even remember to turn the car on to heat the Suzuki with a canvas roof. Later that night, in the middle of the night, I had another flashback. I did the next day and then the three following days.

Lilith and I had a short conversation about this after the first day but were too busy to have an entire conversation. The next morning, she called me to tell me that her father had had a heart attack and died. As challenging as it was to shift my focus to somebody besides me, I was grateful to have something and somebody else to consider. She asked me if I would drive to her dad's home and stay with her that night. I did. The next day, she mentioned to me that she was about a month behind her menstrual cycle. We tried to remember if there were any times that we had unprotected sex. It took us about thirty minutes to recognize that there had been one night. We decided that the day after her father's funeral, she would come out to the farm and stay for the weekend, and we would do a pregnancy test.

On Friday night, Lilith drove out to the farm with groceries, clothes in her overnight bag, and a CVS bag with two pregnancy tests. We had dinner with Charles and Karla. After everybody finished their tea and coffee, Lilith and I walked down the four steps to my bedroom and closed the door. We looked at each other nervously. "Are you ready for this, Michael?"

"No. But I'll not be any more ready in fifteen minutes or fifteen days. Might as well do it now so that we know."

We each took one of the kits and read the directions silently. When we finished, we looked at each other and discussed the process. Lilith entered the cramped little bathroom in my bedroom and came out three minutes later, holding the first test. The first test had two lines, which signified she was pregnant. We had a brief discussion and decided before we discussed this that we should take the second test since she had already bought it. We went through the same process again with the same result.

We sat at the end of my bed next to each other, staring at the wall. We didn't say much, but we held hands. "Are you ready to talk about this, Michael?"

"Yes. Let's talk about it now. Do you want to go first?"

"Would you mind going first?"

"I can go first." I paused to gather myself. "A part of me is excited about wanting to be a father and having a child with you and for Jonathan and Daniel to have a younger brother or sister. And I'm scared for many reasons. I don't feel like I'm ready to be a father or a partner yet. As I mentioned to you previously, I haven't wanted to have kids because the men from both sides of my family have been incredibly violent and hurtful, and people with alcoholism and/or addictions. I love you, Lilith, but we're just getting to know each other. I think that's all I have to say for right now." I gripped her hand a little tighter. I exhaled and did my best to make eye contact with Lilith.

Lilith took a deep breath, let out a big sigh, and gripped my hand tighter. "I love you too, Michael. I have enjoyed being with you so much, and I think you're such an incredible man who would make a great father to our child, stepfather, and role model for Jonathan and Daniel. But I want to be clear. I've spent the last twelve years raising two children on my own and don't have it in me to raise another child alone. I'm not willing to have a child without you committing to me and it." Lilith stopped there. We sat in silence. "I don't expect you to be able to give me an answer tonight, but my belly is starting to show, and Daniel asked me the other day if I was pregnant, and I lied to my son. I don't want to lie again." She reached over and kissed me. I did my best to kiss her back, but I was still primarily paralyzed, numb, and stiff.

This was the first big flinch.

Starting with my visit to Morris County Child Protective Services, I experienced flashbacks of being molested by my brother as a child multiple times. Along with being the boyfriend of a woman whose father died suddenly, finding out that we were pregnant all in five days felt like an earthquake for both of us, individually and as a couple.

Lilith and I only had a little conversation the following week. We were both

                    Raised by Wolves, Possibly Monsters

busy and needed to catch up on all that had transpired the previous week. We decided I would come and spend the weekend with her and the boys, which sounded both lovely to me because I needed some love and support and enjoyed playing with the boys, and scary as hell because I knew Lilith was waiting for me to give her an answer on whether I was ready to commit to her for the rest of my life.

I had spoken with Karla and Betsy privately about Lilith's pregnancy. Even though I talked with them independently, they answered almost identically: "This is your chance, Michael. This child belongs to you and needs to be brought into the world. This child is your chance for redemption and healing. You need to do this!"

I knew that they were right. I could feel it in my bones and my belly. The fear was immense! I could also feel that in my bones and gut. My therapist, Lauraine, almost jumped out of her chair at the idea of me being a father to a newborn, a stepfather to two boys, and committing to Lilith at that point in my recovery. She wasn't wrong either. All three people I looked to for guidance were accurate and on target. And that was the problem because they came to different conclusions. Betsy and Karla focused on my spiritual well-being and Karma. Lauraine concentrated on my recovery and mental and emotional stability. I focused on the upcoming weekend and the impending conversation with Lilith.

As I have called it for the past twenty-nine years, this was The Big Flinch. I lost my only opportunity to become a father, stepfather, and partner to Lilith. There was no other reason besides being scared and flinched.

"I love you, Lilith; I'm just not ready to make all of these commitments simultaneously, especially while I'm going through these flashbacks. I just can't say yes right now." I then cried as hard as I had at any point in my adulthood, then or now. I knew everything about my decision-making process was fear-based and that my world was about to crumble.

Lilith and I hugged. We cried. We hugged. And we cried. Then we got under the covers and held each other, crying, and fell asleep in the middle of the day. As we were falling asleep, she whispered in my ear, "I love you, Michael. I was sure you would say this, and I prepared for it. I am still tragically disappointed, but I understand. I know it's a huge commitment that I'm asking you about, but like I said, I can't do this by myself again. I don't have it in me." Lilith gave me a gentle kiss on the lips.

We walked in the woods about two miles from her home the following day. Lilith told me she had done some research and that there was an herbal medicine woman in Brooklyn who had created an herbal form of abortion. It was safe and simple and did not involve any knives. I supported her as best I could, even though not one part of me wanted her to void this child. Our child. She called the woman the next day and ordered the herbs. They were delivered a few days later, and she followed the five-day protocol. We talked a lot during those couple of weeks. "I can feel that it is dead inside of me. I called the herbalist in Brooklyn, and she told me it might take two or three days for it to get flushed out of my system. It feels awful." I did what I thought was the right thing to do: to rub her back, hold her hand, kiss her, and tell her how much I loved her. None of it felt like the right thing or the truth. It was the best that I could do. I don't use that phrase often because it is rarely accurate or honest. For the most part, I think very few of us do the best that we can do or even close. I have compassion for what I and we were going through, and every part of my being knew that this was happening because I was full of fear and not listening to my Higher Self or any other aspect besides fear. This was not the best I could do, but it was the best I could do based on the decision I had made out of fear. As much fear as I felt in my body, shame was the most prominent experience I felt when I woke in the morning, went to bed at night, and woke up at three crying.

The fetus didn't flush. It turned out that Lilith was still going to need to get an abortion. We made an appointment for December 23rd.

Just like in the movies, there were several Holy Rollers with their crosses and signs outside telling us that we were doing the work of Satan. I wanted to tell them to fuck off and that the baby was already dead, but I didn't have the energy, and what energy I did have, I wanted to offer and share with Lilith. As cliche as it sounds, we walked into the waiting room, and it literally felt like we were at a morgue. Every single woman in there looked utterly miserable. We sat next to each other, holding hands. Nobody spoke in the waiting room. I was the only male present in a room of eight women. Most of them looked aged twenty-one or younger. A nurse called Lilith's name third. I prayed the whole time she was in

                          Raised by Wolves, Possibly Monsters

the other room.

When she came out and was in great spirits, I knew Lilith was doing her best.

I've never been able to explain to Lilith or anybody else accurately, but from December 23, 1993, I was never able to have intercourse with Lilith again comfortably. Being inside of her meant death, fear, and shame. Eventually, I stopped having erections. Soon after that, we stopped having fun together. Ultimately, it was unbearable for us to talk or be in the same room.

The following night after the abortion clinic, which was Christmas Eve, the four of us went to one of Lilith's cousin's houses for a Christmas Eve gathering. On the way home, the snow turned into ice, and we got into a minor car crash. My Suzuki skated on ice, and a car skated even more on the ice and ran into my Suzuki. My car wasn't drivable. All four of us were physically unharmed. The officer who did the accident report offered to give us a ride to the station so we could figure out our plan. It was now 2:30 a.m. on Christmas Eve/Christmas Day. I called as many people as I could to come and pick us up, and finally, one of the staff members at Y.A.P. agreed to pick us up and drive us to Lilith's house. So, there was an abortion on the 23rd, a car crash on the 24th, and two miserable adults with two exhausted children on Christmas morning.

Lilith and I were alone in mid-January, sitting on the floor before her fireplace. "Michael, I'm going to put you out of your misery and do for you what you haven't dared to do for me. I'm going to break up with you because if I wait any longer with you hating me, not having sex with me, and looking at me the way you do any longer, I'm going to drown. So, I'll break up with you, so you don't have to do it." I don't remember what I said, but I remember I went into some long dissertation about love and struggles and shame and flashbacks. It was all factual, but it was a bunch of bullshit at the time.

None of this sat well with me after we broke up. Shame for not being the man I needed to be for me, Lilith, the boys, and our unborn daughter quite literally haunted me. She visited me several times, in meditations and dreams, before she died, and let me know she was a girl and her name needed to be Susie. Lilith had the same dreams.

My lack of ability to stand up tall was antithetical to everything I learned in AA, meditation, and my Reiki practice. It became clear I was not as far along in my development as I perceived. I initially chose to express this by being even more of an advocate for the kids and families I was working with at Y.A.P. I turned heads with increased boldness in ensuring they were heard and respected. I made an internal commitment to standing for the women in my life and whoever would be the next woman I loved. Looking back, part of what occurred with Jemma a few years later, in 1996, may have resulted from this commitment, but I overcompensated.

More than anything, over the next year and a half, the principles of AA clearly stated we make amends whenever possible without harming others, and I knew I had an action to take. I waited until I knew I would not make the same choice again in similar circumstances. I also understood that I am human and will make mistakes and flinch throughout my life. To make amends is to change, not just say you're sorry, only to make yourself feel better. The amends raised the bar on acceptable male behavior, and I took it seriously. As men, we support women by showing them our humility and respect. Lilith deserved to hear me say how I quit her and us and that what I did was not OK. I also wanted to share with her that she did nothing wrong, which was on me. There was a part of me that hoped she would like us to try again, but no matter what might happen, I knew that making amends was about doing what was needed to honor and respect Lilith and our relationship.

A year and a half later, I called Lilith and made my amends. It was short, straightforward, and to the point. When I completed my amends, Lilith was as I remembered her: thoughtful, mindful, and present. "I knew I'd be getting this call from you someday. I knew you were the kind of man and human being that would want to make this right. I'm glad that I was right about you, Michael. I forgive you and love you and will always love you. You touched me in a way that nobody else ever has."

     Raised by Wolves, Possibly Monsters

The Beginning of My Formal Journey with Reiki

 THE REIKI TRAINING on January 25 and 26, 1995, was my first group energy experience. I had previously experienced little snippets at the Tibetan Buddhist Learning Center during meditation and chanting. However, this was the first time I experienced it in a small group of people in a living room together. The participants were Karla, David, me, and Victoria, with Betsy as a facilitator and Reiki Master. Karla was about six months pregnant with her second child, William. He also received all four Attunements.

The training was intense. The Reiki Attunements were each unique, experientially, and profoundly impactful. By the time we had made it to the third and fourth attunements, my mind felt like I was in a different body in a different world. I felt everything slow down dramatically and was fully aware of my senses as if I was dreaming with colors, textures, temperatures, and a deep and slow rhythm. I remember standing up, and my legs felt heavy and wobbly and, at the same time, mushy and grounded. It was likely that I was going to fall over without having any fear about doing so. As the training went deeper, I noticed how differently I was walking. My typical thirty-something Italian male from Newark, New Jersey, persona was getting replaced by something lighter and more mindful. My voice was softer and more straightforward.

The experience that stayed with me the longest from that weekend was the feeling of Reiki energy flowing through my hands. Like everything else that was brand new to me at the time, I had trouble trusting this beautiful, magical thing that was happening in me and through me, and somehow, it wasn't evil or violent. Witnessing and experiencing other people's responses to me putting my hands on them or near them was alarming in a positive way.

I have practiced some form of Reiki daily since January 25, 1995. I am still amazed that this statement is true. It seems impossible. It seems extraordinary. Reiki has been a life-changing practice for me in many ways, known and unknown.

In every Reiki training that I have participated in where Betsy was the facilitator, at some point, whether it be First Degree, Second Degree, or Reiki Teaching Master Training, she pauses before saying this: "We have to put Reiki in the center of our lives. That is our practice. Reiki has to be in the center of our life."

I have intended to keep Reiki at the center of my life. There have been periods of my life when that has felt predominantly true, and there have been times when it feels barely true, if not false. The first few months and years required discipline, intention, and focus for Reiki to be even close to the center of my life. And then it became less intentional unconsciously. Today, Reiki is more at the heart of who I am than something that I "do."

Aimee the Bleached Blonde Teenager

MY FIRST SIX weeks of Reiki were an explosion.

One day, I was getting the store ready for opening. I was sitting at my desk counting money. Aimee, a nineteen-year-old salesperson who occasionally worked with me, was at our store that morning. Aimee and I did not like each other. We actively disliked each other and found it hard to be in the same room. This morning, she entered the back room, turned around the chair next to the desk to face me, and sat down.

She burst into tears, "I just got back from the oncologist, and they have confirmed that I have cancer. I will start chemo and radiation in two weeks." Aimee's head and mane of bleached blond hair fell into her hands as she cried. I stared at her and tried to figure out what to do. I disliked her enough that I didn't want to touch, hug, or hold her hand or anything.

"I'm sorry to hear that, Aimee." That was the best I could do on my own. Reiki took over, "I was just trained in something called Reiki a couple of weeks ago. It's a vibrational healing method, and we put our hands on people. I'm new to it and don't know what I'm doing yet, but if you'd like, I can put my hands on your head or shoulders." Part of me was hoping she would say no so I didn't have to touch or connect with her intimately.

Aimee took her hands away from her face and sat up with blue eyes full of light and energy. "Last night, I couldn't sleep, so I just kept watching TV and changing channels, waiting for anything that would give me hope before going to the oncologist today to get the results. I was so freaked out I couldn't stop crying and shaking. And while I was flipping through the channels at 2:47 in the morning, there was this documentary about Hands-on Healing. I watched the whole thing, and it was amazing. It was like a breath of fresh air. For a minute, I had hope, and I was able to fall asleep. As I drifted off to sleep, I remember thinking that even though I don't believe in God, having one of these Healers in my life would be helpful. So, I prayed to God that somebody would appear. It turned out to be you!"

"That is amazing. Again, I'm new to this, so no promises. I am still trying to figure out what to do. I've never worked on anybody but myself, except during the training."

"Please, Michael, just try."

I had been sober long enough and meditated and prayed sufficiently to know that these are the situations when God or the Higher Power takes over, and it's essential to get out of the way. I nodded at Aimee slowly and nervously, got up, and stood behind her. I went through the protocols to connect with Reiki and have Reiki flow through my hands. Much to my surprise, they got warm and tingly in fifteen seconds. I put my hands over her head while staring down at the brown roots of her hair, which briefly returned me to my judgmental self. I asked for Reiki to flow through me, and it did. I slowly lowered my hands and put them on top of her head. I could feel the energy flowing through my hands, her head, her skull, and her whole body, all the way down to her feet! I stayed like that for a few minutes, but it felt much longer. I slowly took my hands off her head and put them on her shoulders. And the energy was even more focused and intense. I could feel my hands and her body vibrating and radiating.

After a couple of minutes on her shoulders, Reiki guided my hands so that my left hand would be back on top of her head and my right would be on the back of her neck. I gently slid it under her hair and held it on the base of her neck. This time, I felt the energy come in through my left hand, through her skull, down her spine, and straight to her feet. I felt like I was guiding it with my right hand even though it wasn't moving. And then the energy stopped. Not abruptly, but it stopped. I asked Reiki to flow through my hands again, but nothing happened. I sensed we were done, even though I didn't know what "done" meant with Reiki.

I slowly walked around Aimee and sat at my desk, looking at her. I didn't know what to do next, but before I could say anything, I noticed her face was bright, shining, and clear. She looked safe and full of vitality. "How are you doing?" I only spoke loud enough that she could hear me because I didn't want to startle her. Her eyes were closed, and she looked like she was in a different universe.

She slowly opened her eyes, and they were full of life and hope. "My God, that was amazing, Michael! I never felt anything like that in my life. I felt like I was being tickled with a feather by God. Thank you so much! What did you call that again?"

"Reiki. It's called Reiki. Reiki is spiritually-guided universal life force energy."

Aimee stood slowly, and we made eye contact. It made me a little uncomfortable because it felt close and intimate. She leaned over and hugged me with tears of joy while holding me. I started to tear up myself but hid it from Aimee. That hug and moment felt so beautiful. I remember being grateful for Reiki, the Reiki lineage, and God. I also hid from her that my body had gotten turned on, and if she leaned any closer, she would know that, too.

Nine days later, Aimee showed up at the store. She was not scheduled to work that day, and I was confused and braced about whatever she was doing there. It was mid-afternoon, and I was in the back room filing papers when I saw her out of the corner of my eye. Before I could turn around, she leaped into my arms, hugged me, and kissed me on the cheek.

"I just got back from the oncologist for the second time this week. He said it was a miracle that all my cancer had just disappeared as if it had never happened. They did all the imaging twice this week, and it's gone! I don't have cancer, I don't need to do chemo or radiation, and I'm not going to die at nineteen years old! I just left there and haven't even told my family yet. I wanted to come and see you first. Thank you. I don't know what you did or what that stuff you did was, but you saved my life!" Tears were rolling down both of our cheeks. She kissed me on the cheek again, "Thank you, Michael. I don't know how to thank you enough. Thank you for saving my life." Aimee pulled me back into her arms again and hugged me again.

 Raised by Wolves, Possibly Monsters

I was a little more composed this time and could hug her back. As we released our hug, she took both of my hands, held them, and made eye contact with me. Her face was only about six inches from mine. Somehow, in two weeks, this teenage girl went from an annoying, self-centered, self-absorbed, attention-seeking brat to a fantastic grown woman with beauty, strength, courage, and joy. My whole being was turned on in all the ways a human can be turned on.

That was my first Reiki experience after the training. My second Reiki experience happened on the way home from work when driving down Cat Swamp Road.

I was cruising around through the hills and curves of the 3.2 miles of Cat Swamp Road. The police car lights were flashing. A car was angled off the right side of the road, and it looked like the front end was knocked in by contact with a deer. I could hear the ambulance's sirens approaching from a distance. When I pulled up directly next to him, some part of me just eased my foot onto the brakes, slowly stopping my forward progress. I looked at him, and then he lifted his head just enough to turn and look at me. Without even thinking about it, I felt Reiki flowing through my eyes. My hands lifted, and Reiki flowed through them as well. I could hear the police in the background saying, "Okay, keep it moving. We need to make room for the ambulance," but something else was happening. That man and I made eye contact for about thirty seconds, but we connected. Let me correct that: Reiki happened between us. I nodded at him when it felt like we were done, and he nodded back at me just barely.

I started to move forward slowly, and then one of the officers approached the deer with his shotgun. He was about to put it to sleep so it wouldn't have to be in pain on the side of the road. I had the same experience with the deer. I pulled up next to it; it lifted its head and made eye contact. Reiki flowed through my eyes and hands. That was held for fifteen to twenty seconds till the sound of the shotgun echoed through the valley and my heart. Reiki guided me to stay there a little longer while another officer told me to keep it moving. I pulled away, and when I got home, I heard everybody was in the living room. I said nothing about what had taken place. Twenty-nine years later, I still am not capable of expressing these kinds of experiences well. This brings us to the third profound Reiki experience that was early in my practice.

I used to play volleyball at a local high school gym on Wednesday nights. I had been doing so for several years and was close and friendly with the rest of the regulars. Nina, the woman in charge of opening and closing the gym, informed us that the following week, on Wednesday, we wouldn't be able to use the gym because they were doing some work on the floor.

On Tuesday night of the following week, I looked in the Warren County newspaper to see if anyone had a pick-up recreational volleyball game. On Wednesday night in Hackettstown, they just started a pickup game at the elementary school. When I walked into the gym, which was also the theater and the cafeteria, I noticed that it had a low ceiling, low, ripped nets, and apparently low-skilled people in the room, which created disappointment. I thought about just turning around and leaving. Fortunately for me, there was one particular person who caught my attention. So, I decided to stay.

The volleyball sucked. I did my best to play nice and have a good time. Besides, I wanted to show off to a woman, Abby, who caught my attention; what a good sport and playful guy I was. Abby's sister, who was also playing, brought her daughter, who looked about eight years old, and played by herself on the stage while we played volleyball. Somebody on the opposing team tried to spike the ball, and I blocked him. The ball landed on the floor, followed by a scream and the thud of the girl landing near the stage. The girl's mother and her Aunt Abby both ran over. We all followed. The girl's mother was rubbing her head and screaming for somebody to call for help. While we huddled around her, some guy ran down the hall to find a pay phone.

I stayed in the background because I didn't know anybody and didn't want to get in the way. The girl was crying intensely, and her mother was freaking out, as we all were on some level. Without thinking about it or knowing it was happening, my hands floated up in the air about the height of my chest. I faced the girl and felt Reiki flow through my hands. About fifteen seconds later, the girl stopped crying, lifted her head, and looked at me. All of the fifteen or so people who crowded around them looked at me as well, and without me knowing it, my hands were still facing the girl. She sat up, wiped her nose, and thanked me. I froze and didn't know what to do. Everybody looked at me, trying to figure out what I was doing with my hands, why the girl thanked me, and how she was

     Raised by Wolves, Possibly Monsters

now magically ok.

I didn't know what else to do, so I said, "Great. I'm glad she's okay. Let's go play volleyball!" Everybody looked at me differently for the rest of the night.

That was the third of my profound Reiki experiences early in my practice. These profound experiences do not happen to most people, but they did with me. I have no explanation for this; it's shaped my perspective on Reiki moving forward. The bar of what is possible through Reiki was super high, and I have felt inspired and guided to many more of these experiences over the years. I am blown away and startled by the force of love and healing I have witnessed every single time, as if it was my first experience.

Home and Community

 A FEW MONTHS later, I left everything behind and went on another adventure. I was guided to quit my job, let go of my loft by the river, sell my Suzuki Samurai, and give away everything so I could backpack across the country.

Quitting my job, giving most of my physical possessions away, and backpacking across the country was a scary decision for me on many levels. I had achieved the closest thing I had to stability in my life since age ten through sobriety and recovery. I loved my job at Y.A.P., my home by the brook; studying Social Work was inspiring and full of direction toward the man I knew I was becoming. Reiki had created deep roots in me on being human and interacting in the world beyond my self-centered needs and wants. I was building relationships with people in several areas of my life that felt solid and supportive.

My parents, who grew up during the Great Depression, raised us with financial insecurity. Whenever my brother or I did not finish every bite of food on our plates or did not care for a bike or any other material possessions in a manner they felt acceptable, we would receive a sermon aimed at shaming us into eating what was still on our plates. Having "things" was evidence of success and being better than other people, evidence of winning and putting these things into a storage locker, not knowing what or when I would return, petrified me, as did giving everything else to various local charities. And I had minimal experience with backpacking! The question came up internally, "Will I survive without the recovery com-munity, my sponsor, my therapist, and the people I worked and studied with?" I can feel my stomach tighten as I reflect on this time. And I was clear that it was necessary even though I understood the risks.

Betsy and Karla were super supportive of my journey. Lauraine was concerned but offered support despite her concerns. My AA friends and sponsor were responding similarly to Lauraine. My family thought I was doing this to hurt them; my mother eventually came around and got excited about what I was about to do and looked at me with panic in her eyes.

I waited a few weeks before giving my notice at the Youth Advocate Programs.

I had lunch with Jeff Fleischer, my supervisor at Y.A.P., the week before I hit the road. He wanted to ask me more about my trip and what I was doing besides the brief phone call we had the previous month and the discussion at my goodbye party with all of the other directors in the tri-state area.

The conversation was interesting, fascinating, and full of nuggets for me. This one in particular. "Michael, I know you're heading out in a few days, and this is our last time together. Working with you and witnessing your growth and development as a person and Program Director has been a pleasure. I know you'll head out with your backpack regardless of what I say, but I want to share what I learned when I made a few trips like that in my thirties." Jeff took a bite of his taco, started to put it down, lifted it back up, and took two more bites to finish it before continuing. I have always respected someone who takes the next bite of their taco, burger, salad, or ravioli before they continue. "I learned two signifi-cant things; I believe you will as well. There's no place like home, and we can't live without community, very well or very long.

"As you know, I have lived in several countries worldwide, backpacked, and stayed in many hostels, which brought me back here. Anyway, I hope that's helpful." And with that, Jeff picked up his other taco and started crunching away, as did I.

Even though I lived in New Jersey and was heading west, I started my journey from Shenandoah National Park in Virginia. My friend David was moving to

Florida and suggested we launch together and camp for one night in the park. He left in his black Honda, and I went with my black backpack. I was very confident up to and including when David drove away. It then occurred to me that I was about to embark on a journey that I was unprepared and unqualified for.

I took a moment to pause, breathe, and connect with Reiki. I closed my eyes briefly and opened them to see the mountains, hills, and blue sky before me. There was a mix of awe, awful, and awesome. Even though it was faint, feeling Reiki energy and the Reiki lineage within me was enough for me to take those first few steps off the campground and into the forest. I was internally focused on being centered, grounded, and aligned, so much so that I tripped over a large root of an old oak tree and almost fell entirely on my face with seventy-two pounds on my back. I caught my balance at the last minute physically and emotionally. There was no space for me tripping on roots, rocks, or anything else. I needed to hike fourteen miles that first day; it was almost noon.

I stayed focused and steady. I ran into some people along the trail, but there were few. A few hours later, I came to a place where people were kneeling by a creek, others hanging out and taking a break seated on fallen trees. I wiggled out of my backpack and excitedly kneeled before the stream to splash water on my face and hair. A few handfuls made it down my throat as well. I enjoyed the cold, fresh water on my body and throat. I sat there squatting for a few minutes, inhaling the cooler air and hearing the water trickling. My eyes were closed and filled with gratitude, hope, and possibilities.

A middle-aged woman with a man gently tapped me on my right shoulder. I was startled out of my world of water. I turned around, and she held her index finger before her lips, gesturing for me to be quiet. When she knew I understood what she was referring to, she slowly moved her finger to point across the creek from me at the brown bear about forty yards away, drinking from the same creek.

I slowly and quietly put my glasses back on my face to assess the bear and the situation. In my peripheral vision, everyone was starting to tiptoe from where we were hanging out. That was a good idea, so I did the same. I was cautious when putting on my pack and did so slowly, not to draw any attention to myself or my movements. So far, so good.

As I started my retreat, I took a quick inventory of how important it is to pay attention to where I'm walking so as not to trip and fall and keep an eye on the bear while doing so. I have no idea if I did an excellent or miserable job, but I successfully navigated, creating distance between me and the brown bear. About ten minutes later, I returned to walking with my usual steps. The brown bear did not leave my consciousness for the day.

About an hour before dusk, I reached the point where I had to navigate through the side of the mountain over some large rocks. This was not a skill I had practiced previously; more importantly, never in my life, even in childhood, had a good balance on rocks and logs. I took it slow and did my best. I twisted my ankle on the side of a large white and black stone. When I returned to the dirt trail, I could feel the inflammation beginning in my right ankle. I walked for about another forty-five minutes and submitted to the fact that I was not going to be able to get much further, and better find somewhere to set up camp for the night and make sure I got a good meal in and, even more importantly, a good night's rest.

After dinner, I cleaned my pots and pans, dried them, and packed them up pretty high to avoid attracting more bears. By this point, my ankle was throbbing, and I was excited to get inside my blue and white tent and look out the mesh window at the stars.

I was just about to fall asleep when I heard loud thumps. I couldn't identify the sound at first, but as it got louder and closer, I could tell it was a large animal. As it got closer, I lay on my back and practiced Reiki and meditation to calm my system. There wasn't anything else I could do. I asked for the Reiki energy to expand beyond me and my tent to create safety for myself and others. This significant thing that felt like what I saw earlier today at the creek and stomped like something that would weigh that much and had enormous feet walked right past me to where my pots and pans were hanging, as well as the food. It messed around in that area for a few minutes and then came over by me. It was sniffing the outside of the tent, and I could feel the heat of its breath. I was afraid I was going to pee inside my backpack and would, therefore, have to sleep in urine for who knows how many days, weeks, or months. I was able to keep my urine inside my bladder.

Of all of the potential outcomes I imagined in this situation, the bear lying

    Raised by Wolves, Possibly Monsters

down next to my tent about two arm's length away from me was none of them!

It just hung out there next to my tent. I didn't do anything, didn't move, just hung out. Time slowed ruthlessly. It felt like it was twenty or thirty minutes; what I believed to be a bear was lying beside me. In clock time, it was three or four minutes. It just simply got up and thumped away the same way it came. When I could no longer hear or feel its steps, I stood outside my tent to pee and fell asleep within a few minutes.

I woke in the morning to a woman identifying as a park ranger asking me if I was okay. Since this had been my first night alone, I was disoriented when I opened my eyes and saw the shadow of a human being next to my tent. She again identified herself, "Hello? Are you okay?"

"One moment, please. Let me just put on some clothes."

"Take your time."

I grabbed a pair of shorts and a shirt and wiggled myself out of my mummy sleeping bag. I unzipped the opening, and while doing so, I put on my glasses and saw a park ranger in uniform. "Good morning" was all I could say.

"I wanted to check in with you because you are less than a hundred feet from the trail, and we don't allow camping within 100 feet of the trail. I looked at your permit, and you're about three miles short of where you were expecting to be. Were there any problems or challenges?"

I laughed. "Yeah. While I fell asleep last night, a bear came by and laid down beside me! It didn't do anything; it just hung out, and then it left. I ended up here because I twisted my ankle along the side of the cliff about a mile back. I could feel it swelling and wanted to get off my feet and rest to make up that distance today."

"Wow! So glad that nothing bad happened. In the future, you will need to hang your cooking gear and food much higher than you did. You're fortunate, Sir. How is your ankle?"

"I have no idea." I looked around for my boots outside the tent door, put them on, and strung them up. I turned over to get up and could feel that my ankle was weak. It didn't hurt, but I didn't feel I could put total weight on it. "Not so good. It doesn't hurt much, but it feels wimpy." I was walking around in the vicinity to test it and see if my ankle would loosen up.

"I can see you're not putting full weight on it. Consider leaving the trail about two and a half miles up on the left. You only have to walk about a mile to get to the town center when you leave the park. You can find somewhere to stay for the night to take care of your ankle."

"Thanks. I want to see what my ankle's going to be able to do right after I make some breakfast and break camp. Can you show me where to exit on the map if my ankle hurts?"

"I understand your need to keep going. I'm the same way but be careful. If you push your ankle too much, too soon, you might be laid up for a week or two. According to your permit, it looks like you're embarking on a pretty serious hike this week. Hate to see you laid up in some Motel watching shitty cable TV wishing you were on the trail instead of laid up with ice packs on your ankle. Be smart, Sir. Don't let your ego get in the way of your safety on this journey." Her voice was soft and tender in that last sentence. I thanked her for her time and advice, and we said our goodbyes.

After breakfast and breaking down camp, I did a few minutes of Reiki and meditation before throwing my backpack over my shoulders. I also took a moment to offer Reiki to my sore ankle. I reflected on her last sentence and how somebody could apply it to their life. "Don't let your ego get in the way of your safety on this journey." I looked back at where I had made camp the night before, paused to take in what felt like an epic moment of recognizing I survived a bear twice the day before, and made it through day one of that journey that she suggested! Don't let my ego get in the way of completing my journey. I followed her recommendation and found my way out of the park into a local neighborhood.

God, Please Help Me

UNBEKNOWNST TO ME, one of the humorous aspects of backpacking cross country in the summer of 1995 was that the movie *Forrest Gump* was remarkably popular. I had never heard of it. As I moved from town to town and street to street, people, especially children, would start walking with

   Raised by Wolves, Possibly Monsters

me in groups and ask if I was "walking for peace." I found it inspiring that somehow, "intuitively," they all knew I was walking for peace, mostly internally. I was disappointed and tickled when I finally saw the movie and understood the reference.

Six months later, the backpacking portion of the adventure landed me thirty miles south of Deming, New Mexico, a couple miles from the border. Betsy and one of her primary students, Scott, lived in an intentional community. I spent ten days staying in the spare bedroom in her double-wide. Things and experiences feel blurry from my time there in the desert.

I remember nightly dreams being vivid and full of fire, volcanoes, demons, gold light, Reiki, and bridges—lots of bridges. Most nights, I woke up out of breath and full of sweat, even though it was 40 degrees outside. My heart was pounding, and my eyes felt like they were bulging. The dreams were horrifying, and I felt like I was the battleground of a spiritual war. I wasn't part of the war; my body and soul were where the war was being fought and what the war was being fought for. The monsters were circling me again. I remember walking in the desert alone in the afternoons with naked blue skies and vegetation no higher than my waist. What was 40 degrees at midnight was 80 degrees at noon. I felt like I was being watched by somebody or something whenever I ventured out into the desert. I stopped walking in the desert by myself.

I did, however, take a walk to the border between the United States and Mexico to watch the activity and "listen" to what was taking place energetically. I felt sad and challenged, but mostly just sad. I was not very clear on what the sadness was about beyond witnessing that an arbitrary border can create so much hatred, violence, fear, and distrust.

Betsy and Scott spent the days training me. The best way I can describe it was boot camp for spiritual warfare. I did not like any of it! I was scared, shaken, and challenged on a deeper level than I can recall previously, possibly ever. I remember having these fantasies and inner conversations in my head. The basic narrative was like this, "Why can't I just be a Reiki Practitioner and heal people and make people and animals and rooms feel well? Why do I have to get involved in all of this "other stuff"?" I deeply longed for the arrogance and naivety that had sustained me just two weeks before. I was acutely aware that I now had experiences and training that would not allow me to return to that naivety again. Trust me, I have tried.

Betsy would facilitate a Reiki Master training in Webster, Texas, just outside Houston. She asked me if I would drive her from New Mexico to Texas. As much as I loved being in the desert and in that community, I had a deep exhalation mentally, emotionally, physically, and energetically when we passed through Deming, and I knew that soon, we would be on the eastbound highway.

The ride was mostly unremarkable. I was grateful for having a simple job of driving and not having to think about anything else. I was astounded at how big Texas was, even though I had briefly lived there in the 90s!

Being with Betsy in Texas on our way to a Reiki Master Training at Sharon's house, a former nun, was a smooth and straightforward process. All I had to do was avoid a car crash. I was successful in that mission. The Reiki Master Training was potent!

After the training, the next leg of our journey, we drove to Largo, Florida, where Charles, Karla and the kids were now living. I was so happy to see water and smell the salty air passing through Tampa. Parts of me woke up. It has been my experience without exception that saltwater, sand, waves, sun, and sky revitalize, ground, and center me. When we were just a few miles away from seeing Charles, Karla, and the kids, my eyes were getting heavy, and my legs were stiff from sitting and driving. I almost ran a red light into a major intersection. I came damn close to failing at my mission of not getting in a car crash.

Betsy sat up straight and assured me I could make it the last few miles and that we were both okay. She understood how important it was to me to do right by her. After hanging out in Florida for Christmas with the family for a few weeks, I bought a plane ticket to Indianapolis.

Jemma

 IT WAS 1995, and my brother David and I had not talked for several years. When I had backpacked across the States, I met Jemma along the way in Bloomington, Indiana, continuing my journey to New Mexico. When I

     Raised by Wolves, Possibly Monsters

returned to be with Jemma, we became a couple, and I moved in with her. Hearing stories about my brother petrified her, as they should. She made me swear never to let him figure out where I was in the country, let alone her apartment. I agreed, knowing I wanted to keep my distance from him anyway; I was relieved. Jemma and I broke up the following year when she started physically attacking me soon after we were engaged.

On Friday nights, I would attend an AA men's meeting at a church on the north side of Bloomington. It was a fantastic meeting. The sharing and fellowship were exceptional. The handful of men who became my closest friends, who I also played basketball with every Sunday morning, went to that meeting and dinner afterward. Sometimes, some of us would arrive early, talk, and shoot hoops on the basketball court. One night, my friend Terry and I were sort of shooting hoops but mostly connecting. I shared the challenges I was experiencing in my relationship with Jemma.

Terry rebounded a missed shot and tucked the ball under his right arm. He smiled at me, "So, let me see if I got this straight, Michael. You get up in the morning and practice meditation and Reiki. Go to work at the Youth Shelter and Youth Detention Center with adolescents and families in crisis, do some in-home family preservation, ride your bike across town, and work with adolescents on juvenile probation. After all that, you go home and make dinner for you and Jemma, and she attacks you sometimes while you're sleeping but other times while you're awake. Do I have this right?" Terry had a big, obnoxious, sarcastic smile on his face.

"Fuck you, and yes, you have it right."

"Okay. Just want to make sure I have it right." Terry smiled, turned around, and started shooting the basketball again. He broke out hysterically, laughing. I joined him, but I think we were laughing at different things.

The next night, Jemma and I had gotten into one of our fiercest arguments. We were sitting on her white couch with a white blanket covering it when she slapped me and kneed me in the thigh. Jemma verbally tried to egg me on. My girlfriend kneed me again and then started punching me in the chest rapidly with these little taps that she did when she was agitated to release her anger without hurting me. My frustration escalated to anger, and I was now moving into the neighborhood of rage. I felt the warmth in my face and the blood and adrenaline moving through my body. I grabbed Jemma, pushed her onto her back, and held her arms above her head. I climbed on top of her legs so she could no longer kick me. Jemma yelled and screamed at me, but they didn't penetrate my brain. All I knew was that I was sick of her attacking me verbally and physically, and I needed to end it immediately. Decades of violence and abuse were all bubbling up inside of me at the same time.

I pulled her hands together, holding them with my left hand alone. I raised my right hand above my head, cocked, and my fist closed tightly. I saw a vision of me smashing Jemma's face full of blood, and this stimulated me. The vision felt exciting. As I got ready to bring my fist down, a part of me inside said one word, "No!!!"

Something shifted in me, and I paused. That same voice whispered, "I am not this guy. This is not me." All the tension and intensity melted away. I lowered my hand and let go of Jemma's wrists. She looked startled. Her expression was confusion and possibly panic.

"What just happened, Michael?"

I climbed off Jemma gently and deliberately. I turned around and looked at her while walking away. "I'm done. I am not this man."

I went to the bedroom, packed my clothing, backpacking gear, and a few books I had in my backpack, a few more things in my little daypack, said goodbye on my way out, and left. I walked till I found a payphone and called my friend Patrick. I told him what had happened, and he invited me to come and stay on his couch. This action was the first tangible evidence that the monster was not bigger or stronger than me. A new form of masculine strength was rising within me, even if I didn't know it was happening.

Two weeks later, I rented my own house near one of the middle schools where I worked. I had invited my mom and oldest nephew, Carlo, to visit after I settled. We had made all the arrangements without my brother knowing where they were going. I don't remember the story she told him, but it was not Indiana, and it was not visiting Uncle Michael. Lots of drama unfolded in New Jersey the night before they flew to Indiana in the morning. My brother figured out how to scroll through my mother's phone calls on her digital desk telephone earlier that

                    Raised by Wolves, Possibly Monsters

night. There were three calls made to my number earlier. He pushed redial, and I answered, "Hi, Mom! Did you finally get David to leave so you and Carlo can get ready to come here in the morning?"

"You've got a lot of balls thinking you could take my son without letting me know where he's going to be, you piece of shit! Fuck you, and he will see you over my dead body." He hung up, and I stood in my living room with the phone in my hand, listening to the dial tone. That was the last time I heard my brother's voice out loud.

The following day, his wife got a restraining order to keep him out of the home because he had impregnated a fifteen-year-old girl at the church he attended every Sunday. He was moving in with the girl in a new condo he rented.

I continued to enjoy working at Project Breakaway in Bloomington in 1997. We ran a program for adjudicated teens on juvenile probation. We were getting ready to leave to pick up the kids for our after-school programming when I received a call from my mother.

She informed me that David had died of coronary arrest earlier that day. I hopped on a plane to New Jersey as soon as I could. I dozed off on the plane ride since it was a redeye, and I had not slept well since hearing the news. It brought me back to how I felt when my dad died two years before.

I was still backpacking cross-country when my father died. I remember the Friday night I was strolling through Third Street Park in Bloomington, Indiana. I passed the water fountain to meet a new friend when I felt a sharp pain in my abdomen. I almost bowled over with pain and surprise. As I straightened up, I thought, "My dad is gone." I did not know what that meant; he was just gone.

Two weeks later, I called my mom collect from a pay phone. She started hysterically crying when she knew it was me. She shared with me that my father had died two weeks before, and she felt awful that they had to move forward with the wake since they had no idea when they would hear from me again.

I let her know I was not bothered by missing it. I did not share this with her, but I felt relieved that I didn't have to return for the wake. I would not have wanted to stop my journey for this; it did not have meaning to me.

The next day, I woke with deep gratitude that my father had made amends with me before I left New Jersey to go backpacking. As a result, I did not feel like I needed anything else from him now that he was dead. I felt complete.

I called David. My mother said he had cleaned our father's apartment. I wanted my suits and knew they were there.

David was adamant that no suits of mine or my father's were at Dad's apartment. He insisted that Dad must have gotten rid of them. Besides the fact that this was David and most of the words that came out of his mouth were lies, my dad loved his suits, and wearing them brought him great joy. Besides, he had offered to save them for me three months earlier.

I felt complete about Dad, and I felt worse about David. One wolf was gone, the other hungry for more blood.

I woke up as the plane was descending into Newark Airport.

David's wife Gina picked me up, and the same guy who had tried to break into Fair Oaks Hospital with David seven years before was driving the car.

"Mikey, I am so glad you're here. I don't know how to do any of this." Gina paused to steady herself. "The police want to know if we want them to do an autopsy. He was your brother. I will let you decide this."

"Was he still doing coke?"

Gina put her head down in shame, "Yeah. He had slowed down for a while because of the boys, but after all that had happened with him and the police and the restraining order, his pregnant teenage girlfriend, and moving in with her, he started doing more coke than he had in years." Tears were streaking her makeup across her face.

"You and the kids have been through enough. Let's not get an autopsy. The last thing they need is to find out they lost their father to drugs."

"You always know the right thing to do, Mikey. Thank you. One other thing: I am okay with you making decisions on everything else. Is it OK for me to dress him for the casket? You know that's my thing."

"Of course, Gina, that would be great."

Two days later, I walked up to the casket with the incredible relief that I would get to say goodbye to my brother for the last time. I wanted to go up by myself because I was worried that I might smile and hurt my mother or somebody

 Raised by Wolves, Possibly Monsters

else's feelings. Much to my surprise, when I approached the casket, David was laid out wearing my favorite grey pinstriped suit with my favorite blue silk tie on his stiff fucking body. I didn't even get to say goodbye to him without one more fuck you from him.

I bowed to pray, asked God to take him far away, and exhaled, knowing both wolves were now dead. I felt a brief sense of freedom with the few breaths I experienced in front of his casket.

We Are Going to Grow Like It's 1999

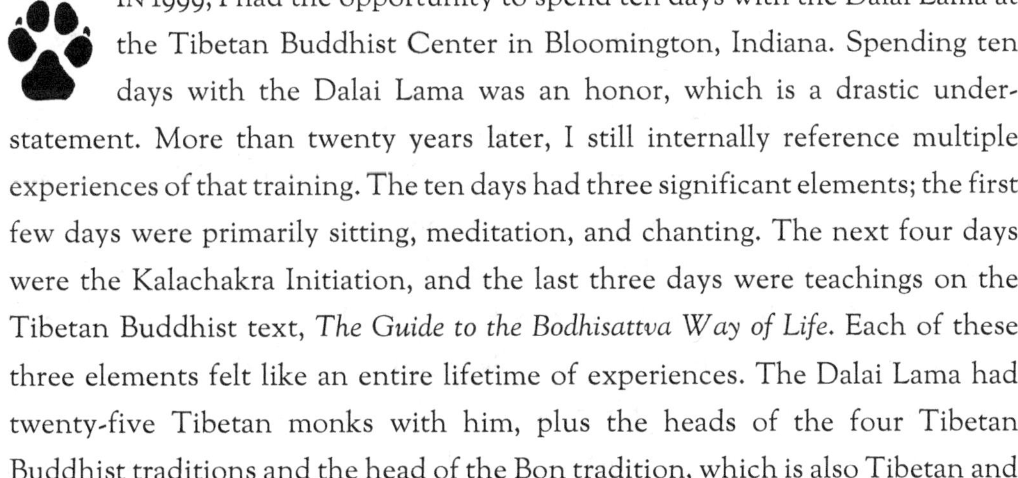

IN 1999, I had the opportunity to spend ten days with the Dalai Lama at the Tibetan Buddhist Center in Bloomington, Indiana. Spending ten days with the Dalai Lama was an honor, which is a drastic under-statement. More than twenty years later, I still internally reference multiple experiences of that training. The ten days had three significant elements; the first few days were primarily sitting, meditation, and chanting. The next four days were the Kalachakra Initiation, and the last three days were teachings on the Tibetan Buddhist text, *The Guide to the Bodhisattva Way of Life*. Each of these three elements felt like an entire lifetime of experiences. The Dalai Lama had twenty-five Tibetan monks with him, plus the heads of the four Tibetan Buddhist traditions and the head of the Bon tradition, which is also Tibetan and predates Buddhism. Four monks worked on a mandala from morning to night for nine days, then released into a river on the property.

Many moments stood out and were extraordinary to me. There is a specific one that feels relevant and valuable to share here. We were about five days into the training when, before lunch, His Holiness announced that we were so far ahead of schedule that he had given his translator a package of index cards. If people wanted to ask him a question, they could write their question on an index card and return it to the translator. He would read through the questions and choose a few to answer publicly the next day. The first three questions were on Buddhism. The fourth one still affects me profoundly in ways I don't quite understand. I will do my best to keep the integrity of what he shared as accurate as possible, knowing it was over twenty years ago.

"Now that I have answered those first three questions, I would like to answer a question that a woman here asked. Before I do, I want to look around the room and say that I'm answering this question for everybody here, not just her, but specifically for the men, because I'm pretty sure all women here have some version of this dilemma. I will now read the question as she wrote it.

"I have been a Buddhist practitioner for more than twenty-five years. I have been married to my husband this whole time, and we have two young men as children. Throughout these twenty-five years, I have gotten up before the rest of my family and found a little corner to sit and practice every day. This practice feels like a monumental accomplishment all by itself. Over the years, my husband has asked a few questions here and there about what I do and why, but he has never shown any interest in Buddhism or meditation, which has been fine for both of us.

"Last year, one of his friends at work got his second promotion in three years. This second promotion was a job my husband had worked hard for and firmly believed he would be offered the position; he was left resentful about being passed over. A few months later, he invited his friend out for lunch. During lunch, he asked what had changed in his life, and he said he had had two significant promotions in three years. His friend answered that he had started meditation, and not only has it improved his professional success, but it has also improved his relationship with his wife and children and his mental and physical health. My husband was surprised and asked his friend more about his meditation practice. My husband then started practicing the form of mindfulness-based meditation that his friend showed him. He became a daily practitioner as well. Many areas of his life have improved since meditating. I've been incredibly grateful to witness and experience all of this, especially in our relationship and his relationship with our kids. A couple of months ago, he started mentioning that he would like to spend three, if not six months, alone in a cabin in the woods to practice meditation and make a full-on solo retreat. There is a part of me that is incredibly excited for him that meditation has become such an essential aspect of his life. I am also resentful and bitter that I've been doing this for twenty-five years and getting up before everybody else in the family so I could meet all of

     Raised by Wolves, Possibly Monsters

their needs without interfering because I was practicing meditation. My question to you: Your Holiness, should I support him in doing a solo retreat in the woods or tell him that he needs to practice at home like me?"

The Dalai Lama looked up, smiled, and laughed. "I don't know who you are, so please don't identify yourself because I think many women here relate to your experience. Here is my advice for you. When you get home tonight, ask your husband to cook, clean, and wash the dishes from dinner. To help your sons with whatever they need help with. Take out the garbage and ensure the kitchen is clean and ready for the morning. When he's done with all of that, to rub your feet and run a bath for you, when you get out of the bath, he needs to tell you and show you how much he loves you and how grateful he is that you have practiced meditation for the last twenty-five years, and supported him, the family, and the community. And if it feels right, tell him to make love to you tonight before you go to bed. And for him to get up in the morning and make breakfast for the kids and you."

He paused and looked up from the card and his thoughts. "This is 1999, and it's about to become a new millennium. At this time in history, we are needed in the world. Monks and nuns can spend their time in monasteries, but for the rest of us, our work here is in the world, our communities, and our families! I'm on a different path that was chosen for me before birth. For most people, you need to do your work in the world!"

I tear up every single time I recall that moment in the retreat. I am choked up right now while writing about it. Whenever I think about the answer to that question, it reminds me of who I am and who we are. Our work is here in the world. I often get lost in thinking that I am "special." For me, it's bullshit! I am not any more special than anybody else. We are all unique and needed, and we count! Every single one of us is needed, and everyone counts!

A Silent Retreat for "A Couple of Days"

 WHEN I LEFT Bloomington in 2001 to study with Betsy in Florida, I was scared, excited, and awake. I knew I wanted to learn how to keep Reiki at the center of my life, but I also knew I needed support to accomplish this. I brought the same Rand McNally map that my mother and nephew Carlo used to track my journey cross-country just a handful of years before.

I got lost a few times, all of which cost me a few hours here or a few hours there. I drew some attention along the way. People did not expect to see a guy riding down local roads in a Suzuki Samurai with a U-Haul trailer on the back. When I entered Florida, there was an adrenaline rush. Then I remembered how big Florida was, and I was far from my final destination.

It was great to see everybody and to be near the saltwater, sand, and beaches again. It was evident by the second day after I returned the U-Haul trailer and stashed all of my stuff in their garage that I was in a headspace that didn't lend itself well to being with three generations of the family, including two young children. I found a converted double-wide that a previous owner had built an addition onto. One side of the structure was double-wide, and the other was built directly on the ground. It was small and simple, and it felt perfect for me to spend my mornings in meditation and practicing Reiki and my afternoons practicing beach volleyball and swimming.

After I moved all of my stuff to this peculiar tiny home, Betsy and I scheduled to meet up a few days later at a picnic table by the beach in Clearwater. I rode my bike to meet Betsy, and there was a nervous anticipation in my belly.

"How's it going over there?"

"So far so good. None of the neighbors bother me or pay much attention to me. But mostly, it's all good so far. Getting in some good volleyball on the beach during the afternoons!"

Betsy looked at me as if she was taking inventory. It looked like she was gazing up and down my body and scanning. She looked mildly concerned. "Michael, I'm pretty sure you didn't drive up all this way and pack your stuff to play volleyball. I sense it would be good for you to spend a few days in a silent retreat in your home. Pick up whatever groceries you need and lock yourself in

 Raised by Wolves, Possibly Monsters

for a few days. How does that feel to you?"

It felt like panic. I replaced the panic with resentment, bitterness, and disappointment. I thoroughly enjoyed meditation and Reiki in the morning, beach volleyball most of the day, and settling in and being quiet at night. I drove all this way, partially to play volleyball on the beach. I knew she was right, but the resistance was strong. Many of the decisions I made over the years with Betsy were born out of my need to do what I thought she would approve of; this was one of them.

"Yeah, that's what I need to do. I have rice and beans at home, and some vegetables for salad. I'll pick up some spinach and make sure I have eggs for breakfast." I never considered during that conversation that I would be diving into a three-day solo silent retreat.

Betsy was still looking at me seriously and inquisitively. I could tell by her expression that something didn't feel right, and she was trying to figure out what it was. "Let's meet at the cafe at the organic market at the same time four days from today." Betsy smiled and stood up, "Looking forward to hearing how this experience goes for you!" She did a slight bow of her head, I returned the same, and she walked away with her orange T-shirt and long blue denim skirt. Betsy often said that, when possible, you should dress in a way that doesn't draw attention when you are away from home. If everybody wears a T-shirt, wear a T-shirt.

I spent way too much time deliberating on how much spinach to buy, which brown rice would be best, whether I should have an extra bag of lentils, whether it was okay to pick up a dozen eggs, or whether I should go vegan. After I left Betsy, I noticed that it took me an hour and ten minutes to buy the equivalent of two grocery bags of food. As I pulled into the driveway of my temporary home, my heart started beating fast, my pulse fast, breath shallow and fast. My resistance to opening the car door was intense. I sat in the driver's seat for a few minutes, taking breaths with my eyes closed and my hands on my chest and belly, offering Reiki. A few minutes turned out to be forty minutes. I smirked at the fact that I had now spent almost two hours avoiding entering my home and beginning this silent retreat "for a few days."

When I made my way into the back door, I could feel my hand release the metal knob as the screen door slammed behind me. I was now alone in my home for the next seventy-two hours. I started putting my groceries away, and then I got an unmistakable message, "It's time to sit in the rocking chair and be still." The retreat started.

It was agonizing and hysterical observing how much I desperately needed to read the *USA Today* sports section, listen to music, and walk down to the beach to look at the stars and the moon. But I sat there. I was hungry even though I had just finished lunch, but I just sat there. Ice cream. All I could think about was ice cream, specifically coffee ice cream. I just sat there.

That afternoon, I got up once to urinate, fill up my water bottle, and bring it back to the living room to sit in that chair. I don't know if I did a lot of "meditation," but I sat there. I put my hands on my body and did a complete sitting Reiki treatment on myself. I did some breath counting, which calmed me down and even brought focus to my mind and thoughts. But mostly, I just sat there and obsessed about all the other things I wanted and "needed" to do. As the sun set, I yearned to go to the beach and stare at the water, the stars, and the moon in the distance. My mind's eye created that landscape, and I just "stared" at those elements without moving from the chair. I was beginning to get hungry for dinner. I checked with myself to see if it was okay for me to eat, but it wasn't. So, I sat there. I had brought a battery-powered red plastic wall clock and hearing the seconds tick away felt like punishment. As the evening wore on, it felt like the clicks were louder and louder. I noted that I would take the battery out of the clock whenever I got up again.

It was pitch black when I got up to make dinner. After eating, I put both bowls on the floor beside me and put my hands on my belly. I focused both on Reiki and my breath to the belly. Since my watch was in the bedroom, and I had taken down the wall clock when I made dinner, I had no idea how long it was, but about two hours. I went into the bedroom to get the composition book I bought the day before and started journaling what had happened so far: to sit in the chair, not do anything, and watch my thoughts wander and call them back. Breathe to the belly. Put your hands on the body. Close your eyes, but don't fall asleep. Stay in the chair. Keep breathing . . . And that was the first half day of my first solo silent retreat.

     Raised by Wolves, Possibly Monsters

The next couple of days were very long. It seemed like an entire day had passed, and it was only 10:30 in the morning. I kept thinking of ways to game the system and have things that generally take just a few minutes to take hours. I scrambled eggs in the morning for twenty minutes because I had to make sure they were fried so there wouldn't be any white spots. Suddenly, it seemed essential to floss twice daily so I didn't build up any plaque. Then, there was a sense of urgency around washing off all the pencil messages on the walls from who knows for how long they were there. This process took a whole morning, and it could have worked better. I decided to go to the paint store and buy supplies to paint over all of this to clear the energy in the living room. Then I remembered that if I couldn't talk, how would I be able to communicate what I wanted to purchase and how much? And could I justify going into a store when I'm supposed to be in Retreat even though the purpose is to balance the energy in the room where I'm doing most of the meditation? That mental argument took much of post-lunch afternoon "meditation time." Eventually, each day, at some point, I just submitted. No more shenanigans. No more washing the walls. No more investing more time and energy ridding my scrambled eggs of whites.

I only remember a few specifics of those first few days outside of my commitment to being distracted and submitting. When it was time to meet with Betsy, a part of me was disappointed that I completed this retreat. I appreciated without noticing how simplicity felt supportive and, well, simple. Just sit in a chair and close your eyes. If you feel like doing Reiki while sitting in the chair with your eyes closed, invite Reiki and put your hands where they need to be on your body. If you feel like you're supposed to do your meditation lying down so you can do an entire Reiki session slowly, lie down on the Reiki table or your bed. If you're thirsty, drink water. It seemed important not to drink anything with sugar, even fruit juices that were 100% fruit juice. I wanted to regulate my energy from peaking and crashing.

When I found her seated with a small piece of scrap paper and a pencil, she had a big smile. "I'm anxious to hear about your retreat!"

It felt good to experience Betsy's passion and enthusiasm for my work.

"I don't know how to describe it. Somehow, in three days, I went from deep despair to inner peace to deeper despair, total peace, to complete acceptance and lots of adolescent resistance that sometimes felt like actual defiance!"

Betsy smiled and chuckled. "Sounds like a solo retreat to me! Do you have a sense of what you need to do next?"

I had not considered something called "next." There was only making it through the moments, sometimes less than moments. It felt like boot camp for life using the principles of one day at a time or one moment at a time that I learned in AA and NA. I sat for a minute and paused. I asked my Higher Self to be present and guide me through the Divine Love and Wisdom of Usui Reiki. Much to my surprise, I blurted out in a very neutral voice and affect, "I don't think I am finished with the retreat yet."

"I'm so glad to hear you say that, Michael. I sensed you weren't done, but I didn't want to push something on you. It was a pretty big deal for you to agree to this as it is. Do you have a sense of how much longer you need to be in retreat?"

"No. But to dive into this and do some work, I need to paint the inside of this house. It feels like painting the walls is part of my process. Between painting and retreat, I need another week before we meet again. Does that feel okay?"

"That sounds about right! Do you know what colors you have to paint the walls?"

"I do! A combination of what Tibetan Monks wear on their robes. The walls will be burgundy red, and the ceilings are in yellow gold. It will look weird, but it feels like what I'm supposed to do here." I felt so strong, clear, and focused.

Betsy nodded her head, affirming my plan. My teacher was giving me that look that she gives when she's taking stock and assessing. She stopped nodding and considering. "I have not seen you this way before, Michael. I feel good about the work you're doing and going to do on this retreat. You're going to need to take some notes for reference in the future. It's also possible that it may be helpful to other people at some point." Without discussing it, we both settled into a silent meditation with direct eye contact right there amongst the hustle and bustle of the Organic Market Cafe.

One hour later, I was back at the mobile home carrying cans of paint, paint brushes, rolling pins, drop cloth, and sandpaper. While painting, the brush-strokes became my meditation. As the day wore on and I knew I was nearly done with the hallway, I started on one of the walls in the living room before dark. I

         Raised by Wolves, Possibly Monsters

cleaned the area, sealed the paint cans, and cleaned the brushes and rollers. I enjoyed the experience and felt incredibly present with the paintbrush and paint. I felt like Ralph Macchio in *The Karate Kid* with Mr. Miyagi shouting, "Wax on, Wax off, Paint the Fence, Side to Side."

I had a simple dinner of quinoa and spinach salad. I sat in the rocking chair, waiting for instructions. It took a little time. I was sitting there for less than twenty minutes when my body just stood up without me thinking about it. I went into the bedroom. Next to the bed, on the night table, was a little blue wooden box with my rosary beads inside.

I returned to the living room and was about to sit in the chair. I picked up the chair and moved it next to the Reiki table. I kneeled on the floor in the center of the room and started reciting the rosary. It was 10:47 at night when I stopped. I had been kneeling and reciting the rosary for approximately three hours. I would have sworn on a Bible, a Torah, or any other sacred texts that I had been practicing the rosary for about thirty minutes.

This list is how the next series of days went.

Lie in bed and complete an entire Reiki session with meditation.
Oatmeal for breakfast.
Sitting meditation in the rocking chair with distance Reiki.
Walk around the block several times in walking meditation.
Simple lunch.
Paint, paint, paint. Pay attention to every stroke and movement.
Evening walk or sit on the stoop as the sun sets.

I practiced the rosary at night. It became an incredible experience. I felt present, connected, and grounded—such a simple practice.

After the rosary, I would sit in the rocking chair and write. I took detailed notes on my process, experience, and the downloaded Teachings.

Each day became longer. I woke up in the dark between 4:30 and 5:30 and would go to bed between 11:00 and 12:00. Every bone in my body was stiff, but it didn't matter.

I did end up painting the bedroom. That night, I slept on the living room floor so as not to breathe in too many paint fumes. I had so much fun painting the ceiling bright gold. It felt like I was painting sunshine into this gross and yucky home.

I felt anxious the morning I met Betsy for lunch, knowing I was not done. A week and three days were the beginning. I had received guidance that I was to stay in the house for the next two weeks after seeing Betsy and getting groceries. I was scared and not convinced I would tell Betsy what the lineage directed me to do.

There she was, sitting at the same table, in the same seat, wearing the same light turquoise skirt and a tangerine-colored T-shirt. She looked earnest. When I sat down, she intently wrote notes on an index card. She looked at me, acknowledged I was there, and returned to her writing. I couldn't see what she was writing, but I could see that she was making a list of some sort. When she looked up, she said, "How are you doing?"

I started laughing. "I have no idea how to talk about what's happened. I know I painted the walls and the ceilings, and the space has been transformed. I know I've had long, intense, powerful days and nights. And I know that I'm not done."

"Too bad you don't have a camera. I want photographs of what you painted. You are creating a prototype for cleansing and rebalancing meditation and retreat spaces. And no, you're not close to done. You're just getting started." Betsy twice made eye contact with me. We again looked into each other's eyes, sitting there quietly. I felt like we were having a full-length conversation in silence. She would break eye contact every few minutes and put a line through something on her list. When completed, we both nodded in a simple bow to acknowledge the moment.

Betsy asked me what I had been working on and what I had learned. I spoke for ten minutes straight without stopping. My voice had no affect or intonation, just smooth, steady, and focused. Betsy would cross off another item on her list every minute or so. When she crossed off the last item on her list, she spoke. "Good work, Michael. You covered everything on the list this week. When do you want to meet again?"

"I don't think we need to meet next week. Let's meet the following week at the same time."

			Raised by Wolves, Possibly Monsters

"Okay. Make sure you have enough food, so you don't have to go back out. Keep up the good work!" She stood up and offered a simple bow. I nodded in response, and then she left. I gathered what I needed from the store with more thought and intention since I would be away for two weeks.

We met every two weeks for the next couple of months. Every time Betsy came with a list on an index card, she would fill out the index card as I arrived. We would sit silently, and then I would share what I had learned and worked on during the previous two weeks. We would talk till Betsy crossed off everything on the list. I came to understand that Betsy was keeping track of all the Teachings that were transmitted between our meetings to make sure I was receiving all the Teachings.

I was two months into my retreat of "a few days." Betsy and I went through our standard procedure of silent conversation, and then I spoke about my work and teachings. When I stopped, Betsy looked disturbed, possibly distraught. Her eyes were darting back and forth with what appeared to be desperation. She was waiting for me to continue. Even though it didn't feel like it was any of my business or that I had permission, I glanced over at the index card and saw two lines scribbled without a strikethrough. I understood what she was responding to. I had missed two Teachings!

She stared at me intently, her eyes seeing right in and through me. Betsy seemed genuinely concerned when I didn't speak: "What happened, Michael? You did not receive two Teachings this week, and I'm concerned. Has there been a breach in the conduit between us? Have you not been doing your work? Have you been staying connected to the Reiki lineage? What happened?"

If you were walking by, you would have thought that this woman might have been my mother, and she would have been extremely angry with me. Betsy was not angry with me at all. She was deeply concerned that one or both of us had been compromised. We spent a few moments checking in with ourselves, each other, and our connection.

About five minutes later, Betsy's gaze softened. "You look connected again. What a relief. I was concerned, Michael. We can't let this happen again! We will probably only get one opportunity in this lifetime to do this work the way we are doing it. We can't be careless or casual about it. We both need to be one hundred percent in this for it to be effective and successful. Too many other energies do not want this work to happen. What we are doing is incredibly important. I know you know this, but I'm speaking to the part of you missing beach volleyball, flirting with pretty girls on the beach, and swimming in the ocean. We need to stay vigilant and focused! The consequences of not doing so might be irreversible. We must continue to be present and pay attention no matter what! Do you hear me?" Her voice trailed off as if it was a question, but it wasn't a question but a demand and an expectation. I nodded my head yes. She thanked me for my commitment and my relentlessness. Betsy got up and gave me a simple bow. "I'll see you in two weeks." And she was gone.

I wasn't ready to leave yet. I wanted to soak in the force of the message we had received and the importance of our commitment. I had a very simple conversation internally with myself around volleyballs, bikinis, waves, and naps on the beach. The message was clear: I should do what I must do right now, and there will be time for all of these things later. I was fighting back my tears because we were in a public place. There was an element of shame in what I was experiencing about being distracted the last couple of days before meeting with Betsy, but the predominant feeling was–Holy shit! Without paying attention, I almost fucked this whole thing up!

I felt ready to take on the world one breath at a time when I got up.

My experience, both of myself and other men who have devoted a significant amount of time and energy to doing inner spiritual work, is that along the way, many of us forget that all of this is about love and connection. We focus on details like how long we meditate, how many days we meditate, what teachings we receive, how present we are while driving and walking, how "detached" we are from the chaos of human existence, etc. We forget this is to become more loving, compassionate, empathetic, and connected. It's about being connected to ourselves, the Earth, all the humans, and other living species on this planet, and being open-hearted and willing to be firmly immersed in the world's mess.

For many years, I measured my spiritual development and growth by how many hours a day I invested in spiritual practices like meditation, Tai Chi, Qi Gong, Yoga, and other practices. Today, I understand that some of this work was a spiritual bypass. I had found a new system after choosing to be abstinent from

     Raised by Wolves, Possibly Monsters

alcohol and drugs. Meditation and Reiki were terrific and helped me grow and develop in ways I could not imagine. They also became a way to avoid unwanted emotions, thoughts, and feelings. If I was angry, I could practice Reiki on myself. If I was sad, I could practice Tai Chi or Qigong. If I was scared, I could practice sitting or walking meditation. If somebody wanted to engage me in conflict, I could breathe into my belly and get present in my feet so I could detach. In this context, detachment was a combination of numbness and separation, without allowing myself to experience the pain and suffering of life and, more importantly, the joy and connection! Being in the mess is part of it.

To look at this from another lens, Betsy used to say regularly, "It is necessary to learn how to be comfortable with being uncomfortable." I recognize how this sounds but I became very uncomfortable when Betsy spoke or wrote those words.

A bypass is a systematic way of avoiding the process of becoming comfortable with discomfort. Having some peace while experiencing uncomfortable feelings, thoughts, or emotions can help our nervous system regulate and know that we are present and can handle the situation or feelings. We want to train ourselves not to feel the need to hide or mask our feelings but to create opportunities to be with them. Our spiritual practices, as extraordinary and essential as they are, can be spiritual bypasses. My experiences, personally and professionally, have demonstrated that this is more common among men than women.

As I moved deeper and deeper into this solo retreat, it was becoming harder and harder to avoid and hide from feelings, thoughts, and emotions that I did not want to experience. Don't go in the water if you don't want to get wet. Don't commit to a long, silent retreat if you don't want to know your thoughts and feelings.

I Am Relentless

ONE OF THE things I learned about myself during those months was that I am a powerful, courageous person committed to growing and learning. Like the ocean, I am relentless! Wave after wave of joy, happiness, and peace, followed by waves of sadness, pain, and fear. There is high tide, low tide, and no tide. The waters of my mind, body, and soul would become choppy, calm, uneven, and unexpected. But more than anything else, I am relentless. My relentlessness is expressed typically through creativity, resourcefulness, and adaptability. All three of these characteristics were trauma responses to growing up in a home with an actual real-life sociopath. I needed to learn to be silent and invisible when that would create safety. I needed to be loud and the center of attention when providing protection. I needed to be funny and charismatic to feel safe and in control. I would be stiff and numb if none of the above worked. I have always felt comfortable being in charge, a worker bee, a go-between, the creator, the follower, the loner, and the connector, among other characteristics and parts, to survive and continue doing what I wanted to do however I wanted.

I now know that all of these characteristics were trauma responses. And I am still affected by my past, despite all that I have learned and experienced. I become incredibly uncomfortable when people talk about my resilient, creative, adaptable, and resourceful nature. I feel this way, not because it is untrue but because of the pain, suffering, and fear that created the need for me to be able to change and morph from minute to minute, depending on what I perceived would protect me. For the record, it is also why I became an addict and alcoholic. There is a built-in cost to be able to morph and adapt to anything and everything, even though these are admirable qualities.

It is very popular for people to talk about addiction as the opposite of either safety or abstinence.

If you have never read or seen the work of Johann Hari, I encourage you to do so. He is a Scottish writer and journalist. His first book, *Chasing the Scream: The First and Last Days of the War on Drugs*, has suggested the opposite of addiction is connection. That is my experience as well. People with addictions of all kinds are searching and longing for connection, connection to self, connection to others, and connection to the Earth. When we lose the ability to connect with ourselves and others, many of us find an addiction or obsession to connect to. Being connected to cocaine or mindless sex or feeling ugly is better than not being connected to anything.

Back to the Retreat.

When I opened my eyes, it was still dark out, and my large digital LED clock

Raised by Wolves, Possibly Monsters

said it was 4:47 a.m. I turned over and attempted to return to sleep, but a little voice inside of me whispered, "Lie on your back and do your morning meditation right now while practicing Reiki." I groaned at the idea of starting back up again, knowing I hadn't fallen asleep until nearly 1 a.m. the night before, but I did it anyway.

I started with my hands on my head, breathing to the belly. I was using Breath Counting on this particular morning of meditation. One in, one out. Two in, two out. Three in, three out . . . Go to ten and then return to one and start again. Anytime you lose your way or get distracted, you begin again at one as if nothing happened. Fifteen minutes in, I noticed that the intensity and focus were more potent and clearer than usual. This brought a smile to my face. Then, I needed to remember where I was, return to one, and start a new set of ten breaths again.

In what felt like an hour or possibly even two hours later, both hands were on my belly, and I felt present and centered in my Second Energetic Center, which most people call the Belly Chakra. Without giving me much thought, my right hand moved to the center of my chest to work on my fourth center, which most people call the Heart Chakra. I remember being in this position for quite a while. I felt safe, comfortable, and at peace for quite a long time. Now and then, my eyes would open slightly to let in some light. I noticed a spider with a small web directly above the bed in contrast to the golden yellow ceiling. Since I didn't have my glasses on, I wanted to watch the spider to see if it moved. Watching the spider became a new meditation where my gaze was. I stayed with the spider for quite a while. As it became lighter, I realized it wasn't a spider. It looked more like a palmetto bug stuck in the wet paint while drying!

I decided to move back to paying attention to where my hands were on my belly and the center of my chest. My left hand moved down to my first center, which most people would call the Root Chakra or the Base Chakra, and my right hand stayed in the center of my chest. I soon felt solid, secure, and rooted. I recall feeling energized and more like an oak tree than a human. Eventually, I moved my right leg into a figure four to work on my hips, thighs, knees, calves, ankles, and feet. I then did the same thing with my left leg and foot. I did a quick scan with my hand over my body to see if anything else needed attention. The meditation and treatment felt complete. I glanced over at my red LED clock before I put my feet on the floor, and the clock said 10:13. I had been lying on my back practicing meditation and Reiki for over five hours.

I was overwhelmed with the thought that a human being could meditate mostly in the same position without a water or bathroom break for more than five hours. I felt disoriented and shaky when I put my feet on the floor. I became wonkier when I realized that I was that human being. I sat there for a minute or two on the side of the bed, looking at the crimson-red walls before standing. It felt like something significant had just happened, and before going to the bathroom and "starting my day," I wanted to take in the moment. I had the urge to get out my journal in the little cubby hole on the right-hand side of the headboard, but now that I had moved my body, I really, really, really had to pee. I noted that I would go to the bathroom, brush my teeth, wash my face, and then take notes. I wrote thirteen pages with my blue Bic pen. The ugly battery-operated red plastic clock I had taken off the wall several months before said I was taking notes for an hour and twenty minutes. Writing that much in an hour and twenty minutes was impossible. I wanted to sit in the rocker and meditate before making tea or anything to eat.

Of the four or five months I was in retreat, this was the day I intended to leave as a reference point to look back at what took place. Except for eating for about an hour and a half and writing in the morning and at night, I spent the entire day inside, alternating between sitting and lying down in meditation. I did about fifteen hours of meditation that day. The number itself is mind-boggling; what is more critical for me when I reference that day in my mind is that a mind, in this case, mine, is capable of paying attention, being present, and still for that long.

Since I did not know I would be doing any solo retreat, no less an extended one, there was not a lot of tension, expectations, or anxiety about this under-taking. Three days became ten days, which became three weeks, which became a month, which became three months, which became somewhere between four and five months. All I know is that it was one season when I started the retreat and a different season when I ended it. Somewhere during that retreat, the state of Florida had its first "freeze" in something like sixty years. I saw people outside during the day in snorkel jackets in the upper 40s. I was in a long-sleeved shirt because that's what my body was comfortable with.

          Raised by Wolves, Possibly Monsters

The Retreat ended as unceremoniously as it started. Charles knocked on my door, and when I opened it, his face looked pale. "Hi, Michael. I know I'm not supposed to come here, and you're not supposed to talk, but I want to let you know that three days from now, there will be a hurricane here, and everybody in your town must evacuate. We all talked about it and decided that you should come and stay with us. If you want, you can stay in a room by yourself and continue your retreat, but we're all afraid that since you're so close to the water and in this double-wide with a house glued onto the side of it, you are not safe."

I asked Charles a couple of questions about the hurricane. He provided many precise details and spoke without much anxiety or drama.

I quickly checked in with my body and Reiki, "Okay. That makes sense. Is Friday morning okay?" I hesitated, then laughed. "Wait. What day of the week is it?"

"Today is Tuesday. Yes, that would be great. There's one other thing I need to share with you. I'm leaving tonight for my job in the UK for two weeks. I tried to tell them I wanted to be home with my family because of a hurricane, but they would not let me change my travel plans. I would feel so much better knowing you were there with them. Karla, Betsy, and the kids are pretty freaked out. I think you being there would be a calming presence for them. And thank you for this. It means a lot to me, Michael." I extended my arms, and Charles and I hugged. It was the first human contact I had had in nearly five months.

On Friday morning, I packed up the most important things to me. I put my bike on the back, and before getting in the car, I stood underneath the carport and took a minute to thank the home, the space, and the time we had together. I bowed when I was sure nobody was walking by, and then I got in the vehicle and left. Since I was not supposed to arrive for a few hours, I rode by Clearwater Beach and parked the car. The beach and the ocean looked incredibly ominous, like something from a Stephen King movie. Dark clouds, dark sky, dark air, dark water, everything looked dark, and it was only 9:00 a.m. A chill moved through my body. I now had a sense of what might happen. I internally connected with Reiki, invited Reiki to expand beyond my mental limitations, and sat with Reiki flowing out to me, the ocean, the town of Clearwater, the city of Largo, and the neighboring communities. It felt clear, clean, and sad to turn the ignition on the car to leave; I felt solid and ready.

I arrived at their home twenty minutes later, and everybody jumped all over me with hugs and kisses and hellos and more hugs and more kisses. Alia brought me a dish of blueberry and corn muffins that her mother made that morning, especially for me. I had not had any refined sugar products since Christmas. I initially was going to say no, but it had an instinct in my body that I was here, with the family, during a natural event with the possibility of death and danger, and it seemed essential for me to be with them. However, they were doing whatever they were doing. And that meant sugar, cable TV, watching movies, eating junk food, playing in the backyard, swimming in the pool, wrestling with the kids, picking vegetables from the garden, and loving everybody. I enjoyed one of each of the muffins.

We all have different moments in our lives that when we look back, we can point to a few of them and say, these were when I was special, possibly spectacular or extraordinary. The next forty-eight hours was one of those times. I have no knowledge or understanding of how easy it was for me to shift from one world to another, but I did. I brought joy, fun, and playfulness to a home that was scared, nervous, and struggling with what could go wrong. I remember afterward when I was leaving and packing up my Suzuki again, Betsy walked out after me and thanked me for being "The Pied Piper" that everybody needed. The hurricane was not awful. It did some damage, but not tons of it. We ended up not getting the worst of it. Other parts of Florida, Mississippi, and Louisiana had much worse damage.

I returned to my little mini-retreat center, ready to dive back in. It was not meant to be. I had completed my retreat. Done. Finished.

I took a day to ensure that I was clear and that no shadow part of me or my resistance was manipulating me and my thoughts. The following day, I was clear that I was done. And it was clear that I wasn't going anywhere. After several months in a solo silent Retreat and several days with extended family during a hurricane with small children, I had to take a few weeks to play on the beach!

My days consisted of several hours of meditation in the morning, journaling and taking notes, eating lunch, and then riding my bike to Clearwater Beach and playing volleyball for several hours on the beach. Four weeks later, I was ready to

          Raised by Wolves, Possibly Monsters

move out. I called my landlord on a pay phone and told them when I was leaving. I left it in better shape than when I arrived and painted the walls and ceilings with peculiar colors. I packed everything into my car, rented another U-Haul trailer, and stuffed it like the last one. I wondered if this was the same damn U-Haul trailer I had gotten here with. I drove to spend a day and a night with Betsy, Charles, Karla, and the family before heading north towards New Jersey.

My mother had gone through a tough time without being in contact with me and knowing if I was okay. I also wanted to see her and my nephews. When I hugged everybody goodbye, Betsy walked me out to my vehicle again. I don't remember what she said or even if she said anything. What I experienced in her facial expressions and energy was an abundance of love, gratitude, and respect she had for me and what I/we had just completed.

The Sopranos

AS I LEFT the Gulf side of Florida, I intended to go east and drive up the Atlantic Coast. After a half year on the Gulf Coast, getting my feet and body in the Atlantic sounded lovely. I took Route 4 through Orlando, just for kicks, since I had not been there since I was in my teens smoking hash before going on the rides. Merritt Island seemed like a nice place to spend a day, so I stayed there for the night.

I returned to my car after the sun went down the next day. I drove on Route 1 for a bit, then got on I-95 North, destination New Jersey/New York!

I had been on the road for just a few hours when I saw a guy with his thumb out on I-95 North. He looked like an utter and complete mess; therefore, I picked him up.

I was correct. Kevin was a complete mess at the low point of his life. It's no surprise that he just got out of a few days in jail and was detoxing from cocaine. You could see in his skin how fiercely his body was trying to excrete toxins with welts and lumps up and down his arms and legs. He smelled grosser than he looked. He told me that he had been wearing the same clothes for about five days, if not longer, and twice had shitted in them while high. I made a mental note that

I had a carload of my clothes. Giving him clean clothes and stopping at a rest stop for him to clean himself in the bathroom would be a gift to me, not him.

Before we hit a rest area to stop, I sensed he needed an opportunity to share uninterrupted. He talked nonstop with little bouts of crying from just north of Daytona to Savannah, Georgia. I pulled off at the rest stop, grabbed a couple of sandwiches, and handed him some clean shorts, underwear, a T-shirt, and a bar of soap. We met back at my Suzuki about twenty minutes later. We ate our sandwiches and potato chips on I-95.

While listening to Kevin share earlier, he said he wanted to go to Elkins, Maryland, where his family lived. He hadn't seen or spoken to them in thirteen years. He said he was ready to visit and get clean and sober. Every part of me was on board with supporting this process. For the rest of our drive at night to Elkins, I supported and encouraged his decisions. When we got to the exit near Elkins, he started freaking out. We pulled off the road and did some breathing together. When he was calm enough for us to speak, I asked him where he wanted to go. He said he was not ready to be brought to his parent's house but would like to get near to walk there. He wanted to smoke a couple of cigarettes and regroup before seeing them. I was suspicious about his ability to pull it off as planned, but he planned to make it. When I dropped him off, he started crying again in gratitude for the ride, support, and clothing. He asked me for a hug, and he cried in my arms for several minutes until we said our goodbyes. As he walked away, I invited Reiki to surround him with love and protection.

I was exhausted and found the first place near the water to get some rest. I called my mom from the dingy hotel and told her I was coming her way. She was excited and thrilled. I was too. I was also concerned about what it would be like trying to interact with her, my nephews, my sister-in-law, cousins, and friends after being in retreat. It seemed prudent to keep my conversation simple and basic.

I saw the iconic New Jersey Turnpike signs and felt the memories—Atlantic City, Wildwood, Glassboro, Trenton, Philadelphia, and my favorite, "Jersey Beaches." I stayed on course. I wanted to make it to my mom's before hitting heavy traffic on the Turnpike, as tempting as the Jersey Shore was and still is. Many of my adolescent memories occurred on the Jersey Shore. None of them

          Raised by Wolves, Possibly Monsters

resembled the TV show. The Jersey Shore was where I first experienced being attracted to and interacting with girls who were not living near me. I sometimes feel my hormones wake up on sand beaches, especially in New Jersey.

Being with my mom and staying on her couch for several days was enjoyable. It was nice seeing all of my family. Even before I went on retreat, our life experiences were much different. They asked simple questions, and I gave simple answers that met our needs. My two nephews went a little deeper, and I responded accordingly.

I called my friend Marissa, who was still living in Manhattan. She could not contain her excitement about hearing from me, and she wanted me to come into the city to meet her boyfriend and watch a TV show with me.

"A TV show? I don't watch too much TV these days."

"No. Michael, you have to see this. I could tell you about it, but you will need more than that. You just have to trust me. If you can get into the city, Yuri and I will take you out to dinner wherever you want to go and whatever you want to eat if you return to my apartment to watch this show together. He's excited to meet you as well."

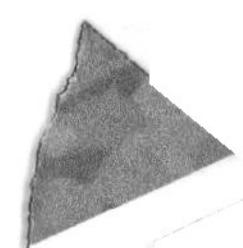

Regardless of her request and the necessary effort, I rarely said no to Marissa. This time was no exception. We made plans the following night for me to meet them in the city. We went to Marissa's favorite diner near her apartment on the Upper East Side. When I finished my bagel, Marissa asked what I wanted for dessert; we would take it to her place and watch TV. Part of me was annoyed that we would stop our conversation and watch TV. Yuri and I were getting to know each other. I enjoyed talking about my retreat with somebody who lived in the regular world but was genuinely interested in hearing about my experiences. The other part of me thought it was hysterical that I was coming into the city to watch TV with her and her boyfriend.

While walking to her place, they told me about the new show they wanted me to watch: *The Sopranos* on HBO. Marissa was convinced the show was based on the crime family I used to belong to. I was skeptical.

We enjoyed ice cream, apple pie, popcorn, and *The Sopranos*. I sat up straight when they got to the scenes about the recording studio the mob characters bought and used as a front. All these fictional characters and conversations were a replica of real-life characters and conversations that I witnessed or was a part of!

Watching experiences from my earlier life be made into a fictional story on HBO was bizarre! On the subway ride home, under the Hudson, to my mom's apartment, my mind was flooded with memories that now felt different. Before, these memories were saturated with shame, embarrassment, and deep, deep pain and sadness about who I was and what I did. I could see them as actions of a different person than I had become. I felt relief to no longer be that person and felt compassion for the young man I had been. A few years later, I tried to watch *The Sopranos* to see where the story went. It went in directions I knew nothing about that seemed purely fictional. I lost interest. Anytime somebody brings up *The Sopranos*, a belly laugh emerges.

Turtle Island Center

 AFTER SPENDING TIME with family and friends in the New York-New Jersey area, I headed west back to Bloomington, Indiana, without a plan, with the U-Haul trailer still on my Suzuki.

I stayed with a couple of people here and there and rented a room for a month or two while Indiana University students were out of town for the summer. I ended up living in a vegan, intentional community called Turtle Island Center on the outskirts of Hoosier National Forest. The community wasn't a perfect fit for me, but it seemed a simple and easy way to live near Bloomington, out in the country, with people who appeared to have a similar perspective on life.

I lived in a double-wide trailer on the edge of a small cliff called The Edge. I shared the space with a couple named Betty and Pete and a guy named Ralph, who was in his twenties. Ralph was a former competitive collegiate swimmer and a current hardcore Earth activist.

A young woman named Ellie Mae slept in a small backpacking tent.

The community's founders were Cecily and Bart, who had a young child, Mayan. Other community members, such as Beatrice and her adolescent daughter Madisyn, were active and part of the consensus decision-making process but did not live on the property.

Living down the street at Turtle Island Center was a bedridden man in his early eighties. His son Dallas was also a community member but not involved in decision-making most of the time.

I enjoyed being part of a community that shared meals, hugs, sweat, growing food, decision-making, caring for the land, and most importantly, love and support. We had a running joke that the biggest challenge for us as a community was childcare and dishes, just like most homes worldwide with young children.

Turtle Island Center was the first time in my life that I had the opportunity to experience being naked with people, whether it be swimming, walking, dancing, or eating, where nudity was not a sexual experience, at least not intended to be.

It was also my first experience with group consensus decision-making. On Thursday nights, we would enjoy a meal together and then have a sharing circle that included small, medium, or large decisions that needed attention. It was a slow, deliberate, respectful, and valuable process. I was getting my first taste of how much space and energy my voice and presence can take up in small groups, and I was helped by not being able to do so in this group's process.

Another aspect of this community that was very helpful for me was my new practice of not being in the center of the group. I liked sitting on the side or even in the back. I enjoyed being able to choose to practice being still and quiet when conflict or chaos appeared in the community, and I would offer Reiki to the group.

One of the community members found out that Haines Foods, a supplier of organic and healthy food products, had a factory in the area. It turned out that every day, they would fill their dumpsters with outstanding cases and bags of grains, legumes, pasta, crackers, and other dry goods. We would go dumpster diving these items and soon became a food bank for people in the area to get food for free. It felt beautiful to share food with people in need.

Some of those groups of folks "in need" were a family of raccoons! They used to rip open the screens of the double-wide, climb in, and attack the sixty and eighty-pound bags of grains and legumes. It was frustrating to wake up and see food all over the floor. We kept changing the thickness and even used galvanized steel screens, but none worked. We finally landed at sealing the windows under the part of the house that was accessible and closed at night. Before we got that far, I awoke and stumbled into the kitchen one night. I turned the light on in the hallway, and five raccoons were looking at me, their faces full of oatmeal, rice, quinoa, and crackers. It was hysterical and bizarre and even a little bit scary.

It was challenging at times living in a vegan community. The challenge was not eating a plant-based diet. That was not hard for me. The zealots were the problem for me. Those folks who saw life through one lens: if you kill and/or eat an animal or anything that comes from an animal, you are evil and terrible.

I am typically skeptical when groups are entirely convinced they are right. For many years, it has been my opinion that although they are typically at opposite ends of the political spectrum, vegans and pro-lifers are mirrors of each other. They both seem convinced there is no other opinion than their own and since we are dealing with keeping something alive or not killing it, they don't have to do anything. They don't have to raise anything. They don't have to save anything. They don't have to care for anything. They don't have to spend any money on anything. They don't have to give any time to anything. All they have to do is be angry, protest, and be one hundred percent convinced they are entirely correct and there is no other story but their own. I had one particular experience that has stayed with me.

One night, we were at one of our community meals. I was conversing with a young woman who would come to many of our community dinners. She was one of several people sarcastically labeled as "Freegans," people who were vegan and went anywhere they could get free meals that other people had to buy, grow, prepare, and serve without offering their time, energy, or financial support. This particular Freegan named Kara spent time with several young men in our community. She would meet them at one of our community meals, they would hang out, and she would go home with them, which was often one hundred yards away, in a tent and would stay with him for the next month or two; they would be a couple, they would break up, and then she would start the cycle again with another guy. She had that clueless hippie chick who smoked weed too often vibe. Kara wore the stoned hippie chick uniform of a cotton skirt of paisley or Indian-style patterns with a tank top or a T-shirt. At times, it felt like all these young

 Raised by Wolves, Possibly Monsters

women went to some training to ensure they all wore the same uniform.

Kara had asked me about my ten days with the Dalai Lama. She followed up with several interesting and thoughtful questions, listened, nodded her head, and was fully engaged. Our conversation lasted about twenty minutes when Kara asked me a question that still swirls around in my head, not because it was intriguing, but because it was not.

"I have a question for you, Michael. Like, how can the Dalai Lama be like spiritual or deep or like have any wisdom, if he eats meat?"

I heard her clearly, but my mind wouldn't accept it. I asked her to repeat herself, and she repeated the same thing, this time with more force and attitude. I replied, "Well, you know he's Tibetan and came from Tibet. Because of their environment, they're unable to grow many vegetables and fruit."

Before she replied, she gave me that expression, "How could you be so stupid not to understand this?" and had her palms facing up. "Yeah, but, like, he hasn't lived in Tibet in many years, and he still eats meat. So, like, he can't be very spiritual if he eats meat. And he's kind of a hypocrite. Like, Buddhists don't believe in killing any sentient beings, and he eats meat, so along with not being very spiritual, he's kind of like a hypocrite."

I started to launch into a monologue that morphed into a tirade and landed at a rant. I realized I was wasting my time and energy. Kara reminded me of the distinction between something a Rabbi once said about practicing Hebrew law. "Michael, it's important that we understand and practice the difference between The Spirit of the Law versus the Letter of The Law. Things are not black and white, nor do they apply to every person in every situation."

Teachings and principles can be lost when we become tangled in rules or dogma. The ego takes over when this happens.

The community founders had decided to go on a six-month sabbatical to Belize. Bart, Cecily, and Mayan were getting ready to leave, and they asked Ellie Mae if she would come with them to help with childcare while they were there. Ellie Mae agreed. The day before the four of them left, Ellie Mae and I had a conversation sitting on the ground next to the double-wide I was staying in. She was excited and energized about going and the opportunities. She also had concerns that they might need to respect her boundaries and time, and she might not get to experience the area, culture, and people.

I was about to answer, but Reiki took over. "I hear you, Ellie Mae, and understand your concern and fear. It's reasonable. I encourage you to be open to the possibility that the situation may change, and you may need to do your own journey. You may need to leave them and explore and discover independently. Please leave space to be guided to something different from what you agreed. You do not owe them anything!" Ellie Mae shed a tear or two, and her face got red. She leaned into me, and we hugged, sitting cross-legged on the ground.

"Thank you, Michael. That means a lot to me, and it feels true. Like you always say, I have to be present and pay attention. I will do that!"

The following day, we said goodbye to the four of them with lots of hugs and tears. I felt sadness that Ellie Mae would not be around. She was my closest friend in the community, even though she was twenty-one and I was thirty-nine.

After Bart and Cecily left, our community became more close-knit and egalitarian. I became a more substantial presence in the community; again, I never trusted them individually or as a couple. That distrust was subsequently proven to be correct. After one heartfelt and emotionally painful check-in after our Thursday night community meeting, Beatrice shared that three credit card companies and the FBI had contacted her, given that Bart and Cecily left her as the emergency contact person. She told us they owed well over a hundred thousand dollars and had purchased an extensive collection of guns.

Beatrice had the keys to the large trailer where they stored their stuff. It turns out that their "stuff" was $130,000 worth of gun purchases on credit cards that they had no intention of paying as a direct action against corporations and banks who funded the manufacturers. The purchased guns would be off the shelves and out of the hands of people who wanted to use them. No one would have access to them as long as they were in this storage trailer. They had also purchased a $30,000 tractor. Over the next few months, the FBI interviewed us all. During this time, we had no way to contact Bart or Cecily. They had left Belize for Honduras.

Besides being furious at them for their actions and being protective of my friends who were petrified of having the police, FBI, and investigators roaming around the property and asking questions, this reminded me of my experiences

     Raised by Wolves, Possibly Monsters

as a low-level mob guy and drug dealer dealing with the Secret Service years earlier. This time around, I was clean and sober. I felt scared, overwhelmed, powerless, and betrayed. A part of me felt vindicated for being distrustful of Bart and Cecily. This was the first situation since the retreat that left me profoundly angry. I did my best to channel the rage to protect my friends by directing blame to Bart and Cecily during interviews with special agents.

A few months later, the community collapsed.

As Betsy was facilitating a five-day retreat in New Jersey called The Healing Apprenticeship, I decided to go. I planned to show up with just my backpack since I had stored several other items in my friend Terry's garage. Betsy invited Ellie Mae to come. The retreat was going to start the first week of October 2001.

The Decade of Death

THE TERRORIST ATTACKS of September 11, 2001, hit New York and New Jersey hard, leaving few locals untouched by the tragedy. That energy of grief and loss infused the retreat and might have contributed to my strong vision there.

It came to me in one of our meditations that my mother was going to die in the next six months. Of course, this scared me. My mother had been battling cancer in various parts of her body on and off since 1972. I had spoken to her just a few days before Ellie Mae, and I got on a train to New Jersey. She was in good spirits and mostly feeling well, except for a cold. She had been to the oncologist she had worked with the month before and got a very clean prognosis. This message of her impending death caught me off-guard.

When our retreat was completed, I contacted my mother to see how she was doing, and she said her cold had gotten a little bit worse; maybe it was the flu. She would go to the doctor the next day for a checkup. My mother found out she had pneumonia. I encouraged her to contact her oncologist, Dr. Sanfilippo, even though she had recently seen her. She resisted, so I called Dr. Sanfilippo myself. I tried not to sound like some weirdo, but I'm unsure I accomplished that goal. However, I convinced her to call my mom and ask her to come in for more tests.

My mother went to see Dr. Sanfilippo, and they did see that the cancer had spread to her liver and metastasized. I hoped my vision in retreat was incorrect, but I was devastated when she called me back and gave me this information.

Between the pneumonia and cancer spreading, and she was now obese with diabetes, I asked Dr Sanfilippo not to push my mother to start chemo or radiation again. Let her live out her last few months as best she could. As someone who had been with my mother through so many ups and downs over the years, it was tough for her to let go of trying to save my mother one more time, but she agreed that was best.

My mother died on March 25, 2002. She was the last of eight family members to die in twelve years, which I call the Decade of Death. During those twelve years, my grandma, aunts and uncles, my father, my brother, and then my mother died. My mother was the last and the person I was closest to in my family. At the end of this period, there was not one living member of my family from the generation before me. What was left were three cousins, Carmen, Carla, and Charlie, their seven children, and my two nephews, Carlo and Anthony.

When my mother died, it felt like twelve years of people dying compacted into one large chunk of grief and loss. I was devastated. Several family members who passed before my mother did not create significant loss or grief inside me; sometimes, I felt relief. My father died while I was backpacking cross-country. I remember the Friday night that turned out to be when he died, although I didn't hear about it until a couple of weeks later, having a sharp pain in my belly and inability to walk or breathe well. My father was not in excellent health, but there was no expectation of him dying anytime in the next few years. I am grateful that before I headed west, we had an intimate conversation where he shared his regrets as a parent and took responsibility for some of the mistakes he made along the way. It brought us closer together. If we had not shared that conversation, I would have had resentment and bitterness for many years afterward. When my brother died, I felt a sense of relief and release. It was very challenging being his brother. I was alive during thirty-six of the forty years of his life, and pretty much at any given time, I had to endure legal, physical, social, mental, emotional, and energetic abuse, if not worse.

My mom was a whole different story. We were close and spoke weekly,

     Raised by Wolves, Possibly Monsters

except when I was backpacking across the country and during my silent retreat in Florida. She was a stabilizing force in my life, sans the first few years after my parents separated and divorced. I loved my mom very much and appreciated and respected the struggles and challenges she endured and fought through from birth to death. She instilled in me a deep appreciation for the healing power of quality meals, making mealtime peaceful and enjoyable, getting people together over food as a means of connection, and, more than anything else, putting love into food is a love language.

Even though my mom had minimal education, she wasn't brilliant and kept a pretty simple life of an Italian woman from her generation and social class; when it came to food, my mother was one of the most experimental and adventurous people I have known. There wasn't anything with food she wasn't willing to try to eat and create at home. It's funny for me to think that my little Italian mom from Newark, New Jersey, used to make tofu in the 60s, Chinese stir fry, Japanese dishes, Hungarian dishes, Vietnamese dishes, Mexican dishes, Spanish, and at her core, she made excellent Italian food that was both simple, delicious with piles of vegetables all over the table. I was eight when my mother started teaching me how to cook. By the time I was twelve, I could prepare whole meals. My mother felt it was essential for boys to know how to cook, clean, do laundry, buy clothes, and do all other household chores so they didn't grow up incapable of caring for themselves like my father. I am grateful that my mother raised me to have domestic skills, just like she would have done if she had daughters instead of sons.

Since going through the Decade of Death, I have not had the luxury of assuming that I, or any of the people I love, will be around tomorrow, the next day, next month, or next year. I certainly don't think about the fact that they may not be around; I don't assume it. I don't live in fear, anticipating death. I don't live in the assumption/illusion that we will be here beyond right now.

I have missed my family, specifically my mom, and wished more than once that we could have had more time together. What if she had lived another twenty years? We would have had twenty years more of conversations, hugs, meals, arguments, gossip, reminiscing, sharing, crying, and laughing. Twenty more years of me knowing her and she knowing me. And how much I have changed and grown in these twenty years. How much deeper and more fully I experience life and my emotions and feelings. What would it be like if my mom had passed just a few months ago, and we had done all of those things and more for another twenty years? It is a call to be present in our time with our beloved. Having this new perspective helps me have even more compassion for the deep sadness, loss, grief, and confusion people experience when someone they love dies.

Come to Wisconsin

A FEW MONTHS after my mother had died, I was on the phone with my dear friend Beatrice, one of the fantastic people from Turtle Island Center. She encouraged me to pack up my car, formerly my mother's, and come to Wisconsin. "Come stay in our living room. Madisyn and I will care for you so you can grieve with us before deciding what to do next." So, I did.

I left New Jersey four days later and headed for Madison, Wisconsin. I had never been to Wisconsin, and all I knew about it was that it was similar in size to Bloomington, Indiana, and it had a large university. The University of Wisconsin-Madison has approximately 36,000 students. Paying to have my mother cremated, tending to her finances, and cleaning out her apartment had cleared out the little bit of money I still had. I wasn't sure I had enough money to make it to Wisconsin. I did. The red light telling me I was low on gas glowed as I approached Madison. It was 2002, and I had no GPS or cell phone. I was still using the same Rand McNally map my mother and nephew Carlo had tracked my journey across the states almost a decade earlier.

Beatrice and Madisyn were thoughtful and kind to me. I did not know how much I needed to be loved and cared for. During the six months in New Jersey, I split my time between my dying mother and a circle of twelve-step meetings I became part of. I did not know how much I had been affected by being around people who all seemed to believe they knew the only way to get and stay sober was in AA. I was grateful for the distance moving to Wisconsin created from that community. I have never been to an AA meeting since.

Let me help you with the math. I had been an active member of the AA community for the first thirteen years of my recovery and have not for the last twenty-plus years since. The only time that I miss being part of the AA community is when I move to a new town, and I don't know anyone. One of the many remarkable aspects of a twelve-step program is you instantly have friends wherever you go. I have not missed all of the coffee and sugar and being in close contact with people who either smoke a cigarette or still smell like a cigarette. I have not missed the somewhat cultish system of believing that AA and the twelve steps are the only "right way to get and stay sober." I have not missed people thinking I am something special because I live a healthy life. I have not missed being around people utterly consumed with their thoughts, emotions, and experiences. Something about the AA culture supports a self-centered way of experiencing the world. I am grateful for my time in AA, literally none, I repeat none, of the gifts, friends, and life that I have today exist if not for the meetings, the twelve steps, and the people that loved me, supported, and kicked me in the ass when needed. I also wouldn't be who I am today if I did not decide to live my life without AA. As a counselor, I recommend people seeking recovery to AA regularly. My instinct is that it will help most people struggling with alcohol abuse and alcoholism. I am also aware that many people think AA is not what is best for them, and I will refer them to other programs and systems.

One morning, over breakfast about six weeks after landing in Beatrice's living room, I shared with Beatrice that I was considering staying in Madison. She supported that decision, and we discussed opportunities and situations that might benefit me. Later that day, she received a phone call from her landlord, who said the woman who had lived in the house next door was planning to move the following month. He wanted to know if she knew anybody that would be a good tenant. Five weeks later, I became Beatrice's neighbor.

Many things happened during my five years living in the house next door to Beatrice. One was staying in the neighborhood, and Madison, longer than Beatrice and Madisyn, who moved a few years later. Another was the opportunity to create a vast garden of fruits, vegetables, and herbs across the street. It was the first time since living in Turtle Island Center that I could apply several permaculture methods I had learned.

The second significant experience of my time in Madison was finishing my undergraduate studies and earning a bachelor's degree. I attended five colleges/universities, and it took three decades, but I did it.

The third and most significant event of my time in Madison was working for the Urban League of Greater Madison for five years, where, in spite of myself, I received intense training on institutional racism and white privilege. The staff at the Urban League was excellent, diverse, and relentless in their commitment to racial equality and education. What impressed me the most, on a personal level, was that every one of the staff members was patient and supportive of me despite my cluelessness and even more forceful and impactful in making sure that I did not continue to be that clueless!

Another Experiment

WHILE BECOMING MORE engaged with the community in Madison, I noticed that what I was experiencing in meditation and Reiki and what I was experiencing out in the world needed to be in sync. I was gaining awareness that both race and gender needed a systemic update. In meditation and Reiki, I was a thoughtful, kind, and supportive person who understood on a deep level that women need to be loved, seen, cared for, and respected for who they are, not solely how or what they are in connection with my needs and desires. I brought this up in meditation for guidance, and I was spiritually directed to choose to be celibate for a little while. I had an internal flinch around other times I was guided to do something "for a little while," and it never turned out to be "a little while." This time was no different.

I needed to make guidelines for what qualified as celibacy for my current needs: no flirting, kissing, physical intimacy, sex, or masturbation. It felt like a tall order, but it was necessary. I wanted my parts to match and feel closer to what my Higher Self needed me to be.

At first, it was super challenging, especially the no-flirting component. Flirting has always felt like part of my identity and a means of connecting and getting affirmation of my attractiveness and masculinity. Flirting was so embedded in my way of being in the world that I had to tie a mental string around

 Raised by Wolves, Possibly Monsters

my finger to remember. I brought this into my daily Distance Reiki practice and asked the Reiki Lineage to help me be aware of this pattern as it was expressing itself. I began to get turned on by every woman I saw, no matter where I went, what I was doing, or who she was! I felt like an adolescent boy again in an adult male body. It became comical how much of my days were flooded with desire and lust. This experience created a firm focus and intention to practice celibacy on a deeper level.

In reflecting over the years since this experiment, I know that suppression and spiritual bypassing had been part of my process. I didn't know yet how to allow myself to experience unwanted or uncomfortable emotions, thoughts, and feelings without needing to hide from them. My parts got louder and louder the longer I was committed to remaining celibate.

As I became more explicit and firmer about not flirting or engaging with women I was attracted to, ironically, they flirted with me more and more fiercely. I now qualified as unavailable, making me more desirable or attractive. The stronger and clearer I became, the more aggressively they pursued me. I wish I could tell you that this created empathy and understanding about what it is like to be a woman, but it didn't, at least not that I am aware of. I was too excited to keep my commitment to register. The primary teaching I received during the year and a half, or two years, of practicing celibacy is how much more women respected me. They saw me differently when they were not a target of my desire and objectification. This awareness was the next step in learning to be a friend and safe man to the women I interacted with, regardless of the environment or circumstances. They did not have to set and maintain boundaries with me.

The end of this experiment was the beginning of briefly dating a woman who had to do all the initiating because I was vacillating between dating her or staying celibate. She was not aware of any of this till we kissed. She laughed and enjoyed knowing I was interested in her enough to make this transition. After my experiment with celibacy, I felt more confident being around women I felt attracted to. I now understood that I could make choices and did not feel as controlled by my desires. I could choose to flirt or not flirt, kiss or not kiss, date or not date. My genitals were no longer the loudest voice in my internal conversations, which was such a relief.

A Free Reiki Clinic on a Saturday Afternoon

ONE OF MY favorite places in Madison was Willy Street Co-Op. It was a cooperatively run market large enough to do all your grocery shopping and still feel like your purchases support the local community. Sometimes, I would host Free Reiki Clinics in their Community Room. People would sign up at the customer service counter. I met with nearly a dozen folks that Saturday, but I will never forget one person in particular. She walked in without knocking or signing up, dressed to light up a stage and smelling like an issue of Cosmopolitan Magazine fresh off the newsstand. She entered as if we were all waiting for her. While I finished with my last clients, she explored the artwork on the walls. They walked out the door to the left, and I was now alone with her. Her looks and scent were intoxicating. I forgot what and where I was. There was just her and that energy that permeated her being. I felt electricity immediately but was committed to Reiki and her emotional safety.

"Hi. I am Allison. Sorry, I am so late. They said you were finished at 5:00, but I hoped you would let me get a treatment or session, or what would you call it?"

I reached out to accept her greeting, "A session, but treatment is fine, too. My name is Michael. Nice to meet you, Allison. Please sit down here." I gestured to the small circle of brown, metal folding chairs used as a space for conversation before and after sessions. She sat right next to me; everybody else sat across from me. This made me nervous. Allison knew the power she had over all men. I was not an exception. She felt dangerous to me because of the power I gave her.

"I do not know anything about Reiki. I saw a flyer on campus about what you were doing and wanted to see what it was. I'm sorry I'm late. I tried to get here earlier but had some things to do. So, can you explain what Reiki is first?"

"Reiki is a Japanese-based healing system, typically expressed through laying on of hands. Reiki is generally translated as spiritually guided, Universal life-force energy. As you just saw with the women who were here, Reiki allows folks to keep their clothes on, and the touch is gentle and supportive. There doesn't have to be any physical contact at all for Reiki to be effective. I often experience entire Reiki sessions without touch. Reiki Counseling is common not to have physical touch."

    Raised by Wolves, Possibly Monsters

"No, I think touch would be good. Since it's late, I know you want to leave, and I have to prepare for something tonight; how about we do it? I rode here on my scooter in the cold just for this. I decided to show up because it felt like something I needed to do for reasons I do not know."

"That's fine. I want to let you know that I will not touch any part of your body that is covered by a bikini unless there is a special reason to do so."

"I trust you; you can do whatever you need to do. I'm here for a reason, and I'll go with it. What do we need to do to get started?"

"Thank you. You can get up on the table, lie on your back, and relax. It will take a moment for me to get ready. Then I'll come over and join you. Your job is to stay present and pay attention. Reiki sessions do not include regular conversation. We can do the session in silence, or there may be guided dialogue if we feel moved. What you share with me can only help me support you, but silence is fine, too. OK?" Allison nodded yes and took off her black leather jacket, revealing her marooned V-neck sweater. After she got up on the table, Allison let out a slow, deep sigh, allowing herself to become comfortable and relaxed. I am glad I had a moment to focus and connect with Reiki.

I stood behind her head, hesitating, before placing my hand on her. Her scent was very powerful, and now I could smell her freshly shampooed chestnut-colored hair glistening from the light above the ceiling. I asked Reiki for help and gently and slowly placed my hands on her head like usual. I felt her relax under my touch almost immediately, which was surprising due to her high energy level. I carefully placed my hands over her eyes and third eye so as not to mess up her perfectly applied greenish-blue mascara and deep red blush on her cheeks. She was strikingly beautiful in her red sweater and brand-new tight-fitting dark blue jeans. I noticed the red lipstick on her lips. I again asked Reiki for help and received it; Allison was not present for my pleasure.

My hands moved to her throat, sliding down to her collarbone. A minute later, they moved to the top of her chest to connect with her heart center. They stayed there for a few minutes before Reiki spoke through me in almost a whisper. My voice was slow and low, "Allison. You do not need to be perfect. You are enough just being you. You are good enough, pretty enough, skinny enough, smart enough, kind enough, and a good enough friend and daughter."

She instantly had tears rolling down her cheeks that smeared her mascara. I wiped them away with my right hand, leaving my left hand on her upper chest. I let her cry a little more freely; resistance was slipping away. "Being beautiful has sometimes been a burden for you, yes?" She nodded her head up and down as her tears flowed to her shoulders. "You have worked hard to look the way you do, and now it is your drug. You do not know how to be just yourself anymore. Does this feel true to you?"

"Yes," she said, her tears more forceful now. "My whole life, I have been the prettiest girl in every room. I know this, and it has become all I am. I am smart, talented, and creative. I rarely get noticed for anything but my pretty face and body. It is my identity. More than identity, it is my existence. I feel like I am here just to be looked at. All women hate me. Guys just want to have sex with me. They don't care about me or who I am. They just want me to fulfill their fantasies of being with "the hot girl." It has gotten to the point that I cannot leave the house without my hair and make-up done perfectly because I must have every man notice me. I didn't used to be this way. I used to like the attention, but that was it. Now I feel like a slave to my looks."

She let herself completely submerge into the experience. I held one hand over the same spot and the other resting on her belly. I could feel the support she was receiving in her belly from Reiki; the energy was clear, clean, and strong.

"Michael, I miss me. I miss my Soul. I miss feeling my body; ironically, my body is such a focus for me and everybody else, but I rarely feel my body. It's like it is not mine anymore. It belongs to everybody else like a museum exhibit, instead of the living human being inside."

"What do you want to be different, Allison?"

"I need to reclaim my body and life! I need to let the real me come out again. I can't keep living this way; I am a slave to my looks and the reactions I receive. Guys fall in love with me almost immediately and then are stunned when they find out I am an actual, real person with feelings, thoughts, and needs, not just their fantasy in the flesh. They look like they have seen a ghost when I speak intelligently and am not just a living mannequin. They run and don't come back. I am good, but nobody cares to notice, and women are the same way. They want to be friends with me to meet good-looking, successful men. They never care to

     Raised by Wolves, Possibly Monsters

get to know me either." More tears flowed.

"Has it always been this way?"

"Like I said, I always received attention for my looks, but I was different then. I was grateful I was pretty and had an attractive body, but I still felt like a whole human being. I did not feel different or special. I just had an easy way to meet people without having to do anything besides be pretty. Most of the time, I feel ugly these days, not my face or body; I, the person inside, feel ugly. This is not who I am! What can I do to be myself again? I want to be more than just the drop-dead gorgeous girl with the great tits and ass! I know most women would kill to look like this, and I should be happy, but I am not. Nobody understands."

"I think you have already started the process by showing up here. You let your Higher Self guide us from the minute I placed my hands on you, so something is ready to shift inside you. I encourage you to listen to that voice that speaks loudly and clearly about you being a whole person. Trust your Inner Voice to guide you and direct you on how to go forward from here."

"Thank you. I feel that voice inside me, too. I used to feel this regularly; it's good to feel it again. I feel like I do not have to look perfect all the time now. That seems clear. I want to show up and be myself, no matter my appearance. I feel like I can do that now! What a relief! I don't have to be a Cover Girl constantly." Allison let out a massive sigh of relief. I could feel her exhale in my belly. We settled back into silence through Reiki.

The rest of the session was silent. I did not place my hands in all the usual places, just the belly and bare feet. Thirty minutes later, we finished our session. We debriefed about the session. Allison changed topics after looking at her platinum Gucci watch. "Michael, I would like you to be my special guest for the show that I lead tonight. Will you please come if you are available? It would mean a lot to me since you now have me prepared for opening night. My way of saying thank you to you."

"I would love to be your guest." She gave me the details of her performance. We looked into each other's eyes and hugged warmly, allowing enough time for the exchange to shift back and forth between us several times.

Allison said, "I'll see you later," and left.

I started packing the table and materials, still feeling charged from the powerful experience. I acknowledged that I had participated in something of great value and had a more profound connection than your typical free public Reiki session. There was more to her than meets the eye. I breathed in the grace of such force and gratitude at meeting and connecting with another member of my tribe is a great honor. That Allison presented herself as a starlet was not lost; it stirred a pot inside me that needed stirring.

The session with Allison was my first understanding of the drop-dead gorgeous syndrome and its often hazardous effects. As a man, I have assumed my whole life that drop-dead gorgeous women have all the privileges that come with their physical appearance and no consequences, which is not accurate. She was not the only woman I have connected with who has paid consequences for how we men see and treat them. We often confuse our desire or attraction as something they are doing, not our own experience that has little to do with the object of our desire. Allison was an excellent teacher for opening my mind to the drop-dead gorgeous syndrome. This experience was about fifteen years ago. I have had the opportunity to share it with other women and men so they might also gain knowledge from my experiences with Allison and the drop-dead gorgeous syndrome.

This experience further cemented into my psyche that the ultimate method to balance lust is to see the person as a real-life human being by connecting with their Higher Self. This process transitions quickly from lust and objectification to love, compassion, and empathy. Shame melts away; replacing it is a deep desire to connect and care for this incredible woman before me. I was also learning that I was capable of both feeling attraction to someone and being fully present and connected to a deep part of them and myself at the same time. This commitment felt like an essential step in embracing my feelings and honoring the man inside of me who wants everyone to experience safety, respect, and acceptance for who they are. Knowing we would not meet again, I felt great love and admiration for Allison.

Raised by Wolves, Possibly Monsters

Intuition Is Only Valuable if We Listen

 MY WORK AT the Urban League was ending. I was exploring other opportunities and was considering being a caretaker at a historical mountain lodge in North Carolina about an hour south of Asheville. Before I left Madison in 2009, there was one more significant event.

I was heading to the East Coast again the following year to meet with Betsy at the farm. I had seen a ride board online and found a young man from Milwaukee driving to the East Coast and looking for somebody to share the driving and the costs. We exchanged emails and a phone call.

That Saturday, I took a bus from Madison to Milwaukee. He picked me up at the bus stop and drove me to the house he and his friends lived in, which he was moving out of. It was about three hours before we left. He was that clueless and disorganized. When everything was done, and he said goodbye to his friends, we walked to the car. When I put my hand on the door handle of his blue Ford, a firm and clear voice told me, "Do not get in this car!" There was no other information; just don't get in the car. I hesitated and stepped back away from the vehicle. I felt scared and a little embarrassed. I had gone through all this effort to find this guy, to get here, wait three hours, and do all the other necessary preparations for me to work with Betsy. I wasn't going to back out now. A small voice inside me said, "This must be your resistance." That voice told me what I wanted to hear: to get in the car and go to New Jersey.

I had offered to drive the first leg. Somehow, that would change whatever reason I wasn't supposed to get in the car. I drove the first six hours, and we made it to the Pennsylvania border on Route 80. It was 1:00 in the morning when I'd asked him if he would be willing to switch since we needed to pull over and get gas anyway. He enthusiastically said yes. I pulled into a gas station, filled the tank with gas, and we both went to the restroom, emptied our bladders, and walked around for a few minutes to stretch.

I don't think we were fifteen minutes into him driving before I fell asleep. An hour later, I woke to the screeching of tires and opened my eyes as we ricocheted off one of the tires of the semi-double tractor-trailer that was turned over on its side jackknifed. We slid off the road to the left, and the car stopped with the two front tires on the grass and the two back tires on the pavement. The point of impact was about three feet from me on the front right quarter panel. The car was totaled. I was lying on my back and needed to unlock the seat belt. I verified all of my body parts were still attached. I turned to my left, and he kept asking me if I was okay. I was trying to remember who he was, whose car I was in, and where we were going.

I managed to unlock the seat belt, sit up, and take in the car's damage. It was a mess. I opened the door to get out and fell to my knees. I stood up again, and by the time I was entirely on my feet, several other cars had pulled up next to us since there was nowhere to cross the highway because the double trailer was taking up all three lanes.

The police and ambulance were there, along with two fire trucks, in minutes. Even with the truck on its side, the semi-driver was hanging out the window; it was apparent the driver was in bad shape. He died a few hours later. After the police officer took our statements, he asked us where we wanted to go. We looked at each other without knowing what to do. We weren't friends. We had no plan on what to do next now that we were in the middle of nowhere in Northwest Pennsylvania on I-80. He recommended that we get a room at a local hotel and get ourselves checked out in the morning since neither wanted to be taken away in the ambulance. We didn't know what else to do, so we said yes. He called dispatch, and the dispatcher made arrangements with the hotel, so everything was set as soon as we arrived. We went to pay for the room, which I didn't have the money to spend. After that, we entered the room with my expedition pack, his backpack, and suitcases.

I looked around the room and at him and heard that voice again. "Do not stay in the room with him. You must commit to New Jersey right now!" This time, I listened. I explained to him that I felt like I needed to keep on my journey, and since we were right next to a truck stop, I would ask the person at the front desk to help me make a sign. I was going to hitch a ride to New Jersey. He tried to talk me out of it for a second but gave up when he realized he had no chance to do so. We wished each other well, and I left.

I was outside for less than thirty minutes before I got a ride since it was bright and early.

Raised by Wolves, Possibly Monsters

The crash's impact shook me mentally, emotionally, physically, and energetically. When I returned to Madison a week later, I received a Shiatsu treatment from a dear friend who is a Shiatsu Practitioner. She identified that I had a mild concussion, if not worse, and my spine needed attention. I saw her twice a week for the next month, and the tightness and soreness in my back and spine were pretty much gone.

During those first few months, I noticed my behavior and actions were unusual and peculiar. More than once, I would find myself standing in the living room watching TV with a cutting board and a knife with partially cut vegetables, not knowing why I was standing there, how I was standing there, and why I was watching TV. I had trouble sleeping and meditating for a couple of months. My body became nervous and tense anytime I closed my eyes. Being sleep-deprived intensified the anxiety and intensity of my nervous system.

Wandering Around the East Coast

AFTER I LEFT Madison, I took a job as a caretaker at a historical mountain lodge in the Appalachian Mountains of western North Carolina, on the outskirts of Pisgah National Forest. It was a great concept but an awful experience. The owner was rude, aggressive, and violent. I moved out under duress four months after I arrived. I decided to explore Asheville since I had heard about it many times over the years.

While wandering around Asheville and the East Coast in my Astro Van, I applied for a job in Liberia, Africa, running a program for rebuilding communities through soccer/football. My work at the Urban League had set a fire in me to support people of color, especially those whose ancestors were from Africa. I have been an athlete and coach of multiple teams and sports with kids and adults throughout my life. I wanted to unite many parts of my world through a community-based program using futbol to unite people after a decade of war. I had passed through several levels in the hiring process and was one of the last seven people out of the initial 3,200 who applied before I got rejected. I was disappointed because it felt like it was an interesting and exciting opportunity for me.

Somehow, a recruiter from South Korea called me and asked if I was interested in being an English teacher. We talked for a while, and it sounded interesting. At the end of the conversation, he offered me a position conditional on passing the government's requirements for foreign English language teachers. It was a good offer that included a place to live and insurance. I almost said yes on the phone. I hesitated and asked him if I could take a week to decide. He enthusiastically supported me in doing so since it was a one-year contract. If I broke it, there were several financial penalties, including not being reimbursed for my flight out there or my flight to leave a year later.

A friend suggested I look into other opportunities like this in South Korea. I spent the next few days scouring all the opportunities for English foreign language teachers in Korea. When I got down to two, I wrote both with a letter of interest and my resume. One of them wrote back to me and set up a phone interview. I enjoyed speaking with them and the position they offered. I accepted it while on the phone. This took place in June of 2018. It would take about six weeks to go through all of the legal and governmental requirements, and if all goes well, I will start the last week of August.

At this point in my life, I had no responsibilities; I was wandering and couch-surfing and could do everything I needed quickly. They had received all of my materials and were beginning to process them.

In late June, I received a phone call from the recruiter who hired me. My heart sank because I thought something had come up in my records from when I was younger, and they were turning down my acceptance due to government requirements. I had been arrested several times and spent a little time in jail for multiple counts of possession and distribution of cocaine. The mob lawyer had promised me that they had it deleted, but anybody who trusts the government is a bit of a fool. Not that I have an opinion on this subject.

It turned out that it had nothing to do with me. A teacher who was supposed to start in two weeks ran into a snag when passing through the government requirements, and they had to remove their offer from them. They wanted to know if I would be willing to come in twelve days. They gave me a raise of $6,000 to do so. In addition, the recruiter apologetically said, "Within your first thirty days here in South Korea, we're going to have to fly you to Japan for a few days

    Raised by Wolves, Possibly Monsters

so you can apply for your work visa because you have to do it from out of the country. I'm sorry you must go to Japan, but it's necessary."

I did everything I could not to burst out laughing. Somehow, in the recruiter's mind, my going to Japan was unfortunate, and it just had to happen. I was now really excited and saw an opportunity.

"I would be willing to do that. And thank you for being so considerate of my feelings. It will be some work flying to Japan, staying in a hotel, and then flying back a day and a half later. Can we extend our agreement for me to stay in Japan for five days, and your company will pay for my hotel and meals for that whole time so that I'm not exhausted when I return to South Korea?"

She answered affirmatively without hesitating. After getting off the phone, I reflected that I thought I was making a huge ask, but they were desperate and would have agreed to almost anything I asked, including more money. "Yes, we'd gladly do that for you, Michael. If you agree to these terms, I will have the papers you need to sign and return sent overnight, and you will get them in the States tomorrow evening. It is of utmost importance that you sign them and send them back the following day to make sure everything happens on time. I will make your plane reservations as soon as we get off the phone." And that was that. After several months of traveling up and down the East Coast visiting friends, friends I hadn't met yet, friends of new friends, I was about to spend the next year in South Korea!

Hello, Michael Teacher

AFTER SCRAMBLING EVERYTHING together, I took a flight from Newark to Seattle, then a thirteen-hour flight from Seattle to Incheon International Airport just north of Seoul. A driver waited for me at the airport. He helped me with my bags, and we left in the taxi. We went up to the second floor of the four-story building made of solid cement. We found my apartment. It was a decent-sized studio with a mini kitchen and a small bathroom. The floor was a natural wood color with a polyurethane finish. He carried my bags, and even though he didn't speak English and I didn't speak Korean, he

walked me through and showed me everything in the apartment. He had never been there before, nor had he ever been to Cheonan. I thanked him, and he bowed at me. I bowed to him, and he left. It was now a few minutes after 4 a.m., I had to be at school at 8 a.m.

After a day of travel, three airports, and an hour and a half ride in a taxi, I was desperate for a shower. I tried to get the hot water on, but no matter what I did, it did not come on. So, I took a cold shower, waking me up instead of helping me fall asleep after the long journey with minimal time to get to work. It still felt lovely to feel the water running across my body and cleansing off a day of travel. I was grateful to crawl into my new bed and remember to set the timer on my flip phone and the digital clock next to the bed to give me enough time to make it to the school, which was supposedly three blocks from my apartment.

To say that I was cranky when the alarm went off after what seemed like ten minutes is an understatement. That said, I knew I needed to get up and get out of bed. I had thirty-five minutes to get to the school. I brushed my teeth, washed my face, and got dressed. I didn't know what teachers wore, so I wore a pair of khakis and a short-sleeved blue and white striped cotton shirt. I wore sneakers because I didn't know what else to do. I planned to stop for something to eat between my apartment and the school, not knowing how complicated that would be. I walked into what appeared to be something like a Korean deli. One could choose from approximately thirty different items, and the women would put them in a little carton for you to go. I chose eggs, bread, and green vegetables. It was a little spicier than I was prepared for, especially for breakfast while walking to the school. But it was food, and I was grateful.

My supervisor, whom I had never met, awaited me at the door. She was a high-energy and highly anxious woman rushing me upstairs while teaching me to say hello with great detail. She explained that the class would be full of kids, and I would administer an oral test with each of them and place them in whichever of the four classes I thought was the appropriate level. I tested eighty-two kids that morning, wondering how well or poorly I placed them.

The day before, somebody must have taught the kids how to practice saying "Hello, Michael Teacher." More than half of them knew no other English than those three words.

          Raised by Wolves, Possibly Monsters

I was introduced to my co-teacher; we were going to share our students as soon as we completed that task. She was introduced to me as Ashley Teacher, her English name. Ashley was sweet and warm. As soon as we were introduced, my supervisor again rushed me down the stairs to meet the school Principal and Vice Principal in their office. Until now, everything looked like an urban school in the United States, except for the white cement outside. The classrooms looked similar; the hallways looked identical, the bathrooms looked similar, but not the principal's office. She knocked on the door, and somebody shouted from a distance for us to enter. We entered a vast room with a large rectangular table that could seat more than twenty people, traditional Korean-style tall chairs with firm backs, and a Formica or similar black and white table. Along the walls were gold and yellow lamps and sculptures with red Korean calligraphy. I felt like I had walked onto a movie set. The principal, who wore a gray silk suit, looked irritated that he had to come over and speak to me since he didn't speak English and I didn't speak Korean. My supervisor translated both of us. After initial pleasantries and hellos, we did a traditional bow. He asked me to sit at the table where the Vice Principal and his Secretary were waiting for us. They took turns saying hello, welcoming me, and letting me know how excited they were to have me there. A bell rang five minutes into our meeting, signaling it was time for lunch. We all hurried out to the cafeteria, which was down the hall.

Upon entering the cafeteria, several things stood out to me. The first was how orderly it was. Kids from kindergarten to sixth grade knew precisely what to do. Young kids cleared their trays after eating. Everybody waited in line patiently. They got their food, table by table—the kids whose tables still needed to be called on sat and waited at their tables. I was confused because the children were doing what they should be doing.

The next thing was unavoidable for me to notice. One by one, every time one of the younger kids saw me, they froze and stared. This was especially noticeable when the kids walking with a tray full of food would drop it on the floor in disbelief at my presence. My co-teacher told me I was the first non-Korean person to enter this building. Most of the kids had never seen an American or White person before.

OK, this will blow your mind if you grew up in the United States. Every kid ate the same thing with no customization, and they all ate all the food on their plates and bowls! You read that right; every kid ate all the food on their plates and bowls. They would go to the cleaning station and clean their plates, dishes, and silverware, rinse them with the spray gun of warm water; then they would bring it to the station where a woman would take all of the dishes and run them through the dishwasher to sanitize.

This may sound baffling, but I learned that day at lunch that every morning, the cooks came in at 5 a.m. and prepared the food from scratch that day. For the most part, the meal included rice, kimchi, some form of soup, and a main course, which could be chicken, seafood, vegetables, or pork. The food was delicious, well-made, and fresh. I enjoyed the rice, kimchi, cheegae, and orange slices. I did not enjoy being stared at as if I were a Martian by almost every student in the school of 1,200 kids. That night, my supervisor, Ashley, and I went out for dinner after school. I'm not going to lie; I found my supervisor annoying based on how high-strung she was. Ashley was adorable from the first moment we met.

They asked me if there was anything I needed help with. I laughed without realizing they did not understand the sarcasm of my laughter. In my one year in Korea, I discovered that sarcasm is not a cultural norm; therefore, nobody picked up on it. After they looked at me blankly, I explained that I needed help with everything. My supervisor offered to walk back to my place and show me how to turn on the hot water, and Ashley offered to go with me to the grocery store afterward to get what I needed.

A switch on the electrical panel turned on the hot water for the apartment. And that was that. They told me many other things about my apartment, but my mind kept drifting back to a desperate need for sleep and my excitement about being able to take a hot shower later. They showed me how to use the TV and the cable with the remote. They both said they thought I would like to watch Korean dramas, so they kept showing me and circling the three main Korean drama channels on the little chart, even though I did not speak Korean. They showed me how to use the remote air conditioner/heater, which had yet to enter the States. They showed me how to use the washer. And then the three of us walked out and down to the street. My supervisor said goodbye and that she would be back next week to check on me. We bowed, and she left.

                    Raised by Wolves, Possibly Monsters

Ashley took me to the small supermarket between my apartment and the school. She pointed to the building where her apartment was, between my apartment and the supermarket. Everything was close together.

We spent about twenty minutes in the supermarket. I was so exhausted I could not listen to what Ashley taught me. I asked her if we could leave. As we walked back together, she gave me her phone number in case I needed anything and asked me if I wanted to go to Lotte Mart. I did not know what Lotte Mart was to be able to say yes or no. This time, she laughed. Lotte Mart is the Korean equivalent of Walmart. For a minute, I was about to say yes, but then I remembered that I was feeling a little light-headed because I was just so bone tired. I just wanted to go to my place, watch TV for a little while, enjoy that hot shower, and go to bed. Ashley said she understood, and we bowed and said goodnight. I remember thinking this was some punishment or retribution for being such a jerk earlier in life by having me live one block and work all day with this gorgeous woman. A car horn beeped at me, and it took me a second to recognize that I was standing in the middle of the street, staring at the door that she had already gone in. I moved out of the way and apologized to the man driving the beige Hyundai who was complaining to me. I realized he had no idea what I was saying, so I bowed to him. He stopped yelling at me, bowed in his car, and pulled away slowly.

I went to bed a little after 9:30 p.m. and was startled by my alarm at 8 a.m. This time, my strategy was better. I made an egg and toast and drank orange juice. I was ready to do my job. I had no idea what I would be doing or how to do it. I did not speak Korean, so I needed to learn to teach a foreign language and help remember where the bathroom was.

Before I go any further, I want to speak about how outstanding and inspiring it is to work every day in a school with no janitorial or custodial staff. The kids themselves clean the floors of the hallways, staircases, and all the common areas. They wash, scrub, and mop the floors of the bathrooms, toilets, and sinks. Here's the most incredible part. They have fun doing it! Not only are they not miserable, grumpy, and complaining with an attitude, but they also talk, sing, laugh, and play the whole time, making it cleaner than if I was doing the job.

So This Is What It's Like to Be a Teen Girl

AS I HAD mentioned earlier, in my thirties, I realized I was an attractive guy. At times, that created a perspective that made me bigger and bolder; at other times, it made me smaller and quieter. I was never good-looking enough that I needed to hide. I didn't draw that kind of attention as a man. As a woman said about me once, "Michael, you're not the kind of guy that is walking down the street a woman says to herself, 'Damn, he's fine' nor are you the type of guy that when a woman is walking down the street, she says to herself, 'Damn, he's nasty.'" I was unprepared for the response I received just being an American human male in Korea.

I was not prepared for all the women to stop what they were doing when I got on a bus, sit up straight, fix their hair, and smile at me.

I was not prepared for the Queen Bee of those women to come and sit next to me as soon as I sat down.

I was unprepared for women walking on the opposite side of the street, going in the opposite direction of me, doing an about-face, crossing the road, and then walking next to me, striking up conversations.

I was unprepared for the Queen Bee to get up from her seat, stand beside me, and lean her body against mine when standing on a train.

I was not prepared to eat alone in restaurants, and I had young, attractive women whisper and giggle while staring at me and following me when I left.

I was not prepared to wear shorts and a T-shirt, and women looked me up and down with a smirk and a sense of ownership.

I was not prepared for every woman to focus all their attention on getting and keeping mine. They often aggressively told me they were single and had a successful career. They found me "very interesting" while smiling, giggling, and continuously telling me how smart, funny, and exciting I was. Even though I could tell they weren't even listening to me or what I was saying.

I was not prepared for women being attracted to me and pursuing me, knowing it had nothing to do with their interest or attraction.

I was unprepared because they perceived me as wealthy and successful; Michael Swerdloff, the human being, was irrelevant.

 Raised by Wolves, Possibly Monsters

I was not prepared to become shy and quiet when I could tell I was a target.

I was unprepared to be noticed everywhere but still felt unseen.

I was not prepared to learn about the experiences of teens and young women who cannot go in public without somebody wanting them but not being interested in them.

I was not prepared to walk away from women to whom I was very attracted and interested, knowing that no matter what I did or said, they would mostly still see me as their White Knight.

I was unprepared to wonder if what I would wear that day would attract more attention than I could emotionally or mentally handle.

I was not prepared for all this attention from amazing women to become a source of discomfort and shame. I felt ashamed that we had convinced so many of these women that they could have a better life just by being with, marrying, and moving to the United States, even if they didn't like the person they were married to.

I was not prepared for the deep shame I felt for all the girls and women who experienced the same thing as I was, but men had even less interest in them than these women had in me. I understood that my experiences were temporary; this was not true for the women who experience this endlessly. And I reflected on all the times I had noticed a woman and only saw her face and body.

An Accidental Marriage Proposal

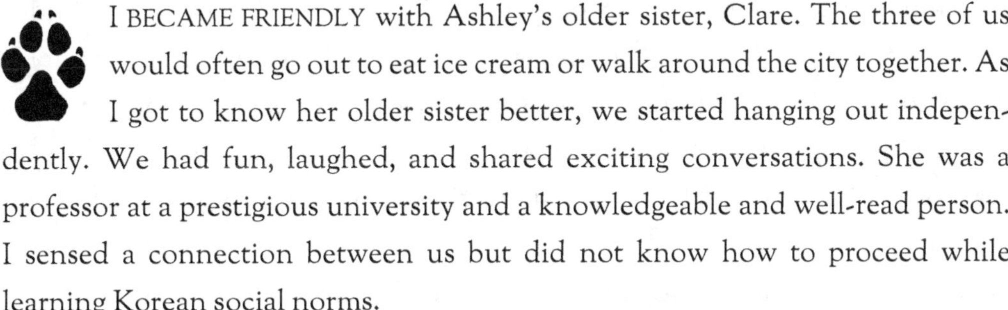

I BECAME FRIENDLY with Ashley's older sister, Clare. The three of us would often go out to eat ice cream or walk around the city together. As I got to know her older sister better, we started hanging out independently. We had fun, laughed, and shared exciting conversations. She was a professor at a prestigious university and a knowledgeable and well-read person. I sensed a connection between us but did not know how to proceed while learning Korean social norms.

I visited Clare in Seoul, and we spent the whole day together. Sometimes, I would go up for dinner and go out afterward, but we always had riveting conversations and enjoyed each other's company. After the fourth or fifth time, I was trying to figure out how to initiate something romantic between us. I didn't know if holding hands was the thing to do, a kiss, or telling her I was attracted to her. I didn't know what to do, and I appreciated her company but did not want to disrespect her or her sister. I was right to be concerned about everything lost in translation between us.

Her younger sister Ashley approached me excitedly one day in the halls. "Michael Teacher, my family wants you to join us in Seoul this weekend! It is our New Year, which Americans call the Chinese New Year. You could stay in my younger brother's bedroom, and you would have your own room. We would eat a big meal, and you would experience some of our traditional rituals. Everybody is excited about you coming and my parents want to meet you. Of course, my sisters were excited when I told them I would ask you, especially Clare."

I asked her a few questions to learn more about the holiday and what the expectations would be. She said they would have to teach me the special bows because we would take turns bowing to their parents on the second day. It all sounded exciting, and I learned that the entire country shut down for three days whenever there was a national holiday in Korea. In each city, one or two convenience stores stay open if somebody needs something, but that's about it. Supermarkets are closed, restaurants are closed, and everything is closed. I said yes, and she said she would teach me the unique bows after school that night and then practice them again at her parents' house.

Two days later, Ashley and I got on a subway to Seoul. While talking, I casually touched my hand on the side of her leg next to me, just below her dress. She flinched and almost jumped. After she gained her composure, Ashley scolded me for touching her leg. That was not allowed ever, especially in public. She said that she would not be able to get married if people knew that I had touched her leg. I apologized and did everything I could not to break down into tears of just how incredibly tragic that was a social norm and how impactful this felt to her. I felt shame and embarrassment, but we worked it out. After she calmed down, Ashley apologized for being so harsh with me. After the fourth time, she could hear that I didn't mean it, apologized for my mistake, and would not do it again. Ashley's eyes were red and wet, and she shared with me that she

     Raised by Wolves, Possibly Monsters

was embarrassed, and her tears ruined her makeup.

When we exited the subway in downtown Seoul, she said we had to walk about ten blocks; even though I was athletic and in excellent shape, I could barely keep up with her and the click-clack of her shoes. I had forgotten that she was late for everything and that following her lead on what time we had to leave Cheonan to get there for dinner was another mistake.

We arrived late for dinner, even while rushing down the streets of people hurriedly scurrying around to get to their families and friends. Nothing had been shut down yet, as tomorrow was the big day. We passed the school where she had graduated with her education degree and the school where Clare got her undergraduate and graduate degrees. Her sister was currently working on her post-doctoral degree.

Her father looked angry with her about us being late, and her mother kept badgering her. Parental scolding is universal because you don't have to understand the language to know what's happening. Of course, they were nice, friendly, and welcoming to me. Neither of their parents spoke English, so the four kids took turns translating the conversation between their parents and me. As much as I enjoyed Korean food, I never gained any appreciation at all for rice cakes. I pretended that I was enjoying them. I did not want to disrespect anybody.

The parents went to bed, and we played card games and Uno for hours. We followed that with the Korean version of karaoke. We had so much fun and couldn't stop laughing at each other. When her younger sister and brother went to bed, she had me practice bowing again with Clare because we would be bowing together. Ashley would be bowing with her younger sister. The brother would bow by himself since he is the oldest and only son, per the traditions. Clare and I had fun and laughed at what an awful job I was doing at this.

The following morning, we had a big breakfast with several rituals that reminded me of Passover; without knowing what any of the traditions were about, they involved food, prayer, or acknowledgment.

After breakfast, everybody had to go and get dressed in "nice clothes." I did not have a suit in Korea; I wore pants, a button-down shirt, and one of the two ties I brought; this was the most formal option. I remember having an internal chuckle at the idea of everybody getting dressed up in traditional clothes but not wearing shoes because it's indoors, as Koreans don't wear footwear indoors; they all wear sandals inside. The son and the father were in expensive suits without shoes.

All three daughters looked gorgeous and were beaming after getting dressed together and the occasion. The son went first through the bowing rituals. Then the two younger sisters, and then Clare and me. Even though I didn't completely understand everything happening, or as it turned out, I understood pretty much nothing, I enjoyed the opportunity to practice a ritual of honoring parents and grandparents. It was a beautiful experience, and I felt connected to the family and Korean culture in those moments. The following two days, we ate meals, talked, played games, and ate and talked. The two of us returned to Cheonan on the subway. I expressed several times how grateful I was for her inviting me and including me in her family's traditions.

We were having lunch with two other schoolteachers a few days later. One of the teachers asked me if I was married and if my wife was with me in South Korea. I had told them I was not married and had never been married. They asked me if I planned on getting married. I told them that if I'd found the right woman and we loved each other, I would be glad to be married. At this point, Ashley started talking with them in Korean. They responded in Korean, were excited, and spoke excitedly and joyfully.

I was about to ask them what they were talking about, but the bell rang, and lunchtime was over. We all returned to our classrooms. After we finished our classes, I walked down the hall to visit Ashley. I asked her what she and the other two women were so happy and excited about at lunch.

"I was just telling them how happy I am that you and Clare are engaged to be married now. You would make a great brother to me. And that way, we can keep you in Korea because we all love you!"

I paused. "I'm sorry. Can you repeat that?"

"They were so excited that you and Clare are engaged and will get married. I told them how excited I was that you would be my brother and that you would be staying here in Korea beyond your contract."

It took us about fifteen minutes to unpack the fact that the weekend's activities were a Korean tradition of asking her father for permission to marry her

     Raised by Wolves, Possibly Monsters

daughter, Clare. After we unpacked, it took another ten minutes to discover how she had thought she had told me this, that I understood, that Clare understood, and that we were both excited about this. I wanted to explode but chose to be careful and sensitive for all of the obvious and not-so-obvious reasons.

We discussed this, and I tried to create a plan to undo it. Ashley informed me that it's not something that can be undone. We got into an argument that ended with her texting her mother and asking her mother for advice on what to do. Her mother called immediately; I could hear her mother yelling at her through her flip phone. This time, I needed help to figure out the tone and intonation of what they were talking about. Eventually, Ashley got off the phone and explained that her mother would try to speak to her father and sister because they all thought I understood, which I didn't.

The following day, Ashley approached me before classes started and apologized for the mix-up. Since it had not been announced to anybody outside the family yet, they could void the agreement, and I was no longer engaged to marry her sister. Now that we did that, Ashley and I had a heated exchange about the situation and how she handled it.

The following week, I emailed Betsy about this situation. She warned me to be careful, "Before I get my foot caught in the door on the way out!"

PART III

Mongolia and Beyond

"Everybody can be great . . . because anybody can serve. You don't have to have a college degree to serve. You don't have to make your subject and verb agree to serve. You only need a heart full of grace. A soul generated by love."

Martin Luther King Jr.

Dreams and Visions of Mongolia

I REMEMBER MY first dream of backpacking solo in the Gobi Desert. I did not register that this was significant or a vision. It just felt like a weird dream. I kept seeing myself in a desert utterly different from New Mexico or Arizona, which are sandy deserts. This one looked more like pebbles and rocks surrounded by cliffs that were rocks. No tourists, roads, signs, or humans existed in these dreams. Next, they started appearing in my meditations; I would also see others walking with me who seemed only sort of physical beings. They were dead people like Mikao Usui, Thomas Merton, G.I. Gurdjieff, Teresa of Avila, Jalalaldin Mevlana Rumi, and several other exceptional humans. Some humans who were part of the process are still alive, like my teacher, Betsy, and friend Ellie Mae. When the visions included other people, it typically appeared that I was walking ahead of them, even though they were guiding me. The visions or dreams did not have me eating, drinking, sleeping in tents, setting up camp, or anything else. I was walking. There was lots of walking. It was not walking to get from one place to the other; it was walking as a means to connect with the Earth, each other, my Higher Self, and Beyond. I sensed that as long as we walked, we would be in our bodies, stay present, and pay attention. Our steps were slow and deliberate. I don't remember speaking in any of these visions or dreams. We were walking as a collective Force.

I sent Betsy an email, and she confirmed what I was receiving. I felt relieved that I wasn't just having weird dreams, and of course, I panicked because, well, who wants to walk alone in the middle of a desert in Mongolia for an extended period?

While all this was happening, I became furious and impatient with my co-teacher, Ashley. I didn't understand why I was so frustrated and irritated with her, regardless of what she did. I was mean, disrespectful, and cold. My poor treatment of Ashley continued throughout the last few months of my contract as an English Foreign Language Teacher. She was one of the people who was utterly baffled as to why I was going to the Gobi Desert to walk by myself for a while. At least some of my friends in the States understood that I had been guided several times previously to do solo spiritual work and process. They still thought I was crazy, but they understood. Ashley came from another world, both literally and in personality. It was not till after I returned to Korea to get my stuff after Mongolia, Kazakhstan, Kyrgyzstan, and Uzbekistan that I understood that I had fallen for Ashley somewhere along the way. Since she did not reciprocate, or I did not perceive that she reciprocated, I felt rejected and created a wall between us. All of that melted away when I saw her again. But I am getting ahead of myself.

With about two months left in my contract, I was sweeping my classroom at the end of the day as we did every day. I was gathering the dust pile together into the dustpan when a sharp pain came across my spine, and I crumbled to the floor in pain. I couldn't move or do anything. I was lying there writhing in pain by myself. Ashley heard me moaning and groaning and came running down the hall, click, click, click, click, click of her heels. As she got closer, I knew that somebody would be able to help me. "Michael Teacher, what happened?"

I rolled over enough to be able to see her kneeling next to me with her eyes wide open and her skin taut with fear. "I don't know. I was sweeping the floor, and then I got this pain in my back, and I fell over." Ashley ran to get help. Eventually, they got me to the clinic down the street. They were not able to see or find anything wrong with me, but they could feel the inflammation and throbbing in my spine and lower back. They gave me painkillers and referred me to go to the acupuncture clinic that I often frequented. I received treatments two or three times a week until my back felt somewhat better. I followed their advice, and it became a little bit less brutal, but the pain didn't go away. I'm sure the fact that I knew that I was only one month from flying to Ulaanbaatar in Mongolia to backpack in the desert did not help my body relax.

I contacted my new supervisor, Helen, to help me find a chiropractor who spoke English. It took her ten days to find one. I took the subway to see the chiropractor. He worked on my spine, shoulders, and neck. He also gave me an injection of vitamin C. He looked concerned when I told him I was about to go backpacking in the Gobi Desert. He did not know why I was in pain or what was the source. I had not yet connected that the car crash that I was a passenger in less than two years before may have been related. I also did not know this was the

            Raised by Wolves, Possibly Monsters

beginning of my body going through a brutal seven or eight years. But first, the Gobi Desert was waiting for me, expecting me.

Ulaanbaatar and Central Mongolia

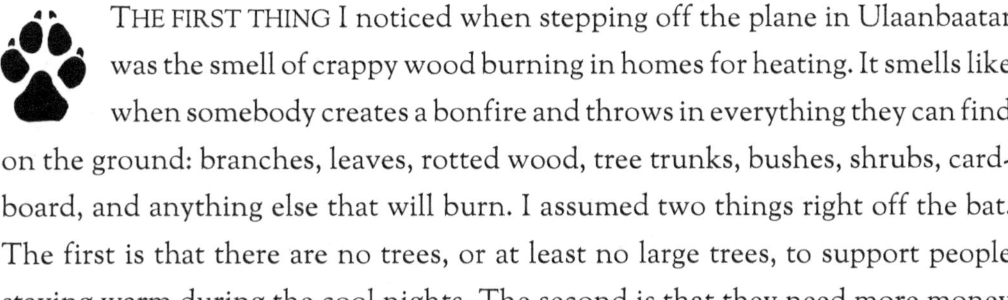THE FIRST THING I noticed when stepping off the plane in Ulaanbaatar was the smell of crappy wood burning in homes for heating. It smells like when somebody creates a bonfire and throws in everything they can find on the ground: branches, leaves, rotted wood, tree trunks, bushes, shrubs, cardboard, and anything else that will burn. I assumed two things right off the bat. The first is that there are no trees, or at least no large trees, to support people staying warm during the cool nights. The second is that they need more money or resources for other ways of keeping homes heated.

I stayed at several youth hostels. Some were Gana's Guest House, Khonger Guest House, UB Guest House, Golden Gobi, and LG Guest House, and others without actual names. I came and left Ulaanbaatar several times; therefore, I had different places to stay for as short as one day and as long as four or five. Ulaanbaatar is one of those cities built for probably a hundred and fifty thousand people but ended up with a million. To offer some context, geographically, Mongolia is about the equivalent in size of Texas. The population of Mongolia is two million people, with about one million living in Ulaanbaatar. The population of Texas is more than thirty million.

One of my favorite memories of Mongolia is the reversed engendered fashion compared to the West. Men wear gorgeous, creative, long, heavy, predominantly silk robes embroidered with many handmade shapes and colors for work. In contrast, women wear plain clothes when working and getting "dressed up." When working, they typically wear heavy black denim jeans, T-shirts, sweatshirts, and a black jacket, often thick, rich leather in colder weather. When they get dressed up, they wear black dresses.

We were scheduled to leave the Golden Gobi at 8 a.m. It was a stretch for me to get myself together and pack in time to reach the waiting van with the Mongolian male driver who was smoking a cigarette and a young Mongolian woman who was not. She spoke enough English to hold an introductory conversation; he spoke none. She was our tour guide. There were going to be five of us taking this tour to and around Central Mongolia and back.

The first one in the van was a woman named Claudia from Germany. She didn't speak much or have any natural facial expressions. A younger Japanese woman named Aya was warm, friendly, and full of energy. She had long black hair, and she and Claudia had neatly packed simple baggage. Aya was also holding a journal and a pen in her hand while we were waiting. I was the third to arrive. Supposedly, an American couple was joining us and staying in one of the other hostels in the courtyard. I was mildly irritated when they were fifteen minutes late because I rushed to be on time. When they were thirty minutes late, I was annoyed. When they were forty-five minutes late, I was frustrated. When they arrived an hour and twenty-five minutes late, I was full-on angry and already hated them before meeting them. In addition, you could smell the vodka oozing out of the pores from five feet away. They both made casual remarks about staying out late and drinking too much, and so and so was supposed to wake them up. Nowhere embedded within this message was "I'm sorry that I was such a shit that the three of you had to sit here and wait after getting up early in the morning and paying to stand here in the courtyard while we were fighting through hangovers from poisoning our body with vodka till 9:40."

We all climbed into the van, and Christopher, the male, proceeded to sit across from me. Mandy, his girlfriend, was in the seat next to him. Aya was sitting next to me, with Claudia on her other side. She looked nervous, gripping her journal and pen tightly with her legs pressed together.

We made it to our first stop before dinner, a relief. One of the local families would welcome us into their ger for a traditional Mongolian ceremony. It was my first time being in a ger. I had been in yurts previously and similar structures, but not a ger made of felt. There was a small table in the center of the room with short legs folded, just like in Korea. Like several Asian cultures, they have sleeping mats that roll up during the day so they can use the same room for other activities like eating, working, and being together. They had simple furniture, including two sets of drawers, a wood-burning stove for heat and cooking, and several folding chairs for sitting when not on the floor or squatting. The furniture and

     Raised by Wolves, Possibly Monsters

wall hangings were tangerine and turquoise with mandala-style artistry.

Our guide, Munguun, translated everything they said and vice versa. The Tea Ceremony was simple. It was predominantly just a gesture to recognize the guests who were present and welcome. We passed around a tiny teacup that we all took a sip of. The mother led the ceremony. They followed the formal ceremony with a more casual one led by the father, which included passing around a mug of vodka. Everybody got a little uncomfortable when I passed the cup to the next person without taking any. The father, guide, driver, Christopher, and Mandy insisted I do it out of respect. Each time one of them said it, I bowed and passed it to Claudia, who was grateful to have the vodka in her hand. If for no other reason than they would stop hassling me. Eventually, they subsided; she took her sip and passed it along. After we completed that tradition, the mother scurried away and returned a minute later with food.

We all sat on the floor around the table and "enjoyed" mutton and dumplings made of sheep fat. There was also dried yak cheese.

After dinner, we were going to go on a camel ride. Before we did, Mandy had noticed the sky as the sun was setting behind us. It was spectacular. We lifted our eyes to glowing shapes of yellow, gold, orange, red, and purple on top of a blue sky. I was grateful that Mandy had noticed this and acknowledged this to her. She grunted back at me. It turned out that most nights, she would be the one who would notice where in the sky it was most beautiful and alert all of us.

We walked to a circular ring similar to horse training. There was a dozen or so camels. Unlike camels I had seen in movies and TV, these were two hump camels. They did a quick demo on how to get on, get off, and ride them. One by one, each of us mounted the camel, rode around the ring twice, and then dismounted. It wasn't long before I realized that we were all getting our practice on the oldest and slowest camel in the bunch. We went to where the rest of the camels were after all five of us had taken our turn, plus the driver and tour guide. We each mounted a camel, and just like that, we were on a forty-five-minute tour of the area on camels! Sitting between the two humps was fun, but my favorite part was being up high. It reminded me of whenever I have been in a semi that was part of an 18-wheeler, looking down at everything we passed. Unlike being in a truck, no metal exists; you're in the fresh air. It was lovely in Mongolia, outside of most men having cigarettes in their hands or mouths all day.

The seven of us all slept in the same ger. We took turns stoking the fire and getting to know each other. Munguun, the guide, had a deck of cards. We played Spades. It was a relaxing way to end the day. While we were all figuring out what beds we would sleep in, Aya came over and whispered in my ear, asking me if it would be okay if she slept in the bed by my feet so that she would feel safe. Of course, I said yes, knowing that having her so close would prevent me from sleeping for at least thirty minutes of fantasies and another twenty minutes of calming down my penis, so I could comfortably fall asleep.

The following morning, we were scheduled to depart at 8 a.m. This time, Christopher and Mandy were only about twenty minutes late and somehow still smelled of vodka. We all knew each other better now that we had spent twenty-four hours together. There was more conversation along our ride. The depth and intimacy increased incrementally. Aya and I became good friends. We discussed meditation, Qi Gong, Reiki, and Waka poetry, which we wrote while in the van. Her warmth and sweetness were a nice balance to the rest of the group, and of course, she had beautiful soft skin with light brown eyes that were always dancing with joy, excitement, and curiosity.

One of the days on this excursion included riding horses through the semi-Gobi, meaning semi-desert. It was random that I ended up with the fastest horse. It was one of those horses that anytime another horse came up next to it, she would go into a gallop, and then again, if another horse came up next to it, it would go into a full run. Without me doing anything, I was always in the lead.

I was far ahead of the group, and they were now out of sight behind me. I came up next to a creek, which is rare in the Gobi or semi-Gobi. On the other side of the creek was an entire herd of yak drinking and eating. One of the younger ones walked over in our direction. The horse I was on took off when it approached us from the left. The young yak took off as well. The horse went faster. As the yak went faster, the horse went even quicker. Panic appeared in my body, and my heart started racing. I realized that we were approaching a cliff. Neither the horse nor the yak was slowing down.

I pulled on the reins as hard as possible, but it was not making a difference. At the point where I could see that we were less than a hundred yards from the

 Raised by Wolves, Possibly Monsters

edge, all kinds of thoughts were running through my head. One of them was to let go of the reins and try to jump off. Fortunately, the yak and the horse knew what to do when you were in a full gallop and approaching a cliff. We stopped completely, probably ten or fifteen yards from the edge. Then, we just hung out as if nothing had happened.

By the third day, we spent our time in the van with heads falling asleep on various people's shoulders and even laps. There was comfort among us, except Mandy and I distrusted each other, which may have been dislike in disguise. Munguun became friendly with me. At first, she was casually flirting with me. She became somewhat aggressive in her flirtation. I reciprocated but was more cautious since she was the guide, and I needed to learn the cultural norms and values. I respected that she was working and was the one person among us who spoke Mongolian and English.

Bordering Siberia

I STILL DIDN'T feel ready to launch into my solo backpacking, and more importantly, I had yet to find a ride to the Southwest region of Mongolia. I signed up for another excursion going north within 60 km of the Russian border of Siberia. One of the people I was traveling with was a woman from Irkutsk, Siberia. Alexandra was the only woman on this trip, along with me and six other men. There was also the driver and the driver's assistant. There were two German friends, two American friends, an Irishman, an Italian guy, Alexandra, and I. All of them were in their twenties or early thirties; I was fifty.

The German men were intelligent, practical, and mostly dull. The two American men in their early twenties, one from California and one from Texas, were more interesting than the Germans. The one from California also had that youthful arrogance after having backpacked for about a year-and-a-half of his life as if he had been doing this for decades. Column, the Irishman, was our one cigarette smoker, desperate for coffee and nicotine every morning and alcohol whenever we had access to it. The Italian guy, Paolo, continually got frustrated that no Mongolian food resembled Italian food or had Italian-style ingredients and seasoning. Of everything we did as a group, I was by far the slowest and least motivated to do the extra work needed for safety and success. Being grounded and centered through Reiki was my contribution to the group. They did not always receive that as an "asset," but I proceeded to do so.

One of the aspects I enjoyed about traveling without a guide was that the drivers had their route, and when we arrived at each destination, they hung out in the van or wherever we were sleeping that night. We appreciated planning and having adventures each day as a group.

We could go by horse, van, or foot on the next leg of our journey. We collectively wanted to go by foot, knowing that it would take two days, the equivalent of a one-hour ride in the van. I was excited about getting my first genuine opportunity to go backpacking in Mongolia, even if I was far from my destination.

We were making good time as a group. Everybody seemed to be mindful of each other's needs and taking care of themselves. Column was not as conscious as others. He was a cigarette smoker and smoked several cigarettes while we were hiking. It was rather annoying to smell cigarette smoke enter my lungs while I was in the middle of nowhere in Mongolia, with the sky so clear that I could see the sun and the moon simultaneously. I felt violated and invaded by his cancer sticks.

I let the group know I would hang back a bit slower and create some distance, wanting to be alone and away from the cigarette smoke. I generally stayed between 100 meters and a hundred yards behind the group. I ensured I could hear or see them at all times. All of this was true until they heard and eventually saw me.

I needed to lower my head to get my pack under a sizable horizontal limb of a tree about six feet high. At the time, I was still five foot nine and a half, and my pack was a good foot above my head. I didn't bend far enough as I was bending, and the top of my bag hit a wasps' nest!

About ten seconds later, my body was invaded by wasps. I was screaming at the top of my lungs. Kevin came running full speed with his pack on. He threw it off his back when he was about twenty feet away from me and saw what was happening.

   Raised by Wolves, Possibly Monsters

"Michael! Take your pack and all of your clothes off now. They are stuck on your body, and they can't get off because of your clothes." He watched me having trouble unbuckling my pack while being stung repeatedly. The young man came over and did it for me and helped me get my clothes off. It was not till later that I realized he was putting himself in harm's way by helping me without flinching for a second. After my clothes were off, he pushed me in the opposite direction and told me to run, which I did. He was right behind me as we kept running for about two minutes. By then, the rest of the group returned and saw us running. One of us was naked without a backpack, and the other one clothed without a backpack. John heard what Kevin instructed me to do and started asking questions. We waited about ten minutes, then Kevin and John returned and got our packs and clothes.

We counted since it was easy to do while I was naked, and I had been stung thirty-seven times. Of those thirty-seven, three or four were multiple bites, so it was probably closer to forty-five or fifty stings. My body went into shock a few minutes later when we found a clearing, and I felt safe. I was shaking, cold, and scared. Other parts of my body were hot, sweaty, and clammy, and I could still feel my heart rate accelerated. It felt tragic to be standing in this clearing on top of a steppe with a fantastic view of hills and the sun-kissed mountains in the distance. It took about half an hour, or at least it felt that long, for everybody to help me become calm, eat food, and drink water. We decided to have lunch there since it was midday, bright and sunny. We also wanted to take the opportunity to regroup and recalibrate our route.

Now that I was calmer, many parts of my body, especially my face and throat, swelled. Even though Kevin said it was impossible, I could feel the toxicity of the collective stings in my body. I was feeling light-headed and unsteady. Paulo offered to carry my pack to begin the next leg of our journey until I felt better. I appreciated the offer; initially, I resisted, but then I accepted humbly and gratefully.

Even without a pack, I still had trouble keeping up with the group. My body was having a strong response to both the traumatic experience, all of the toxicity in my body, and, of course, my body's response to the toxicity—one by one each, one of the group members except for Column offered to carry my pack. We hiked for a few hours and set up camp for the night in a clearing with a magnificent view of the mountains. Some of them had snow caps, some of them had green caps, some of them had both, and all were gorgeous and majestic. I could appreciate it even with my physical and emotional distress and discomfort.

We had one more day on foot before we rode horseback. It was a very long day, and we were exhausted when we reached the campsite to spend the night. Paolo was complaining about not having pasta. Column was complaining about not having a beer and running out of cigarettes. The Germans were complaining about the two of them complaining. Kevin and John were complaining about how slow everybody was. Alexandra was complaining about having to spend another day with all the guys. I was complaining about my back, as the discomfort and sometimes pain was increasing daily.

We did have one box of pasta and decided to cook that so Paolo would be happy. Our Italian friend was momentarily excited until he saw Kevin heating a jar of marinara sauce. He was pacing around our camp, muttering in Italian what seemed like he was cursing about every ten words. We were all punchy and cranky. It was cold. History has told me that I feel even colder than the temperature dictates when I'm tired and grumpy.

We sat around the fire, eating penne with store-bought marinara sauce, mostly in silence. We needed more energy to engage in conversation. Instead of us all setting up our tents, we would just set up the two larger tents and squeeze in like sardines to conserve energy for setting up and breaking down tents and for warmth. I cleaned pots and dishes with John while everybody else set up tents.

Five minutes later, we were all inside our tents. The tent I was in had Kevin to the left, and John, Alexandra, and I were to the right. It was tight but cozy. I felt uncomfortable as soon as we were all zippered up in our sleeping bags. At first, I just felt a little uneasy. Then, my breath was feeling labored. I couldn't stop wiggling in my sleeping bag, which was challenging in my light blue and gray mummy bag, which had no room for wiggling.

Alexandra asked me what was going on and why I wasn't trying to fall asleep. I explained that I was trying to fall asleep, had trouble breathing, and was uncomfortable. The two guys complained and told me to be quiet so we could get some rest. I turned over onto my left side, facing away from everybody,

     Raised by Wolves, Possibly Monsters

hoping that would help. About a minute later, I felt Alexandra's hand on my shoulder and stillness. Then I felt her move a little closer and put her arm entirely around me with her hand on my chest. Initially, this felt supportive. That lasted only momentarily. I became uncomfortable and even more uneasy. I was still squirmy, and my breathing was getting more labored by the minute. I waited till I could hear everybody in the tent still, quiet, and breathing evenly, then I got up, grabbed my glasses, water bottle, sleeping bag, and mat, and crawled out of the tent. As I pulled the zipper down to close it behind me, Alexandra stirred, "Michael, where are you going?"

"I'm feeling claustrophobic. I'll be okay. I'm just having trouble breathing in there where everybody else is. Go back to sleep."

She started speaking but fell back to sleep.

I set up my mat and sleeping bag between that tent and the fire on flat ground. It felt nice to be outside and in the fresh air but still warm inside my sleeping bag and close to the fire. I wasn't ready to fall asleep yet. I opened my eyes, and even with my glasses off, I could see stars and the moon shining brightly. Seeing the moon helped me calm enough to settle into my sleeping bag without squirming. It only took about ten minutes to fall asleep.

I woke up a little while later while it was still dark. I could not tell if I was awake or dreaming because I heard wolves howling in the background. My best bet was to open my eyes and look up at the stars and moon again to ensure I was awake. I was. I appreciated having the stars and moon to keep me company.

As I returned to sleep, I again thought I heard wolves in the background, unsure if I was sleeping or awake. I pulled the little flat on the top of my mummy sleeping bag a little further over my head, so I was completely covered and fell back asleep. I was not fully asleep when the wolves approached our camp. Again, it was hard to tell what a dream was and what real life was until I heard their footsteps and breathing around me. They circled me a couple of times, and I could feel them smelling and checking me out. I did simple breathing, Reiki, and prayer. What else could I do in a situation like that? What was I going to get up and run naked in cold weather with a pack of wolves chasing me?

They seemed to lose interest in me and gained interest in the cans and other food supplies that needed to be thoroughly cleaned but weren't. I could hear the cans and dishes knocked around, chewed on, and growling sounds. None of this did anything to create a sense of safety for me, but I was glad they had a distraction. When they ate whatever they could from the picnic table, they wandered back to me. I could hear them breathing, and then I listened to their footsteps move over to one side of me and then the other. One of them howled. They all howled. And then they all took off from the same direction they came from on my left.

When I could hear them no longer, even though it was cold as hell, I needed to sit up, get on my knees, and pee on the ground next to me because I was holding it in the whole time. I remember for a split second thinking about what it would feel like to pee in your pants but actually to pee in a sleeping bag. Fortunately, I was able to hold it in until they left.

I settled down, got on my knees next to my sleeping bag, and prayed once more. I crawled back into my sleeping bag to fall asleep even though it was starting to get light out. I turned onto my belly, leaning on my elbows to look at the water in the distance; this felt comforting. A couple of minutes later, everybody was out of the tents in their sleeping attire, trying to figure out what had happened, why I was sleeping outside, and if they really heard wolves howling during the night.

I had a hard time explaining any of it, but the one part they all seemed to understand was that I said my back was hurting and I needed space. As exhausted as I was when I went to bed, I was significantly more exhausted now, but I had to put on clothes so we could go horseback riding.

The following two days of our journey were on horseback. This time, I ended up with the slow horse. We needed to stay focused and keep moving to ensure we reached where the van drivers would be with the van the following day.

We needed to go higher up into the mountains on day two. Sometimes, I didn't think the old horse I was riding had it in him with some more challenging climbs, but he did fine. After lunch, we needed to cross a river, and some of the horses were skittish, mine being one of them. He eventually went through, as did the rest of them. When we reached the other side of the river, which was moving rapidly and forcefully, our group split into two groups for the remainder of the day. It was not intentional, or maybe it was, the Europeans were in one group,

 Raised by Wolves, Possibly Monsters

while the Americans were in the other group, with Alexandra joining the Americans. We were all excited about the possibility of camping at a "Resort Center" in "teepees" by the shoreline of a large lake, Khovsgol Nuur. I think we all had a fantasy of swimming after a hard day. None of us had prepared ourselves for how cold the water was! Kevin and I went in a little past our knees, looked at each other, and returned.

After weeks of eating crappy food, it was such a treat to have a meal of borscht with fresh bread! We laughed and relaxed after dinner in the Retreat Center. The trip had been a grueling seven days, although enjoyable, and many opportunities for connection with each other, the land, and ourselves.

While we were getting ready to leave in the morning, the retreat center owner offered me a job to run the retreat center. For a moment, I considered it. Why wouldn't I want to live in a teepee on a beautiful property with a lake at a retreat center? Well, the answer was easy—the food. I loved Mongolia, and I loved Mongolian people, not the food. It was lovely having borscht the night before and the night before that. But there's only so much mutton that I can eat. I thanked him for the opportunity and joined the rest of the group.

I finally felt ready to do what I had come to Mongolia to do. As soon as we packed up all our stuff, we headed back to Ulaanbaatar. It was now time to put that vision/dream in motion.

The ride back took a few hours. The group energy felt unified. We went through a lot together in a short period, survived, and primarily thrived. In my mind, while leaning my head against the side of the van, I was putting together the plan to get to the southwest corner of Mongolia to a small town named Altai.

While everybody was unloading their gear and discussing their travel plans, Alexandra walked over to me with sadness. "You're going to leave on your trip tomorrow, right?"

"Yes, I believe so. I still have to find a way to get there, but that's the plan."

"I have enjoyed getting know you, Michael." Her English was not as fluid or grammatically accurate when Alexandra was experiencing strong emotions. I did not mind; I took it as a compliment, an act of love.

"Me too. It's been great traveling and talking with you as well, Alexandra. I think you're beautiful and amazing."

I walked around the city, trying to find transportation across the country. Everybody I spoke to advised me to take a bus heading west at 7:15 a.m. the next day. That bus would get me about 150 km West on the only road that traversed the country from east to west.

I went to a couple of the bazaars to get supplies, such as carrots, apples, and peanut butter, and I found a few protein bars. I needed a warmer cap to wear and found a reversible hat made of camel wool; one side was solely the color camel, and the other was the color camel with a white stripe along the bottom. I had never worn camel wool before and had no idea how comfortable it felt. It was like having a blanket on your head. I went to a place in the city with good quality Goulash to ensure I had a lovely meal before leaving. I felt I was preparing for something epic, not just a bus ride.

I checked in with myself to see what was going on. One of the more practical voices in my head wanted to ensure that I purchased everything I needed in the capital city since I had no idea what would be available. This answer satisfied most of me, except the part that knew this had nothing to do with bus trips, towns with no supplies, or being adequately prepared. I was scared. I wanted to offer the parts of me trying to control the situation that would ease the fear and anxiety. It worked fine for those parts of me. My core was terrified that I was leaving the city of Ulaanbaatar to intentionally go to what might be my death. No number of carrots, apples, peanut butter, or protein bars could convince the backpacker part of me that everything was going to be okay.

At 7:20 a.m., while waiting to enter the bus doors, I paused to learn the social rules of who gets on the bus and when. It was evident that there were almost twice as many people as seats, and that was before about fifteen sacks of carrots, potatoes, and onions passengers loaded into the back three rows of the bus about eight feet high. I was the only non-Mongolian on the bus. They all looked at me strangely. Occasionally, one of them would try to interact with me speaking Mongolian. I only knew a few sentences, and it didn't sound like they were the correct reply to their question. Several older women got up from their seats and insisted that I sit in them. I refused. Eventually, about five stood up, and almost two rows of empty seats had nobody in them. A couple of men mumbled something and sat in the empty seats, and the older women snapped at them

          Raised by Wolves, Possibly Monsters

sharply. They got up and moved to another side of the bus. It took me a bit to catch on, but they would sit when I took one of the seats. As much as it went against my social instincts, as soon as I sat down, the rest of them sat down and made room for each other so that none of them had to stand. Several had small children on them or near them.

I then experienced something for the first time that I would often experience in various situations and environments over the next few weeks. The woman sitting next to me, who had a young child of probably three or four years old, who I assumed was her granddaughter, just plopped her granddaughter on my lap while she dug into the bag that she was carrying and looked for things. The girl leaned into me and curled up on my lap as if we had known each other our whole lives, and I had cared for her many times before. I was confused and taken aback by the ease with which she accepted being placed on the lap of a man she didn't know. She started talking to me in Mongolian, and when I didn't understand, she took my right hand and started drawing pictures of what she was trying to say on my hand with her index finger. I had no idea what she was trying to communicate, but I enjoyed having her use my hand as a whiteboard or a blackboard. When the grandmother finished what she needed to do, she reached over and took the girl from my lap. The girl made noises indicating that she didn't want to, then pleaded something to her grandmother. Her grandmother looked at me briefly but very directly and deliberately, then looked back at the girl, and then she nodded to the girl. The girl then put her head on my chest, put her arms around me, and promptly fell asleep about a minute and a half later.

The feeling of this girl, whom I would not be able to communicate with verbally or probably see again or know her name, but who was completely safe with me, was not something I had experienced at home. It felt touching, beautiful, and lovely. The force of her love and safety made my eyes leak salty water.

About two hours later, the bus driver yelled something, and everybody stirred. He pulled over about two minutes later, and everybody got up and left without their bags, food, or luggage. However, most people had their toilet paper rolls in their hands. Mongolian toilet paper is light brown, and it feels like something between newspaper and some form of soft cloth that stretches and is absorbent. In Mongolia, you bring a roll of toilet paper everywhere you go because none of the stores or restaurants have toilet paper in their bathrooms. Even in the city, there are little "stalls" that you can use as a toilet on street corners and in alleys, but they don't have any plumbing or toilet paper.

From some of the other trips I had taken in vans, I understood that some places qualify the Mongolian version of a rest stop. In essence, everybody stands in a line on the side of the road on the pebbled desert and urinates. People that need to squat, whether by urination or defecation, walk about fifteen meters, and there's a yellow flag-like barrier that has two thin metal posts in the ground holding it up where you squat behind, do your business, wipe your ass, and then pull your pants back up. It doesn't keep you hidden; it just gives you the illusion of being hidden.

Over the next few weeks, I learned that any time a man was watching women pee or women on the other side of these little yellow-cloth barriers, all the other men and women would yell at him. There is something utterly comical about having all of these people in the line urinating while yelling at each other. About five minutes later, the bus driver whistled, and as if we were robots programmed, everybody stopped what they were doing and got back on the bus in the same places we were sitting before. We stopped again about two hours later for the same process. The third time we stopped, the bus driver whistled, and everybody grabbed their things and got off the bus. While departing, on the right, I could see it looked like we were a couple of hundred meters from a town's outskirts. We had gotten somewhere, but I had yet to learn where we had gotten to. I felt finished with the group excursions and Ulaanbaatar. I was on my way to Altai in the Gobi Desert.

The Journey to Southwest Mongolia

 ANYONE WHO HAS traveled to Mongolia has come across and seen Ovoos. Ovoos are Mongolian stone and stick cairns. You can find them on the top of hills and mountains. They typically have strips of blue fabric hanging all over them to help you identify that they are Ovoo. The blue

          Raised by Wolves, Possibly Monsters

stripes may have other significance, but I am unaware of them. They have been part of Mongolian culture before Buddhism or Shamanism. Most Mongolians follow the traditions of Tibetan Buddhism, with His Holiness the Dalai Lama as the head of the tradition. When one approaches an Ovoo, we walk around it three times, followed by an offering to the pile. A rock, pebble, or stick will do.

Along with the offering, we share a wish. These cairns pay tribute and gratitude to the spirits and ancestors for protecting the surrounding land. I saw them most commonly during a pass on hills and mountains.

I enjoyed the experience when I was with groups of people following the Ovoo rituals. However, when traveling solo, I would sit a few feet back cross-legged on the dirt and sand and meditate until I felt complete. The connection with the land, the sky, the Earth, and myself was apparent and palpable. It also allowed me to pause and step outside of what I was doing or what I thought was important.

It took me a couple of hours to find a ride going in the direction I needed. It was hysterical and frustrating being sent from one person to another person to another person to another driver to another bus to another van to another driver till I finally landed at three Mongolian men who were going a couple hundred kilometers west.

They were drinking vodka when I arrived, when we left, and all along the way. One of the fascinating experiences of traveling through Mongolia in a motor vehicle is that since there aren't roads, you are predominantly traveling in the desert. It is only sometimes obvious when you're about to hit a large rock that would cause a big bang and a flat tire. Most drivers have two, if not three, spare tires for the ride. In addition, because it's dry and hot, and vehicles have to work so hard on unpaved surfaces, most journeys include a radiator leak or burst. They often have several gallons of water and a backup radiator as well. These are the things that all drivers have: a surplus of tires, a surplus of radiators, a surplus of water for the radiators, and a surplus of vodka for driving.

We were several hours into our journey, and it was approaching dark. When we had gone through all three back-up tires and a radiator, they decided to stop. They parked in an area where they perceived another vehicle might come by that night or the following day.

The guy in the backseat with me kept bugging me to drink. When I kept refusing, he started making jokes about me, and initially, the two guys in the front seat would laugh with him. As he got drunker and drunker and more obnoxious, they started yelling at him to stop. Eventually, he fell asleep from drunkenness. Several times during the night, I woke up with him lying on top of me, the first time and second time on my shoulder, and the third time on my lap since. I felt like there was a warm bottle of vodka lying on top of me by how much he wreaked of vodka.

Early in the morning, we heard a vehicle in the distance. We got out of the car and waved them down. One of them got into the Russian Jeep, along with two busted tires and the initial leaking radiator. They returned about three hours later. It took about an hour and a half to do the work necessary to continue.

The next afternoon, we arrived at a small town whose name I had never found out. Calling it a town would be an overstatement. There was a gas station, a small grocery store, and twenty-five small homes. They needed gas, supplies, food, and more vodka. Even though I was in the middle of nowhere, I determined I did not feel safe continuing with these men in the Kia Jeep any longer. My prospects of finding a ride were slim. I banked on my assumption that people passed through this little stop along the way regularly. The two guys in the front seat seemed happy that I was leaving, but the drunk guy in the backseat continued to yell at me even while I was walking away from them, and I was about two-hundred meters from the gas station. I just wanted to get away from them. When I saw they had pulled out, I walked back by the gas station to the general store to get supplies.

Another exciting aspect of Mongolian life, both for natives and foreigners, is if you're walking on the side of the road and you wave, every single car, truck, or motorcycle will pull over and negotiate a ride for a price. Whether they are a family of seven, a sheep herder transporting sheep, a grandmother with her grandchild, or a woman on a motorcycle, all of them will pull over and instantly become a taxi. In essence, anybody with a motor vehicle, a horse, or a camel is a taxi driver!

It only took a few hours of sitting on my backpack and grazing on food before a solidly built man and an older woman stopped. We negotiated a price, and I pointed to the map where I was going. I ascertained that they were going mostly in that direction. I hopped in the back, and off we went! It was such a relief to be in a vehicle with people who weren't drunk or in the process of getting drunk. They were both friendly, and we communicated as best we could with linguistic obstacles. They genuinely tried, as did I. We had driven about what I guess was two and a half hours when they pulled off the road into a little village. It was dusk, and the sun had gone down, but there was still a little light. They drove to a field, grabbed shovels and spades from the back of the Jeep, and started digging. My initial thought was they were going to kill me and bury me right there in Mongolian soil!

It turned out they were harvesting carrots and potatoes. It was getting darker; they handed me a shovel, and I joined them. I did not express to them, nor did I have a way to do so, that my back was already hurting from not sleeping the night before with the vodka-infused man breathing and leaning all over me to further inflame the issues I was experiencing with my spine and lumbar areas. We dug up carrots and potatoes and put them in burlap sacks. We loaded the burlap sacks into the back where I had been seated. I wondered where I would sit when they talked to each other, and the woman asked me to join them in the front seat. She was smaller than me, so she got in the middle, and I sat in the passenger seat. There were more attempts at conversation. The one thing we could all communicate is that we liked music, and music was enjoyable. We listened to music.

A few hours later, we arrived at a shack with gas pumps and nothing else around it. The driver filled up the car with gas and then pointed for me to join them inside the structure. There were several rectangular tables and benches along the perimeter. I could smell food; I guessed that we were here to eat. It was pitch dark, and we had been on the road for much of the day. They had goulash, which became my default setting when possible. The meal was good. I enjoyed it more because I had spent about twenty-four hours eating mutton and junk food like chips and a few carrots. A man, a woman, and two teenage girls were operating the place. The woman seemed much younger than the man, but it turned out that he was a chain smoker and vodka consumer and looked much older than he was.

After we finished eating, the driver motioned me to come with him back out to the vehicle; he grabbed his bag and pointed for me to grab my pack. I did not know what was happening, but I followed his instructions. He pulled out his sleeping bag and motioned for me to do the same. The benches along the perimeter are for travelers spending the night resting. A few other men showed up for rest as well. By the time we settled in, and the lights were turned out, seven people were sleeping along the perimeter, and the family of four slept in a room off the main area.

The man who owned or ran the place was very drunk. He was pointing and yelling at me while I was trying to sleep, and I kept hearing the word "American" in most of his sentences. The driver and the woman passenger kept pushing back against him, trying to protect me. He then grabbed a broom with a wooden rod and started poking me through my sleeping bag. I was beginning to lose my calm and restraint. He continued, and the man and the woman continued to yell at him. The other assorted travelers were also yelling at him. He became more out of control and lifted the broom over his head, planning to swing it down at me. Both the driver and I jumped out of our sleeping bags and tackled him. He went flying because he could not have weighed over a hundred pounds. He was small and frail. The woman, who I assumed was his wife, came out screaming at him. She dragged him by the collar of his shirt into their bedroom, with him complaining the whole time. The two teenage girls were yelling at him as well. When all of that drama subsided, we got back in our sleeping bags, and five minutes later, everybody was sleeping.

We woke at the break of dawn as there was bustling inside the building. I smelled eggs and something else frying that turned out to be potatoes. We ate breakfast and started loading the Jeep. The other travelers had already left when we were ready to go. What caught my attention was the family of four scurrying out of the building, getting into a Jeep, and leaving before we did. I don't know why I found it funny that this rest stop was now closed since there was nobody there. We turned left out of the parking lot on our way.

It had snowed all night, and the road itself was reasonably safe, but everywhere around us, the snow piled high due to the wind, which created snow drifts that were often twenty or thirty feet high. About a half hour later, we noticed that the family of four was a couple of hundred meters off to the right of the road

     Raised by Wolves, Possibly Monsters

in a snowdrift. The driver turned right and headed in their direction through the heavy snow.

When we arrived, they were all in a state of panic. The Jeep driver had a chain in the back. I remember thinking at the time, no matter what situation came up, it seemed like he had whatever was needed in the back of the vehicle, even though I didn't know anything was back there. They connected a chain from the front of the Jeep that we were into the back of the other Jeep. The chain was about six feet long, and they doubled it back, so it was about a three-foot extension. The guy who attacked me the night before got in between the two Jeeps, giving directions to the driver of the Jeep that I was in, who was now in the driver's seat of their vehicle. All four females were standing outside of the Jeep some distance away. I was standing about three feet to the right of the drunk guy. My brief history with him convinced me that this would go poorly somehow. It did.

There was a lot of snow on the ground. As the driver was slowly going in reverse and the tires were spinning a little bit, the drunk guy kept waving for him to continue to go backward; the wheels caught a little bit of tread and jerked back directly into the drunk guy, who was now doubled over, appearing unconscious!

I was screaming at the top of my lungs and banging on the door for the driver to pull forward. He finally understood what I was saying, and I ran back to catch the drunk guy as the Jeep pulled away. I made it there just in time to catch him falling, but I'm not sure it would have mattered since there was so much snow the landing would have been soft. It was obvious his shoulder was dislocated because it was hanging. The two adult women came over and decided it was best to lie him down in the snow and help him wake up, which he did a minute later. He didn't know where he was or what was going on. There was much discussion and planning, but I didn't know what any of it was. All I knew was that five minutes later, the driver, the two adult women, and the drunk guy were all in the front seat of the vehicle I was traveling in. The drunk guy was barely conscious, and he was lying across the two women in the front. We had put down the back seat and rearranged all of the potatoes and carrots to create, in essence, a bed for us to lie on. However, there was only enough room for two people to lie down. The two teenage girls were lying on their backs with their feet towards the back of the Jeep and their heads towards the front seat. They pointed to me to lie on top of the one to the right, who looked to be the older of the two and probably fourteen or fifteen years old.

I didn't understand what they wanted me to do, but eventually, I figured out that they wanted me to lie on top of her. So, I am lying on top of this teenage girl with my body in between her legs and my head on her breasts. I could tell that she was very uncomfortable. I could not discern how much was mental, emotional, or physical. I saw a tear or two in her eyes, again not able to determine how much of that was having an old, strange man lying between her legs with his head on her breast or what I assumed was her father or uncle unconscious with his arm hanging.

About fifteen minutes into the ride, just like earlier in the week in the tent, I became claustrophobic for the second time and the first time in decades. I started freaking out, kicking my legs, and screaming, the driver pulled over. I crawled out of the vehicle and landed on the snow-covered road. I climbed on top of the Jeep and started untying my backpack. I yanked it down, threw it on my back, and started walking in the direction we were headed. The driver looked scared and ran after me, confused and deeply concerned, evident by his scrunched-up forehead and eyebrows and the panic in his eyes. He just kept yelling cold and snow, cold and snow, cold and snow. I used hand signals and breathing to show that I was claustrophobic and couldn't breathe. He put up his finger, communicating to wait a minute. He ran back to the Jeep, and they rearranged everything. This time, the girls were lying on each other, and I was on the right side by myself, with at least a little more space and breathing room. He convinced me to return to the vehicle, and I grudgingly submitted.

A couple of hours later, we pulled into a small village that appeared to be a simple, former Soviet shelter of sorts with six white, concrete buildings/homes and a larger one that turned out to be a cafeteria and community center. Everything "just woke up" when we arrived, people running from all different directions, helping the unconscious guy out and making sure he didn't get further hurt. They used a table as a stretcher to bring him into the community center. A minute later, a doctor appeared and was looking at him. The doctor spoke some English and afterward communicated to me that the guy had a concussion, several of the bones in his arm and shoulder were fractured, and he

    Raised by Wolves, Possibly Monsters

had a dislocated shoulder. He told me to sit down and that we would all eat soon. He said I could stay in the bedroom with his sons, and they would sleep in the same bed so that I would have my own bed. Everybody was lovely, and their response to having strangers arrive with an unconscious man who was injured was endearing and heartwarming. After we ate, the man received medical treatment, and his arm was now in a sling. We all went to various small white cement residences.

The doctor and his wife showed me to their home, the first one on the left, and directed me towards the bedroom. Their two sons were twins. Mongolia, like South Korea, has a lot of twins. The boys asked me all kinds of questions, with their dad being a translator. It was cute. A few minutes later, the lights were out, and I was sleeping in a room with two boys, probably around ages six or seven.

Again, everybody was up at dawn, we enjoyed a freshly prepared breakfast, and the three of us left soon after. The family of four stayed there. There was a lightness and feeling of relief between us that morning in the Jeep. I did not understand what they were saying, but I could still figure it out. I imagine it was something like, "Holy shit! We almost killed that guy by accident, and what the hell were they doing in the middle of that snowdrift anyway? Then we made it through this American guy freaking out in the Jeep, and we found a village to stay in for the night. The guy squished between the two vehicles is going to be okay, and somehow, we're on the road again, and it's bright and sunny, and the sky is blue, and there's snow everywhere, and we're okay, and life is good!" At least, that's the narrative I wrote by witnessing their expressions, energy, and tone.

That night, we made it to the city of Altai, which is different from the town of Altai, which was my destination. This Altai was their destination. He dropped her off and then brought me to a hotel. He negotiated a fair price for me and helped me carry my backpack to the room I would be staying in, even though I didn't need help. He was a beautiful and kind man. We said goodbye, and then he put out his hand. I received it and shook his hand. He seemed overjoyed. He then pulled me closer and hugged me tightly. I shared another beautiful minute with a lovely man. He left, and I went to get something to eat. I was vacillating between moments of extreme excitement and extreme fear and panic. I was aware that tomorrow, I would need to find a way from the city of Altai to the town of Altai. Therefore, the real journey was about to begin. It briefly crossed my mind that this might be one of my last meals. I had two servings of goulash.

As someone who has done several long treks and expeditions, going into a desert solo without a tent seemed insane. And to everybody else, for that matter. That's what I was told to do via Inner Guidance. I picked up carrots, peanut butter, an apple, and protein bars at the grocery store.

I found a place where I ate a large breakfast with several eggs, potatoes, and something that was a cross between ham and Canadian bacon, as well as two glasses of orange juice. A couple of women were selling fresh-made flatbreads, similar to Naan, on the side of the road. I also bought one for no reason but to reorganize my pack. The last detail to coordinate was how to get from the city of Altai to the village of Altai.

I wandered around the bazaar for a few minutes to see if there would be an easy way to connect with a ride. There wasn't. I was impatient, so I pulled the straps on my backpack tighter and headed out on the only road through town. The road lasted about five blocks, and then it was the crumbly dirt of the Mongolian desert. Lastly, I took a deep breath, connected with Reiki, connected with God, connected with my Higher Self, and then began walking slowly and deliberately with purpose.

I had walked for about thirty minutes, give or take, when a family packed into the front of a truck with their whole life stuffed into the back of the truck bed, including all of the pieces that make up their ger, passed by. The kids all waved hello. I waved back and started walking again after the dust the tires had created subsided. About two minutes later, they stopped. I saw many young hands sticking out the window and waving for me to come. I walked faster. The door opened when I approached the vehicle, and four children and their mother piled out of the truck. They started giving me obvious and precise directions on what they wanted to happen, not knowing that I needed help understanding every word they said. Still, I followed where they were pointing to and where their eyes were focused, and I understood that they wanted me to put my backpack in the truck's bed. I took my bag off and crawled onto the side of the truck.

I was seated in the front next to the mother, who was in the middle of the

     Raised by Wolves, Possibly Monsters

front seat. We were not even two minutes into the drive when two kids had crawled onto my lap from the back seat. Five minutes later, another of their siblings joined them; the fourth one fell asleep before he had a chance to think about coming up. And then they carried on as if I wasn't there.

When they pulled up to the village of Altai, they drove to a little side street, where an older woman awaited them. She looked startled when she saw me in the truck. I guessed she was the grandmother. Everybody piled out, and more instructions, more directions. The kids ran in with the grandmother, and then the mother motioned me to get back in the truck, following her. The three of us drove two blocks to a large, abandoned building. They pulled up next to the building and pointed for me to go into the building. I climbed on the back of the truck, got my backpack, and jumped back down. She hurried into the building and kept waiting for me to follow her. She brought me down a series of hallways of what I assumed was, at some point, an apartment building with a school or a school with some bedrooms for staff or janitors. She ushered me into the room she thought I should be in, for reasons I have no idea, because it didn't look different from any other rooms. She waited for me to put my backpack down, which I did, and she again scurried away, wanting me to follow her, to what ended up being a kitchen that looked unused for years. For some reason, she thought I needed to know where the kitchen was, which I assume did not have gas, electricity, or any other way to use it. The last stop was the bathroom, which also looked like nobody used it for years. After she was satisfied with showing me where everything was, she smiled, waved goodbye, and left.

I was trying to figure out what to do with my stuff, whether it was safe to stay there, illegal, or anything else problematic. While trying to figure it out, I walked around the building out of curiosity, and I heard some footsteps and some women talking, so I headed back to the room where my gear was. The woman was back with another woman, who was her sister, and two younger women. The two younger women giggled and looked at each other, exchanging glances when they saw me, and then they held hands and giggled some more.

I had spent enough time in Asia to know what that was all about and did my best to ignore it. Until one, and then both of them, started interacting with me in simple English. They asked me where I was from and what I was doing. They took turns asking questions, and whichever one was not asking questions slowly looked me up and down several times, blushing and hiding their head between their friend's or sister's head. The older women were giving them instructions and telling them what to say to me: come to our house for dinner, and we will feed you tonight. I said yes, and one of the older women said something to the younger women, and then they repeated, "My Aunt wants me to come here many times, see you ok, building use no more. I see you safe." As soon as she finished talking, she and the other girl had a quick exchange and more giggling. She pointed to her sister, "Sister, come too." She pointed to the floor, meaning "here." I nodded and said "Okay." The four of them left with the two younger women giggling, grabbing each other's arms, and playing. It made me a little nervous.

I put down my mat and sleeping bag, created a pillow out of several shirts and a sweatshirt, like I always did, and set up the space to take a nap. I fell asleep as soon as I put my head down. I woke up sometime later with the two young women standing at the threshold of the room, watching me. I have no idea how long they were there!

When they saw that I was awake enough to see them there, "We see you okay." Then they giggled and left. They did these two more times that afternoon, and then the third time they came after that, "We eat food." I put down the pen and the journal I had been writing in and put it in my sleeping bag. I gathered another sweatshirt and put on my boots. In between their visits, I took a brief walk through the village and then circled the town's perimeter a couple of times to get oriented. I was grateful there was an Ovoo; I needed help getting grounded. The three of us left, and as we were walking to whichever home we were going to, they were both on my left-hand side and giggling. Then, one of them pointed to a building on our right, "New School." Then she pointed back to the building I had been in, "Old School." I nodded in acknowledgment.

It was a lovely meal; I don't remember anything we ate. I was mentally preparing to leave in the morning to go somewhere, which I did not yet know where that was. After the meal, the two young women walked me back to the old school. There was a man in one of the rooms smoking. They yelled at him, and he left. I thought it was hysterical. A grown middle-aged man got yelled at by

	Raised by Wolves, Possibly Monsters

these two young women, and he ran as if he was being pointed at with a rifle. The three of us went to my room. They just stood at the threshold, watching me. I was trying to figure out what they were looking for, wanted, or were thinking. They didn't say anything to me or each other; they just stood there. A few minutes passed, and I felt more uncomfortable with each passing minute. They talked briefly, then one of them said goodbye, and the other stayed in the doorway to the room. She stood there for a minute. "I stay here, you safe." I did not know how to respond to this, how long she would stand there, if I should invite her in, or what to do. She just stood there.

I started reorganizing my backpack to do something so that I didn't have to look at her looking at me. A few minutes later, I felt a tap on my right shoulder. She was standing next to me, looking at me with excitement, anticipation, and something similar to confusion. I turned around, and she pointed to her lips with her right index finger and then pointed to my lips. "I kiss you." I did not know what to do or say. I had no idea if she was fifteen or thirty-three. Mongolians have beautiful, golden, soft, and lovely skin, so it was almost impossible for me, as an outsider, to know how old any of them are except for those who are chain smokers with lots of wear and tear.

While I was trying to figure out what to do, she moved closer, pressing her chest up against mine. As she was about to kiss me, I put up my right index finger "No kiss." She looked startled, not necessarily disappointed, just startled. I don't know what narrative she had in her head, but I think me saying no to kissing her was not any of them. She stepped back two or three steps. She put her head down in what appeared to be shame and/or embarrassment. I put my hand over my heart; she gave a semi-smile, and from behind her shame and embarrassment. "I come back see you safe." She nodded her head. She was back about an hour later, this time with her sister. It was pitch black at this point. When they were walking down the hall, I was hoping it was them or the two mothers and not somebody wanting to cause me trouble besides wanting to kiss me. They stood at the door's threshold for a couple of minutes, holding each other's hands tightly. The one who tried to kiss me earlier pointed a finger at me. "You okay?"

"Yes, me, okay. Thank you." I put my hands together and gave them a half bow. They smiled and gave me the same half-bow with big smiles on their faces.

"Okay, bye-bye." and left. The building was now quiet, as was the little village. After knowing they were far from the building, I walked out the back door so I could pee before going to bed. I woke in the morning with the two of them standing on the doorway's threshold. There was no actual door to the room. I realized that these two young women, who might have been teenagers, were staring at me, not knowing that I was naked in my sleeping bag. I was grateful that they didn't know that, but I did not know how to tell them to leave so that I could get dressed. "Hello." I did not know what else to say.

"We bring food." They reached down and held out various breakfast foods, such as fruit, coffee, and apple juice. They were waiting for me to come and take it from there.

"Thank you! I'll eat food soon." I pointed to a shirt and my Levi's, "I get dressed." I realized that my sleeping bag had slid down a little bit, and they could now see I wasn't wearing a shirt. They were both staring at my chest, looking at each other, giggling, and then grabbing each other's hands. Their faces turned red. So did mine. They giggled again and then just ran away. And that was that. I got up, got dressed, and ate the breakfast that they brought me; that was enough for three people, which I was grateful for because I was leaving as soon as I had my shit together.

The First Steps

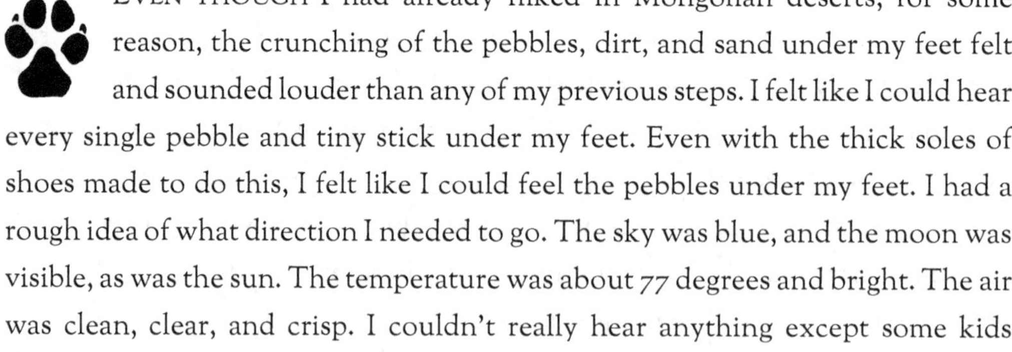 EVEN THOUGH I had already hiked in Mongolian deserts, for some reason, the crunching of the pebbles, dirt, and sand under my feet felt and sounded louder than any of my previous steps. I felt like I could hear every single pebble and tiny stick under my feet. Even with the thick soles of shoes made to do this, I felt like I could feel the pebbles under my feet. I had a rough idea of what direction I needed to go. The sky was blue, and the moon was visible, as was the sun. The temperature was about 77 degrees and bright. The air was clean, clear, and crisp. I couldn't really hear anything except some kids playing in the distance.

I approached the Ovoo, took a breath, and released it. I stepped forward,

     Raised by Wolves, Possibly Monsters

beginning my trip around the Ovoo, and started my first trip around. My second trip around, and then my third trip around completed, I kneeled with my right knee, signed the Reiki symbols in the air with my right hand, silent prayer, and bowed to something or somebody. I was now ready.

I lifted my backpack onto my back and stood tall. For reasons I know nothing about, I stuck my chest out as if I was getting ready to go to battle. I was.

The first couple of hours were impressively uneventful. I was mostly walking, breathing, watching, and paying attention. I was struck by how few forms of life there were. A little dry, prickly bush here, a little patch of five or seven blades of something like grass over there, a dead tree off in the distance, that was about it. Nothing was moving but me and whatever my feet came in contact with. The stillness was actually uncomfortable. The concept of nothing else alive within eyesight felt eerie and uneasy. The lack of life was a reminder that there was a reason that everybody thought I was committing suicide; nothing lives here except snow leopards now and then, which did not give me any comfort to think about.

As I moved further and further from the village, I became aware of how loud my footsteps sounded when I reached what felt like the center of two hands surrounding me. The cliffs on my left and right created something like an echo from just my feet walking. Now and then, I would make a sound or two to hear it reverberate.

A Sound

I FELL INTO the rhythm of walking, walking, and walking. I counted my footsteps as Thich Nhat Hahn had instructed in several of his books. 1, 2, 3, 4, and back to 1. 1, 2, 3, 4, and back to 1. Since there were no other distractions besides my brain, I decided that instead of counting to four and returning to 1, I would count to 10 and return to 1 as I did with sitting meditation. After about fifteen minutes of this practice, I felt fully present. I felt aligned from head to toe with myself, the Earth, and everything around me. Time and space became part of the background. There was just me, my feet, the Earth under me, and my next step.

I heard a peculiar sound coming from somewhere. I could not place the sound or direction since everything would bounce off the cliffs in all directions. Each "fishbowl" was only 100-200 yards long before entering another one; sounds seemed to come from everywhere and nowhere. I guessed the sound was coming from before me, but I wasn't certain. I continued to walk, but I needed to be more tenuous in my steps and breathe more naturally. The sound was getting incrementally louder; it grew from what sounded like possibly just a little bit of wind in the distance to now would qualify as a whisper. It still sounded pretty far away, whatever "it" was.

A few minutes passed, and the sound continued to get louder. I was getting nervous.

I didn't know what else to do with this sound but to keep walking. Isn't that what I was sent here to do?

The sound got louder, and now it was about the volume of two humans having a normal conversation. And then I saw it in the distance. Between my bad vision and the length of its body, it looked like a dog with wings. I could not believe that the sound I heard for several minutes in the distance was a bird! As it got closer, I was able to identify the bird as a hawk. The sound that kept reverberating from one fishbowl to the next fishbowl to the next fishbowl was its wings flapping! I listened to the bird's wings flapping for five minutes before I could see it! By the time it was over my head and circling me, it was louder than two humans having a regular conversation. It was just a hawk flapping its wings. After it circled me once, then the second time, it passed, and then the same process happened in reverse. I heard the flapping, and then it got softer and softer, and finally, I turned around when I couldn't see it anymore. Then, there was a gentle breeze in the distance. Then it was hearing my feet crunch the Earth beneath me again.

That first day was primarily walking. I had no profound spiritual or emotional experiences or visions. I could see the Sun finishing its day's journey across the horizon. I had my initial pangs of anxiety about where and how I was going to sleep. After several hours of being very intentional and focused on my feet and the Earth underneath it, my mind was writing all kinds of scenarios

    Raised by Wolves, Possibly Monsters

about the different ways that I would die in the Gobi without a tent or any form of shelter. The most frequent story in my head was me lying on top of my backpack for comfort, and at some point during the night, the hawk whose wings I heard flapping far in advance, and after its sighting swooped down and started munching on me. I tried to run away, but how far away could I get in a desert surrounded by cliffs with a sixty-five-pound backpack?

More Sounds

FOR THE SECOND time that day, I heard something way before I had any idea what it was or where it was coming from. This time, it sounded like a military troop off in space at the end of a challenging day, dragging their feet through the dusty soil with their heavy boots. Since I knew that wasn't what was happening, I wanted to know what kind of animal would make that sound based on my experience with the hawk earlier in the day. Like the hawk earlier in the day, I could not come up with anything that resembled the truth.

I didn't have an actual route of where I was going. I was trying to "listen" for guidance; I figured I would tentatively and carefully walk in the direction of where I thought the sound might be coming from, which was in between these two cliffs on my left, but still going south as guided. What was funny was that as I got closer to the sound, I didn't get any closer to figuring out what was making the sound. That was until about ten minutes later when the path weaved between two cliffs to the right, and as it was bending around, I deduced that the sound was coming from the right above me. I looked up the hill, and on top, I saw an entire herd of sheep, much to my surprise! It looked like there were at least fifty, if not seventy-five of them. It was extraordinary to be standing between these two cliffs, looking up at the sheep who all moved to the cliff's edge to look at me.

I had that feeling when standing or sitting somewhere, and a deer pops up in front of you, not knowing you are there, and it just stares at you, and you stare back, and neither one of you does or says anything. Except it wasn't a deer; it was an entire meadow of sheep about 250 feet above me. I continued standing there looking up at them, not knowing what I was expecting to happen or not happen, but I should stand there and look at them. I looked away for a minute and noticed that about 150 yards away, to my left, there was a path going up to the top of the hill. While I was contemplating whether that choice would be beneficial or not, he appeared.

The sheep parted ways as this gorgeous man in a long blue silk robe on top of a brown horse with a white stripe just above its eyes came through to the edge of the cliff. He said hello to me in Mongolian, and I replied in kind. He began talking to me in Mongolian, thinking that I understood more than the very simplistic few phrases I had picked up. I stretched my hands to express something I didn't understand; he nodded his head and mumbled some things in response. He pointed to the right where the path was to go up the cliff. He snapped his whip, and off he was towards the trail with the entire herd following him. When he got to the trail, he cracked his whip again twice, and then they stopped. He turned the horse around to look at them and shouted something in their direction. They turned around and went back to where they were before. About forty seconds later, he was right next to me. He had such a beautiful face.

He tried again to communicate with me in Mongolian; the only things I understood were food, family, and ger. When he realized verbal communication would be ineffective, he nodded and pointed off behind a cliff. When he saw me looking in that direction, he started to move slowly, waving for me to follow. The pass was narrower than most other passes I had seen. When we made it to the other side of the pass, I turned left, and there was their ger and a complete base camp with a woman and two sets of little twin boys by her side. Everybody stopped what they were doing when they saw me, and a girl popped out from behind the ger. The man and woman exchanged several back-and-forth verbal replies. After they had finished whatever they were discussing, she nodded, looked towards the ger, and started walking in that direction. She looked back at me as she approached the door and nodded, implying that I should follow her.

The five young children, all probably under age six, just stood there stunned, staring at me without movement or sound. The man on his horse started speaking to me, but I didn't understand. As he left, he motioned for me to go to the ger. The woman invited me to follow her.

I entered the ger, and then the five kids followed me and stared. The woman

     Raised by Wolves, Possibly Monsters

pointed to where she wanted me to sit, which was next to a turquoise and orange table with six-inch legs. She handed me some tea and very stale bread. She was stirring a stew or soup that was already on the fire. Like many families, they did not have beds, cots, or benches. They just had roll-up mats on the floor when they were ready to go to bed at night and rolled them up in the morning. They had simple furnishings if you can call them that. There were two chests of drawers; one was horizontal, and one was vertical. A light wood cabinet was packed with dishes, drinking glasses, and silverware.

About five minutes later, she went over to that cabinet, grabbed a ceramic bowl and a spoon, and with her ladle, she filled it up with what appeared to be a broth with chunks of meat and dumplings. There were a couple of pieces of shaved carrot as well. As she handed me the bowl in a very soft, welcoming tone, she talked to me in what I assumed was, "Here is some food; please enjoy it as our guest." The five kids stood inside the door, watching all of this in amazement and silence. That changed when we all heard what I assumed was the father and the horse galloping and then arriving outside of the ger. The kids ran out to greet him, and the six of them returned moments later. By the time he walked in the door, the woman had filled another bowl with the soup and handed it to him upon his arrival. She then fed the five kids and herself, and we sat at the table. The seven of them were having continuous conversations, but the two sets of twin boys were primarily talking to each other, not as much with the girl and the two adults.

After dinner, I witnessed something I never would have imagined in the middle of the Gobi Desert in a hidden ger. The woman reached into a cabinet, brought out something that looked like a Game Boy, and handed it to the one set of twin boys who took turns playing it. She gave them a command, and they gave it to the other set of twin boys, then she gave another command, and they gave it to the girl to play with. Each kid had about five minutes with the handheld video game, and she took it from them. She played whatever game it was for the next hour and a half. A Game Boy in the middle of the desert! No TV, no radio, but a Game Boy.

When she stopped playing the game, she gave another set of commands to the five kids. They grabbed eight mats and spread them out across the floor.

There were four small mats for the two sets of twins that were the row above the four other mats, three adult-sized and one for the girl. The girl's mat was all the way to the right, followed by the mother, the father, and me. They all pointed for me to get on the mat. They started bringing me blankets; I pointed to my back-pack, pulling out my sleeping bag.

For some reason, that made both of the adults really happy to see, and they seemed pleased that I had that with me. I realized that I was not going to be able to go to sleep without urinating first, and I didn't know what the protocol was for that. I just put my boots on by the door without tying them, walked out, walked a hundred feet to get around the cliff, and then peed, looking up at the nearly full moon. While I was doing so, I didn't hear him approach me, but the father appeared and stood next to me as well. It was actually a sweet little moment. There was no conversation, no eye contact, just two men standing in the middle of nowhere urinating before bed. We both finished, went into the ger, and crawled into our bedding next to each other. I fell asleep while they were talking. I did not realize I was that tired.

At some point later, I heard some noises and identified them as horses arriving with humans. There were no lights on in the ger; they had already put the candles and oil lamps out. Everybody woke and stirred simultaneously, and one of the sets of twins jumped out of their mats and hurried over towards the door; as it opened, a man that I assumed was their father appeared. The boys were excited to see him. Everybody got busy moving mats around. All the way to the right was still the girl, her mother, the father, me, and the two men were next to me. Ten minutes later, everybody was sleeping again.

In the morning, we had full bowls of soup and tea, identical to what we had the night before. There was a brief conversation about what I was doing and where I was going. I wanted to help with cleaning up, and the woman and the two fathers all looked at me with fierceness in their eyes. I backed away, and everybody settled down and continued their business. A little while later, my pack was back on my back, and I was heading through the pass and off to the left with the sheep above me on the right making noise as I briefly passed them.

I felt solid and grounded, and I would have described myself as ready for the day and whatever was going to happen at the time without knowing what was

		Raised by Wolves, Possibly Monsters

actually going to happen. It would have been impossible to be prepared for this. That said, my steps were strong, solid, and firm.

After surviving the first day solo, I felt revived and confident. I could feel a living, working faith building inside of me. I walked for about thirty minutes and then found a nice size rock to plant my butt on, practice meditation, and align with Reiki.

While I was sitting there feeling connected to my Higher Self, the Earth, and Beyond, my mind reflected on the Divine Masculine inside me. That differs from the words I would have used at the time, but that feels most accurate. It occurred to me at that moment that whatever questions I had about my masculinity or "being a man" dissolved. With my ego in check and not needing anything to build it up, I could sit with how few people, or men, could do what I am doing the way I'm doing it. I was doing this based on my instincts, my trust in myself and Beyond, and a physically strong body that Betsy referred to as "The Horse" that drives the body.

At that moment on the rock, I understood that I was in the middle of something exceptional and that very few men would embark on or survive. Instead of building up and feeling bigger and more prominent, I experienced a sense of being carried and directed, and I wasn't doing this on my own, nor could I! I had experienced similar things before in moments of greatness. In every one of those moments, not that there have been that many of them, I always felt very simple, clean, and straightforward. This was one of those moments.

Before I got up to launch for the day, I took a moment to acknowledge and be grateful for what I defined as God, my body, my Teachers, mentors, friends, and family, and all of those who had gone before me and were with me at that moment. The gratitude inside and beyond me was incredible and palpable!

As I stood up, I paused to look around and take in my surroundings: the coarse soil, the sand of the Earth, the little dried and knee-high sun-abused bushes here and there, the cliffs made of reddish clay, the sky above with a handful of clouds, and the fresh, clean air. I sensed there was an opportunity to do something special. I had no idea what that meant; I just knew that something special was about to happen. And it did.

When my backpack was back in its rightful place on top of my body and strapped in, I could feel my teacher, Betsy, standing next to me. A few steps further, I could feel Ellie Mae on the other side, my right. Next to Ellie Mae, Sensei Mikao Usui, the founder of Reiki. On his right is the Divine Feminine in the form of Quan Yin. To her right was the great Buddhist practitioner Bodhidharma, who was the founder of the Zen lineage. To the left of Betsy, our teachers G.I. Gurdjieff, Laozi, Zhuangzi, and to his left, the great Persian teacher and poet Jalalaldin Rumi. One by one, they all lined up to my left and my right. Some I was able to identify, others I couldn't. They lined up behind me in a row. They, too, were flanked on their lefts and rights. It felt like the entire center of the fishbowl was walking with me, or maybe it was that I was walking with them. We were walking together in unison. One Breath. One Step. One energy. One sensational and unbelievable presence.

As we continued, others walked from the back to join us in the front line: Mary, the Dalai Lama, Thich Nhat Hahn, Pema Chodron, Jesus, Joseph, Mohammed, Abraham, John the Baptist, Teresa of Avila, Joan of Arc. I tried my best not to get lost in the awe of who was present. I tried not to be the little boy meeting his favorite athlete, musician, or whoever he fantasized about becoming or meeting. But I was that boy. Some soft voices in harmony were chanting like Gregorian or Benedictine monks and nuns surrounding us. I didn't know who it was coming from, but it was part of what we were doing. There were footsteps, breaths, and the soundtrack to our journey caressing our ears and hearts.

They were with me the whole morning. When the sun was directly above us, I felt hungry and thirsty. My sense was to keep walking. Just keep walking.

It was a warm day, and the temperature was probably near 80 degrees. I wanted to remove a layer of clothing, but I did not want to stop and interrupt the energy. I kept walking,

At some point, it occurred to me that I was not sent here to die, at least not in the usual sense. I was sent here so all of them would have a physical body to be present with on this Earth plane. They weren't there for me; they were just there. I was sent to be the physical body. Another large dose of humility filled my chest and belly. None of this was because I was special or had extraordinary gifts; it was because I had a physical body and was willing to show up and say "Yes!" I did not attract nor manifest any of this. I happened to get tapped on the shoulder; even

     Raised by Wolves, Possibly Monsters

though I spent weeks and months fighting the visions, meditations, and dreams, I didn't do anything to make this happen besides being willing to do what I was told. I did not hold or create any intention for any of this.

I accepted an invitation.

At some point mid-day, they left. As simply as they appeared, they disappeared.

I kept walking.

Even though I could see where the sun was on its journey for the day, I felt confident and safe, knowing that I was going to have somewhere to sleep that night. While I was sitting with that and letting it wash through me, I thought I had heard something on my right side above me. I looked in that direction and had to put my hand in front of my eyes to cover the sun. I saw a shadow of an object on top of the cliff with four legs, two ears, and a tail. At that point, I couldn't tell much more about what it was or anything else. I waited a moment for my eyes to adjust. And for a brief second, terror erupted in my body. On the top of the cliff was a snow leopard after I remembered to breathe again.

I looked around at my physical environment to assess my potential options. That didn't take long because there wasn't any. I looked back up at the snow leopard, and now there were two others on top of the cliff. The three of them were looking in my direction, ears pulled back and tail low. They were not yet in a crouched position, so I knew they were not ready to attack me yet.

There wasn't much else for me to do, so I realigned and connected with my Higher Self, the Lineage, and all of those who had been with me moments before. I sensed they were still with me, and once again, they needed me to take a leap of faith and do as I was told. So, I started walking again with slow, deliberate movements and my head facing forward.

As connected as I was, I could not resist that part of me that needed to know what was happening on top of the cliff. I looked up to the right. The sun wasn't as bright in my eyes by this point; it was slightly covered by the ridge on my left, and all three snow leopards were seated. They watched me. It had not occurred to me that I had not looked to my left to see if any snow leopards were there! Slowly looking to my left, I saw three snow leopards almost exactly across the fishbowl from the others.

I smiled and almost laughed out loud. Now that the snow leopards were on both sides, there were six of them. If they decided they were going to kill me, I was going to die. There was nothing to think or worry about at that point. I might as well keep walking. So, I did. I kept walking. As I approached the far end of the fishbowl, I again lifted my head to the right, and those three were gone. I lifted my head to the left, and those were also gone. I had a brief moment of panic, thinking that maybe they had come down the cliff already. I didn't know it, and they were nearby. I stopped and did a slow 360, looking around as my eyes adjusted to the light behind me instead of in front of me. I did not see a snow leopard or anything else behind me besides a few dried-out shrubs. I continued walking.

When I had passed through another two fishbowls, I was acutely aware that I had been holding in my urine pretty much the whole day because I didn't want to shift anything that was happening. Obviously, I wasn't going to stand and pee in the middle of the fishbowl while six snow leopards watched me.

Since I had stopped, there was no harm in drinking water and eating a couple of carrots dipped in peanut butter. It felt good to let the water go down my throat after being in the dry and dusty desert. Just as I was about to put my pack on my back again, I heard another sound that I wasn't able to identify in the distance. It sounded like a motor. The noise only took about a minute to get to me this time. It was two men on a gold motorcycle. For a minute, I thought it was another energetic presence until they were about twenty-five feet away, stopping next to me.

They said hello. I said hello. The guy in the back pointed to me, my backpack, and then the tiny space behind him on the back of the seat. I pointed to my backpack and then made a gesture of confusion, not knowing what to do. He got off the motorcycle and put out his hands to take the backpack from me; he got back on the bike with the pack between them. He motioned for me to get on the back. At this point, there were only a few inches. I was about to say no and ask for my backpack, and then I started laughing at what I had experienced in the last two days and that being on the back of a motorcycle in the desert was probably the least dangerous thing that had transpired so far. They looked at me strangely because I was laughing. I didn't care. I got on the back, put my hands around his

     Raised by Wolves, Possibly Monsters

waist, the driver kicked the clutch, and we were off. Three men and a backpack all fit on a small motorcycle in the middle of the Gobi Desert. As we were cruising along, now and then, I broke out laughing again for reasons I did not know of. It felt ridiculous and funny and joyous.

They pulled up next to a ger an hour and a half later. I got off, and the guy handed me my backpack before he got off. Then the driver took the motorcycle and drove it to the back of the ger. About a minute later, two adult women and a pack of kids appeared. Ten minutes later, the whole pile of us were eating dinner inside their ger. I spent the night with them, as I had the night before with another family. There were nine of us sprawled on mats throughout the yurt. Also, like the night before, it was only a few minutes before I was completely asleep and did not feel like I moved. We ate breakfast, and I left. I was about twenty steps away from their yurt when my eyes started to tear up with gratitude and joy.

And this is how it went for the next few days. I honestly can't tell you how many days I was by myself crunching on the earth of the Gobi Desert. It may have been three, it may have been seven. The day I was walking under a bunch of power lines, which was bizarre in the middle of a desert, a Jeep pulled up next to me. The vehicle had a man in his forties or fifties and a younger woman, probably in her late twenties or early thirties. It was funny; they pulled up next to me as if it was customary to see a foreigner backpacking alone in the middle of nowhere. She said casually, "Hello! How are you doing?"

I don't know what surprised me more: her English was reasonably solid, or she was approaching this as if we were both in line in the grocery store, and she was commenting on the bag of carrots I was carrying. "Hi. I'm doing well. How are you?" I didn't know what to say or how to interact, so I followed the traditional dialogue and didn't have to figure it out.

"My name is Muutaafa, but most people who speak English call me Sylvia. Do you remember me?"

Well, now I needed clarification. I stepped up next to the passenger window to get a closer look at her. My mind was scurrying, trying to figure out if I had ever seen her before and where. It occurred to me that I had met her at the bazaar in Altai, and they had offered me a ride as a taxi, but they were going in a different direction than I wanted on a different day than I needed. She had flirted with me somewhat aggressively. I remember blushing then, and I also started blushing in the present. I looked at the driver. He had an annoyed and irritated expression on his face. I didn't know what it was about, but looking at her seemed much more enjoyable, so that's what I did. "Yes, I remember you! My name is Michael."

"Well, it looks like you haven't died yet. That's a good thing." She started laughing. I didn't find it as funny, but I laughed anyway. She was correct; I did not die yet—at least not my body.

"No! You are correct. I am not dead."

The driver barked something at her; she barked back. They had a tense exchange quickly for a minute or two. Muutaafa had a defiant look on her face. She looked at me with that look that some women have when they've decided that you are theirs, and there's nothing you can do about it.

"Why don't you throw your backpack in the back and come jump in the front seat with me, and we'll get you back to Altai. That's if you're ready to stop walking around in circles in the desert by yourself, waiting for a snow leopard or dehydration to kill you?" She stared at me. The driver started barking at her again. She turned around, pointed her index finger at him, and yelled back at him. Without knowing what words they were using, I was able to deduce that he didn't want me to come, and she told him he didn't have a choice but to shut up. I'm sure it was something like that.

"Well? Are you going to get in or not? Are you just going to stay here walking along under the power lines?" Muutaafa's eyes connected with mine. I don't think I answered her. I just removed my pack; she got out of the brand-new Russian Jeep, took my pack, stuffed it in the back, slid to the front seat, and motioned for me to join her. As soon as I sat down, she slid to her right to press her legs, hips, elbows, and shoulders against mine. The guy was again pissed off and complaining. He ground the vehicle into first gear. I was done with my solo backpacking in the Gobi Desert.

I took a day to recover. I thought I would need a few days, but I only needed one. It was an incredibly anti-climactic completion of this journey. I felt strong, like an oak tree, and more solid than at any point in this life. The loudest feeling for me was there was a call for me to answer and show up, and I showed up, and

     Raised by Wolves, Possibly Monsters

they showed up. Every part of my being was now experiencing what it was like to be in my Divine Masculine energy and being. Even then, I understood that I may never have an opportunity like this again. I may never be called upon to stand in that way with all the beings who walked with me earlier in the day. And oh my, the gratitude. I was clear that the next thing for me to do was to get to the farthest western point of Mongolia and then fly to Kazakhstan. I found a ride reasonably easily in a bus packed with humans. I had two children falling asleep on my lap at different points, and once more, I felt the gratitude that they had accompanied me through the Gobi.

The Altai Mountains

I ASKED ENOUGH people to discover I could take a flight from Olgii over the Altai Mountains to Oskemen, Kazakhstan. There were two flights a week, and I only had a little time to spare if I wanted to leave in the morning. I got a taxi to the airport, which was incredibly tiny; it was a hangar with an indoor ticket counter. Dark clouds were coming in our direction. The flight was supposed to leave at 7:20, and everybody was purchasing their tickets and sitting in the waiting area. They made an announcement over the PA system, and everybody stood up and walked outside. I thought they were going to the plane to board, but they all left in taxis. There were three employees from Arrow Mongolia and me. It took some work, but I figured out that they canceled the flight due to the weather and would leave the following morning at 7:20. I would redeem my ticket then.

I returned the following morning, and there were no hiccups. I was excited to fly over the Altai Mountains in a small prop plane. In addition, there's a point where China and Russia meet at the Western border of Mongolia. It's only 12 km from Kazakhstan. The idea that you could potentially pass through four countries in five minutes excited me.

Kazakhstan

WHEN WE LANDED in Oskemen, I looked out the window, and all the people working on the tarmac were pale-skinned humans with blond hair! After almost two months in Mongolia, seeing only white people with blond hair made me laugh. Everybody on the plane looked at me as if I were strange. I eventually understood that Osterman was one of the cities that, in the Post-Soviet Era, continued as a predominantly Russian city.

The first thing I did when I left the airport was to ask a taxi to take me to somewhere where I could eat borscht. I had borscht for lunch at a pub and then borscht for dinner at another. The dinner borscht was green; I did not know there was such a thing as green borscht. My education continued. After the dreams, meditations, visions, and treks to the north, south, central, and then southwest Mongolia, the intensity of my time solo in the Gobi, I was now in a different country. By the time I had finished dinner, I had seen more white people on that day than possibly the previous fifteen months collectively.

My time in Kazakhstan was an opportunity to recuperate, recalibrate, and digest my experiences in Mongolia. I also met, traveled with, and stayed with various people from the Couchsurfing Network, which allowed me to write about my experiences in Mongolia.

I reached the City of Osh, which borders Kyrgyzstan and Uzbekistan. My time there was quite bizarre. I came into town on a bus that dropped me off in front of a youth hostel, where I booked a room. I was exhausted from all of the travels and decided it was time for a nap before I would do anything. I woke up with somebody knocking on my door. They wanted to tell me that the power had gone out in the city. I walked up and down the main street a couple of times before realizing only two places had power. One was a small dingy bar, where one could be greeted by an assembly line of drunk men smoking cigarettes. The other option across the street was a restaurant that looked rather fancy. Since I had few choices and was hungry, I chose the fancy restaurant even though I was dressed pretty messy and hadn't showered in a few days.

Raised by Wolves, Possibly Monsters

Power Outage

THE HOST LOOKED me up and down several times and appeared confused about what to do with me since my jeans were ripped and dirty, my shirt sweaty and oil-stained, my face looked ragged, and I hadn't showered in several days. She consulted with the other hosts, and eventually, they both decided to seat me at the only available table, which happened to be in the center of the room. Everybody else was dressed nicely; many of the men were actually in sports coats and ties. As far as my experience there, like everywhere I went in Asia, mostly attractive young women paid attention to me. A few minutes later, a man who introduced himself as the owner asked if he could sit with me for a moment. I didn't feel I had a choice, so I said yes.

He wanted to explain to me why the hosts were confused and nervous. It's a high-end restaurant, with an upstairs space for weddings and a downstairs with a nightclub. "Generally, they don't have people wanting to eat there dressed as I was, but they didn't know how to say no without offending you. I'm glad they came to me and let you in."

The server recommended several dishes, including rice, chicken, and lamb, in traditional Turkish seasoning. I said yes, and about two minutes later, she served a gorgeous and aromatic meal. When I was nearly finished eating, the owner came to join me again. He wanted to invite me upstairs to see a traditional Kyrgyz wedding reception. This sounded interesting, so I said yes. He brought me up a tiny staircase through the kitchen that I barely fit through. When we passed through the doors into the main hall, I was astounded by this massive hall with high ceilings and gold trim housing a wedding reception of more than 500 people! The men wore elegant formal attire. The women wore colored gowns and dresses, and each one was different. They all appeared to be handmade specifically for the women wearing them.

When we entered the room, we drew the guests' attention. He had already asked the bride and groom's family if I could see what was happening. The bride came over to say hello and had her sisters and what I assumed was a bridesmaid all flanked by her sides to greet me. They had bright, shining faces full of excitement and warmth. One of the sisters spoke a little English and asked me if I could stay there for one moment, and before I could answer, she ran away. She returned briefly with a young, gorgeous woman in a turquoise and gold-trimmed silk gown shimmering as she approached us. She introduced herself as Gulnara, the bride's cousin. She spoke excellent English.

Initially, I had difficulty responding to her because she looked like a living angel. I would not have been surprised if wings had appeared behind her and she had slipped away through the high ceilings. She was translating between the bride and myself, who insisted I join them for dinner since it was being served right then. I explained that I had just eaten dinner downstairs and was full. She would have none of that. A moment later, they ushered me to a table on the left. They were all round tables made of marble, each one holding sixteen guests. Everybody scurried so Gulnara and I could sit beside each other and talk. She introduced me to the folks at the table, and the establishment owner went downstairs to get my daypack, which I had left in the restaurant. He paid the bill for me and brought my backpack up so it would be safe. I was still having trouble talking with her due to her radiance.

She explained the Kyrgyz customs, why such and such were dressed one way, and why somebody else was dressed another way. She taught me about the symbolism of the murals on the walls and how the couple getting married were each from families only a step or two below royalty. None of that surprised me. I felt like I was at a royal wedding. Along with being intelligent, exciting, and radiant, Gulnara was quite engaging. She had two graduate degrees and was working on her PhD in Psychology. Her minor was Women's Studies.

We had barely finished our delightful meal when it was time for everybody in the room to slow dance with a partner to join the bride and groom in their first dance. My host invited me to join her, and while we were dancing, holding her hand with one hand and my other hand around her waist, Gulnara whispered in my ear that I was the first man to ever put their hands on her body that wasn't a family member or doctor. I asked her if she liked it, and her smile became even more radiant as she moved closer to me. I continued to have thoughts in my head that she was a fantasy, and this was not real, not this vast massive restaurant and venue, running on multiple power generators of a dark city, not that I had just randomly ended up in the middle of a Kyrgyz wedding, dancing with this

     Raised by Wolves, Possibly Monsters

extraordinary being in a woman's body in my arms. It all felt like a fantasy. The way I figured out that it was real, a moment after she moved closer to me and she started blushing, my penis woke up, and she jumped. It was both adorable and embarrassing. She regrouped so she could dance with me again, but at no point did she come nearly that physically close to me again during the wedding.

After the group's slow dance, the band started playing an upbeat song, and everybody shifted from slow dance to celebratory dance. That included Gulnara and me. We were both happy, having fun, and full of joy. When we were done and returned to the table, the owner came by again and whispered something in her ear. She then explained to me that there was going to be a religious element of the wedding ceremony, and only people who were committed Muslims were allowed to be present. She told me he had invited us to go downstairs to his nightclub for free if we wanted to continue dancing. I told her that was a lovely offer, but I felt terrible taking her from her cousin's wedding. She said she would be right back without explaining. She returned with her jacket and purse a moment later, grabbing my hand and walking towards the door back through the kitchen and another set of stairs. We landed in the middle of a nightclub with white walls covered with fuchsia, purple, and gold lighting and a DJ playing high-energy local pop music and American pop and hip hop. The song "Low (Apple Bottom Jeans)" by Flo Rida came on. Gulnara jumped up and down excitedly and begged me to dance with her. I could not resist; I said yes, and then she and I were dancing; the dancing got closer, and then, out of nowhere, she started grinding on me. This time, when my erection started forming, she moved closer as if she was expecting it, possibly wanting it.

We danced to a few American pop and hip-hop songs and then sat down. And a whole other personality erupted out of her. The well-cultured, educated, sweet cousin did fine dining and conversing on the third floor and became **a** bold, playful club girl without notice. The owner returned and told her that her family was looking for her. She pulled me back onto the dance floor and was again intimate and sexual with me. And I loved it!

Gulnara pulled me close to her, put her arms around my head, and whispered in my ear, "I have to go upstairs. Will you meet me outside tomorrow for lunch so we can play, and I can show you around?" While I was trying to take in what she said, she leaned forward, pressing her chest against mine, "Please?"

Of course, I said yes. Gulnara was excited and hugged me, then held her arms out so we could make eye contact; she hugged me again, grabbed her things, and ran upstairs. It took me a minute to gather myself. I grabbed my little pack, threw it on my back, and left the nightclub. Much to my surprise, the power had returned to this city of Osh, and the streets were alive with people buzzing, restaurants and stores with neon lights, and music playing. As I walked the streets trying to take in everything happening in search of ice cream, all I could think about was Gulnara's dancing eyes, full cheekbones contrasting her soft lips, shiny black hair, fantastic smile, and her even more unique energy and radiance. And her fragrance. I felt like I could still smell her dancing right before me. I fell asleep that night, seeing her eyes and smelling her fragrance. I woke up happy, joyful, excited, turned on, and curious. I wondered what an afternoon with Gulnara would be like.

Power Flowing

GULNARA STARTED SHOWING me around the city. She had only been there once before and was in town for the wedding. But she spoke the language, knew the culture, and knew how to research where and what things were. We walked and talked and walked and talked. I learned about her PhD research project on the psychological effects of Islam on academic women. We both discovered that most of Osh's "points of interest" were not very interesting. And we also found out that we were interested in each other. I found out that she had never kissed anybody outside of her family. She found out that I had never kissed a Muslim woman before.

At 5:30, she announced that she had to take a taxi back to the hotel for a family dinner ritual the night after the wedding. She asked if I would meet her at the club at 9:00, and I said yes again. She gave me a half hug and ran into the back seat of an orange taxi.

I stood outside the club with thirty or so other people milling around, drinking, smoking, flirting, and doing the things people do outside of a club. At

          Raised by Wolves, Possibly Monsters

9:20, I was getting ready to leave since Gulnara had not yet arrived. I picked up my backpack and heard her and her cousin screaming out of the back of a taxi, making a U-turn in front of the club. "Wait, Michael! Wait!" The three of us went inside and downstairs to the club.

The white walls with colored lights and music pumping through the PA did not seem as interesting to me as the night before. The night before, the idea that I was eating dinner below a massive ballroom and above a nightclub thrilled me. I had no idea they existed, especially while the city was without power, and they were running off a generator. Tonight, it was just a club; there were no surprises. The three of us sat and talked; her cousin Fatima was initially cautious and guarded. While sipping her second blue cocktail, she started loosening up and flirted with me to see how Gulnara would respond. Gulnara responded by moving her chair next to me, sliding her hand into mine, and holding it tightly. She got up and led me to the dance floor. This time, Gulnara was freer and playful. She felt like a woman who had decided she didn't care what anybody thought about her.

I enjoyed Gulnara rubbing up against me, grabbing my hips while shimmying and shaking in her red skirt with shiny gold pinstripes. Her white top, which initially buttoned up to the top except for the first button, lost the following button first, and two songs later, the third. Gulnara was showing cleavage and even snippets of her bra while dancing with her arms up in the air pressed up against me. Her cousin came out to the dance floor, barking commands and judgments at her and how she dressed and danced. I did not need to speak their language to know when a woman was suppressing another woman for choosing to be free.

It was really fun and exciting to watch Gulnara laugh and shake her chest and hips at her cousin playfully to get her to stop complaining. In English, full of energy and enthusiasm, she said, "We're at a nightclub in a town we don't live in. Nobody knows us here or knows about Michael being from the United States. We may never get to dance like this again. Have fun and let go!" She shook her hips and breasts again, turned to me with her face sparkling with excitement, putting her arms around my neck. I put my arms on her waist, and her eyes lit brighter. Her cousin started yelling again, and Gulnara pulled us about ten feet away. Her cousin stomped back to the table to finish her cocktail. I was not sure what form of alcohol was in her drink because five minutes later, she joined us on the dance floor. For a brief moment, my mind and body got excited with a fantasy of making love to these two amazing, talented, gorgeous, and virginal Muslims later that night. That didn't happen.

Five songs later, the three of us returned to our table to catch our breaths. The two of them verbally exchanged back and forth several times with some English sprinkled in, allowing me to figure out that her cousin wanted to leave, and Gulnara was not ready to go. Her cousin didn't want to leave her alone with me, "Because he's an American man and they don't care about Allah, all they want is flesh and sin." Gulnara kept stating that she would get home on her own by taxi and that I would protect her. Her cousin kept saying that I was the one she needed protection from. It was bizarre that they spoke this part in English as if I wasn't there. Her cousin gave up, exasperated, hugged her, kissed her on the cheek, grabbed her purse, and walked up the stairs and out of the club.

She and I were alone. Gulnara was turned on and on fire, and I had no idea what to do with this. My conscience said to take care of her and make sure she didn't do anything she would regret tomorrow. My heart said make passionate love to her. Those parts were expressed while we were sitting, talking, and dancing. When she was shaking her ass against my genitals on the dance floor, my conscience faded away. That's when my desire grew, and I became bold.

The club was getting ready to close. It was a Sunday night, and all clubs and bars ended at 11:00. The fresh air felt terrific, and being away from the loud music was delightful. Gulnara and I leaned against a building next to the restaurant and club. Well, to be exact, she had her back to the building leaning against it, and I was standing close to her, holding her hands. I let her know I wanted to kiss her. She blushed. I asked her if that was a yes or a no. Gulnara said she was embarrassed in front of all these people and that she had never kissed a man before and didn't know how to do it. In typical mansplaining fashion, I gave her instructions on how to kiss. She slapped me in the chest. I could not tell if she was being playful, offended, or a combination. Either way, she kept her right hand on my chest, which felt nice. I don't think that she even knew that her hand was rubbing my chest until I looked at her hand, and she realized she was kneading my

     Raised by Wolves, Possibly Monsters

muscles. Gulnara flinched and pulled her hand away. She apologized for putting her hand on my chest, and I explained that I liked it very much. This beautiful person informed me that she was not allowed to do that. I asked her again if she wanted me to kiss her, and again, she blushed and turned her head away.

"I'd like to kiss you, but only if you want to kiss me. Please let me know what you want me to do or not do."

"I want you to kiss me. I'm just embarrassed in front of all these people. Nobody has kissed me on the lips since I was a child. When you get close to me, and I think you'll kiss me, I start giggling because my cousin's brother and I used to kiss each other when we were little kids as part of a game. That was the last time somebody kissed me on the lips."

"Would you like to walk away from everybody here so that you don't feel like they're watching us?"

"I promised my cousin that I would not go anywhere alone with you while I was drunk. I don't want to break my promise with her."

"Are you afraid I'm going to do something to you that you don't want to do?"

"Maybe a little. We have heard many stories in our village about American men and how they treat women, especially when they are travelers here visiting our country."

I took a breath and connected with Reiki. I asked Reiki to create a bubble around us for love, safety, and connection. "I'm sorry to hear that. I wish it were untrue, but it is true in many cases. I don't want you to feel scared. Let's stay where people are around here, and we won't kiss. Is that the best for you?"

"Thank you! That's very nice of you." She smiled, moved towards me, and kissed me on the cheek, somewhere between a peck and an expression of romantic affection. It was my turn to blush. Somehow, that felt more intimate than kissing on the lips. It could have been the spontaneity and innocence. At that moment, I aligned with how special she was and that whatever my desire said, I wanted to respect her choices. I asked her if a hug was okay, and she hugged me as she did with some of her cousins the night before when saying goodbye to them.

"I have to go now, Michael. We will get up early in the morning and have a five-hour drive to return to my village. I want to stay in touch with you, but I don't know how. Are you on Facebook?"

"Yes, I am."

I'm not sure what was happening with her, but quiet tears rolled down both cheeks. I asked her if she was okay, and she waved me off from asking any more questions, so I didn't.

"It was nice to meet you, Michael. I hope we can be together someday. Good-bye." Gulnara put her arms around me and hugged me tightly. She was now fully crying, and before I could say or do anything else, she released me and ran into the back of a taxi, waving for him to pull out. Gulnara waved at me as this extraordinary woman left, her eyes full of tears. I have written many narratives in my head over the years about what she may have been experiencing, especially the year or two after we met. I had no clue what was going on inside of her. However, somehow, she became a Facebook friend of my co-teacher Ashley from when I worked in Korea, and then she sent me a friend request a few days later. We initially wrote each other a few love letters through Facebook. Over time, the messages became less frequent, and six months later, they stopped. Deep down inside me, I knew that what I wanted from her was not what she wanted from me.

This is one of the benefits of daily meditation. We can experience desiring things that may not be respectful, honorable, or loving to ourselves or somebody else, and we can choose love, honor, and respect at any moment. This was one of those moments. It felt honorable not to write to her anymore.

Pass!

THE FOLLOWING DAY, I was ready to cross the border into Uzbekistan. Everybody told me the best way was to take a taxi to the Kyrgyzstan border and then travel by foot. They told me other things, but I didn't listen because I thought I would simply be walking across a building from one side to the other and ending up in Uzbekistan. That's not quite the way it happened.

I put on my backpack with my passport in hand when entering the little station with metal walls on the Kyrgyzstan side of the border. I was the only

    Raised by Wolves, Possibly Monsters

person in line from somewhere other than Kyrgyzstan or Uzbekistan. Most of the people looked me up and down. They wore regular clothes for daily functions, and I wore sandals, shorts, and a tank top. When it was my turn to be processed, the people behind the metal framing did not speak excellent English, but we still worked it out. It took me longer to process than the previous seven people ahead of me. I was grateful to be finished with that and looked forward to finding a taxi that everybody said would be on the other end after processing.

I walked out the metal door on the other side and was surprised to find just sand and dirt for about 100 feet leading to another similar metal-sided building. I now understand a "No man's land" between countries. When I was halfway between the buildings, enjoying the warm sun on my body and excited to be entering a new country, three military men standing against the fence next to the Uzbekistan processing center started yelling things in my direction, "American!?!" I looked around. "American?" It hadn't occurred to me that I was holding an American passport in my right hand, no matter what answer I gave. Finally, I answered, "Amcrican." They replied, "American?" I again answered, "American." This time, they replied as a statement instead of a question, "American!"

The men had automatic weapons with bullets strapped across their bodies. They kept barking commands and pointing their guns at me. I froze. Then they yelled, "Pass. Pass. Pass!" at me. I thought that meant I was supposed to pass everybody in line, so I stepped to my left and started moving towards the entrance to the small green metal building. Five more uniformed men appeared from behind me, and now eight of them all pointed their weapons at me and yelled various commands in what I assume was Uzbek, meaning for me to come towards them.

I literally thought I was going to be shot and killed right there. I believe I even did a quick prayer to God that my soul be taken care of in death. They formed a circle around me. They kept yelling, "Pass. Pass. Pass!" I eventually figured out they meant passport. With my left hand, I pointed to my right pocket, slowly took out my passport, and extended my hand. One of the officers grabbed it from me. While he opened it and looked at it, two other guards started barking orders at me, and I figured out that they were pointing their weapons at my backpack and wanted me to take off my gear; I obliged. They pointed towards the ground, so I placed my bag on the ground. They pointed for me to step back, and as I stepped back, they attacked and pulled apart my pack. Everything stopped in both countries' processing centers. Nobody said a word; nobody moved; it felt like nobody was even breathing.

I am still trying to determine what happened all these years later. A few minutes later, one of the guys looking at my backpack barked out some command in what I thought was in my direction, and I again froze. He was talking to his comrades. I have no idea what they said to him, but they all stepped away from me simultaneously and put their weapons down. Two of them pointed their guns at my possessions near my backpack on the ground and waved them toward it. I assumed that meant it was time to collect all my stuff and return it to my backpack. As I was gathering my things, two of the younger soldiers clicked the safety on their weapons, took their guns off their bodies, placed them on the ground away from me, and smiled at me. They started handing me things to return to my backpack as if we were old friends. When everything was inside, my hands were trembling. I had trouble zipping up the sides of the backpack; one of the men reached over, gently touched my hand with his left hand, and zipped up the pack with his right hand. I got ready to pick up my backpack when the other guy asked me to wait a minute. He picked it up, stood behind me, and put my backpack on my back while the other closed all the clasps in the front. Then, the one who had barked a command at them a few minutes before barked another command, and the two men pointed towards the line. They escorted me to the green metal building to begin processing in Uzbekistan.

They knocked on the door to the entrance as if everybody wasn't watching through the thick double-pane glass windows, and two guards from the inside came to unlock the door to let me in. Now, all four escorted me to the front of the line and barked commands. All the people going through processing stepped aside so I could go to the front. They barked an order to the person behind the metal frame, looked at my passport briefly, typed something on the computer, and stamped my passport, "Welcome to Uzbekistan." And then, I was ushered out the other door by two more guards. As I walked away quickly before anything else bad happened, they all started saying in Central Asian voices, "Bye-bye, bye-bye." And that was that. I was now in Uzbekistan. Alive.

                    Raised by Wolves, Possibly Monsters

Not a Bachelor Party

 ONCE AGAIN, I was an unexpected participant in a wedding ritual. This one was a bachelor party in the city of Tashkent. I was in the country for less than an hour. I made a new friend because a hostel in the Lonely Planet guide to Central Asia did not exist, and he was helping me out. He was headed to his friend's pre-wedding gathering of young men and asked the groom if he could invite me. The groom enthusiastically said yes.

We arrived at a multi-level, partly traditional, and partly modern Islamic building made out of some form of white stone with a turquoise dome on top. Everything looked clean and cared for. While we were walking up the outside stairs briskly since we were late, Jahongir pointed to the left in the direction that the women were meeting on the third floor; we were meeting on the second floor on the right-hand side. Interestingly, they met in the same building and did the same process.

He opened the two enormous wooden doors into the building and pointed to the circular staircase we ran up to the right. When we were on the second floor, he opened another set of wooden doors, and in the center of the room was a large round table made out of stone and strong, solid legs also made out of stone. There were eight young men; the one I was with was in his mid-twenties; the rest of them were probably twenty-one or younger. They looked soft, delicate, and beautiful. They all stood when we entered, and Jahongir introduced me. They were kind and tried hard to greet me in their limited English. Their intention was warm and inviting.

They were wearing clothes that were either bone or off-white, with gold embroidered collars. The table was set with something similar to rice pilaf, which is very common in Central Asia, roasted chicken legs, hummus, flatbreads, steamed and sautéed vegetables, and several bowls of fruit. There was more fruit than anything else, which caught my attention in contrast to an American "bachelor party."

They were socializing and not ready to begin any rituals yet. I did not need Jahongir to translate that; it was evident by the way they kept looking at each other, looking at me, then looking back at each other, and sharing with sparkles in their eyes about having a guest from the United States.

About ten minutes later, Jahongir whispered in my ear that the groom was about to lead a prayer; all the men listened and replied something similar to Amen. Jahongir shared with me that in the next element, each one of the men in the room would offer a prayer and a wish for the groom for his wedding, wedding night, and future. One other thing of note: there was no alcohol on the table. They had several ceramic pitchers of water or fruit juice that seemed similar to mango but not mango.

Jahongir translated as each young man offered their prayers and wishes to their friend. In short, except for Jahongir, none of them had ever had sex or even kissed a girl/woman. They had yet to be on a date. He was the first one to get married, and it was an arranged marriage. He had just met the bride the week before. It was sweet and lovely to hear them share with him their wish for the first night with his wife. All of them blushed and laughed when they talked about it because they had no experience with anything they were talking about. I enjoyed the purity and excitement that they shared about their friend's love life and starting a family. I don't think I was ever that innocent or pure, even as a five-year-old.

After all the men had their turn around the circle offering their prayers and wishes for the groom, he stood up with his water glass in hand. They joined him standing, as did I. Jahongir translated his "speech," which, in essence, was, "I'm so grateful you are here, I love you all, and I am so excited and nervous about being married to this beautiful woman I get to spend the rest of my life with." I was not the only man in the room with trouble holding back their tears. It all felt lovely and authentic.

He raised the glass, as did the rest of us. We all clicked glasses to drink water, and he invited everybody to start eating. As we were all sitting down, he decided to stand up again and asked Jahongir to translate to me directly. "Thank you, Michael, for joining us. It is such an honor to have you here, and since you are an elder and you know a lot more about life and women than me, it would be a great benefit for me for you to share your experience with me and the rest of us. In our culture and religion, we are not taught much about love, romantic love, or sex. We have to wait till marriage. Would you be kind enough to share anything with

     Raised by Wolves, Possibly Monsters

me and the rest of us you think would be helpful?"

I was honored by the thoughtfulness and respect they were showing me. If they only knew about me and my past, I would not have been treated the same way, not that it mattered. When I was about to start talking, he motioned for me to stand up, which I did. "I am grateful to be here and that you let me join this beautiful sacred ceremony and ritual. I have never been married, but I have had girlfriends and partners. So, I can't give you any marriage advice. I can tell you that women like to know that they matter, they're valued, and that you respect them. They get hurt and angry when they feel like we've taken them for granted, especially around sex, childcare, and attending to a home if that is what they do. And always, always let them know how much you love them. Thank you again for letting me participate in this beautiful ritual and say a few words. I'm humbled."

I gave a bow even though I knew I was in a culture where bowing was not part of their tradition. I had no other way to demonstrate to them how honored and respected I felt to be present. He thanked me and then instructed the men at the table to serve me food before anybody else ate. I was a little uncomfortable and asked Jahongir about this. He told me that the groom is generally served first by all the other men, and they all begin together. He was firm that I should accept the offer, let it happen, and receive respect. I nodded at Jahongir, shook my head at the groom, and nodded to all the men.

At that time, all of them except for the groom took turns putting food on my plate of whatever was in front of them: the chicken legs, the rice, the vegetables, the fruit. I never felt so welcomed and attended to in such a genuine and un-dramatic way at any point in my life. When my plate was complete, they each got up individually and filled the groom's plate. After his plate was full, he prayed, and I heard the word "Allah" twice or thrice. Then, he opened his hands so everybody could start serving themselves and eating. The following two hours were eating, laughing, sharing, and true brotherhood. They did another round of sharing a prayer for the groom. He thanked everybody for coming, especially me, and they started to disperse. One by one, they all came by and offered me a handshake and then a hug. At that moment, my internal narrative was straight-forward. "I want to move here to be around kind, gentle, sensitive, and loving men."

On our way out, I said goodbye and thanked each of them. I felt like I was glowing. Jahongir and I made our way out of the building into his car with my backpack patiently in the backseat.

Ten minutes later, Jahongir pulled up to a different hostel, not in the Lonely Planet Central Asia guide, and helped me get my things inside.

As I settled in, knowing I would stay there for a few days, I showered, journaled, and got on my knees for prayer and meditation. My heart was open with love and gratitude.

Bukhara

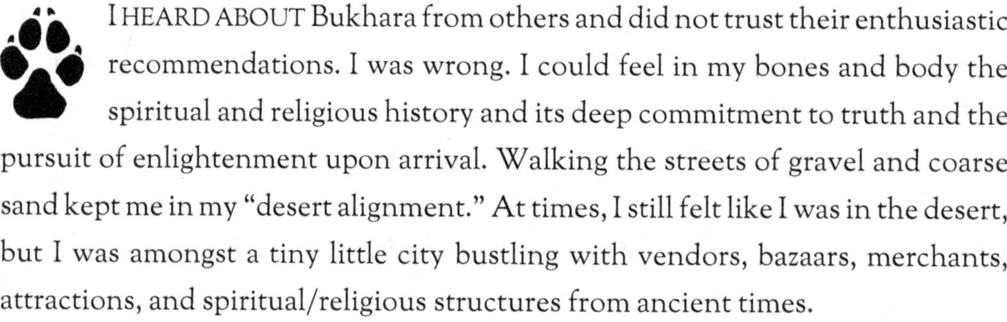 I HEARD ABOUT Bukhara from others and did not trust their enthusiastic recommendations. I was wrong. I could feel in my bones and body the spiritual and religious history and its deep commitment to truth and the pursuit of enlightenment upon arrival. Walking the streets of gravel and coarse sand kept me in my "desert alignment." At times, I still felt like I was in the desert, but I was amongst a tiny little city bustling with vendors, bazaars, merchants, attractions, and spiritual/religious structures from ancient times.

One of those places is Chasma Ayub Mausoleum, the Spring of Job. The prophet Job struck his staff in many places from Oman to Bukhara, causing a spring to appear, the water of which cured him of boils and ulcers. The mausoleum contains a small water management museum and a tap to enable pilgrims to drink from the spring. The energy inside this small museum was clean, clear, and balanced. The water from the spring was similar, with a higher vibration flowing through. I drank a little and washed my face with the water. I left feeling cleansed and purified, but not before I sat and did some meditation first. I enjoyed the opportunity to connect even further back into our history. There were few visitors while I was there, and I embraced just sitting and being in the space near the spring. I understand that many people use these mausoleums for intellectual and historical curiosity. For me, it is about connecting to the lineage and past Teachers and Prophets.

     Raised by Wolves, Possibly Monsters

After leaving the Spring of Job, I walked deeper into the city. Several people had tables on the side of the road selling their crafts and clothing. One woman under a small, stucco footbridge was selling silk robes and dresses. I felt a strong pull to this gorgeous fuchsia, dark and light gray, and maroon striped robe that I could not walk away from. I am not the type who typically feels drawn to these things, but the robe felt special to me and seemed necessary to buy for reasons I didn't know then, knowing I would now have to find a way to include it in my backpack.

I visited several temples, mosques, churches, and this teeny synagogue, supposedly the oldest in Asia. It was a beautiful little space with about twenty seats, a gorgeous ancient Torah with stucco walls, and architecture from that time in history in Bukhara. You have to ring the buzzer outside the synagogue and be greeted by an older man and a young man. I could tell they needed to do a screening by the various questions they asked me, wanting to know why I wanted to visit and even wanting to see my passport. The reminder of how careful many old Jewish synagogues have to be about guests and visitors who may be violent or destructive. I sat for about fifteen minutes in the synagogue, praying like I did everywhere else. Both men were sitting in the end seats, watching me. I was uncomfortable while they were observing me during such a sacred and intimate moment. I did not stay as long as I wanted; it just didn't feel like being there and being present was okay. I'm glad I was able to sit and pray, and I wish the world were a safer place for Jews.

Every day in Bukhara, I visited a mosque in the morning and a church in the afternoon, sometimes multiple mosques and churches on the same day. The architecture was gorgeous, the care and attention to the spiritual structures were inspiring, and the energy was supportive. In addition, as I walked around several times, I felt the life force energy seeping out of me. I sensed that the history of religious violence in the area took a toll on me. It was an odd experience to be in structures that felt supportive and full of vitality and walking around near them felt depleting and draining. This was my experience of Bukhara in general: beautiful, sacred, and focused, and the ache and pain of centuries of violence and hate. Bukhara will always be with me.

Samarqand

I WAS ABLE to get a bus from Bukhara to Samarqand. As we approached Samarqand, I was excited about the beauty and architecture of the city. Bukhara was simple without frills; there were few modern buildings, and the remodeled ones were remodeled in a way similar to the architecture of the time they were initially built. Samarqand had fancy lighting, water fountains, modern turquoise domes on top of mosques, landscaped grass and shrubs, paved walking paths and sidewalks, and the people were dressed more like those in Tashkent, not Bukhara. Tashkent also had beautiful hotels and restaurants near Central Square, as well as more popular mosques and attractions.

I stayed in a guest house between a motel, hotel, and motor lodge, even though there was nowhere to park. I didn't have a car, but I noticed that everything was set up just like an American motel where you would drive your car right up to the parking space in front of your room, but there were no parking spaces, and everybody walked. It was two floors shaped like a U. The center area was not enclosed and had beautiful plants and vegetation. I enjoyed the environment and the way it looked.

The next afternoon, I was going to leave Tashkent and fly to Incheon International Airport in South Korea, where I had left all the stuff I had not taken to Mongolia with Ellie Mae. She was staying in my apartment till hers was ready.

When I arrived at the airport, I realized that the two $100 bills I had gotten at an ATM two days before had been stolen from my wallet. I was out of money. I got on the plane on time and headed back to Korea.

It was good to see Ellie Mae and be in a familiar place.

Ellie Mae was staring at me intently. "I wish Betsy could see you as you are right now. I think it would bring tears to her eyes, and I want to thank you for going to the Gobi for all of us. I didn't know till you were there why you were going and that it was for all of us to be there in the only possible way. Michael, I don't think I've ever seen you look so comfortable in your skin and full of masculine energy. You feel confident, solid, and grounded." We hugged, and I said goodbye to Ellie Mae again. Ellie Mae and I have had to say goodbye multiple times during our friendship. Every time, it feels jarring and sad. Our bond is

Raised by Wolves, Possibly Monsters

intense and nourishing. I always feel that we may never see each other again, but history tells a different story.

I reached out to Ashley, my former co-teacher, and we decided to have dinner together. There was a foot of snow on the ground already, and it was coming down heavily. I waited for her out in the street. After being in warm and dry climates, including deserts, it felt beautiful to experience the fresh, clean, and moist air of a full-on snowstorm. When Ashley came out, she hugged me in her pink down jacket zipped up to her chin. She hugged me and let me pick her up and twirl her around. Ashley was giggling and squealing in delight. I felt utter joy in her presence and her body in my arms.

We walked hand in hand down the street to our favorite bulgogi restaurant. When we entered the restaurant, we stopped and looked at each other. Our faces were full of excitement, warmth, and appreciation for being together. We both shared how good it was to see each other and then paused. Nobody was speaking, but we were looking into each other's eyes. We've never talked about it, but I wanted to lean forward and kiss her. Thirteen months later, I had figured out how much I adored her.

We stepped inside the restaurant together and sat in the far right corner. We had so much fun and felt close and intimate. When Ashley had gone to the bathroom in the middle of our meal, I took a second to reflect and question why I had never allowed or facilitated her and me having this kind of relationship previously. I felt sad because the answer was simple: fear. Fear of rejection, fear of complicating our work together, and fear of some of my darker desires ruining this loving, warm, sweet, and almost innocent woman in her late twenties. I did not trust myself. When she returned, she could see that something was different. I never did share with her what was going through my head. All I said was that I wished we had spent more time together like this while sitting and working beside each other daily. She enthusiastically agreed.

Saying goodbye to Ashley was hard. Even though we talked about her coming to visit the USA and possibly me coming back, we knew that none of that would happen. Neither one of us was going to leap.

I had dinner with Ashley and Helen, our supervisor, later that night before leaving for Incheon one last time. Along with the three of us, a new couple started working at one of the schools. It was a little awkward to have these two new people with us while the three of us were getting ready to say goodbye. When Ashley and I said goodbye, before we even hugged, the tears created black and red lines all over her face. I could feel the tears dripping down both our cheeks while we hugged. I whispered in her ear, "I love you, and I will miss you."

"Me too, Michael Teacher. Me too."

I was about to say goodbye to Helen when she asked me if I wanted to get ice cream with her and give me a ride back to my apartment. I said yes. We were parked in her car outside of the ice cream shop when she asked me a question that took her three times to say before I understood what she was asking me. My American brain could not process the query.

"When a man and a woman are in a room together, how do you do it?"

"Do what?"

"You know, talk, watch TV, or eat together. How do you do it when you're in a room together?"

"We just watch TV, talk, and hang out." I was frustrated at her stupid question. "I don't understand what you're asking, Helen." There was irritation and impatience in my voice.

"Michael. If you are in the United States and you and a woman are alone in the room, how do you not have sex?"

I knew now what she was asking and why I couldn't understand it. The social structure of Korean life does not permit men and women to be in a room together without somebody else. In their minds, if a man and a woman are left alone together in a room, they will have sex because they can't control their urges.

"Ah. I understand now. We've been doing it our whole lives; it's not new to us." I paused for a moment to reflect on how contrasting our experiences were. She literally had no idea what it was like to hang out with men anytime you want, anywhere you want, as long as you know that you can trust him and he's safe. And vice versa. And I have no idea what it's like not to do that. To not have dinner at my friend's homes or for them to come to mine. Or for us to watch TV together. Or to lie on the floor in front of a fireplace together. Or to stay up till four in the morning drinking tea and sharing our hopes, dreams, and challenges. "I'm sorry that you've never had those experiences. I can't imagine what it would

   Raised by Wolves, Possibly Monsters

be like to have never been alone with all of my female friends for the last thirty years."

Helen stared at me blankly as if I was speaking a foreign language, which, in reality, I was. "So, you're saying if you and I hung out tonight in my apartment together, we would be able just to hang out and not have sex?"

I started laughing and then realized how insensitive that was. "I'm sorry I didn't mean to laugh. Yes, we could even fall asleep on the couch, watching TV together and not have sex. That's not our kind of relationship, especially since you're my former supervisor, and I will probably write to you for references in the future."

"So, you're saying nothing would happen."

"Something would happen. We would hang out together, talk, and laugh just like you do with your female friends, and I do with my male friends. The only difference is you wouldn't take off some of your clothing while we're hanging out, and I would close the door to the bathroom when I have to pee. Otherwise, it wouldn't be any different."

Something about this made her uncomfortable. I asked her about it, and she brushed me off. We said goodbye a few minutes later when she dropped me off in front of my apartment. I would pick up my two suitcases, take a taxi to the train station, and leave for Incheon International Airport as my last night in South Korea. I started feeling my eyes become red and watery. We hugged goodbye, and I got out of her car. Twenty minutes later, I was on a train to Incheon International Airport.

The Bay Area

 SINCE I HAD no plan or schedule for what I would do when I returned to the States, it was easy to land in San Francisco to visit and spend some time with two Reiki students who were also dear friends. My intention was after spending time with them, I would fly back to the East Coast, where my van and a handful of boxes of things I put in storage waited for me.

It was great to see Vera and Adele. We did a combination of exploring the area, catching up, and Reiki. They both offered to do Reiki on me, for which I was grateful. My back and knees were starting to hurt more regularly. They both independently noticed stuck energy, inflammation in my knees, and tightness in my lumbar region. After the Reiki session, they looked at me and were disturbed by something. We talked about it, and they expressed that they had never felt me so solid in myself, and my body felt broken and tight. The fact that they both noticed this caught my attention. I had known that I was struggling with discomfort and sometimes pain in my back, but I assumed it was from all of the backpacking and sleeping in uncomfortable places. It had not registered that something was different in my body and needed attention.

I noticed the solitary item on Adele's refrigerator was a postcard advertising Ecstatic Dance on Sunday mornings in Oakland. They responded enthusiastically when I asked about it and convinced me to go with them on Sunday morning. They thought I would love it and we would have fun together. I tried to explain to them that I don't dance, but they were clear that it didn't matter, so I agreed to try it.

On Saturday night, Vera let us know that she wasn't feeling well and couldn't make it. On Sunday morning, Adele informed me she wasn't feeling well and couldn't go either. I took BART, the subway system, to Oakland, as directed by Adele. I found Sweets Ballroom, the venue where the dance would be. It was a beautiful old building with dark brown steps and a dark brown wood railing creaking as you walked up to the second floor. When I walked into the room, I was surprised by how large it was, with incredibly high ceilings and lots of windows and light. The music had yet to start, but several hundred people were already present in various shapes, sizes, and colors. People wore everything from slacks and button-down shirts to hippie clothes with tie-dyed shirts. There were a few young women wearing skirts and topless.

I was overwhelmed by the number of people and considered turning around and leaving. The DJ started playing lush, soft, and reflective electronic music similar to New Age but with more substance. One by one, people sitting on the side talking, other people stretching, people walking around, and the people socializing stopped what they were doing when the music started and made it to the room's central area. Some were on the floor lying on their backs, others were

    Raised by Wolves, Possibly Monsters

in various yoga poses, and some were standing and letting their bodies sway slightly from side to side. I was not ready to join, but I enjoyed witnessing everybody collectively joining.

As the music raised in tempo, folks on the dance floor raised their energy and level of movement. Watching how the DJ guided the energy in the room through rhythm, texture, and energy was beautiful. I had been a DJ twenty years earlier but hadn't done it in many years. I had never experienced DJs having such presence and connection with the dancers and movers on the floor. When the tempo was between medium and high, solid percussion drove the beat, and three young women came to support me in standing and making my way onto the dance floor. They danced with me, or should I say they put me in a circle and surrounded me with warmth and attention. After a few songs, my body moved more, and I connected to what was happening. They bowed together with their hands in front of their chest and moved to a different dance floor area. I saw them do the same thing with a couple of other people alone. I thought it was sweet and lovely that they were, officially or unofficially, the greeters of people who were by themselves, helping them feel safe and comfortable on the dance floor. It's a beautiful way to encourage inclusivity.

I had a great time at the event, and several dancers invited me to an outdoor picnic afterward. I told them I did not know such a thing was happening and didn't bring any food. They encouraged me to join them; there was plenty of food to enjoy.

The picnic was also lovely. The people were kind, thoughtful, and intelligent. The whole experience was fantastic, and I made a mental note that whenever I returned to the East Coast, I would try to find something similar.

That turned out to be a short time. I took a flight to Newark a few days later. Since nobody knew that I was back, and I wasn't ready to engage in the chaos of my family yet, I had a very simple Christmas at a Couchsurfing host's home. On the 26th, I took my stuff out of storage and wandered around in my van in the middle of winter. I spent the next month wandering around New Jersey and NYC with a combination of sleeping in my van, staying with Couchsurfing hosts, friends, and family, and finding cheap last-minute hotels to stay in on Priceline. More importantly, I found a barefoot freestyle dance in Manhattan called the Barefoot Boogie online. I called the contact number on their web page and spoke to a guy named Kevin, who encouraged me to meet him for pizza before the dance the next night in Manhattan. I said yes, and we made plans.

Barefoot Boogie

MID-AFTERNOON, KEVIN called me and apologized that he wouldn't be able to meet me for dinner, but he would stay at the door waiting to greet me at Insight Meditation Center, where the dance would be. I thanked him for the phone call and started planning to go into the city for dinner before going to the dance.

The dance was at 28 West 27th Street in Manhattan. I found a sushi restaurant to eat in that was empty on a Saturday night. I was about to turn around and leave, but something told me to stay. I'm glad I did. I ate my dinner in complete silence, without any hustle and bustle. About halfway through my dinner, this remarkable woman, full of presence, beauty, and a pile of red hair, entered the restaurant and sat a few tables away me. I could not keep my eyes off her, even though I tried hard not to. I had agreed that if a woman were in a restaurant or something similar by herself, I would not stare or gawk at her so she could enjoy whatever she was doing without having to deal with my gaze and energy. But she was striking in her army boots and an army jacket, although she didn't look like somebody in the military. She looked like somebody who was either a model or an actress by the way she carried herself.

We had both asked for our bills and walked out at literally the same time. We were walking on the same side of the street in the same direction. When I arrived at 28 East 27th Street, the number was on the wall, but there was no door. She saw me staring at it and trying to pull a wooden board as if it were a door. She stopped and looked at me curiously. "Are you okay?"

"Thanks for asking. I'm supposed to go to something at 28 West 27th Street, but there doesn't seem to be a place to enter."

"Well, that's because that's 28 East 27th Street. I think I'm going in the same direction."

     Raised by Wolves, Possibly Monsters

"I'm going to something called the Barefoot Boogie at the Insight Meditation Center."

"Really? That's where I'm going!"

"No way!"

"For real. how about we go and find it together?" I appreciated how she made it sound like she was trying to find her way around the city like me, as opposed to me being lost and not having a clue. We started walking together, and it turned out that Sabrina *was* a model, an actress, and a professional dancer. To whatever degree, I was intimidated by her being stunningly gorgeous with little or no effort or attention to her appearance. I had a fantasy in my head of Sabrina and I being romantically involved. After ten minutes of connecting with her, that fantasy disappeared based on not feeling her equal, which might have been true for all eight billion of us after spending ten minutes with Sabrina. She is that spectacular. I quickly shifted my intention to getting to know her and sharing our stories and lives. Sabrina was intelligent, creative, strong, confident, and set clean and clear boundaries. I found it easy to connect with her and feel safe.

That night began my journey into freestyle, conscious, and ecstatic dance. A month later, I was one of the DJs. Six months later, I was co-coordinator with Kevin. Six months after that, I was co-coordinator with another person who was also new to the dance community, Maggie, who is one of my best friends today. Even though my first experience was in Oakland, this was the launch into movement, music, and connection for me. A little over a year later, I went to the annual Dance Camp hosted by Dance New England, the organization that Barefoot Boogie is a member of. It was held at Camp Robin Hood in New Hampshire. I've gone all thirteen years since then, except in 2020, when we had a virtual dance camp instead of the in-person one due to the COVID pandemic. I've met all my closest friends at a conscious or ecstatic dance event or Dance Camp. I currently work for Dance New England as a Program Manager.

Brynn

 I RETURNED TO the East Coast after a year and a half in Asia. I was a creative director at an Indian recording studio that recorded Hindustani and Carnatic music in Edison, New Jersey. The musicians were great, and the owner was kind and thoughtful. In addition, I was picking up a few DJ gigs here and there.

I can't imagine Brynn and me ever launching if all the following elements were not true. To begin with, when somebody survives my experiences in Mongolia, going on a date with a fantastic woman does not seem nearly as daunting. Secondly, divine masculine and feminine beings being present is helpful in surviving such an experience. Last but not least, for right now, the faith and trust that I would be all right was so profound and prominent when the Hawaiian Airlines plane landed in San Francisco that I felt like there was nothing in the world I was not capable of. There was no arrogance, ego, or self-inflated machismo, just an inner sense of power, strength, and feeling one hundred percent supported.

I met Brynn through an online dating site called Spiritual Singles. I remember the day her profile appeared on my screen. My heart was racing, my face beamed, my energy buzzed, and my genitals tickled. I hadn't even started reading her profile yet. Just seeing her image stirred up my whole being! I remember the thought in my head was, "Write her and write her now. Be clear, direct, and authentic. You must get her attention!" I did, and in the morning, I received a response from Brynn.

Over the next few days, we exchanged emails, which grew in length with each day. Emails became texts; texts became phone calls, and phone calls became Skype. The interesting thing about all this is that Brynn lived less than forty-five minutes from me by car. We could have gone on a date.

We made plans for our first date. On Friday night, I would take the train from Edison to Princeton, where Brynn would meet me. She would drive us to an Ecstatic Dance event north of Philadelphia. We planned on eating before the event near the dance. That would give us enough time to get used to each other's physical presence in the car.

    Raised by Wolves, Possibly Monsters

I took the train to Princeton. Five minutes later, I noticed a blonde woman who looked nothing like Brynn reading on a bench by herself. My heart sank. Somehow, even on Skype, she had tricked me. She wasn't who she pretended to be and didn't look anything like her photographs and the visual images on my screen.

At that moment, the woman put the book down, took her sunglasses off, and stood facing me. I found her even more attractive than the photographs and video. She slowly walked towards me, but my legs wouldn't do anything. I remember standing there frozen, smiling as happy as could be. When she got about ten feet away, my legs started working. As we walked towards each other, she put out her arms to greet me with a hug; without thinking, I went right past them and kissed her on the lips! Not a cute little hello kiss or nice to meet you kiss. This kiss was an "I want you, I need you, and I'm going to have you" kiss. I wish somebody had taken a video of this couple, who still had not spoken to each other in person yet, in a deep, intimate, passionate kiss while dropping the things in their hands on the black paved surface. Several minutes later, I remember gently moving my head back a few inches, making eye contact with Brynn's excited and loving brown eyes, "Hi! I'm Michael."

"Hi! I'm Brynn."

We giggled, smiled, and stared into each other's eyes like we had never seen another human. I noticed that we were holding hands, and our hands were trembling. We were still determining what to do next.

"Hi, Brynn. Before we go anywhere else, can we sit on the grass over there? How does that sound to you?"

I wasn't sure she heard me because her gaze was still completely locked in without movement or response.

She leaned forward slightly and whispered, "Do I get to continue to make out with you over there on the grass?" Brynn kissed me.

"Yes!" I kissed her back. Nobody moved. Nobody breathed. I don't remember breaking our embrace, but somehow, we were both sitting on the grass on a blanket that was in her bag, staring into each other's eyes and kissing. It was fifteen or twenty minutes before we began a conversation.

We started talking and got a chance to get to know each other and be in each other's energy. We confirmed our plan for the evening, grudgingly gathered our stuff and the blanket, which Brynn folded perfectly, and went to her car. We pulled out of the parking lot, and Brynn asked if we could stop at her home quickly to go to the bathroom since it would be a long ride. She wanted to show me her house quickly, too, as she had just had the stucco exterior walls painted two months before.

She parked on the street, and we left everything we needed in the car. I stood in the living room of her home, looking around. It was simple and tasteful: lovely wood floors, a beautiful walnut dining room table and chairs, and no TV. I don't know why that made me smile, but it did.

Brynn came out of the bathroom and showed me where it was, and it was my turn. It was nice to have a moment to myself to empty my bladder and get grounded. I walked out of the bathroom to tell her that I liked the mirror with the natural wood framing. Before I could do so, Brynn was kissing me and pushed me against the wall. Everything in my body was on fire. I was present and could feel Brynn's presence meeting me there. We didn't move from that place, but we did switch several times who was holding who against the wall. In the middle of Brynn licking my left earlobe and me caressing her upper back and right butt cheek, "Shit! I left my keys in the car with the window open and all of our crap, including my wallet and your backpack!" We both laughed and ran out to her car, which was still there with everything inside, which facilitated another round of laughing and kissing and hugging and groping, this time in front of her home.

We decided to eat in downtown Princeton and then drive to the dance. It was a lovely walk to the Thai restaurant that Brynn had just called for reservations at along the way. Dinner was amazing. She grabbed my wrist as we exited the restaurant and said, "There's this great gelato place just one block away that I'd love to show you. Do you like ice cream?"

"I'll go wherever you take me. And I love ice cream!" So, we got gelato. We landed in front of a chapel when we finished our ice cream and walked through her favorite part of Princeton. "I love this chapel. Sometimes, instead of eating, I sit here during lunch since my office is just a few buildings away. Can we peek our heads inside quickly? It's so beautiful in there."

"I'll go wherever you take me; I love churches." Brynn kissed me, took my

 Raised by Wolves, Possibly Monsters

hand, and guided me in. There was a unique service going on. We sat in the last row holding hands while Brynn pointed to various pieces of stained glass and iconic paintings of angels. I felt her move closer to me. Our legs, hips, and elbows were connected while seated. I already knew I was in love with Brynn. I also knew that Brynn was in love with me. My mind wandered, and I fantasized about getting married in that church. At the end of the service, while leaving the church, Brynn whispered in my ear, "I have always wanted to get married here at this church." It sounded like she was asking a question, not making a statement. We both smiled broadly, sharing the same fantasy of standing by the altar across from each other in that chapel on the Princeton University campus.

As you may have already figured, Brynn and I never made it to the ecstatic dance. We spent the moonlit night walking, talking, sitting, kissing, and walking and talking until we landed back at her place.

Once there, we made a mutual agreement not to have sex that night so that we could get to know each other better without the expectations or complications of sex on our first night together.

Brynn pulled me to the floor. She curled her head around my shoulder to my lips and kissed them gently. About thirty seconds later, we were lying on top of each other on her hardwood floor in the blanket like a burrito. We both fell asleep there for about a half hour. We unrolled the burrito, which was comprised of Brynn and Michael. Brynn took my hand and brought me up to her room. She handed me an unopened toothbrush, and we silently brushed our teeth. After we both finished our bathroom routines with a smirk here and a giggle there, we both went to her room together for the first time as if we were robots programmed with only one destination.

I took a moment to look around her room with its sky-blue painted walls, a few pieces of art, and semi-famous prints. There was an oil-painted dancer in a red dress with black hair on canvas, and that caught my attention. On the far side of her room, away from her king-size bed, was her desk with many things on top of it. It was nice to see somewhere in her house where everything wasn't perfectly in place. She did not expect me to be in her room tonight.

"I'm sure all of the crap on my desk is interesting, but I'd like you to look at something that you might find more interesting." Somehow, without me knowing it, Brynn had removed all of her clothes and was naked except for her crimson-colored underwear. I smiled and took in this beautiful human being who was standing in front of me. I could see and feel her confidence and vulnerability staring me in the face. "That's the response I was looking for."

I took a few steps towards Brynn, and with each one, I removed another article of clothing: the pink button-down shirt and the tank top underneath. While I was getting ready to unbuckle the white cotton belt and my shorts, the woman in front of me raised her right hand and index finger, signaling me to pause. I gladly obliged. Her face, neck, and chest all got slightly red with excitement as she scanned my torso full of dark hair. She nodded when she wanted me to continue. I felt incredibly turned on, knowing she was turned on watching me. I took my time, the belt and then the shorts. I was now standing naked except for my red cotton Calvin Klein boxers as Brynn and I took in each other's bodies and presence.

She put out her hand as an invitation. I took her hand and moved closer until our chests met, as well as our lips. We climbed onto and into her bed. The sheets felt clean and crisp, with her soft white comforter smelling like it dried on a clothesline out back. She handed me her underwear as a statement. And then I took off mine and gave it to her. It felt like a ritualistic ceremony. More smirks, more giggles, and more bodies pressed against each other. This time I could feel my semi-erect penis pressing against her pubic hair. I let out a deep exhale. When Brynn responded and smiled, I realized I had expressed that out loud, not just in my head. The rest of the night was a combination of exploring each other's bodies and skin and hearts and minds and souls and genitals until we fell asleep in each other's arms. I woke up in the morning with the same mostly full erection that I went to sleep with. This time, Brynn put her hand on my pubic hair and started running her fingers through it.

"Morning, Michael. Is your proposal from last night about no sex or orgasms still applicable this morning?" She moved her legs in a manner that offered invitation and consent. As we continued exploring each other's genitals, we found new ways to connect and tenderly acknowledge each other's desire and vulnerability. I invited Reiki to be present to support those connections and our intentions.

   Raised by Wolves, Possibly Monsters

The next few months were some of the best months of my life. Our connection, love, and enjoyment of each other grew weekly. Brynn saw me and loved me. I saw Brynn and loved Brynn. Reiki was holding us each step along the way.

That first weekend, on Sunday afternoon, we walked around downtown Princeton and stopped inside a clothing store. We were both looking around casually. I remember seeing these cool shorts made of soft, bone-colored cotton with thick, flat drawstring ties. I picked them up and put them down a couple of times.

"Why don't you get them if you like them so much?"

"They just seem expensive for shorts to wear around the house."

"Why don't you at least try them on to see if you like them enough even to consider it?" Her eyes glistened, and her cheeks were full of vitality when I walked out wearing the shorts with my sandals. "Michael, you look so good in them! You wouldn't have to wear them only around the house; they would also be great for the beach. And for hanging out in my backyard eating brunch on Sundays."

"Wow! You have lots of plans for me and these shorts. Maybe another time." I changed back into my olive green shorts. Walking around with Brynn was fun. We had similar default settings in presence and style and walked at a similar pace. Even though Princeton is a small community, wherever we walked, Brynn was physically connected to me, whether it be holding hands, her arm around my waist, and now and then, her hand would be tucked under my arm. I don't think I had ever experienced a woman I had dated embracing me as a person while we were in public so enthusiastically. It was evident that Brynn wanted people to know that we were together. There was no showing off; she adored me and wanted others to know. I appreciated Brynn enjoying me that way.

One night, I was going to DJ at the Barefoot Boogie in Manhattan, and Brynn wanted to come with me. I was thrilled at the idea of my new friends in the NYC ecstatic dance community meeting Brynn.

About forty-five minutes into my set, an older guy who was a regular was dancing with Brynn. They had danced together for a few songs and started playing more intimately and closer. For a split second, I felt jealous, and my feelings quickly shifted to being turned on mentally and physically. Brynn would look over every two minutes to check and ensure I was okay with what she was doing. I was. I enjoyed seeing Brynn having fun, enjoying herself with somebody else, and witnessing somebody else totally turned on by Brynn!

On the ride home in the Holland Tunnel, Brynn asked if we could talk about something. I said yes without knowing the topic. I knew the topic, but it felt important to say yes without asking questions first. I knew this was going to be a challenging conversation for her.

"Michael, I know we talked about this on our first date, that I get extremely jealous easily. Do you remember that conversation?" I nodded my head yes. "And do you remember that I said that if I get jealous, it's not because I don't trust you. It's because I have trouble trusting men based on my history." I nodded my head again. Brynn took a deep breath and let out a sigh. "I want to talk about tonight when I was dancing with Joe. Are you sure you were OK with how we danced and how close and intimate we were?"

"Absolutely! It was fun and turned me on. I never get to see what you look like when you're turned on because I am part of what we are doing."

"I am trying to believe you, but it's hard because it is different. I would lose my shit if you were doing the same thing with some random woman on the dance floor."

"I know, Brynn. At first, I was jealous, but seeing you alive and engaged was fun and exciting. And I understood, even then, that we are different, and it would not be good for us if I did the same thing."

"And you're OK with that imbalance?"

"I am. We both have different strengths and challenges. You feel super comfortable with being naked in front of me, your body, and your physical appearance. As you know, I sometimes feel self-conscious about those things, and you don't hold that against me. You are thoughtful, gentle, tender, and supportive when you sense me getting tangled up that way."

"Yes, that's true. So, are you truly OK with us having different boundaries when flirting and interacting with others?"

"Yup." I could see her looking me over, trying to find some speck of hidden contrary energy.

"For the record, I get great pleasure out of seeing a handsome man like you

 Raised by Wolves, Possibly Monsters

still feel a bit cautious sometimes when you are naked. Men tend to be either agonizingly cocky or paralyzed by being self-absorbed and feeling inadequate. It's refreshing to be with a man who is more in the middle but can still show up! It even turns me on."

Brynn and I started making plans for me to move in with her. We felt a bit rushed, but we were both willing to take the risk of being together under one roof. She had the better roof and everything else.

A few weeks later, Brynn decided we would go away the weekend of my birthday. We stayed at a cute bed-and-breakfast Brynn had picked out. Brynn returned to that store with the cotton shorts I liked. From minute one, they were my favorite shorts. A decade later, they are still my favorite shorts. Sometimes, I cry when I put them on because I miss Brynn. Other times, I cry when I put them on as a reminder of our shared love and connection.

Another weekend, we were out to dinner at Brynn's favorite restaurant in Princeton. I was munching on a large fruit tart when Brynn took a deep breath and sighed before speaking in what appeared to be her studying my face and body.

"Sweetie, I continue to fall even more in love with you by the day. I've been excited about our plans for you to move in with me. Sharing a home and a bed thrills me on many levels. And even though the miracle of miracles is starting to happen, my trust and faith in you continue to grow, and I am rarely jealous when I see you talking to another woman, even if she is attractive. I never thought it would be possible again to experience that kind of trust with any guy." Brynn paused, taking an even more extended breath with a slow exhale, closed her eyes briefly, opened them, and continued. "Of all the extraordinary people I've ever met, there are so many aspects of your life that you are exceptional and fully committed to, and this inspires me. There is one you are not committed to at all, which concerns me. And I want to understand it because it seems incompatible with who you are."

"Okay . . ."

"You are 'all in' in everything you do except for your job and career. It's as if money and your future don't matter to you. And in knowing you, that doesn't feel true. Help me understand why these don't matter to you?"

I had to clear my throat and steady myself. Brynn's perspective was not anything I was prepared for as she was leading up to this point. I remember my hands being in a tight fist on the side of my chair and a tightness in my lumbar and neck. I could feel my temperature rising rapidly. For a brief minute, all I could think about was how to annihilate and destroy Brynn. To say that I was caught off-guard by my response would be an understatement. My physical and emotional responses were surprising. She had presented her concerns to me respectfully. I was not accustomed to feeling like this.

"Just to clarify, are you asking me if money and the future don't matter to me, or are you asking me if that's true and why they don't matter to me?" I was trying to stall from wanting to kill her, to the best case scenario, return to deeply loving her. I was unsuccessful in the latter and only marginally in the former.

"Well, really both. If both matter to you, the second part of the question is irrelevant." There were some mild sharpness and edges to how Brynn spoke that were new to me.

"Well, on some level, money and the future don't matter to me. You know most of my family has died, so you can't count on the future, and there are so many things more important than money." I knew I should have stopped right there and not said another word. I knew whatever was about to come out of my mouth would be hateful and harmful and had nothing to do with Brynn or what she was asking me. "Not everybody wants to work forty or fifty hours a week at a job they can't stand with a boss who is an asshole."

"Really? That's where you want to go with this? You want to give me shit for working at a job that pays for the home you stay in and want to move into, the bed we sleep and make love in, the car that you love that takes us to the beach, Philadelphia, and the City. And that job is paying for the dinner that we just ate. Plus, the grad school classes at NYU. I never felt I was being taken advantage of or disrespected about the imbalance of our economic situation until now. I am grateful to have earned enough to enjoy and share my lifestyle with you. We have different gifts; this is one that I can offer. We both know if we walk into the kitchen, the food will taste better if you make it than if I make it. How dare you, Michael! How dare you!"

Brynn got up, walked to our server, and handed him her credit card. He

     Raised by Wolves, Possibly Monsters

returned it to her where she was standing, and she left. There was no drama, no theatrics; she just left. I sat alone at the table with the fruit tart she paid for. I couldn't decide which was worse: to take a minute to finish those last few spoonfuls of the fantastic fruit tart or get up to try and catch her while she was just down the block. I chose the former, knowing it would only worsen things, which it did. All four spoonfuls felt like pouring salt on Brynn's wounds. I put down the spoon and left.

The physical symptoms would increase dramatically over the next few years, and they began to express themselves in the form of lumbar pain, hip and knee pain, but more than anything, back pain. I started to run after Brynn. The exchange and the present tension only made my back feel worse. I stopped running and tried to walk fast. My lower back was starting to throb. I needed to walk even slower. Tears were beginning to form in my eyes and throat. How am I going to make this better? How can I fix this? What did I just do?

I went to her front door tentatively. "Brynn?" I walked through the living room and into the kitchen and didn't see her there. I returned to the base of the dark wood steps and was about to call out her name again, but I chose to walk up the steps slowly and quietly to avoid agitating things more. The door to the bathroom was closed, and I could hear her slow breathing swishing around the tub. She must've run home to fill the bathtub so quickly. I knocked gently on the door to the bathroom. "Brynn?" I spoke softly and gently.

"I'm taking a bath. Can I have a few minutes to myself?" She sounded defeated. The tears in my throat and eyes were making themselves known. I cleared my throat to the best of my ability: "Of course." That was the first night Brynn and I went to bed together without the presence of love surrounding us. It was the worst night I chose not to include Reiki in bed with us.

Brynn whispered, "Are you up?"

"Yes."

Brynn turned around to face me. She leaned her forehead into mine so our noses would touch. I could feel her tears rolling down both our cheeks. I was aching, knowing that I was the cause of this goddess' pain and sadness. I wiped her tears away and kissed her forehead softly. I licked the one tear still rolling down her cheek and tenderly kissed her forehead. She kissed me back with gentleness and warmth. "I love you, Michael."

"I love you too, Brynn."

"I want to talk about last night, but I need to feel you inside of me first. Can we make love?"

"I can't imagine anything I would rather do at this moment than be inside of you and you inside me." We moved our bodies enough for me to enter her. I asked Reiki to fill my penis with healing energy. It was vibrating, pulsing full of life and fire while also still. I heard a barely audible "Yes." We didn't move. We stayed in that position for quite a while, and without warning, we expanded together. We went from silence and stillness to roaring, pressing, and holding through the release as the feminine energy expanded within us, meeting with the masculine energy and keeping us grounded. Yeah, we were going to have that other conversation soon enough. But at that moment, bodies, love, presence, and beauty were connected with God.

I desperately want to tell you that I wrote Brynn and told her that I had figured it out. That we continued to make love and more love. I want to tell you how I dug deep inside myself to overcome my inadequacies, ego, and fears. I want to tell you I grabbed hold of the lessons and teachings I had received and expressed them fully. I want to tell you the masculine energy flowing and radiating out from me that was discovered in the Gobi Desert, and Central Asia took over. I want to tell you my Higher Self had taken the hand of the little boy inside of me, who was scared of failure and losing Brynn so intensely that he hid under the covers in my bed. I want to tell you that love, connection, and commitment won over fear, resistance, and protection. But this isn't the kind of story where the author provides a Hollywood ending. I want to tell you that love triumphs over fear and trauma, which they did, but not yet. This story has a beautiful finish, but not how they would do it in Hollywood.

Later that day, Brynn and I talked. I was vulnerable, honest, and open with her. She demonstrated the patience, compassion, and empathy I was hoping for. I remember we went for a walk to get ice cream; she was fighting for us so tightly and fiercely that I felt our love and connection could withstand anything, even fear and self-sabotage, mine and hers.

We'd come to an understanding. I needed to understand what Brynn wanted from me. I thought she wanted me to have a traditional career and income like hers. She wanted me to treat my job and work as I did with everything else: the same courage, passion, and commitment. On a practical level, Brynn didn't need me or want me to change my morals or values, especially those I wouldn't enjoy or feel inspired by. All she wanted was for me not to be another line item expense. Brynn wanted me to move in, cover my end, and have enough left over that sometimes I could pay for dinner, a hotel, or other fun and exciting things. She didn't need us to be economic equals. I was able to hear all of it. I felt like we were over the hump.

"Michael. I am so proud of you. All these conversations around money and careers have been tough for you. Now that I understand this is connected to your history with your father and brother and how all three of you tied economic success to your masculinity, it must have made you feel like I was attacking you as a man. I have the highest regard and respect for you as a man and what you've done with your life, despite how you were raised and what they taught you."

Brynn paused. She pulled my hand a little closer to her and tightened the grip. I could feel her love and affection in my skin and bones. "You are not the first man I have met who has struggled with me being more economically success-ful. I was programmed in the same culture as you. The man is the breadwinner, and that's the end of the story. I've also had my work to do in this over the years. I've had my resentments around earning more and typically having a more stable income. You're the first man to hear all that, regroup, and meet me somewhere that feels good for both of us. I'm glad I felt safe enough to share with you that I felt like I was being taken advantage of and that you would never offer to pay for anything we were doing or bring any food for us to cook when you came over. It never occurred to me to ask you."

"Thanks, Brynn. I feel much better about all of this, but I still struggle. I was not aware of how much my identity and masculinity are tied to money, especially in relationships with women. I'm grateful that we were able to hear each other." I leaned over in her direction, and we kissed. I felt a few tears drip on the bone-colored cotton drawstring shorts Brynn had bought me for my birthday. Brynn and I loved each other and were good for each other.

Somehow, after both having multiple orgasms and making it to the top step of the second floor, whatever understanding we had reached evaporated. We got into a fierce argument that ended with Brynn breaking up with me and me sleeping on the couch. We were both mean, hurtful, and downright unloving. I remember standing on the steps arguing and thinking in my head, "I hate her so much I hope she dies." I left in the morning without connecting or speaking about what had happened.

A month later, we tried again.

The moon cooperated, shining brightly in its complete and glorious beauty. After finishing the coffee gelato, Brynn took my hands with a soft, tender, and barely audible voice, "I'd like you to spend the night if that feels good to you."

I kissed her. She kissed me back. "Yes." Brynn took my hand and led me upstairs. It felt like she was leading me to her room for the first time. There was more tenderness, more vulnerability, and more love.

Brynn woke in the morning crying. She could not speak coherently enough for me to know what she was crying about. Her pain emanated from the whole room. I felt crushed by it. "Michael. I can't do this. I've tried this before when I loved somebody, and I knew we couldn't work it out, and I kept trying to force it. I'm not going to do that this time. I can't do this any longer." Brynn returned to crying with her head nestled under my right armpit. She kept sobbing and sobbing and sobbing. Occasionally, she would stop, whisper, and tell me how much she loved me and couldn't do this. I could feel my eyes getting red and watery. My heart was getting twitchy. I didn't know what to do. One thing felt clear: I would not leave her bed until she asked me or told me to do so. I wanted to drink every moment together before we were apart.

She cried and cried and spoke about how she failed all of her relationships, and she would never find a partner, and this is what she always does, and the pattern would never break, and she loved me, and she couldn't do this.

At some point, I started laughing. I don't know what I was laughing at; I just laughed. Brynn was in tears, Michael was in laughter, and it continued for an hour. I needed to get up, shave, shower, and put on a suit because I was DJing at the Hoboken International Film Festival awards ceremony with a room of 500 people in suits and gowns.

Brynn kept crying, repeating, "I love you, and I can't do this. I love you, and

            Raised by Wolves, Possibly Monsters

I can't do this." I was sitting up with my back against the wall. The breeze tickled my back, watching Brynn, who was utterly heartbroken. Hollywood heartbroken. And I was paralyzed. I couldn't get up. I couldn't see anything. I couldn't feel her. I couldn't love her. When I noticed I had sixty-three minutes to get to the film festival, which was fifty minutes away, I told Brynn I needed to get up and go.

I leaned over and kissed her head, telling her I loved her and had to go.

Several times during the event, I texted her, asking her if she was okay. She did not reply to any of them. When I loaded my BOSE system into the car and pulled out of Hoboken, I called her, and she didn't answer. I tried five minutes later, but she didn't answer. I left her a voicemail pleading for her to text or call me and let me know she was okay. She called me and told me that she was alive and had no plans to kill herself, but she was not OK and still lying in bed crying. She said she couldn't talk, said goodbye, and hung up.

Eleven days later, I texted Brynn asking if we could get together to talk and tie up some loose ends. She thought that would be a good idea. We set up a time for the following Sunday afternoon to meet in a park between us. To say that we were both a mess would be a colossal embellishment. Before we even dove into anything or had a chance to sit down, just standing and talking to each other without really being able to put coherent sentences and words together, I dropped my book bag; Brynn dropped all of the things she brought with her that she wanted to include in her closure process. I suggested we walk around the park first to get grounded and create some safety.

We sat at a picnic table. Brynn asked if I could go first. I shared with her all of the things I wished I would have done differently, how I wished I could stand up and walk through my pain and fear. More than anything else, I wanted Brynn to know how much I loved her and how deeply I always will.

We were both silent and still. We knew there was nothing else to say or do. Every part of me wanted to tell this fantastic woman how much I loved her, that we should give it another try, and that I would do better, but I couldn't because I was not convinced I could do better. At least not yet.

We stood up, hugged each other awkwardly, shared a few tears, said goodbye, and kissed each other on the cheek. As Brynn walked away, she briefly took my hand, held it, and let go. Brynn was gone.

This was ANOTHER Big Flinch. Through my loss, I learned that loving another person is the hardest thing a human can do. I look back and see that I wasn't ready to change to be with Brynn. I knew I wanted to find a partner who aligned with all of me. I finally realized that a genuine and sustainable connection must be rooted in who I am, not in who I might be.

Ellen

 I HAD DATED a few women after Brynn. They were awesome women but had no chance because I had not moved on from Brynn. I compared them all to Brynn, and they were not her.

I attended Dance New England's Summer Dance Camp for the first time in August 2011. I met many lovely, open-hearted people that first year and every year since.

In my second year at Dance Camp, a friend from the Barefoot Boogie had come to camp for the first time with an old friend from Brown University named Ellen. I found this hysterical a dozen years later, but Ellen did not register with me the first time we met. Over the next few days, we had several intense and intriguing conversations. Ellen was super intelligent, interesting, and a force of nature. When she was getting ready to go home at the end of camp, she hugged me and said with little affect, "I have a really big house in Providence, Rhode Island, that just me and my daughter Angela live in Michael." I had no idea what that meant or why she shared this with me, so I replied, "OK. Thanks." And she left with me standing there curious what the ___ that meant.

Ellen and I dated, then became partners, with me moving into that four-bedroom house in Providence with her and Angela two years later. As my body continued to get worse and worse, our relationship suffered. We had not been together long enough to withstand one of us going through a major health crisis while we were still creating our foundation and trust. I struggled with not feeling like a man and feeling inadequate. I could not contribute much besides cooking, washing dishes, picking up Angela after school, and being in pain. My pain and

          Raised by Wolves, Possibly Monsters

shame took a toll on all three of us. I moved out and into the Providence Zen Center. I am intentionally sharing the bare minimum about our relationship then because Ellen is one of my best and most trusted friends today. I want to honor what we have today without sharing our past dirty laundry. We deeply loved each other then and even more today. I can't imagine my life without Ellen in the center of it. She is one of the people in what I refer to as my core group of friends. Ellen and, to a lesser degree, Angela are the people who witnessed my physical decline and the havoc it wreaked mentally and spiritually up close in a way no one else did. I wasn't the same man they met just a few years before.

I Don't Want to Tell This Part of the Story

 MY BACK AND knee pain had progressed and was spreading further up my spine, including my hip joints on both sides. I went to chiropractors, doctors, osteopaths, Reiki practitioners, bodyworkers, acupuncturists, orthopedic surgeons, orthopedic spinal surgeons, and orthopedic specialists. Spinal orthopedic specialists who wanted to do spinal fusion surgery and put four metal rods in my back were consistent with all of the rest of them; I knew that what they were saying was wrong with me and that what they prescribed was incorrect. I did not know what was going on in my body; I just knew it wasn't what they believed was true, undeniably.

As things got worse, I started walking with a cane. Then they got worse, and walking with a cane was even more challenging. This strong, active, powerful, athletic man, full of vitality, was now the equivalent of most people in nursing homes. It was brutal. My enthusiasm for life was shrinking weekly. The reflection I would get in people's eyes when they saw me continue to have less mobility and more pain told me everything I needed to know. It seemed easier not to spend much time with people.

People gave me all kinds of incredibly condescending and judgmental analyses, including things like karma from when I was a drug addict and criminal, resentment from childhood, sexual trauma, unresolved issues with my father, unresolved issues with my mother, unresolved problems with my brother, and unresolved issues from all of my girlfriends, unresolved issues from early recovery, unresolved issues with my parent's divorce, unresolved issues with everything you could think of that a human being could experience. What was worse, several of my friends offered the same kind of "support." I was utterly exhausted, with everybody telling me what was wrong with me, which was an unresolved issue with one thing or another. The few friends that didn't go down this road were treasured.

The next annoying thing in my journey towards a crumbling body was that every new person I met who noticed how much physical pain I was in and that my body was starting to take on an unusual shape would ask me if I had ever heard of or gone to a _____. You can fill in the blank with any of about twenty-five different modalities. For some of them, I was a teacher and facilitator. It did not matter if I answered yes or no; they would still go on a ten-minute rant "teaching me" about whatever the modality. The rant would be even more extended if they were white and male. When I would share with them that I had either explored, practiced, or was a teacher of the thing for the second time after their rant, they would promptly ask me questions solely to prove how I was doing it wrong; otherwise, I would be healed. And if they were a white male, they would then give the same rant/mansplaining that they had just done five minutes previously, almost verbatim. After a few years of this, I just started answering the question no and pretending to be interested in listening so that they would only give the rant once.

Here is a partial list of the practices, lifestyle, and treatment modalities that "helpful people" would ask me if I tried or practiced that were normal aspects of my life, some of them for years or decades.

Meditation
Reiki
Qi Gong
Yoga
Physical Therapy
Chiropractic care
Acupuncture

     Raised by Wolves, Possibly Monsters

Bodywork

Fasting

Dance & Movement

Green leafy vegetables

Hypnosis or E.F.T. (tapping)

Walking barefoot

Swimming

Running (Yeah, somebody actually said that to me)

Sex

Suicide (Really?)

Gluten or dairy-free diet

Vegetarian or vegan

High protein diet

Whole grains & whole foods diet

Past Life Regression

Prayer

Heavy painkillers, after I mentioned I was a recovering addict!

And the one that created the greatest anger inside of me: "Have you heard of the law of attraction?"

Yes, I have. I am fully aware that middle-class, healthy white people who grew up in suburban, affluent neighborhoods with educated parents, still married, living in their own homes, with grass in their front and back yards, quality schools, and had the opportunity to go to university and or higher, "attract" success. I mean, what else could they possibly do? When you start the other team's three-yard line, it's not a miracle to get a touchdown. The law of attraction is the whitest supremacist spiritual New Age nonsense I have ever heard in my life. So yes, I have heard of the law of attraction. And what is it that you think I attracted after fifty years of spectacular health that one day, my body started crumbling? Do you really believe that a human being would "attract" being in pain night and day for seven years, losing seven inches of their body, and not be able to walk at their mental, emotional, spiritual, energetic, and karmic peak in life to that point? If I was going to attract all of this pain, mental, emotional, and physical, don't you think I would've done it when I hated myself and everybody else in my twenties and early thirties or even late teens? Why would I "attract" all of this after I worked through the bulk of my mess and karmic consequences? It is borderline comical that these gorgeous, healthy, middle-class white people think that they have what they have because they "attracted it." As if having one of your parents or grandparents found a way to earn money is a skill set.

Since I am condensing this process and experience dramatically, we are talking about somewhere between six and seven years. Yes, you read that right. *This lasted for about half a dozen years or longer!*

I was demoralized, embarrassed, grieving, and experiencing betrayal, resentment, bitterness, self-hate, and shame. I felt deep shame that somehow, I let this happen to me, that I had failed as a human being and healer. I was an embarrassment to the Reiki community in my mind. I was an embarrassment to the meditation community in my mind. I was an embarrassment to the Qi Gong community in my mind. I was an embarrassment to the dance and movement community in my mind. I was an embarrassment to the recovery community in my mind. I was an embarrassment to everyone who loved, cared, and invested time and energy in me. I was an embarrassment to my Teacher Betsy. I was an embarrassment to all of my students and clients. I was an embarrassment to our species. I had given up on the idea that things would ever be better. I had resolved, or possibly submitted, to the fact that I was going to be in pain every single day for the remainder of my life and that I was going to have to learn to be stronger, braver, and more powerful to survive.

At one of my visits to my primary care physician's office, the nurse told me that I was five foot three inches, an inch shorter than last time I had been there. The data was not penetrating. I told her she was wrong. She measured me again, and I was 5 foot 3 inches. I told her she was wrong and that I was 5 foot 9 and a half. She measured me again. She told me I was 5 foot 3 because she was 5 foot 3 and we were the same height. The data would not penetrate my brain.

My primary care physician was committed to my well-being. I felt grateful that I had found a doctor who cared that much, even though I was new to his caseload. He sent me to most of the people on the list above. He just didn't know what else to try, so he referred me to an endocrinology center that primarily

          Raised by Wolves, Possibly Monsters

focuses on diabetes, but they do other work as well.

"Michael, I just don't know who else or what else to send you to. The Hallett Center is just a shot in the dark. I don't know how or if they can help you, but I don't know what else to do, and I don't want to give up on you. I don't know anybody at the Hallett Center for Endocrinology, but I will give you a referral because I've had past patients tell me good things about them." I grudgingly agreed to give it a try. As long as he continued to try to find ways to help me, I made an inner commitment that I would keep showing up for whatever the next thing was going to be.

I went to the Hallett Center, which, the following year, became Brown Endocrinology and is now Brown Medicine. I filled out the paperwork as I did at every other place, sat, and waited.

Enter Dr. Ricardo Gabrielle Marques-Correa.

"Hello, Mr. Michael. My name is Dr. Ricardo Correa. I have good news for you! I have looked at all your tests and labs, and everybody who has given you a diagnosis is completely wrong. The good news is that you have a tumor in your body!"

I was standing before him when he said this, and I fell into a chair, and he caught me and guided me safely. How can having a tumor be good news?

"Michael, I was a resident at the National Institutes of Health outside of Washington, DC. They do amazing research and work on people in the endocrinology unit there. I used to be one of the people who were able to diagnose Tumor-Induced Osteomalacia. I believe you have a tumor that causes all of these problems. If I'm right, the tumor can be surgically removed, and you will no longer be in pain." He now had my attention. Most of what he said went right by me, but it left an imprint in my body because later that day and night, I remembered what he said almost verbatim.

He said two significant things without knowing it. The first was, "If I am right." He was the first doctor who didn't assume a hundred percent that they were right. The second was, "You will no longer be in pain." I had heard similar versions of the second statement, but he said it without arrogance, cockiness, authority, or any other form of "I know better than you, and I am right." He said it with softness, gentleness, and warmth.

"So, what did you call this again?"

"If I am right, we have to run one test, but it's very simple; I believe you have something called Tumor-Induced Osteomalacia. And with your permission, I would like to refer you to the National Institutes of Health to see if they are willing to take on your case."

"Okay. What is the other test?"

"It's straightforward. I will send you to get some bloodwork, and the one thing we want to test that nobody has tested so far is your phosphorus level. We will run another test that other people have run just to get the most current data we can, but the phosphorus level is the thing that I want to know about. If you're willing to do this, I will write you up for lab work, and you can do it downstairs. They will get the results in a few days, and then we can schedule another appointment to discuss them. Is that okay with you?"

He asked another question. He wanted my consent, not just my submission to his authority and power. He actually wanted my consent.

A week later, I was sitting in Dr. Correa's office again. This time, it was a different experience because a part of me felt droplets of hope and excitement. Those were really dangerous words for me at that time—dangerous words— dangerous feelings. Hope and excitement meant I was about to have another round of bone-crushing Soul defeat and disappointment. I was playing with my fingers and fingernails, waiting in his office for him to arrive.

He knocked on the door gently, "Mr. Michael, is it okay for me to come in?" More respect and consent.

"Yes."

He walked in; his face was shining and glowing, even more than the previous week. He reached out his hand to shake mine with his right hand, and with his left hand, he motioned for me to stay seated so I wouldn't have to get up. As he was shaking my hand, he could not contain his excitement. "Mr. Michael, my suspicions were confirmed. Your phosphorus level is ridiculously low. I want to talk about this more, but I want to ask again for your permission to refer your case to Dr. Rachel Gafne and Dr. Michael Collins at the National Institutes of Health. They are the two people who have been researching Tumor-Induced Osteomalacia. Since I used to work on the unit, I can email Dr. Gafne directly. If

Raised by Wolves, Possibly Monsters

that's okay with you, I don't have to go through the whole system."

I could not pronounce osteomalacia. I couldn't even remember those three words, even though Dr. Correa had now repeated them several times. I did not know what the National Institutes of Health was. Full transparency: I didn't realize what phosphorus was. What I did know was my body sitting up straight and my eyes tearing slightly. This was different. I still had no idea what he was talking about, but something felt different inside me. And I trusted this beautiful, small, and gentle man.

"That would be great." I took a deep breath and exhaled. I took another deep breath and exhaled again. "I know you explained a lot of this to me last week; please repeat what this condition is, what the National Institutes of Health is, and what the treatment would be if I had it?"

"Thank you for asking, Mr. Michael. I will start at the beginning and go slow. If you have any questions, please just ask them." Dr. Correa took his time. He was with me for almost an hour that day. Three times, nurses knocked on the door, came in, and asked when he would finish because he had other patients waiting for him. Each time, Dr. Correa answered, "I'm with Mr. Michael right now, and as soon as we're done, I will let you know. Are there any other doctors available to meet with my other patients? Our conversation is important, and I don't want to rush it." Each time, they left frustrated. He did not let it affect him. He returned to making eye contact and giving me his full attention and presence.

What I understood was that somewhere in my body, there was a tumor that was probably benign, sending information to my parathyroid, which is made up of four little pea-sized glands on the thyroid. They inform my body about how much vitamin D, calcium, magnesium, and phosphorus it needs at any moment. If I had this condition, this tumor sent false information to the parathyroid, and the bulk of my phosphorus, calcium, magnesium, and vitamin D were all eliminated through my urine. And since those four vitamins and minerals are the essential building blocks to the health and well-being of bones and soft tissue, my bones had changed shape. They were pressing against each other, causing close to twenty-five fractures I had throughout my ribs, hips, spine, knees, and feet!

I didn't understand the science, but I did understand that my bones felt perceptibly stronger when he spoke about those vitamins and minerals. I asked him to go ahead and send the referral to the National Institutes of Health, which he told me was the largest research hospital in the world. Since the federal government funds it, no insurance or money is involved. All of my testing and treatment, and if needed, my transportation, would be covered without me paying one dollar. It seemed too good to be true. Fear and doubt crept back in. He apologetically said he needed to meet with his next patient but wanted me to return in two weeks to continue our conversation. I want to repeat that a medical doctor wanted me to come in to continue our discussion. Not for more testing, treatment, diagnostics, or any planning; he wanted to make sure I understood what was going on and the potential process. It was as if he thought I was human and deserved his time, knowledge, experience, and attention.

The Call

IT WAS A regular Tuesday afternoon. I was on my way back to the Zen Center, where I'd now lived for the past three years, one of them as Director, and I needed to get gas. I had just finished pumping gas when I saw my iPhone alerting me that a call was coming from Maryland. I knew it would be quicker to grab the phone than to prepare myself, adjust myself, and land in the driver's seat before the caller hung up. "Hello, this is Michael."

"Hi Michael, this is Rachel Gafne from the National Institutes of Health. Dr. Correa may have mentioned that I might be reaching out at some point. Do you have a few minutes to talk?" My heart was beating and thumping, and excitement ran through my bones and veins.

"Hi, he did tell me somebody would be calling at some point. I just finished pumping gas. Can you give me a moment to pull my car out of the way?"

"Sure. But if this is not a good time, I could call it another time at your convenience."

I turned on the car and eased myself into the seat. "No. This is a great time." I pulled my car to the side of the gas station on that warm, sunny afternoon,

     Raised by Wolves, Possibly Monsters

turned the car off, and settled in. "I'm ready now. Thank you for waiting."

Dr. Gafne briefly introduced herself and explained why she was calling. I was startled that she was the one calling me; she was not a receptionist, not an appointment coordinator, nurse practitioner, secretary, or administrative person; she was THE person. After she finished her two or three-minute introduction, she asked me if I understood everything she said and if I had any questions. I told her I had many questions but wasn't ready to ask them yet; I wanted to let her do her thing.

"Before we go any further into this, it would be helpful if you could tell me the things you have lost in your life due to your medical condition that would be most important for you to have back. It will help me understand if we can meet those needs partially or completely first."

I was startled again that she wanted to know what was important to me and what I wanted to have back in my life before she wasted *my* time. Not me wasting her time, her wasting my time. "What a great question! This is not hard for me to answer. The list goes through my head almost daily in some shape or form.

I want to swim again and walk on the beach without extreme pain.

I want to dance comfortably without being in pain for several days.

I want to bike ride again.

I want to be able to have sex without being in debilitating pain for the following week or worse.

"Thank you, Michael. That's helpful. If you do have Tumor-Induced Osteomalacia and we're able to find and remove the tumor, all of those things are possible in varying degrees. I can't promise anything to you or even that we will be able to find a tumor if you have one. It is hard to find these tumors; they are typically very tiny, and sometimes we cannot find them." Her honesty, integrity, and humility were inspiring and still are. We spoke for about forty-five minutes on the phone, asking me many general and specific questions, and I asked her many general and particular questions.

Right then and there, while we were talking on that October afternoon, she told me that she was pulling her schedule up on the screen of possible times I could come to the NIH for testing and diagnostics. We figured out that the only two-week period between then and February was December 6-20. Dr. Gafne said they might not need the whole two weeks, but they would need ten days unless there were no signs of T.I.O. or a tumor anywhere. She was unequivocal in stating that they would not be doing any treatment while I was there for this visit. She explained that boundary respectfully. This visit was for testing and research only.

"I can see through all of the notes I forwarded that you have had this for many years. I'm sorry that you struggled for so long. I know that some people with T.I.O. cannot work or receive income. How would you get to Bethesda, Maryland, and would you need economic support?"

"I think it would be too long of a drive for me. I think flying from Providence would be best, but I don't have the money to afford that."

"Okay. That's not a problem. Here are the next steps. Our unit research nurse, Lori Guthrie, will call to officially schedule your visit here. In addition, I will send an email to our on-site travel agency. They will arrange for your flights and for you to be picked up at the airport and brought directly to the NIH. Do you have any other questions now?"

"No. I don't have any other questions at this time. I want to thank you for your call and for how you've treated me. This has not been my experience with the medical profession in general."

"I'm sorry to hear that, but unfortunately, we hear that a lot. I wish it weren't so. Thank you for taking the time to talk with me, Mr. Swerdloff. If you don't hear from the travel agency or our research nurse by tomorrow afternoon, let me give you my cell number so you can call me directly. We look forward to seeing you here soon enough. Hopefully, we can help you." We said our goodbyes, and I clicked my phone off. I wasn't ready to do anything yet, so I just sat there in the car next to the gas station, digesting and breathing, digesting and breathing.

When I felt ready and capable of driving again, I turned on my car and eased my way out of the parking lot towards the Zen Center. I reflected on who and how to share this new information and possibilities with the residents and other members of the Zen Community at Providence Zen Center in Cumberland, Rhode Island. By telling them, their excitement would raise my hope all by itself. Hope with chronic pain and suffering is not always welcome and helpful. Sometimes, hope can be dangerous.

            Raised by Wolves, Possibly Monsters

On the first day of my stay at the NIH, each team member made their way to my room to greet me and ensure that all of my needs were attended to. If it weren't for the fact that it looked like a hospital, the care and attention felt like I was at a five-star hotel near Central Park in Manhattan.

Dr. Gafne was even more authentic and genuine in person. She had finished her workday and wanted to connect with me before she went home. Later that night, Dr. Michael Collins, who was studying T.I.O., sat beside me on the side of the bed while we spoke.

The following morning, I met the unit Social Worker, Lisa Felber. Lisa was great! Along with letting me know all of the art and social activities that I could participate in while I was there, she told me about a room on the first floor with four donated chairs, each with surround sound running throughout the chair and costing about $25,000. When you reserve one of those chairs, someone will offer Reiki if you'd like. That was the first thing that I scheduled.

Lisa went over everything I had shared with Dr. Gafne on the phone back in October that I was hoping to experience. We talked through each one; she asked specific questions to get clarity and took notes on all of them. Then, she asked me a question I wasn't unprepared for or had considered. "Mr. Swerdloff, if we can find the tumor, assuming you have one, and we can remove the tumor, and your body starts healing and repairing itself, what would you do or at least like to do as a way of celebrating having your life back?"

"What an interesting question! I would love to go to the Caribbean or Indonesia! That would be an amazing way for me to celebrate having my life back."

The following day, they had me up and busy with X-rays, CT scans, PET scans, octreoscans, bone scans, blood work, and urine. And it continued for over a week. Some tests were as short as peeing in a cup or having blood drawn. For others, like the octreoscan, the test was a little less than five hours. I have a fascinating memory of that particular test.

Since it was tough for me to lie on my back on a hard surface for more than five or ten minutes, they knew they had to give me a sedative to scan my body to find this tiny little tumor successfully. I was clear with them about being a recovered addict, and they assured me what they gave me was nonaddictive and that they would monitor me afterward. I lay flat on my back on a narrow surface, almost like a gurney. My hands were at my side, and my legs were straight. The technician lightly secured both my wrists and ankles.

The person who was going to execute the imaging was the head of the Nuclear Medicine Division. I had seen him around earlier in the week when his staff gave me some of the tests listed above. He was a beautiful, soft-spoken, and intelligent man. Since the test would be long and we needed something to distract me, he asked me if I liked music. I told him I did and asked him if he wanted to use my iPhone to play music through, and if so, to hand it to me so I could pick out a playlist. He said he keeps a boom box in his locker for special situations like this, and it does not have a port to hook into a phone or iPod. He said he had a copy of Miles Davis's *Kind of Blue*. When he saw me light up, he told me he would return and ran down the hall. He was back in 90 seconds flat.

Throughout the test, I came in and out of consciousness a multitude of times between not sleeping much the night before or any of the nights before and being drugged. I realize this is not what happened because he and I talked about it afterward, but it felt like every time I came into consciousness, the central musical theme of the first piece of music, "Freddie Freeloader," was playing. Here's the thing: since the test was almost five hours long, which meant the CD played several times from beginning to end, that album was programmed into my brain, especially "Freddie Freeloader." Over the next few weeks and months, whenever I felt nervous, scared, uncomfortable, or anxious, my brain just started playing "Freddie Freeloader" in my head.

Later that night, several team members came in, led by Dr. Gafne and Dr. Collins, with smiles. Dr. Gafne was the one who spoke first, "We found it!" Dr. Gafne told me they would meet with the surgical team in the morning to review the results and create a plan. She told me that the tumor was wrapped around a few of my ribs just outside of my right lung.

The whole team came for the meeting to discuss the plan the next day. There was the surgeon himself, Dr. David Schrump, Colleen Bond, Nurse Practitioner, Cheryl Warga, Nurse Practitioner, and another younger male doctor who was part of the team. I believe he was doing his fellowship, but I'm not sure. Colleen Bond was the one who was leading the conversation and carrying twins in her womb.

          Raised by Wolves, Possibly Monsters

Colleen framed the process in broad strokes. They wanted to remove the tumor from my ribs, but since it was wrapped around three of them, they were going to remove parts of those ribs and replace them with a Gore-Tex patch. The tumor was close to my right lung, and they prepared for the possibility of my right lung being punctured during surgery.

The plan to make sure I was still breathing, if that were to happen, was for me to have another major surgery in advance of this surgery to move my stomach further away from my left lung since it was pressing up against it; this surgery would be a partial hiatal hernia repair. That surgery would take place locally in Rhode Island, and they would give me instructions on how to do that. Because it was pressing against my lung, and all of my organs and glands were squished together and pressing against each other, they were concerned that I would not have enough lung capacity in my left lung if my right lung were punctured. I was acutely aware of my organs and glands being squeezed into smaller spaces. It affected pretty much everything in my life, from digestion to breathing to excretion to blood pressure, and I imagine somewhere in there, it affected my sexual organs as well. Having many problematic areas of my body was not news to me; the information that my stomach needed to get moved was news to me.

They repeated over and over that these major surgeries would be completed back-to-back. It would be exhausting for me, and there would be a relatively long recovery time due to the consecutive procedures done in such a short period. The timeline that they came up with was for me to have the partial hiatal hernia repair done in Rhode Island, or preferably at Massachusetts General, through laparoscopic surgery or robotic surgery, with robotics being the first choice. After that surgery, I wouldn't be able to eat solid or whole food for a couple of weeks and take liquid protein supplement drinks as part of my recovery. As I moved to food that was more and more solid, I needed to continue to up my protein intake. They required me to be strong and stable to perform the surgery the last week in February because they would not be able to do so again till probably April or May.

The team wanted to get this done, as did I, but they weren't the ones who would undergo two major surgeries in a six- or seven-week period.

When they began to talk about removing my ribs, I hit my limit of what I could absorb for the day. My ribs and intercostal muscles had been a source of significant discomfort and often pain in my body. Even though I knew I would be knocked out and have anesthesia, the idea of anybody doing anything beyond gently touching my ribs created deep fear and shallow breathing. I told them that I probably wouldn't be able to continue much longer with the conversation. All four of them received that message well.

Heather, my favorite nurse, checked up on me as they walked out. I appreciated it. Dr. Gafni came by a little later, as did Jamie Streit, the new Research Nurse on the unit. Each one of them gave the amount of time necessary to make sure I understood what was happening, that they were an excellent team, that Dr. Schrump was one of the best in the country at what he does, and that they would all be part of my recovery when I came back. Their care and attention felt reassuring and supportive.

Colleen and Cheryl came back and went over everything again with me. This time, the two of them sat in chairs next to my bed, which was informal and casual. I was appreciative of their knowledge, support, and attention. They didn't leave until I had communicated that I understood the process and that a whole team would support me before, during, and after. And they would want me to stay at least two, if not three, weeks afterward at the NIH for recovery, physical therapy, and rehabilitation. When they left, I was grateful to have the room to myself and nap.

Jamie made an appointment with the travel agency the next day to make all of my transportation arrangements for February. While I was waiting to meet with the travel agent, I realized this was really happening. I wasn't sure how I felt about it, but it was happening.

Lisa, the social worker, made sure she spent fifteen minutes with me before I left to remind me of the five things I wanted to have back in my life and the celebratory trip when appropriate. It was helpful to leave having that as one of my last conversations.

The OTHER Major Surgery

Dr. Lucas Beffa at Kent County Hospital in Warwick, Rhode Island, performed the laparoscopic surgical procedure. The surgery went fine. I felt rushed out the door the following day. I assume my insurance only covered one overnight stay. I felt a little more beat up than I expected. Even though it was explained to me in great detail, and I read an abundance of information on recovery from partial hiatal hernia repairs, a liquid diet with broths and protein drinks felt awful. Every week, I was scheduled to shift my diet to a little more solid food, solid food, dense solid food, meat solid food, and then high protein solid foods, primarily meat and protein supplements. I didn't feel like I was getting more substantial or more robust. The two Nurse Practitioners of the surgical team were concerned about whether I would be strong enough for an even more major surgical procedure.

Colleen and Cheryl pushed me to start exercising, with plenty of movement, physical therapy, and eating a high-protein diet of 60 to 80 g of protein per day. It was funny because I was living in a vegetarian Zen Center. Getting the amount of protein I needed took some effort. Ten days before returning to the NIH, I was still shaky and wobbly. I started to get fearful that they were going to cancel my surgery and have to put it off for several months. The relationship between hope as inspiration and hope as a form of dangerous expectations was making noise within me.

People can say many things about me, and giving up easily is not one of them. Sometimes, the singular thing that makes me successful is relentless intensity. As is typically the case, I rose to the occasion when needed. The other aspect of my recovery they were concerned about was that my left lung had not increased its capacity to the expected level. Lung capacity did not improve regardless of my "relentless intensity."

At this point, I was barely hanging on to my last bits of faith in God and the universe. I was on the phone with my friend Archie Roberts, an excellent therapist, discussing my situation. He brought up the idea of creating a GoFundMe campaign to raise money to pay my bills while I was at the NIH and for the months after surgery needed for recovery without income. He connected with my ex-partner Ellen, another excellent therapist who was a student of Archie's at Salve Regina University in Newport, Rhode Island, to put this together and reach out to many of my friends and family. When they started the campaign, they set it to raise $650. It was $900 before lunch! Archie changed it to $2000. Two days later, it was $2700, and two friends from Dance New England offered to send me a check for a thousand dollars. I had tangible evidence that many humans cared about me when it was all said and done, which gave me and my body the jolt of energy necessary.

Along with the financial support, several members of the Zen Center offered me meals and then created a schedule to bring me meals during the first couple of weeks that I would return. Some people offered to help me in and out of the shower. Somebody cleaned my space every few days—more evidence of being loved and cared for.

Recovery from major surgery number one completed.

Major surgery number two was scheduled for Tuesday, February 27. I was to arrive on Tuesday the 20th for testing and preparations. While I was still wrestling with whether I was "ready" or not, that Monday night, I packed my bag and arranged a ride to TF Green Airport in Warwick, RI. It was time to return to the NIH, where I now put all of my eggs in one basket, namely, the removal of a tumor in and around three ribs. That was my entire plan in life. I had no alternatives or backup plans if it didn't work. It needed to work.

The Return to the National Institutes of Health

THE SCHEDULE FOR preparations and tests began an hour after I arrived. The first test was breathing and respiratory. I continued to fail that test. They said it was a few percentage points higher than before the hiatal hernia repair, but they were still concerned. Their concern had me concerned.

Several of the meetings were scheduled with various palliative care team members. Here's another wish: I wish most therapists, counselors, and psychologists had the same level and quality of active listening and respect for the person they're speaking with as the members of this palliative care team. They took

          Raised by Wolves, Possibly Monsters

exceptional notes on what we agreed on for the rest of the team.

Each time I met with a different team member, they said, "I see that you're a recovering addict, and you've been clean and sober for almost thirty years. That is incredible, Michael! Let's ensure that whatever plan we devise does not conflict with or hinder your sobriety." The words each person chose were different, but the message was consistent. I felt heard. I felt seen. I felt respected. And possibly more importantly, I felt safe knowing I would be cared for based on the three previous feelings.

The plan we designed included me receiving acupuncture every day in my bed for at least the first week after surgery; receiving essential bodywork/massage every other day for at least the first week; either a Reiki Practitioner coming to my room and working on me there or me being taken down to the room with those fantastic chairs with sound and music while receiving Reiki; somebody from their team checking in with me every day in person to see the pain level, and what needed adjustment. In addition, we had to consider morphine or oxycodone if naproxen and Tylenol were making it too painful for me to sleep, function, or recover. We agreed in advance that I would get a minimal dose of IV morphine the first night after surgery to ensure I could sleep and rest because this would be necessary for my rehabilitation.

I met with various physical therapy team members throughout the testing. They mapped out what the process was going to look like. Since I hadn't had the surgery yet or any sense of what my body would feel like, it didn't fully penetrate my brain. It had now been around seven years. The concept of me getting better did not feel real.

The surgery took place on the morning of February 27. When I opened my eyes again, I was in a room by myself surrounded by walls of glass in the Intensive Care Unit. I felt lost and disoriented, and it felt like the right side of my body was stiff, with a dull, constant pain where the incision and the removal of ribs and tumor. There was a completely different team of nurses in the ICU than in the endocrinology unit.

My nephew Carlo, the older son of my deceased brother, drove down from New Jersey to Maryland to be with me the two days before surgery and the three days afterward to make sure I had a family member with me. It was lovely waking up and seeing Carlo sitting beside me, playing with his iPhone. His presence leading up to and immediately following surgery was a gift to me. I am grateful he decided to come and support me that way.

Good Friday

 IT WAS 8:20 A.M. on Friday the 30th. Dr. Gafne and Dr. Collins walked into my room together. They both had similar expressions, but I was oblivious to what they were trying to convey. It didn't take long for it to be clear.

Dr. Gafne's face lit up, and her voice cracked, "Good morning, Michael, I mean Mr. Swerdloff. We wanted to come in before either of us does anything else to let you know that your phosphorus results came back this morning, and they were 3.8, which is normal! It worked! We got the tumor!" I could see and hear her tears of joy.

"We did it, Michael! No more T.I.O.!" Dr. Collins was even more enthusiastic but did not shed any tears like Dr. Gafne and me.

I hesitated before speaking. I wanted to check with myself and ensure I was awake and clear-minded. Four nurses were in the room, standing in a row beside the two doctors. Everyone beaming with eyes glistening and cheeks full of color and vitality.

Once I realized I was awake and coherent, I opened my mouth to speak but couldn't. In my fifty-seven years at that point, I never recall such extreme and potent gratitude. I could only manage this: "Really? Normal?"

The two doctors looked at each other and smiled; Dr. Gafne spoke, "Yep. We asked them to verify the results twice, and you are normal!"

"I think this is the first time I've ever been glad to be normal!" Everybody in the room burst out into laughter, the joyful and effervescent laughter that heals anybody who experiences it.

"We don't get a lot of 'wins' on this unit. Most of the folks we work with have some form of diabetes, and the best we can do is make their life a little bit more manageable. When something like this happens, everybody on the team

    Raised by Wolves, Possibly Monsters

celebrates. They all wanted to come down to be with you when we shared the news." Dr. Gafne lost her bearings momentarily, "Now you can start working on that list when we spoke on the phone in October. You can begin to get your life back."

I ordered French toast with cinnamon and maple syrup, strawberries, two scrambled eggs, and an orange juice for breakfast. They had me booked up for the bulk of the day with testing to ensure everything was going as planned, including two different physical therapy sessions. While waiting for my breakfast, I texted my nephew Carlo, who had returned to New Jersey the night before. I then texted my core group of friends from the conscious dance community. My gratitude and joy expanded by sharing my moment with the people closest to me.

The various teams kept me busy for the next few days. The surgical team wanted lots of imaging of my bones and body. The endocrinologists wanted to know about the chemistry set that was my body. The palliative care team wanted to know about the pain in my body. And the physical therapy team wanted to know how my body was functioning and how they could improve it.

When I felt solid enough, they let me go to my two favorite restaurants in the area. One was an Italian restaurant in Bethesda named Olazzo on Norfolk Avenue for pasta and sausage. The other was Nando's Peri Peri in DC. The Peri Peri chicken was yummy. I enjoyed being out in the world after being inside for fourteen days straight, except for a walk around the property a couple of times.

Recovery at Providence Zen Center

WHEN I RETURNED to the Zen Center, the community was excited to see me and hear about my progress. They were also confused because now that I was getting "better," I walked around with two canes instead of one. I was instructed to practice walking with two canes thrice a day for twenty minutes and then add to it every few days. After about a week, I was walking with two canes all the time as my strength and flexibility increased. This process was to shift the gait of my legs while walking.

The two local physical therapists I worked with, Paula Silva and Jessica Claiburgh, let me know when it was time for me to get rid of the two canes and start walking without any canes. At first, my hips, in particular, hurt, as did my lower back. Little by little, each muscle became stronger and stronger. I progressed to going out without canes for the first time in about five years!

I can't say this often enough or loud enough. The people in my life were so supportive! I do not remember any point that I had felt so supported, cared for, and accepted as in those first few months after surgery. I started to work on simple movements and dance to find out what my body could do. At first, it wasn't much or long. Spring was moving into early summer, which meant the annual dance camp for Dance New England was coming up in just a few months in the first week of August. The previous August, many organization members pooled their money and bought a Girl Scout camp in western Massachusetts called Camp Timber Trails. It is a beautiful location with over 400 acres of predominantly forest that we call our own.

In previous years, the organization had rented space for the eleven-day camp each year in various locations over the last forty years. We were now at our own space with a challenge: it was much more rustic and spread out. This dynamic meant I needed to get my body stronger over the next few months so that I could participate at least a little bit. Even if that meant the only thing I did was DJ some dances at night, hang out and eat with friends, and do a little swimming in the lake. I am one of those people who does well when I have a target. And this was an immense target.

My walking was getting stronger and becoming more stable in the water. I was starting to dance a bit, even when, sometimes, at local dances, some of my friends had tears in their eyes that I was moving my whole body. I started practicing yoga regularly. This was a huge help. Between meditation, Reiki, yoga, semi-regular bodywork, and acupuncture, there was an increase in strength, flexibility, and stamina each week.

One of the teachings of my recovery from T.I.O. is that my body functions better when I engage in something I enjoy or have fun. During those painful years, the state of my body and nervous system created patterns of tension and bracing. Learning to get to a place of comfort and reduce inflammation while not

    Raised by Wolves, Possibly Monsters

relaxing or enjoying myself was a work in progress. Fortunately, this is not true today.

One of my fondest memories of those first six months was seeing friends at dance camp who saw me walking without a cane and being able to dance, breaking into tears of joy on witnessing my recovery. I still have many of their expressions and tears imprinted in my mind. This was the most extraordinary evidence of being loved and accepted that I have ever experienced in my life. It never would've occurred to me that people crying with joy at the miracle of my recovery would be a highlight in my life, but it most certainly has been and continues to be!

PART IV

What It's Like Now

"The sage has no mind of his own.
He is aware of the needs of others.
I am good to people who are good.
I am also good to people who are not good.
Because Virtue is goodness.
I have faith in people who are faithful.
I also have faith in people who are not faithful.
Because Virtue is faithfulness.
The sage is shy and humble – to the world he seems confusing.
Others look to him and listen."

Lao Tzu, Tao Te Ching 49

(translated by Gia-Fu Feng and Jane English)

Five Years Without Hugs

 I FIND IT incredibly challenging to describe to other people what it was like not to be able to be hugged. It's not like I was some big hug nut or that I ran up to people, wrapping my arms around them. I was prudent with my hugs but fully hugged the people I loved and felt safe with. That was before the intercostal muscles tightened, and the ribs started fracturing in multiple places.

I had read information and research on hugs and their importance, why they're important, what hormones are released, etc. I read all of that stuff. I would share this information with many clients I have worked with. That was before I went half a decade without being able to hug other human beings or them being able to hug me. Let me correct that. That was before I went half a decade without being able to embrace other human beings or for them being able to hug me without me paying a considerable cost for the experience. Eventually, my "hugs" were more like a precursor to COVID hugs, where both people put their arms out like they're hugging but don't hug. I guess this made me a pioneer in COVID-19 hugging. Funny, not funny.

The sad part of all this was that I eventually didn't even notice that I wasn't hugging people anymore. Not hugging became an accepted norm in my life. Now and then, I'd be lying in bed, uncomfortable and irritated that it took me twenty years to be able to let people I love and care about hug me without my body stiffening or going numb. It felt like a cruel joke. I remember one morning thinking it would've been better if this had happened a decade earlier, while hugs were only sometimes enjoyable or pleasurable. Why did it have to happen after I could enjoy and feel safe?

Along with being unable to hug people safely, I had to decide to stop laughing! Laughing was even more physically uncomfortable than hugging. I remember the first time I laughed in a half-decade without pain. The impact of no hugging or laughing was not truly understood until they reappeared. I had forgotten about them to the degree that they didn't even cross my mind when Dr. Gafne asked me during that first call what I wanted back in life. I encourage anyone who reads this paragraph to hug somebody today, and please make sure you laugh. Really laugh. They are such treasures and gifts whose importance is only noticed when they are gone. These simple but profound experiences are an incredible source of joy and gratitude.

Let the Changes Begin

ONE OF THE strangest experiences of that first year and a half of my physical recovery was feeling my bones get more substantial. I did not know a human being could experience that that was something, but I did. I took calcium supplements for the first two years, and a local endocrinology team monitored my progress. I don't have the vocabulary to describe what it feels like to experience your bones getting more substantial, but I felt it. Every few months, I felt my bones more prepared for incidents like falling on the ground or tripping over something unexpectedly. As my bones became denser, my nervous system relaxed more and more.

I have had multiple experiences of going up several flights of stairs in various places that were challenging and frightening for me previously and doing so with ease and comfort. It would startle me when I reached the top of the steps and noticed my body was not bracing.

My bone density increased, and my muscles became more substantial with increased flexibility. This was a slow and gradual process that most people around me noticed before I did. As mentioned earlier, daily Reiki and yoga practice helped. I was committed to daily yoga practice. In January 2019, I added a movement and dance practice following my morning yoga in the living room. Little did I know then that having a morning dance and movement practice would be part of my survival during the early stages of COVID-19 in the United States. I could dance and move daily, no matter what was happening. No matter how much pasta and rice were missing from the shelves. No matter how close I came to running out of toilet paper. No matter how many contradictory and scary statements the mainstream and social media shared. No matter how long I went without seeing my friends physically in person or touching each other's bodies. I

          Raised by Wolves, Possibly Monsters

could dance, and I could move.

I needed fresh air and to be outside and look at something different, so I forced myself to walk in the snow in March and early April, even though I still did not have good physical balance. But I did it every day. It was vital to my recovery, development, and ability to stay somewhat sane in an incredibly isolated time and place. I refused to go into despair! I had been through hell multiple times in my life and just found my way out of it the year before. I was not going back to hell again! It was just not an option!

Between meditation, Reiki, yoga, walking meditation, and dance/movement, I went into semi-retreat during the first two months, possibly three, of the pandemic. As tragic and brutal as what was happening around me, including to multiple friends and clients at this point, I was doing spectacularly. Parts of me that I had not experienced in half a dozen years were starting to show their head and remind me of who I was. The experiences since then have created more compassion, empathy, and resiliency, as if I needed more of the latter.

A COVID Couples Counselor

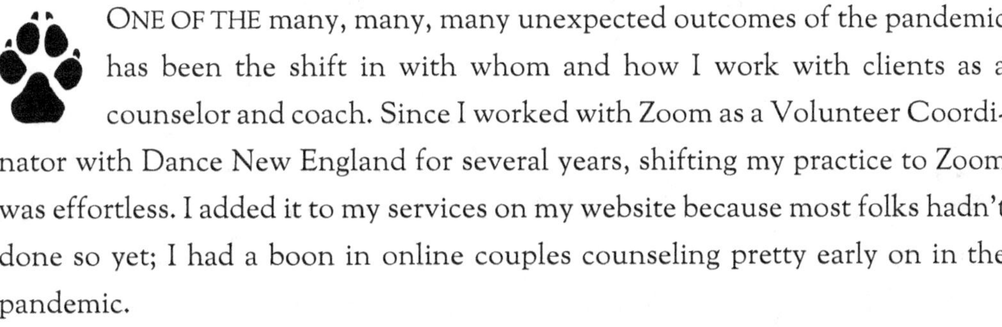

ONE OF THE many, many, many unexpected outcomes of the pandemic has been the shift in with whom and how I work with clients as a counselor and coach. Since I worked with Zoom as a Volunteer Coordinator with Dance New England for several years, shifting my practice to Zoom was effortless. I added it to my services on my website because most folks hadn't done so yet; I had a boon in online couples counseling pretty early on in the pandemic.

Before the pandemic, my general ratio of individual clients was ten to one or two couples, and once or twice a year, I would work with a family. That turned upside down through Zoom online counseling. For the last two and a half years, many of my clients have been couples all over the United States. I continue working with individuals and families. I would've never predicted this because of everything I do; it's what I had the least experience with. I did in-home family counseling and crisis intervention. I have decades of experience working with adolescents and teens in their homes and the community. I have been working with individuals since the mid-90s. I would work with some couples along the way, but I didn't have much experience. I decided to take an online course in couples counseling through The Gottman Institute to expand and improve my skills. They are leaders in research and treatment of couples.

When I first started meeting with so many couples, what surprised me the most was how organically effective I was without knowing what I was doing! It turns out I'm an outstanding couples counselor.

When I think about working with couples, many things inspire me to support and motivate couples to invest in their individual and collective well-being. At the top of the list are the consequences of a poor relationship, or one in which separation/divorce is needed, which affects many people. Inspiring people to improve their relationships or create a separation that respects themselves and each other is vital. Working with individuals also affects multiple people, but with couples, it expands exponentially. I love the work and feel alive and valued when I see them begin to trust, love, play, and become affectionate again with each other without even noticing that they're doing it.

Riding the Waves of a New Body

ELLEN TEXTED ME to ask if I wanted to go to the beach with her late one Wednesday afternoon. It was a silly question because I always want to go to the beach. We decided to go after 4:00 since there is free parking and entrance to the beach at that time. Ellen suggested we go to Sachuest Beach in Middletown or Second Beach. Again, the answer was yes, but this time with more enthusiasm.

Even though I had lived in Rhode Island for more than five years, I had only been to Second Beach a couple of times at this point. The beach itself from the parking lot is too long of a walk for somebody who has mobility issues, but I was ready to give it a try.

As we walked towards the beach, I could feel the tension in my body, fearful of walking through the sand for too long of a distance comfortably, which might

     Raised by Wolves, Possibly Monsters

ruin my experience of actually playing in the water. The sand was firm and packed, so walking was easy. My body relaxed when we got to the part where you could see the water, the skies, and the sand. Second Beach is about 1 mile long and has the most robust and forceful waves of all the area beaches. I had forgotten about this, and my body stiffened again as I noticed the waves crashing again and again. I took a deep breath, and we kept walking.

We plopped our stuff down, and as I was about to make myself a place to sit on a towel, I decided I wanted to go in the water. I invited Ellen, and she joined me.

As is typically the case for me, feeling those first few footsteps into the soft sand as the water trickles above the ankles, my whole body relaxed into this simple sensual pleasure. As the water went up past my waist, I went ahead and dove in. It felt lovely to dive into the ocean without hesitation. As I resurfaced, a wave came crashing and washed me up to the shore. I did not plan on riding any waves, and especially not that wave; despite myself, I got a free ride and survived. This experience gave me the confidence to ride the waves. I spent the next forty minutes riding waves, one after another. I was knocked around, knocked upside down, swallowed mouthfuls of water, and had a body full of joy. About fifteen minutes in, Ellen asked me how I was doing. "I am having so much fun!" I rode waves till my legs couldn't keep me up any longer. I walked up to the beach to join Ellen, who appreciated seeing me experience joy and pleasure in the ocean.

When Dr. Rachel Gafne called me last October, I had not considered nor fantasized about riding waves in the ocean. I had not even considered it an option. This simple pastime started when I was eight or ten years old and produced much joy. It felt like my whole body was tickling and pulsating with happiness and excitement.

In one form or another, I have been riding the waves of this body ever since. Sometimes, those waves come in the form of a fifteen or twenty-mile bike ride on an e-bike that my friend Charlie gave me on a permanent loan. Occasionally, those waves are DJing and dancing with friends for several hours. The waves sometimes express themselves as a hike in the woods accompanied by a deep, intimate conversation. And probably my favorite "wave" does not move at all. When a group of people lies on each other in a puppy pile, I can join them and feel their bodies under, next to, and on top of mine. I am grateful for all these various forms of waves in my life today.

The Reiki Wave

ANOTHER WAVE WAS feeling inspired and comfortable offering Reiki to clients again. It took a while for me to get past my self-judgment and shame to feel like I could still be a Reiki Master after my body had fallen apart the way it did. Then came facilitating regular Reiki Trainings in person and online. The last step in reclaiming my Reiki practice was adding Reiki Counseling back into my services offered. Reiki Counseling is a process of sharing Reiki with clients to slow their brain rhythm so that fear and ego are less of an obstacle. Reiki provides safety to explore aspects of ourselves that feel scary by diving deeper held by Reiki.

The two experiences where I feel most inspired, alive, and connected to my Higher Self are when passing Reiki Attunements to people during Reiki Training and Reiki Counseling. These experiences are when I feel like I am doing why I was put on this earth more than at any other time!

Riding the Waves to Costa Rica

IN THE SUMMER of 2021, I dreamed of visiting the Caribbean, symbolizing my recovery. A friend who grew up in Jamaica had initially recommended Jamaica to me, and then he took his recommendation back and suggested I explore the US Virgin Islands. I got on the Couchsurfing Project website and looked for potential hosts. It didn't matter how long or how many times I looked; it didn't feel right. I looked at other islands in the Caribbean. They didn't feel right, or it would cost too much to be there for more than a few weeks. I had this strong sense of staying at least one month, if not two.

One day, I talked about this with some friends, and Ellen suggested Costa Rica. She had been there several years earlier and was considering returning at

     Raised by Wolves, Possibly Monsters

some point. I internally rolled my eyes at all of the New Agers and hippies there. Later that night, I got online, explored the beaches and towns, and got excited—most photographs combined beach and trees, if not jungle. I kept switching back and forth between looking at Airbnb rentals and Couchsurfing Project hosts. The longer I looked, the more excitement and energy began rising from within. After a few hours, I was convinced I was going to Costa Rica!

Meanwhile, at my job at Dance New England, we had begun to plan our next virtual event. I called my friend Moti Zemelman, an excellent Contact Improvisation teacher, to see if he was interested and available. He said he was busy right now and couldn't focus on this. We were closing our conversation, and I asked him what he was working on.

"I just confirmed that we'll return to Goddess Garden EcoRetreat Center in Costa Rica in February. I want to start planning and promoting the retreat."

"When will you be in Costa Rica for your retreat?"

"The second week in February."

"Where in Costa Rica?"

"Goddess Garden in Cahuita, which is on the Caribbean coast. It's a small town at this gorgeous retreat center. Why?"

"Well, I'm going to be in Costa Rica at that exact time somewhere on the Caribbean coast!"

Ten minutes later, I had committed to participating in Moti's Contact Improv retreat! Since this is what he needed to do anyway, he gave me suggestions on where to stay, what to do, and other helpful hints and suggestions. We were getting ready to get off the phone, "Michael, I don't know if you know this, but Kristen Chamberlin is going to be offering her retreat the week before at the same retreat center?"

"I did not know that! I do remember seeing her leading retreats there in the past. I will give her a call."

Later that night, I called Kristen. By the end of our conversation, I had also committed to going to her retreat at Goddess Garden EcoRetreat Center the week before Moti's. I now knew where I was going to be in Costa Rica for the first two weeks of February. I started looking for Couchsurfing opportunities the week before, and nothing felt right or connected. It made logistical sense to begin my experience at Kristen's retreat.

While all of this was happening, Omicron was spreading throughout the world. I had yet to formally send my deposit to Moti or Kristen, the Airbnb I had picked out in Puerto Viejo, or my flights to and from Costa Rica. I was cautious about seeing how this latest variant of COVID-19 was going to wreak havoc and possibly derail the plan. I woke up one morning in early December, booked my flights and the Airbnb, and sent deposits to both retreats in about thirty minutes! I was going to Costa Rica for two months beginning in February!

Like any exciting trip or adventure, one has to distinguish between the fantasy of what will happen in our heads and the reality of what may occur. The stories in my head included 85-degree weather, monkeys, toucans, interesting birds, lizards, trees, and flowers. The fantasy included me swimming in the Caribbean Sea multiple times daily. Many fantasies had deep healing and cleansing on the black sand beaches and saltwater waves. Of course, there were also the fantasies of amazing Costa Rican women, including flirting, playing, exploring, and mutual orgasms, screaming so loud that the monkeys replied in kind. I also had fantasies of women travelers from all over the world, "open to whatever experiences universe had in store for us." Some of those experiences happened in my bed at night, waking together in the morning—more fantasies of the black sand beaches of volcanic ash, salt water, waves, and naps. Then, there were the fantasies about the two different retreats. Most were about the Contact Improv retreat, feeling safe open, diving in 100%, and connecting with other humans and their amazing bodies in movement. The fantasies of the on Being Human retreat with Kristen showed up more as fears and anxiety than anything else.

The fear of this particular retreat felt deep. The best way I can describe it is that any or all of my core wounds would be exposed, poked, and splattered all over. When I reflected on this, my heart would race, my breathing would increase, and my body would stiffen. I had repeatedly considered canceling and begging for my payment back from Kristen. I returned to the premise that this lined up too quickly and effortlessly for me to let my fears convince me not to show up. That was my goal: show up. Having a PCR and rapid test completed before I left, all of the things related to the pandemic for air travel, leaving the

     Raised by Wolves, Possibly Monsters

United States, entering Costa Rica, and getting to the retreat center created several external obstacles. Showing up was not a simple task, regardless of my fears.

I received a text from my dear friend Ellen. The text was simple: "Hi, Michael. It keeps coming up for me that I need to participate in Kristen's retreat. I know you've already signed up, and I wanted to see if it's okay with you for me to be there." End of text. Beginning of panic.

I love, trust, respect, and feel safe with Ellen as much as anybody on this planet, and she knows me in ways that nobody else does. Translation: whatever fears I had around being exposed and poked now expanded exponentially inside my body and mind. I had images in my head of escape routes and forms of protection and denial that I hoped would create safety for me in showing up for this retreat; by saying yes to Ellen, I accepted that none of them would be helpful or successful. Shit!

I sat with the dilemma of wanting to support someone I love who is incredibly supportive versus my need for some degree of control, or at least the illusion of it, approaching the retreat. I was not able to sit for very long. By mid-afternoon, I replied to Ellen's simple text more straightforwardly, "Yes." The only thing I could think of to do with my body after sending that text was to put on a bunch of layers and go out for a walk by the river in the snow.

Ellen wrote back to me that night, "Do we need to talk about this?"

"No." If you've been reading this book from the beginning, I generally don't reply to anything with one-syllable answers, especially things that include connection, intimacy, and vulnerability. It seemed clear that I needed to stay out of this and let Ellen make her own choices and decisions regardless of the impact, or perceived impact, on my experience. There was also a degree of, "Fuck it! If I am going to show up for this retreat and do the work, I might as well push myself to the edge before I even get there."

It ended up that we booked our flights on the same plane without planning to do so! We were now traveling, planning, flying, and going to the same retreat together! At times, I enjoyed having somebody else go through the process of preparing for the retreat and an extended stay in Costa Rica during a pandemic with a super-spreading variant; at other times, it felt weird, scary, and annoying.

The fantasies of my time in Costa Rica after the two retreats involved me having a lot of time to myself, except for intimate and erotic connections with women along the way that were short-lived or not short-lived. None of those fantasies involved having one of my best friends/extended family members or an ex-partner be part of the process. Again, without talking about it, we both made plans to be in the same area after our retreats. We would be at the first retreat together. Afterward, I would stay at Goddess Garden for the contact improv retreat. Ellen was going to meet with some folks she had been with in a previous retreat in Costa Rica. They would be practicing meditation together. We would both end up on the southeast Caribbean coast of Costa Rica for the following month and a half.

on Being Human Retreat

 THERE ARE SITUATIONS and environments in life where it doesn't matter how many times or how many ways somebody explains what's going to happen; you don't really "get it" until you're physically present in the environment. This particular retreat was an example of that.

Before diving into the Tantric retreat, I want first to roll my eyes in written form. Whenever I hear anybody talking about Tantra, who is white and American, my entire system rolls its eyes multiple times. These eye rolls even happen more so when the retreat is in Bali, Mexico, or Costa Rica. This is probably not the best attitude for attending a seven-day retreat in Himalayan Tantra led by a white female from the United States. If you have never met Kristen Chamberlin before, you would not understand. Kristen is wise, grounded, solid, sensual, loving, intelligent, and a force to reckon with. She is more like an oak tree than a sunflower. Her somatic and trauma work in her private practice is exceptional. Kristen was why I was there. I am interested in Tantra, eroticism, and deep connection, but Kristen was the draw for me. Except for a few silent retreats at the Providence Zen Center, I had not been to a retreat in at least a decade, if not longer. The retreats at the Zen Center were primarily sitting, walking, and chanting. They did not require vulnerability, open-heartedness, honesty, and a

    Raised by Wolves, Possibly Monsters

willingness for deep, intimate connection necessary for the on Being Human retreat.

Most of us met on Friday night at the Adventure Inn, near the San Jose airport, the night before the retreat. We were all taking a van together to Goddess Garden in the morning. The retreat itself formally started on Sunday morning. There was excitement, anticipation, anxiousness, and collective disorientation. For many of us, this was the first time in two years that we were in close contact with people outside of our pods. This was different from my COVID experience. My core group got together every six weeks during the first year of the pandemic for a weekend. However, outside of Ellen and Kristen, I didn't know anybody at this retreat; that's what I thought.

A bunch of us ate dinner together, and while we were finishing dinner, we played a rousing game of Two Truths and a Lie. As you can imagine, playing this game with me is not fair. My life resembles a crazy novel more than someone's actual story.

We had a lot of fun, and it was an opportunity to connect and get to know each other. Kristen had asked me what I thought of us dancing on the patio next to the pool. It was implied that I would be playing music for us to dance to. I asked her to check with the hotel manager to determine if we could use their sound system. They were OK with it, and they did have a sound system. Twenty minutes later, a dozen of us danced by the pool in Costa Rica with the sun down in shorts and tank tops! DJ Mystical Michael had made his first appearance in Costa Rica. It was so fun and gave me a glimpse into what it would be like playing and connecting with this group, even though not all of us were there yet.

The retreat details seem optional to share; many of them were, like I mentioned earlier, you had to have been there. The teachings were excellent; Kristen and her two assistants, Arianna and Michael, brought their education, experiences, and juiciness. We spent the first few days becoming present, grounded, and creating individual and group safety. It was fun witnessing the dance between increased safety and intimacy in myself and others, creating a whole new set of protectors and parts showing up as obstacles to vulnerability and connection.

On the second or third day, Ellen approached me about wanting us to work on our relationship as part of a group process. We had both been aware for a while that some things needed attention between us left over from when we were partners, even though neither one of us knew what those "things" were. I agreed it would be a good idea, and of course, I hesitated. The next day, she informed me that she had talked to Kristen about it and that we would do our work with the group the following day. I was taken aback because she didn't check with me first for consent, but it's possible if she had checked with me, I would've weaseled my way out somehow. On an interesting note, we never did any formal work together that whole week, but somehow, at the end of the week, whatever barriers and parts were in the way between us were gone! We had discussed it and agreed that we were closer at that point than when we lived together as a couple. It felt lovely. We still have no idea what facilitated the shift, and that's okay.

One night, I had a dream about the experience I had with Deborah in Mr. Sobieski's class that began this book. I had not thought about that moment in decades. Later that night, I had another dream. In this dream, I had shared with the group all of the awful things I had done and said, and not done and not said, with girls and women my whole life. I needed to come clean to move forward in this dream. The dream shook me, and I knew it was time to do work around the shame of my past actions and the shame and fear I experienced around attraction and lust. I was not able to fall back asleep after the second dream.

When we all checked in in the morning, as we did every morning, I said I would like to do some work that morning. The specifics of what took place should be left at the retreat for confidentiality reasons, and without context, they may not make sense to those who were not present.

I want to share that I started by talking about the shame, embarrassment, and judgment I often experience around lust and desire, especially with younger women. Kristen did something spectacular.

Kristen facilitated my exploration of what it was like to have these newfound desires, feelings, and responses in my body when I was first attracted to girls. This caught me off guard because that was my first dream the night before. So, I shared those experiences, and Kristen and other group members supported me in discovering and remembering what it was like to be attracted to girls. The

     Raised by Wolves, Possibly Monsters

experiences of wonder, beauty, fascination, joy, excitement, and sense of being fully alive I had buried inside me. We spent the next hour cultivating those memories and feelings; something cracked open during this process. A shell was split, allowing other thoughts, feelings, and emotions to emerge. I felt naked. I felt raw. I felt alive!

A practice inspired by that experience has shifted how I see, and experience being turned on by women I know and don't know. I began to look for who she was and what was turning me on physically. What are her gifts, strengths, beauty, courage, creativity, and divinity? Who is the human inside this breathtaking body?

After both retreats, while walking around Puerto Viejo and hanging out on the beach, whenever I noticed a woman, some part of me got excited; I energetically searched for who this fantastic human was inside this beautiful body. Through Reiki, I connected my Higher Self with her Higher Self. I had these unique, beautiful, and impactful experiences all day and night. In short, I saw her, not just her body and self-presentation. This was a fun practice. I still do it today, but less often or diligently. Any time I feel like I'm objectifying a woman and ignoring the person inside that body, my system notices her. An unexpected perk of this particular practice is that many of the women who received that gaze from me seemed to do something similar to me. They took the time to see me and offer me connection or contact in mutual acknowledgment. Sometimes, it was a gentle nod, sometimes an authentic smile, eye contact, or they mouthed "Hello"; a couple of women broke into soft laughter, and others walked up to me and introduced themselves to me. Talk about receiving positive affirmation from a new practice in your life!

Playa Negra

I HAD READ about the black sand beaches that run from the northern end of Puerto Viejo de Talamanca up to Cahuita. They were part of the reason I was in Costa Rica and, specifically, this region of the country in the Caribbean. The dark color of the sand caused by volcanic remnants has healing properties for the body. The dark sand mixed with seawater produces magnesium, calcium, potassium, and sulfur elements.

Of course, reading about healing and experiencing healing are different. Marketing "healing" is a regular aspect of American life in 2022. I was not surprised when reading about Playa Negra and how often they've referenced the healing properties. I was surprised when I walked, napped, meditated, and swam on these beaches; how different my body felt. The beach's energy is clean, clear, pure, and lively. I made a point to find my way onto this beach almost daily while I stayed in Puerto Viejo. The sparkling of the sun on the black sand is its own experience. As someone who spent much of my youth, teens, and young adulthood on the Jersey Shore, I was accustomed to white sand beaches. Something feels mystical about being on a black sand beach with waves rolling in full of saltwater. I came to Costa Rica for this, nourishing myself in the experience as often as possible. After a couple of weeks, I began needing to feel the salt water and the black sand on my body.

The Next Chapter of Healing

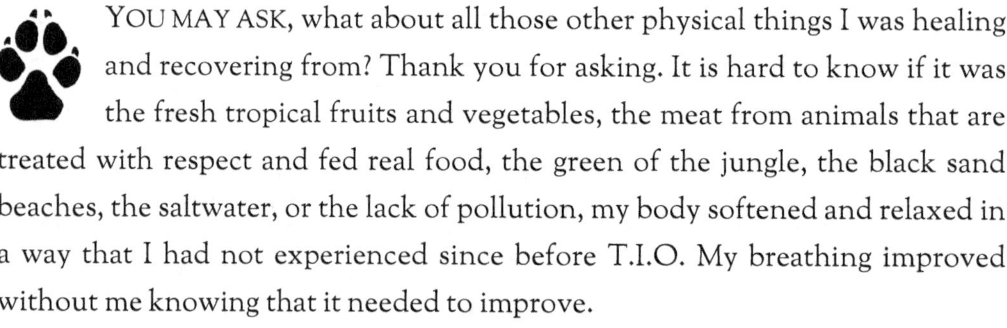

YOU MAY ASK, what about all those other physical things I was healing and recovering from? Thank you for asking. It is hard to know if it was the fresh tropical fruits and vegetables, the meat from animals that are treated with respect and fed real food, the green of the jungle, the black sand beaches, the saltwater, or the lack of pollution, my body softened and relaxed in a way that I had not experienced since before T.I.O. My breathing improved without me knowing that it needed to improve.

I enjoyed being in a semi-retreat. I like doing intense work while still being part of the world. That balance is supportive and feels natural to me. I struggle to create the same elements in my regular life. I also recognize that everything is relative. What I perceive is not being able to reproduce the experience of being in a semi-retreat; many people would interpret my life as being in a semi-retreat or even similar to a fancy retreat. I thrive in this environment—no cold weather, no heavy clothes, and what indoor heating does to my eyes, skin, and body. I get revitalized by intense, focused meditation and other spiritual/energetic practices while having fun, dancing, swimming, and eating ice cream. Connecting with friends and the community, then returning to solitude.

There are consequences to this lifestyle. I am surrounded by incredible and creative people who live alternative and innovative lives. It is not that I am "too alternative or weird"; I am probably somewhere in the middle of weirdness and alternative lifestyle choices among the people in my communities. Focused solitude, time for reflection, and inner work can be obstacles to relationships because not everyone is willing to share their life with a person who has made strong commitments that may appear to be separate from their partner. I find those commitments to nourish and support relationships. I do not struggle with this at all, but some people feel jealous or not as important, creating resentment and distance.

Leaving Costa Rica

 I DID NOT expect that leaving Casita Toucan, the cabana I stayed in for six weeks, and Puerto Viejo would affect me as intensely and deeply as it did. I felt sad and lost. My experience in that home was profound and forceful. I feared I would be unable to capture that commitment and focus after leaving, and the growth and development that took place while staying there would lose momentum. I enjoyed this new lens of seeing women for their divinity, beauty, and sensuality, to feel a kinship with her, and lust and desire. I did not want to lose this thread. It felt vital for my existence and relationships.

The week I was getting ready to leave for Costa Rica, I met a woman on an alternative dating site, Feeld, whose name was Kayleigh. There was a photograph of her with her blonde and light brown straight hair, wearing minimal makeup and light rose shade of lipstick, with yellow fingernail polish and simple clothes. In her description profile, she wrote about her relationship with water and its meaning to her. The other picture she included was of a glass of water on a table. I don't know why this cup caught my attention so fiercely, but it did. It turned out that she lived only 10 miles away! I wrote to her, and she wrote back to me.

Because she was much younger than me and very physically attractive, I was skeptical that she was a scam or selling something. I asked her about it, and her response was, "Really? Does that happen? Do women from Ukraine ever do this sort of thing?"

Her first two questions are what scammers often answer, so that didn't produce any response inside of me. The question about women from Ukraine did. I asked her to explain, and she was baffled by my reaction. There was a burp in the system that led me to believe she was 10 miles away from me and led her to think that I was 14 km away from her. In reality, I was in my bedroom in Rhode Island in the United States, and she was in Central Ukraine, also lying in bed in her bedroom. I'm reminding you that this is late January 2022.

After we untangled all of that and realized we would probably never meet each other and that it wasn't worth our time, we politely both moved on. When I shared with Kayleigh that I was leaving the next night for Costa Rica and was going to be in a Tantric Retreat followed by a contact improvisational retreat, she asked me if I would not mind sending her a couple of updates because she was curious about both. I said fine and forgot about it.

Halfway through the Tantric Retreat, I wrote to her and told her about some fun and exciting things we were doing and how much I was learning and experiencing. We continued writing to each other during the second Retreat as well. We had riveting discussions via WhatsApp, and I appreciated being able to share my experiences with somebody who wasn't part of the retreat or my life. I felt free and safe.

After I finished the second retreat and went to the cabana where I would spend the next five weeks, I began to enjoy our connection, however far-flung we were. It turns out this woman was not named Kayleigh. Her name is Anastasia. She has two daughters, aged sixteen and nine, and works in her local school system. We continued to text through WhatsApp daily, often several times a day.

That changed on February 24, when Russia attacked Ukraine. I believe it was two days after that when she and her two daughters were huddled in a bomb shelter. She texted me and asked me if I would be kind enough to go out in the world and take pictures and videos of a world where a mother and her two

      Raised by Wolves, Possibly Monsters

daughters don't have to hide in a bomb shelter. So, I took photos of waves crashing, people swimming, black sand beaches, monkeys, birds, cats, hedgehogs, lizards, geckos, flowers, and tropical rainstorms. This was how we primarily communicated for the next week. Anastasia and her daughters would alternate between staying in their home or hiding in the bomb shelter, depending on if the air raid sirens were going off.

I have had many roles in life, but none included capturing images of the world and texting them to a person in a crisis like this. I took this role very seriously, and it is among my most significant accomplishments.

Besides the apparent element of sharing compassion and empathy with somebody in an awful and brutal situation, which I would do for anybody, I had the honor of standing as an Oak Tree for her to lean against. This experience felt like the culmination of sixty years of life, being the man who could do this with an open heart. I was offered the opportunity to love somebody I would never meet. The fact that I had regular fantasies of loving, being loved, and making love with her was irrelevant, and I had grown enough that being attracted to her in that way was not an obstacle in any shape or form. I got to show up as Michael Swerdloff.

We shifted our form of regular communication from predominantly texts to voice messages. Anastasia escaped to Poland, traveling back and forth to Ukraine via a long bus ride, making last-minute arrangements, and gathering documents to finalize her work visa for her and her two daughters, who were moving to Sudbury, Ontario. Our friendship continued to flourish. When she was in Poland by herself, and her daughters were in Ukraine with their grandparents, she could talk freely without her children in the same room for the first time since we met. This environment created space for us to begin flirting and playful banter.

This experience only furthered my resistance to going home. I wanted to stay in Costa Rica, but my flight was the next day.

I was fighting back tears when I lowered myself into the taxi for the airport at 5:20 a.m. This magical journey was going to come to an end. I stood in line to check my bag through those winding ribbons as person after person going to Newark International Airport completed stage one before going through security and customs. When it was my turn to go to the counter, I considered turning around and running as if I was being made to go by the government or some secret underground group of spies. I raised my duffel bag onto the metal scale, got my passport out of my pocket, answered COVID questions, and handed my boarding pass. A guy took my bag off the scale and carried it about 10 feet away, preparing to send it with the rest of the luggage. Then, all five United Airlines representatives reached down and simultaneously picked up their cell phones. It appeared scripted and choreographed. While talking to whoever was on the other end, they looked at each other with glances and eye contact, acknowledging that "a thing" was happening. I was preparing for them to tell us that the flight would be delayed another twenty minutes because they were having trouble removing the sewage or the vacuum cleaner broke. After they got off the phone, they huddled together. They continued looking at each other with serious expressions, looking at the line, then looking at each other.

Of all the things that I could have guessed caused their concern and hesitation to act, a cargo plane crashing on the runway, splitting in two, and catching fire was not one of them!

I actually thought she was kidding when she told me this, but one of the other women I was talking to stood so that the rest of her team couldn't see her and pushed a button on her phone, hiding it from everybody else. She was showing me the yellow DHL cargo plane on the runway, split into two pieces and flames! I would not have believed her for a moment if she had not shown it to me.

The staff and passengers needed to figure out what to do. At the check-in process, a handful of us hung out where we were, and everybody else was in the zigzag lines waiting, giving irritated stares to staff and talking amongst themselves. I didn't know what to do with myself, so I started flirting with one of the staff. I know, how cliché. She was intelligent, lively, and cute. She was one of those people who showed up well-prepared, internally and externally, for everything in life. About twenty minutes later, they announced in Spanish and English that the airport was closed due to an emergency. They informed everyone that no flights would depart or arrive for the rest of the day or several days.

The woman who showed me the video inserted herself in front of me; the

     Raised by Wolves, Possibly Monsters

woman I was flirting with went to another station. We were working on finding a flight to leave in the next few days. They were not sure they could clean all the debris on that day or even the next day. They could not find any flights from San Jose to Providence in less than two stops along the way and at least sixteen hours. She had suggested we set up flights for tomorrow, so that it is in the system. She wanted to ensure I didn't lose my flights. She urged me to call United Airlines that night to explain my situation and find better options. I had nothing else to do, so I agreed to her recommendation. What neither of us knew was that later on at night, when I called United to change my flights for the next day, I was on the phone for six and a half hours and fell asleep the final hour till I was woken by the representative coming off hold! It scared the heck out of me. Eventually, after annoying them into submission, they found better seats than what I had paid for on a flight leaving Monday afternoon.

As I prepared to leave Costa Rica, I experienced mixed emotions, thoughts, and feelings. The two loudest were sadness about leaving and joy at what transpired. I felt overwhelmed while reflecting on some of the more potent experiences like being the "on-call DJ" whenever Kristen wanted us to have a dance break, the intimate eye contact, body contact, and heart contact during both retreats, but primarily on Being Human, the discovery, or should I say, rediscovering, of my childhood/early adolescent feelings of wonder, amazement and excitement at the female body and feminine energy, consensually being pushed to all kinds of limits in both retreats in so many different ways, making out with somebody who was born in a male body, making out briefly with two other women at the contact improv retreat, being honest with myself and listening to myself that I was not really able to fully participate in the contact improv retreat due to the depth of my experience in the Tantric retreat, making a bunch of amazing friends between the two retreats, my time alone at Casita Toucan, picking up a couple of young stragglers who stayed with me at various points that needed support, safety and grounding, my time with Ellen, the howler monkeys, the spectacular fresh fruit and so easily accessible, eating pineapples and mango pretty much daily, and of course, the Caribbean saltwater and black sand beaches.

Back to Rhode Island, Which Isn't an Island

 NEWARK AIRPORT HAS always been an odd experience for me, even when it's less than a two-hour layover like this trip. There was a point in my early twenties when I lived in Elizabeth, New Jersey, about four miles from the airport. My brother lived in the apartment building across the street. If it was late at night and we were bored, sometimes we would go to the airport to hunt for attractive young women who were miserable, exhausted, and bored out of their minds waiting for a flight the following day. Sometimes, we were actually "successful." More than once, the combination of their exhaustion, cocaine, alcohol, and marijuana at my brother's apartment somehow made all of their clothes slide off.

From head to toe, I was absolutely against what I was doing, except for my penis and ego. They desperately needed me to feel powerful, sexy, masculine, and capable. Technically, the women never did anything they didn't want, and that was because we undermined their ability to make an informed decision.

I wholeheartedly support the current culture of consent around sexual contact and the use of drugs and alcohol. This concept is easy for me to understand. I have lived it. I have been the predator. I have been the prey. I have been the one waking up in the morning after a night partying in Philadelphia at my off-campus apartment in Glassboro, New Jersey, thinking we left my car in Philly the night before and finding it three days later parked on the other side of the garden apartment complex. So yeah, I get how drugs and alcohol impair the ability to make decisions.

When someone's decision-making ability is impaired, monsters and wolves move in and do reprehensible things to them. When somebody doesn't get a vote about what happens to their body, it is socially, culturally, and legally a crime against humanity.

I had not yet fully healed my painful memories from the past of being at Newark Airport; parts of me were still activated. I experienced shame, excitement, confusion, and more shame. Newark Airport is intense without adding layers of my past to the chaos. It felt jarring to be back in that environment after all these years, while full of love, joy, and openness after having just left Costa Rica.

 Raised by Wolves, Possibly Monsters

I was grateful to get on the fifty-minute flight from Newark to TF Green Airport in Rhode Island. Since I had to go through all the immigration and customs stuff in Newark, leaving TF Green was reasonably effortless.

During my first month at home, I felt lost. I felt like a stranger in my own home, town, and country. This culture felt foreign to me. People cut each other off in lines and on roads. Strangers yelled and taunted each other over where they parked their cars. The pace and stress associated with it felt like an electric shock. Nobody said hello to random people they passed on the sidewalk! They didn't even know somebody else was on the sidewalk to say hello to.

If I hadn't been writing this manuscript, reintegrating into the American way of life might have been even more challenging and taken longer.

My private practice flourished upon my return. I was meeting with more clients than I had in years. I started hosting and DJing local ecstatic and conscious dance events again, which are inspiring, fun, and connective. Even though I missed the black sand beaches, I live across the street from a river, about a half mile from the ocean! I danced daily in my living room with a view of the water after Yoga and Reiki. And, of course, seeing, hugging, and dancing with my friends again was lovely. The weather was changing, and I could ride my bike on the local bike path next to the ocean most afternoons, knowing, soon enough, I would be back in the New England Ocean and saltwater in Rhode Island. All of these elements were part of my reintegration process.

You Have to See the Rabbit

IN HIS BOOK, *In Pursuit of the Great White Rabbit*, Edward Hays writes a parable about being able to stay the course of our spiritual commitments. The parable is about a young monk asking an older monk how he has stayed while others have come and gone. The older monk shares a story about a dog chasing a white rabbit, and all the other dogs in the neighborhood join soon after. However, only the original dog continued after the rabbit.

"Unless you see your prey, the chase is too hard. You will lack the passion and determination necessary to perform all the hard work required by the discipline of your spiritual exercises."

Meaning, you have to see the rabbit!!!

I continue my daily practices and commitment because I have "Seen the Rabbit."

I have seen the rabbit with sobriety; staying sober felt possible.

I have seen the rabbit with meditation; being present and focused was possible.

I have seen the rabbit with Reiki; Reiki flowed through me to others.

I have seen the rabbit with love, kindness, and acceptance, which informed me that I was lovable.

I have seen the rabbit with healing; Aimee didn't have cancer; miracles happen.

I have seen the rabbit with Yoga; I knew my body could be more flexible.

I have seen the rabbit with conscious dance, a connection through movement.

I have seen the rabbit with community, acceptance, and belonging, which are real.

I have seen the rabbit with intimacy; the closeness and connection were not awful.

I have seen the rabbit with trust, letting people in and coming out alive.

I have seen the rabbit with counseling & therapy; exploring the shadow didn't crush me.

I have seen the rabbit with masculinity. I am a man and still feel like a man when I am gentle.

I have seen the rabbit with a connection to my Higher Self, my partners, friends, and family, and my experience of God.

I have seen the rabbit!

Betsy talks about the need to have the experiences, even if for a minute, to create reference points so we have real-life evidence that the practice and process work. The experience that comes to mind was during one of our retreats. We were actively working on creating safety and security in our first center, the root center. We stayed in this meditation for the entire morning. There were a few minutes that I felt entirely safe and solid for the first time without somebody or

Raised by Wolves, Possibly Monsters

something else facilitating that process. I now knew I had the ability and resources to execute a practice for future reference. I could not reproduce this often for the next year, but I knew it was possible. I experienced this more often the following year, which continued over time. I saw the rabbit of inner safety and security. I committed to daily meditation because I experienced moments of beauty and presence, and Reiki because I felt the vibration and love. After all, it shook my whole being.

We have to see the rabbit.

The Ukrainian Woman in Canada via Poland During a War

 ANASTASIA AND HER two daughters were now in Ontario! We began creating a plan as soon as she arrived, knowing that she would need a couple of weeks to get oriented before we could connect in person.

It didn't make sense to me to fly to Toronto, rent a car, drive five hours to Sudbury, spend two days with her, do the reverse, and fly home. I decided to get there earlier in the week since I had never been to Toronto to explore the city and hang out with some friends who lived there.

After staying in four different Airbnb's in five nights and driving five and a half hours to Sudbury, it almost didn't seem real when I met Anastasia in person for the first time. Even though we had done plenty of video calls, and she had sent me plenty of pictures of her, seeing her in person was a new experience. I had a peculiar sensory experience of her standing in front of me, and her face and body didn't match what my mind had created of her through video and still images. We said hello in her driveway and shared a hug. It felt lovely to have her in my arms. Finally, I had the opportunity to smell her fragrance, hear her breathe, and feel the curves of her warm body. Anastasia was a real-life human being.

We spent the next few hours walking, talking, eating takeout food, and sitting outside on the back deck of the Airbnb overlooking the lake, getting to know each other in a new way. Initially, she was more comfortable and relaxed than me. Our differing experiences are where our age gap became apparent. As an attractive woman in her late thirties meeting with a guy in his early sixties, I don't think she had any question that I would find her attractive. I was filled with doubt and feelings of inadequacy.

I had prepared her several times in previous conversations, but she had asked some questions about my physical challenges. I included how short I am with a highly unusual body. This didn't seem to affect Anastasia. My inner narrative about the changes in my body in the last ten years, when we may have felt equal in our physical attractiveness. We are not similar in that regard today.

Our conversations were fun, playful, and fascinating. Anastasia had mentioned several times that she felt she was meeting with an old friend; it did not feel like a foreign experience. Since her daughters were extremely nervous about their mother, who was the only person they knew on this continent, meeting with a guy they had never met before, they kept texting and calling. Both of us were caught off guard by the intensity of their concern for her safety, and we ended our night early to support the kids feeling safe. I drove her back to the house where they were living. We hugged more intimately when we said goodbye and made loose plans for the next day.

We made plans in the morning for me to pick up Anastasia and her youngest daughter to play miniature golf. They had gone to a miniature golf course the week before, and Sasha was excited to play again, even though it was clear that her daughter was shy and uncomfortable with me.

While the three of us played, Sasha became comfortable with me verbally, and her mother became comfortable with me physically. It felt like middle school. She would poke me after a funny joke or give me a gentle elbow to communicate that it was my turn, or she would lean her shoulders and side of her body against mine; I let her initiate and guide our physical touch. By about the fifteenth hole, she was very comfortable connecting with me physically. Sometimes, when Sasha hit the ball, Anastasia would touch me and make eye contact before her daughter could see us. This dynamic felt even more like middle school, but instead of hiding from her parents, we hid from her nine-year-old daughter! After we brought Sasha back to their house, Anastasia and I went out to find food, which we brought to the Airbnb.

Romance, physical touch, and sexual tension were present, along with soft,

     Raised by Wolves, Possibly Monsters

sensual forms of intimacy. We felt close, safe, and trusting of each other. As the sun went down, Anastasia shared how challenging and stressful the previous five months had been. We were sitting on the deck overlooking a lake. My back was leaning against the patio furniture, and Anastasia had her back to me, leaning into me. I held my arms around her and gently held her while she shared. I didn't feel like I needed to say anything; I just needed to be there, hold her, let her share and breathe, and share and breathe. I connected with Reiki and asked for the Reiki energy to surround, immerse, and fill Anastasia from head to toe. I felt like we were floating in the air, connected through the base of the spine, which many people call the Root Chakra, and we were grounded and solid in the space we were physically seated in. I felt love, admiration, and appreciation for this spectacular human being now relaxing and allowing herself to fall into my chest.

I asked her if I could touch her hair and run my fingers through it. Anastasia didn't stop what she was doing. She just nodded yes. Anastasia continued sharing, and I ran my fingers through her hair and lightly massaged her scalp. Beautiful, soft cooing sounds came out of her mouth. I was experiencing incredible pleasure and satisfaction from connecting with her this way, feeling her smooth, thin blondish hair and smelling her shampoo inches from my head. She leaned back, and I kissed the back of her skull. I ran my nose through her hair.

My entire being and body were turned on with Reiki, love, and desire, and this moment expressed three decades of work, culminating at the Tantric Retreat in Costa Rica. This experience was what I had wanted all along, but I didn't know it was what I wanted. My genitals were alive and full of vitality as my penis became firm against her buttocks. It was not a distraction to either of us. We were deeply connected with each other and ourselves, and one could even say we were connected with God.

I could feel her body relaxing more and trusting deeper. After about fifteen minutes, this amazing woman in my arms let go and melted into me. Her body felt like part of mine. Touching her scalp, I felt like I was touching mine. Kissing her neck felt like being kissed. It turned out that the mosquitoes were enjoying our bodies and skin as much as we were enjoying each other's bodies and skin. We moved inside, and it took a little while for both of us to get our legs back under us and get oriented to standing and walking in an indoor physical environment. We started on the couch but ended up on the bed moments later.

Our shared experience was sensual, loving, connected, and intimate in ways that felt new to me. Anastasia asked what I wanted or fantasized about over these past few months. I shared the three things that popped up the most in my mind. That's when Anastasia came alive. It was fun experiencing those fantasies and daydreams in real life. I believe that was the first time I had shared with somebody what I wanted and desired from them, and with them authentically, which would've been enough for me. The bonus was living out those fantasies with her. I don't think she knew how important this was for me. Although seeing how much joy and vitality she received by offering herself and her body to make these fantasies come true, maybe she did. Anastasia's grayish-blue eyes became green during our more passionate moments; they appeared electric or like a galactic being from another world.

The next day, Sunday, I would need to drive back to Toronto with the rental car. Anastasia invited me to their house for lunch so I could meet her older daughter, Dianna, who was sixteen, and spend some time together before I left. When I arrived at 1:00, Sasha was still in bed downstairs while the three of us talked, laughed, and ate upstairs in the kitchen. Dianna felt familiar to me after spending five months getting to know her mother and the last two days being with her mother in person. They share many of the same qualities mentally, physically, and energetically. We connected quickly, and about half an hour later, I didn't feel like I was hanging out with a mother and daughter that I just met. I felt like we were already "something." Dianna and I had fun laughing, playing, and exploring intellectual topics like culture, social programming, education, politics, music, and being human. I felt like I had met another family member in those ninety minutes of hanging out together.

We enjoyed the salmon, potatoes, and salad Anastasia prepared. The salmon was seasoned in a way that felt foreign to me, delicious but foreign. It was a friendly reminder that Anastasia came from somewhere else in the world, a place attacked by another larger country. The three of us enjoyed lunch with Ukrainian salmon style in Sudbury, Ontario, Canada. My heart opened even more, and I felt ready to start crying, but it didn't feel like it belonged in our

     Raised by Wolves, Possibly Monsters

circumstances. I do not think they would understand how honored I felt to be with them in Canada after what they went through.

A loud voice told me to be with them and let them enjoy being safe in this home with me on the other side of the world from where they came from. Let them have this safety and comfort. Be the safety and comfort they need right now. I remember having an energetic nod of affirmation, "I can do this. I can have my feelings and still be one hundred percent present with the two of them, and when Sasha appeared in her PJs, the three of them. I can be their safety right now. I don't have to say anything. I don't have to do anything. I have to be present with my heart open. I am capable of doing this today."

The girls walked me out and showed me the pool in the backyard, and then Anastasia and I opened the wooden fence gate to the driveway. She looked at the girls with that maternal glance, telling them to return inside. I almost burst out laughing because every part of me knew they would run to the front of the house to watch us through the picture window, which they did. They got to the front of the home before we did.

Anastasia and I stood on the other side of the rental car to shelter their gaze a little, but not much. I could tell she was working hard to make sure she made this light and cheerful like it didn't matter or wasn't a big deal. Her eyes said something different. Anastasia's heart was screaming something different altogether. My heart also acknowledged that something unique and beautiful had occurred between us this weekend, and we may not get this opportunity again, regardless of our plans or intentions. We had a simple goodbye, not many words, a hug, and then another goodbye, one more hug, and then she created several feet of distance between us. I could see that she was struggling with keeping it light and simple. Anastasia turned slightly to the left, communicating that she was ready to walk to the grocery store and that I would leave in the rental car. I blew her a kiss and said goodbye. I could see her eyes red and tearing up even before she made it out of her driveway. I could already feel the tears rolling down my cheek as she walked away.

I got in the car with my hands trembling. I wanted to tell her that I loved her, and what we shared was a memory I would carry with me for the rest of my life. I wanted to feel our lips and bodies connect one more time. And I wanted to respect the part of her that needed to feel safe, strong, and independent. I pulled out of the driveway, made a right on Main Street, and then made another right at the gas station heading towards downtown Sudbury. I don't think I was a mile down the road when she texted me that she was already standing in the middle of the road, crying and missing me. We connected for the next 10 minutes, authentically sharing our thoughts and feelings—another magical moment. Anastasia was shaking in a way that she was unprepared for and had not expected it. I knew I would be surprised at my core in the best way possible and was looking forward to it for weeks.

Four hours later, we spoke on the phone while I was driving. I was still about an hour from Toronto. We both needed the affirmation that we would still be connected and part of each other's lives.

Angelina

 IT WAS A typical Saturday night at our local conscious ecstatic dance. We had a smaller group than usual, only about fifteen people, and I enjoyed the warm, inviting intimacy of the group of dancers and movers.

She came in wearing deep red from head to toe. One of the gifts of regularly participating in a local conscious dance event is getting to know who was a part of our community and who was not. It helps us be supportive and welcoming to new folks joining. Angelina was not part of our regular local community. She did what most people do when they show up somewhere new and don't know anybody: they stay at the far end of the room near the door in case they need to escape.

As DJ and host, I like to make my way onto the dance floor and at least make eye contact with everybody, whether I know them or not, at some point. Angelina appeared anxious when I moved to her space on the dance floor, so I kept moving around the room. One of the women in the group energetically connected with Angelina; after that, she expanded her territory to include the whole space.

During the closing circle, she shared that she was new to our dance, had not

    Raised by Wolves, Possibly Monsters

been to any dances in a while, and felt "blissed out." We sat and talked after the closing circle, and she and another woman helped me carry my audio gear to my car. When we were the only two folks left in the parking lot, I hugged Angelina; she accepted and spent the next five minutes crying in my arms. I knew nothing about her pain, but I understood she needed to be held and allowed to let out whatever needed to be expressed. As soon as we broke our embrace, with her face red and her eyes full of tears and softness, she said, "Thank you, Michael. I needed that. It felt like you were holding and surrounding me with Reiki."

After our hug, we decided to go out for pizza and ice cream. After that, we landed at a park on the Brown University campus, walking and talking. We shared our challenges, struggles, and moments of joy. The previous two hours of conversation now made sense; Angelina had spoken about having trouble going to dances, yoga, or the gym. She was feeling anxiety daily and couldn't sleep. She had trouble leaving her home, and her sense of feeling overwhelmed felt monumental when she did.

When walking under the arch to the park, she shared with me that she had been raped recently. I put my arm around her elbow and kept her close while walking. I asked Reiki to join and hold us. We walked and talked, we walked and talked, and we walked and talked. I felt like I was a human body of Reiki. I had none of the old fear or worry that I could not offer her what she needed in those moments. I allowed the love of Reiki to flow through me, and that was all I had to do. I didn't need to fix her, I didn't need to teach her anything, I didn't need to tell her it was OK, all I needed to do was love her, even though I was having trouble remembering her name since we had just met.

When we were sitting in her car at the end of the night, Angelina thanked me "for everything;" I could feel the warmth, gratitude, and shame in her voice.

We hugged again before I got out of the car. "You're welcome. And thank you for trusting me, for all of it."

Tears of sadness and gratitude made driving home a little more challenging. I thought about my life. I used to be the reason girls and women cried in people's arms, but now I have the honor of being the arms in which they cry. If men want to know "what to do" in those moments when women cry, this is it: all we have to do is love them. We don't need to fix them, we don't need to teach them how to do anything, we certainly don't need to give them a Gettysburg Address telling them what their experience is, and we don't need to feel shame for something that one of our brethren did. We need to be with them and love them. When they talk about wanting men to be protectors, this is what they're talking about. When they show up and give voice to their pain and sadness and whatever mess they are experiencing in their lives, what they need from us is for us to be present and to love them. Even if we only know them long enough that we still have to remember what their name is, we can hold them, create a safe space for them, and love them.

The fact that she was half my age, that I found her attractive, and that she was vulnerable had nothing to do with what she needed from me that night. Angelina needed evidence that there was one of us out here in the sea of male human beings who would not exploit, manipulate, or take advantage of her. She just wanted to be seen, heard and loved. This is how we show up as protectors and providers.

Many men think that being a protector is having a bulky neck, chest, and arms so full of muscles that you can't pick up a napkin off the floor, owning multiple guns, and practicing mixed martial arts, but what they fail to understand is, yeah, you can protect her from another man, but who will protect her from you? When she sees you threatening, beating, and taunting other men twice her size, she is acutely aware that you can demolish her if you lose your temper with her as you do with them!

Let's be real. Most women do not encounter bears, lions, snow leopards, tigers, or crocodiles daily. So, the primary thing men can protect women from is other men.

I invite you to breathe that in and let it swirl in your belly for a moment or two. If there were no violent men in the world, women wouldn't need men to be protectors because there wouldn't be anything we would be able to protect them from. It's us; we are the thing they need protection from, not squirrels, cats, dogs, goldfish, infants, girls, or women; it's us. If you want to be a protector, I invite you to learn how to make your presence a safe haven for women.

　　　　　　　　Raised by Wolves, Possibly Monsters

Change Is Real!

IF THERE IS only one thing you receive from this book, my wish is this: change is real and possible; it really is. I am living proof. Specifically, men can change. We do not have to be self-absorbed, adult adolescents our whole lives. We can be beautiful, kind, loving, attentive, sensual, and present. We can love fiercely and hold space for a woman to relax and let down their guard, knowing they are loved, appreciated, and adored. This is not a fantasy or some pop psychology bullshit; it is true: I know, I live it every day. I am not perfect, nor is that my goal. I can stay present with the emotions that terrify me and breathe through and with them. I often can "be comfortable with being uncomfortable." I am the man today I wanted to be as a child when I looked at men that I respected. And . . . I am not done.

My experiences of making love with Lilith, Brynn, Ellen, and Anastasia while holding space for us to connect and feel safe through Reiki are the blueprint for me. Those moments of love and intimacy of mind, body, and spirit are beyond comprehension and are real. They are worth the work all by themselves!

I experience immense joy and gratitude that through Reiki, I can offer safe spaces for dancers to be themselves; knowing they are safe and accepted is miraculous for me. Dancing before all of this happened was simply a way to convince a woman to have sex with me. Now, it is a home for me, a place to exhale, enjoy my body, connect with other amazing humans and their bodies, and be one of the men in the room who stands for and with the women present. What a gift!

What Now?

THIS HAS BEEN quite a journey, beginning with seeing a bit of an adolescent girl's breasts in science class. My path included being petrified of girls, desiring and being rejected by them, hating them, and wanting them as a teenager. My hate became violence, and my violence became shame in my twenties. I had to find a way to numb and silence the shame piled on top of mountains of shame. It didn't matter how much violence, money, prestige, power, alcohol, drugs, crime, and risky, stimulating behaviors I engaged in; none of them could knock out and suppress that shame long enough for me to be a functional person.

I cracked. I fell apart. And I started again. I tried to kill my girlfriend and myself but ended up in a locked mental hospital. When they let me out, it was six weeks of a full-time outpatient program, ten AA and NA meetings a week, and meeting with a therapist twice weekly. I pretty much hated all of it. It required me to learn about myself, who I was, and what I had done. I survived that as well. I wanted to make amends to the girls and women I had hurt; instead, I stood in front of classrooms and auditoriums telling people about date and acquaintance rape and my experiences before, during, and after. In 1996, I was holding down my then fiancé while she was screaming, kicking, and trying to bite me; I pulled my right arm back, made a fist cocked, and was ready to splatter her head on the white blanket of the white couch. I am so grateful for that voice that told me I would never be able to return from this if I moved this arm forward. I didn't.

My work with my teacher, Betsy, was grueling and brutal and felt abrasive. She stood for and with me when I was unprepared to stand for myself. Betsy's commitment to me, my Higher Self, and my well-being was more significant than my lower self and my need to protect myself by creating distance between me and the rest of the world and the dark shadow that was part of me and still is today. Betsy taught me I can be terrified and still stand solid and grounded.

There was that four- or five-month-long silent retreat in the disgusting little expanded double-wide trailer where I painted the walls and ceilings like I was wrapped in a Tibetan monastic robe. During that time in the Gobi Desert, I could hear my footsteps, fear, gifts, and spiritual community with each step.

There is my tribe of core friends that I love, trust, and adore, and they love, trust, and cherish me. Somewhere along the way, I became an activist for women. At first, it was part performative and part commitment. Today, it is part of my amends and my commitment to creating safety for those born in female bodies.

In my mind, I see and feel those moments sitting on the deck at the Airbnb, looking over the lake as the sun sets. Anastasia is in my arms, and I run my fingers

     Raised by Wolves, Possibly Monsters

through her hair and feel Reiki pour into her. I wanted her to feel safe with me while this gorgeous, remarkable, intelligent, courageous, and incredibly powerful, sexy woman was inside my embrace, knowing I was safe with her, my feelings, and my desires, and she was safe with me. Wolves, possibly monsters, raised me. I was healed, and still healing, by the love, respect, dignity, commitment, and persistence of the people in the last three decades who could see who I was and what I was capable of, even though I was utterly clueless about any of it. They didn't care that I was a jerk a lot of the time. They knew I was worth their time and investment. I am unbearably grateful for them and everybody else who showed me that everybody deserves love, respect, and belonging.

Often, I hear Betsy whispering in my ears, "Michael, we need to keep Reiki at the center of our lives." This is my commitment to myself and Reiki.

My journey forward is simple but ridiculously hard: be present, pay attention, stay grounded, and stay connected to Reiki. Sometimes, it is expressed as a DJ at an ecstatic or conscious dance event; other times, it's a dancer on the dance floor. I need to continue to show up and stand with my clients no matter how dark, painful, or traumatic their lives have been. I want to love my friends and let them love me without much resistance, remembering that it is progress, not perfection. And to quietly go about my life as the reflection of beauty, love, creativity, strength, and courage inside us all.

I am living proof that one can let the inner shadow become the loudest and strongest voice, survive, rebuild, and let the light become the most vociferous and vital voice. Most people are terrified of discovering what's behind "door number three" or what their shadow side looks and feels like. I have seen and survived what's behind door number three, and I know precisely what my shadow side looks and feels like. Early in recovery, my goal was to delete or eliminate all of those parts of me as if they were a stain on my blue denim jeans that I could spray with Shout, hoping they would disappear. That has not been my journey. My journey has been creating balance, integrating the shadow, AND my Higher Self. The same skills, traits, and talents that made me a successful criminal and con man are the same skills, traits, and talents that make me an exceptional Counselor, Coach, and Reiki Master today.

I want to thank all the people along the way who showed me the reflection in them of who I was and am. Thank you for showing me how beautiful, extraordinary, and unique I am.

Raised by Wolves, Possibly Monsters

Acknowledgments

There are so many people I would like to recognize that it feels foolish to try to choose a few, but I will honor those directly involved in the process of creating this book:

I miss my mother, who was fiercely supportive of me and always appreciated who I am. My therapist in the 90s, Lauraine, who put up with a lot working with me. Betsy, my Reiki Master and Teacher for many years. Jane, the editor, who I consistently stated that I am not a writer, and she repeatedly reminded me that I have written a book and have two others on the way.

My Vermont friends, Lisa Nigro, Ron Isenstein, and Susanna Baker, who have supported this project in many ways. My core group of friends, in the order I met them: Maggie, Clare, Arnold, Ellen, Heidi, and Jonna. The Grand Poobah. The Conscious Dance Community in Rhode Island and New England. Through these communities and people, I have experienced feeling love, connection, intimacy, acceptance, belonging, and value. Conscious communities provide opportunities for deep healing of wounds in a softer, gentler container. If you have not found your community yet, please do. It changes everything.

And the Divine Presence inside me, you and us.

www.ingramcontent.com/pod-product-compliance
Lightning Source LLC
Chambersburg PA
CBHW060213120726
48004CB00008B/1809